M. + G. Lucchi
Eingangstrasse 9
8304 Wallisellen

D1750458

Preface

The first edition of "Advanced Soaring Made Easy" was compiled with a variety of goals in mind. However, it was mainly intended to encourage enthusiastic newcomers to carry on as soaring pilots and hence improve member retention in our sport. Too many pilots give up after reaching solo status or remain mere circuit pilots. Even after a few successful solo flights they are still far away from realising their full potential.

To the delight of everyone involved, the book's first edition enjoyed such strong demand that a second print run became necessary only a few months after the original version was launched. This soon lead to enthusiastic waves of writing for an expanded second edition. It reinforced our belief that gliding was lacking an up-to-date work for solo pilots trying to make the difficult transition to become either competent cross-country pilots or competition pilots.

Positive feedback from pilots all over the globe - often accompanied by a wish list for additional topics - and various suggestions from some of the world's leading pilots have resulted in substantial additions. The topics already discussed in the first edition were significantly extended and much new content was added. In particular, performance-orientated pilots will notice a greater focus on competition soaring including the all-important psychological aspects. Adding a chapter on technical issues and placing a greater emphasis on modern navigation systems, including electronic flight analysis, has resulted in an all-encompassing work for generations of glider pilots to come.

Gliding is without doubt the most peaceful, most affordable and the quietest form of aviation; forever challenging, but also very satisfying and rewarding. Keeping a glider airborne for hours on end and at the same time travelling hundreds or even thousands of kilometres without the need for an engine is perhaps the ultimate challenge for modern aviators. Real determination to succeed is a good starting point, but good progress in a complex sport like gliding requires some guiding literature. Most readers already know the basics and will use the book as a training aid for guidance from local soaring to advanced cross-country flying and beyond.

A great glider pilot once said: "Gliding is the art of understanding the relationship between sun, wind and terrain". Although this might sound too simplistic it is in essence what this book is all about. Written in plain language it aims to help others discover the true fascination of gliding. For some this fascination is the fun of silent flight, while for others it is long journeys of airborne discovery in total comfort and in an environmentally friendly manner. A glider pilot's greatest reward is a constantly changing impression of our beautiful Mother Earth. We are among a privileged few when we become mountaineers on wings surrounded by otherwise inaccessible snow-covered mountains in places like New Zealand, Japan or Europe. Just as impressive is soaring high over the red earth of sunburnt central Australia and western USA. But whatever the case may be; the peaceful bird's eye view of nature, or a close look at the most spectacular cloud formations in the atmosphere, these are privileges glider pilots will forever treasure and protect.

Gliding is a sport, but it is more than that – it is an absorbing passion difficult to express in words. Therefore the author lets cameras speak and allows readers to experience the third dimension often from quite unusual perspectives. The author's own pictures of memorable gliding expeditions – frequently taken in some of the most inhospitable parts of Europe, Japan, Australia and New Zealand – were supplemented by spectacular shots from almost all other corners of the globe. They reflect the attraction of the sport in an impressive way and will hopefully stimulate interest and curiosity to the newcomer but at the same time provide support, encouragement and background knowledge to already addicted members of the gliding fraternity. Successful glider pilots have managed to transform theoretical knowledge into superior practical skills but even inexperienced pilots can achieve success without major setbacks and disappointments on the way by implementing the information in this book.

About the Author

A 40 year love affair with aviation started for Bernard as a young boy when he visited a model aircraft field. After 15 years of building, flying and later even designing model aircraft he decided to take up gliding and obtained his German licence in 1982.

In 1983 his professional career saw him transferred "down under" to head up his employer's Australian operations. The truly excellent gliding conditions in Australia convinced Bernard to become a private owner of a PIK 20 in 1985, and from then on gliding occupied most of his spare time.

While serving his club as a committee member, president, gliding instructor and state association delegate, he obtained his "Form 2 Inspector Rating" (1991) and his private pilot licence (1992). In 1996 he became a gliding coach and was made a GFA Level 2 coach in 2002. He was later appointed head coach for South Australia and the Northern Territory.

In 1996 he was able to acquire a damaged self-launching open class ASH25 two-seat sailplane. Re-building the aircraft with the help of friends increased his enthusiasm for the sport even further. Since then he has taken his pride and joy to many places in Australia and pilots from many countries have benefited from free coaching sessions.

Over the past 20 years Bernard has retained his excellent contacts with various European glider manufacturers. He and his wife Chris became agents for a number of manufacturers during the nineties. Today they run successful agencies not only in Australia but also New Zealand and Japan with excellent reputations and first class relationships with their customers.

With over 3500 hours soaring in his logbook, Bernard always strives to extract the maximum distance out of any gliding day. He can look back on an estimated 300 000 km of cross-country soaring with his heart set on long distance flying. He holds all GFA distance badges, has performed 6 flights in excess of 1000 km and has set a new Australian record for a 1000 km out & return flight. In addition he has performed one flight in excess of 1100 km (FAI triangle of 1134 km).

Although he is not an ambitious competition pilot, he has competed at national sports class events and has won a number of competition days. He has also won several state championships.

Foreword

With this book Bernhard presents to the gliding community a dictionary for the meteorological phenomena that can keep gliders aloft to fly long distances.

In recent years we have seen an increase in performance of cross-country flying that seemed impossible only a few decades ago. The improved performance and handling of gliders are only partly responsible for that surge. It is most likely that the pilots' tactical decisions and their advanced knowledge of meteorology boosted the long distance and speed records to their present level. Pilots who have developed a basic understanding of gliding theory and have an open eye for the forces of nature can explore and enjoy the almost endless possibilities of modern gliders so skillfully designed and constructed by dedicated craftsmen.

The different chapters in this book explain in detail, with clear illustrations, what glider pilots need to know to maximise their enjoyment and performance. Some lift forces are smooth or weak and others are strong and turbulent. Lift can also be isolated or lined up for long distances. Pilots who have learned to master these great forces with skill and patience can, on certain days, combine several different lift sources for exhilarating flights using all the daylight hours.

Ingo Renner (World Champion 1976, 1983, 1985 and 1987)

This book not only gives a complete overview of meteorological phenomena but it also explains to glider pilots how to take advantage of them. The book details the techniques of soaring in thermals, slope lift, wave, etc., and provides pilots with excellent information that they can put into practice to improve their skills and get the maximum out of the sport of gliding. Pilots who achieve the best performance are those who can recognise the different forces of nature and use them to their advantage.

Perhaps they can use an early morning wave to set off on long distance flights as I have done. I shall never forget my late glides into a sunset from a high climb in a late thermal or from a wave. In high mountains the ice breeze occurs almost every evening and one can enjoy late soaring in the centre of the valleys right up to last light. This is what makes the sport of gliding so special.

To all readers of this book I wish you excellent soaring and hope you gain as much pleasure and exhilaration from gliding as I have over the years.

I would also like to commend Bernhard Eckey on the huge amount of research he has put into writing this book and presenting it in such a useful format. The first edition of his book has been well received but because this second edition looks deeper into many additional topics it will be even more encouraging and motivating to the many supporters of our fascinating sport.

Safe soaring to all

Ingo Renner

Foreword

I imagine if you are reading this foreword you share my love of flying without an engine; in using only one's knowledge of nature to explore the skies and the countryside. Your memories of special flights may include, as do mine, fast flights under high cumulus cloud streets over the flat, dusty, red outback of Australia or gliding over huge forests and lakes in Sweden and vast stretches with nowhere to land in Africa's Kalahari desert.

Then there is passing Mt Cook and looking out across the forests of the West Coast to the sea in the fantastic wave systems of New Zealand or ridge soaring the west face of the Matterhorn peak in Switzerland. Whatever landscapes you have the opportunity to fly over, the enjoyment of the landscape, as well as the satisfaction at achieving remarkable distances and speeds with only the power of nature, are the things that inspire us to keep flying.

Getting the most out of every gliding day is what drives me and gives me the most enjoyment in gliding. To be able to do this, one needs knowledge. But having said this, I believe that to fly doesn't require a special talent. Like any other sport, systematic training can allow anyone to improve their gliding skills.

Michael Sommer
World Champion 2006 and 2008

One of the aspects of the training is the theoretical background. Much of this is already known and many books have been written about the various aspects of gliding. The specific value I see in 'Advanced Soaring Made Easy' is that it, in simple words and in a very practical way, provides all the background for any glider pilot to improve their gliding, no matter whether they just have accomplished their first solo flight, or they are competing at a high level.

I got to meet Bernard a few years ago in Australia. He is more than just an enthusiastic glider pilot who has accumulated a lot of skill and knowledge. I know him as someone who is dedicated to sharing his gliding knowledge with up-and-coming glider pilots - to show people what is possible in gliding. This, together with Bernard's skill in putting things in an easily understandable way, makes him an ideal author of a book such as this.

The first edition of his book has already helped thousands of newcomers to advance their gliding career. However, this second edition expands on a wide range of topics and will be even more beneficial to the many followers of our captivating sport.

However long we have been flying, there are always new things to learn and experience. Each day brings a unique set of conditions, opportunities and challenges.

Even after more than 20 years, gliding has lost none of its early fascination for me. I hope this is how it is for you also!

Enjoy the book!

Michael Sommer

Content at a glance

Chapter 1 Local soaring

As thermals are the main source of energy for soaring, this chapter is dedicated to the location and use of this lift. It includes vital background information, detailed assessments and proven procedures for the benefit of the reader.

Chapter 2 Gliding and weather

This chapter deals with soaring weather, especially the prediction of soaring conditions for the day ahead. By combining meteorological theory with practical examples, light is shed on this difficult subject. Other issues such as sea breezes and favourable soaring conditions for different parts of the world are covered.

Chapter 3 Flight preparation

From checking the equipment to organising a crew, this chapter contains the information needed to get ready for soaring away from the home airfield. Even checklists for various gliding activities are included.

Chapter 4 Extended local soaring

Flying beyond gliding distance of the home airfield is a milestone in every new glider pilot's career. This difficult step is made much easier with the information contained in this chapter. Hints on traditional as well as modern navigation methods are given and recommended training sequences are included. Even meteorological phenomena of interest to the early cross—country pilot are explained and solutions to common pitfalls are given.

Chapter 5 Advanced cross country flying

Guidelines for proven flying tactics and methods for speed improvement form the centrepiece of this chapter. The most efficient methods for extracting energy in climb as well as cruise are identified and proven methods for maximising the average cross—country speed are examined. This chapter even provides advice on reducing the cockpit workload in the interests of increasing efficiency. Also, common mistakes and such subjects as optimum final glide, mountain flying, flight analysis and dolphin flying are put under the microscope.

Chapter 6 Winning the mental game

Mental aspects of gliding such as positive thinking, decision making, thinking ahead, goal setting, self motivation etc. are vital for success and are essential tools for recreational and performance-orientated glider pilots alike. For competitive reasons, it is vital to be a step ahead and have the mental edge over other pilots.

Chapter 7 Flying competitively

Competitive aspects of the sport are discussed in detail here. Valuable hints for improving the performance and competitiveness of the glider are examined and the reader is also introduced to the concept of saving time by shaving off the seconds.

Chapter 8 Let's get technical

Getting the most out of a glider is equally important for competition and recreational pilots. This chapter provides ideas for fine tuning your glider and its instruments for maximum performance. The effective use of flaps is also covered in detail.

Chapter 9 Outlandings

This chapter deals with outlandings and explains how safety can best be advanced. The author provides a long list of easy to follow suggestions and includes a list of dos and don'ts.

Chapter 10 Safety first

This chapter is all about safety. It deals with lookout, scanning, thermalling etiquette, use of radio and proper thermal approach procedures. Issues relating to gliders with retractable engines and manoeuvrability of open class gliders are also incorporated.

Chapter 11 Ridge lift and Slope soaring

The use of ridge lift and related issues are the subject of chapter 11. Flying in areas of suitable topography allows pilots to enjoy spectacular scenery in comfort and safety, provided the advice given in this chapter is adhered to.

Chapter 12 Wave lift

A good knowledge of wave lift can provide for unforgettable experiences. This chapter provides not only background information but also practical guidance. It provides even flatland pilots with the information required to enjoy the pleasures of soaring to diamond heights in the smooth airflow of mountain wave.

To my family

This book is dedicated to my wife Chris and our son Ralf. Both have been very loyal supporters over the years and have given me strength to continue in my many aviation endeavours. No matter how strange the many new challenges or ideas appeared at first my family went through thick and thin with me and have done their best to make it a success.

Without their ongoing support this book would not have been written and many of my most memorable aviation challenges would not have been met.

Over more than 25 years of married life my wife has not only been a first class mentor but also a source of inspiration and help whenever it was needed most.

Thank you both – I could not have done it without you!

The use of icons

To improve reading efficiency and to highlight sections that you should really pay attention to I'm using symbols (or icons) in this second edition.

When you see this icon next to a text passage it means that this section contains information that was not included in the first edition. If the icon appears next to a text heading the enttire section is new.

This icon lets you know that this information is of particular importance.

If you see this icon, feel free to become a selective reader. This section contains information that is only applicable for a particular part of the world.

When you come across this icon you know that I'm about to embark on a technical issue that might not provide essential information at an early stage of a pilot's development.

Training in the vicinity of the home airfield

1.1 Introduction

Whilst the early solo pilot will appreciate my back-to-basics approach, I hope the experts will forgive me for covering the more advanced topics a bit later, although even this first chapter includes a few useful hints for experienced pilots.

To remain airborne all aircraft require energy – this is fundamental. Power pilots rely on a big noise-maker up front plus large amounts of fuel in the tank. By contrast, glider pilots tap into the generous updraughts Mother Nature provides. Once we have acquired the skills to make good use of this freely provided energy we can fly in peace and quiet without spending hard-earned dollars on engines and fuel.

THERMALS are the most common source of energy for gliding. By climbing in them, energy is accumulated in the form of altitude. It is almost like refuelling at a petrol station – well before we run dry we top up again and continue on our merry way. This is easier said than done, especially for newcomers to the sport, but this chapter can assist aspiring glider pilots to improve their thermalling technique and get a better understanding of related issues.

Last launch of the day
Photo:
Holger Weitzel

1.2 Thermal recognition

A basic skill in gliding is to recognize a thermal as we approach it. Generally thermals are invisible unless marked by smoke from a fire or rising dust. This only happens on rare occasions; a good reason to develop our thermal recognition abilities.

We will touch on the structure of thermals a little later, but for the moment we must accept that a thermal cannot rise through the lower atmosphere without leaving some sort of disturbance in its wake. Therefore the first sign of nearby lift is some slight turbulence, and the second is an increased rate of sink. Athough no two thermals are the same, it is fair to say that this sink usually weakens gradually and is soon replaced by a second patch of rough air. This is another indicator of a nearby thermal. When sink gradually turns into weak lift, cruising speed should be slowly reduced in anticipation of good things to come. The airspeed should be kept high enough to ensure a quick and positive aileron response. For a modern unballasted single seater, a speed of around 55 – 65 kts would be fairly close to the mark. On entering the thermal the pilot will notice a surge - a sensation sometimes combined with one wing being raised. This is an indication of a strong updraught which is often embedded in a larger area of buoyant air with less powerful but still quite useful lift. The surge is not displayed by our instruments as quickly as we would like because instruments can only indicate lift after the aircraft has undergone a change of altitude. Only then probes can sense pressure changes and feed this information back to the variometre. This takes about three seconds for even the fastest vario on the market. If you think this is an unacceptably long delay you are not alone. However, the good news is that pilots possess faster reacting and very sensitive body sensors that reduce our reliance on the instruments and on the variometer in particlar. Some of these sensors are located in the inner ear and form part of the body's balance system. In addition, our body's nerve endings also act as sensors. Those in our backside are especially useful. They instantly detect even minute changes in seat pressure. Our brain's clever software program quickly converts this information into an indication of lift or sink and makes it superior to even the best and most expensive variometer. An almost instantaneous "seat of the pants" feedback allows a response time of close to zero.

Some readers may find this hard to believe, but it is a fact that you might want to confirm for yourself on one of your next flights by forcing yourself to consult the variometer only upon feeling a change in seat pressure. Don't be surprised when on every occasion lift is sensed much quicker than all those expensive gadgets on the instrument panel combined. I have tried it on many occasions and have even covered up both my variometers for the duration of flights lasting several hours. Let me assure you that soring without variometer works very well indeed, but I'm happy to admit that the sound of my audio vario provided valuable assistance on those occasions.

Variometers are also fooled by horizontal air motion on the fringes of updrafts. A detailed investigation is reserved for Chapter 8 (Section 8.2) of this book, but the fact remains that all variometers indicate good lift for short periods well before the glider is anywhere near the core of the thermal. If the pilot disregards the seat of his pants and initiates a turn he will find himself in sink near the thermal's outer fringes.

The answer is to trust your instincts and wait until positive variometer readings are confirmed by a distinct vertical acceleration of the glider. In other words, wait until increased seat pressure and variometer readings coincide.

One more point for consideration. In recent years I have had the pleasure of flying with World Record holders and Australian, European and even World champions. What they all have in common is a rather limited interest in their instruments. They do rely heavily on information from other sources such as other gliders in the vicinity, soaring birds, clouds, ground features and – last but not least – changes in seat pressure.

When the presence of a thermal is confirmed by the fastest variometer (usually the electric one) we become interested in an indication of its strength. Our body is only good at detecting changes in vertical airspeed but it can not interpret the rate of climb. Our variometer does come in handy now; in fact it is crucial for an indication of thermal strength.

Let's elaborate on this a bit more and imagine stepping into the elevator in a tall building. As the elevator starts up we can clearly feel increasing g-loads which our brain correctly interprets as an upward directed acceleration. However, as soon as this acceleration subsides and we ascend at a steady speed, our brain is unable to provide further clues. It can't tell whether we are still going up or whether we have come to a complete stop. No wonder we all look at the floor level indicator to find out where we are.

If we agree that our brain can't sense vertical speed in an elevator, then we will have no argument that the same holds true in a glider. Fortunately, the vario was invented for rate of climb indication although it can also be used for thermal selection. A word of warning though: Keeping the eyes glued to the variometer during thermal entry is a bad habit depriving us of other valuable clues including hints from outside the cockpit. It is not only dangerous but it also seriously masks our ability to feel the thermal because the human brain automatically assigns top priority to sight. There is plenty of scientific evidence suggesting that only in the absence of visual clues other stimuli are taken into account. Hundreds of millions of years of brain evolution have probably led to this development for very good reasons, but as far as glider pilots are concerned our preference for visual cues has a very significant drawback. It means that by looking at the instruments our brain automatically disregards the instantaneous "seat of the pants" information.

1.3 Centring a thermal

Having found a thermal and being satisfied with its strength, decisions need to be

The new ASG 29 in its element for the first time
Photo: **Manfred Muench**

made. We need to initiate a turn, but the problem is one of timing. Sometimes we need to roll into the turn very soon after we feel the vertical acceleration but on other occasions we should wait for a few seconds. Apart from our entry speed, the size or horizontal extent of the thermal plays an important role. Usually a swift turn is the right course of action at low altitude, but when high it is almost always best to delay the turn for a while. There are no firm rules here; we need to keep practising thermal entry and make a conscious effort to refine this important skill. Experience counts for a lot and as time goes by we will find it a lot easier to get it right.

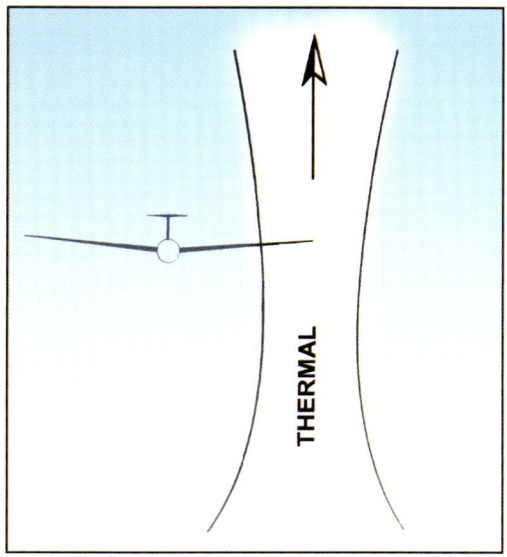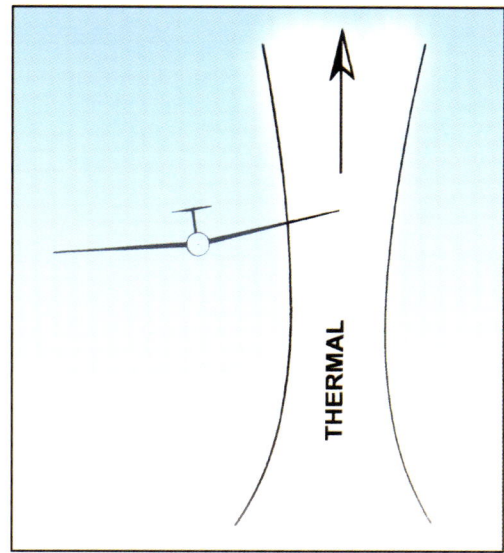

Figure 1: Lifting of wing by thermal (not to scale)

Just as important as the correct timing of our turn is the decision whether to turn right or left. The instruments are of little help here. If our eyes are glued to the variometer, our chances of turning towards the core are 50 percent at best and our chances of turning into sink are the same. With a very light touch on the controls and by looking outside we will often notice a slowly lifting wing while closing in on the core. This is never as dramatic as illustrated above but it can be a useful indicator.

Obviously the rising wing is travelling through more buoyant air, providing a good indication in regards to direction of turn. (Refer to Figure 1.)

By simply banking towards the lifting wing and doing the exact opposite of what our glider tends to do, chances of striking the best part of the lift are increased and the risk of flying through the heavy sink normally found nearby are much reduced. Now it is only a matter of closing in on the core.

Even experienced pilots often assume that the first turn is tangential to the direction of flight. However, even in the most agile of single-seaters it takes about two seconds to roll the glider to a steep angle of bank. The result is

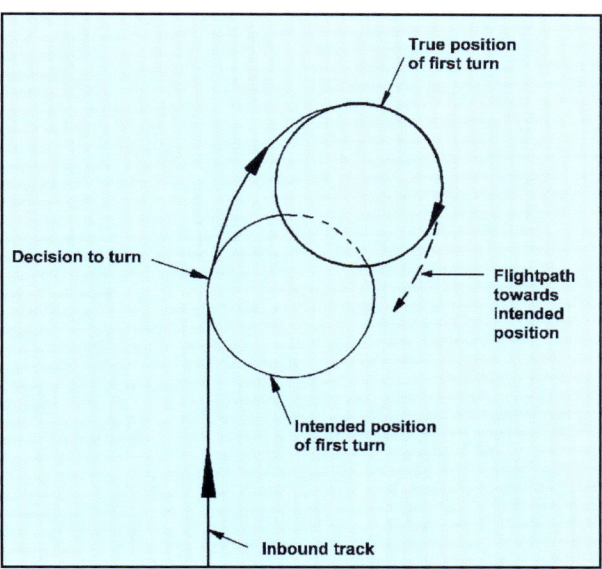

Figure 2: True position of first turn

Training in the vicinity of the home airfield

a flight path as per Figure 2. The time taken to roll training aircraft or open class gliders into a steep angle of bank is almost twice as long due to the slower roll rate. As a result the first full turn is usually completed a fair distance away from the intended position. It is therefore often advisable to level the glider momentarily after completing a 200° turn.

More often than not this moves us closer to the core, which is usually indicated by the air becoming smooth or the amount of turbulence decreasing markedly. Often this coincides with improved control responsiveness and a reduced noise level within the cockpit.

However, doing the exact opposite of what our glider seemingly wants to do means that we must be able to thermal to the right and to the left. If we, like many other glider pilots, have fallen into the habit of thermalling in the same direction all the time, there is no real need to worry. It is a common problem but can easily be corrected without involving instructors or coaches. We simply must gather all our willpower and force ourselves to thermal in the opposite direction for half an hour or so every time we fly. Practising this ensures that within a few weeks we will lose our preference for a particular direction of turn.

Even the best glider pilots do not get exactly into the core on the first turn and need to perform some thermal centring. Two basic rules help greatly when it comes to moving the glider closer to the centre of the lift.

Rule No. 1: NEVER EVER FLY TWICE THROUGH THE SAME PATCH OF BAD AIR.
Rule No. 2: ALWAYS SHIFT YOUR CIRCLE TOWARDS THE STRONGER PART OF THE THERMAL.

Rule No. 1 does not need any further comment, but this basic mistake is repeated time and again. It is simply a bad habit some of us have fallen into and there is only one piece of advice I can give: DON'T DO IT.

Obeying rule No. 2 is easier said than done. However, it becomes much easier if we

INCREASE THE ANGLE OF BANK AS THE LIFT DECREASES AND DECREASE THE ANGLE OF BANK AS THE LIFT INCREASES.

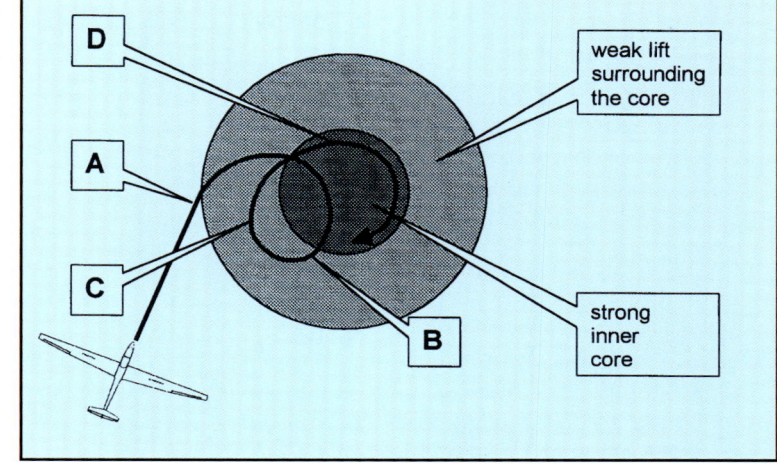

A-B Turning into lift

B-C Steep angle of bank due to weakening lift

C-D Shallow angle of bank due to increasing lift

D Maintain constant angle of bank while in steady lift

Figure 3: Thermal centring when only partly in the core

Centring a thermal by varying the angle of bank is only advisable when just slightly displaced from the core. However, if our turn is partly in sink, we have to take more drastic measures. A major position change is called for that involves a short term levelling of our glider.

This leads us to the so called "Worst Heading" method. It is best employed if we find ourselves a fair distance away from the centre of the thermal (Figure 4). If you think the sketch is too simplistic, you are right. The only thing certain about a thermal is that it is not of a circular cross section, but the described method works most of the time.

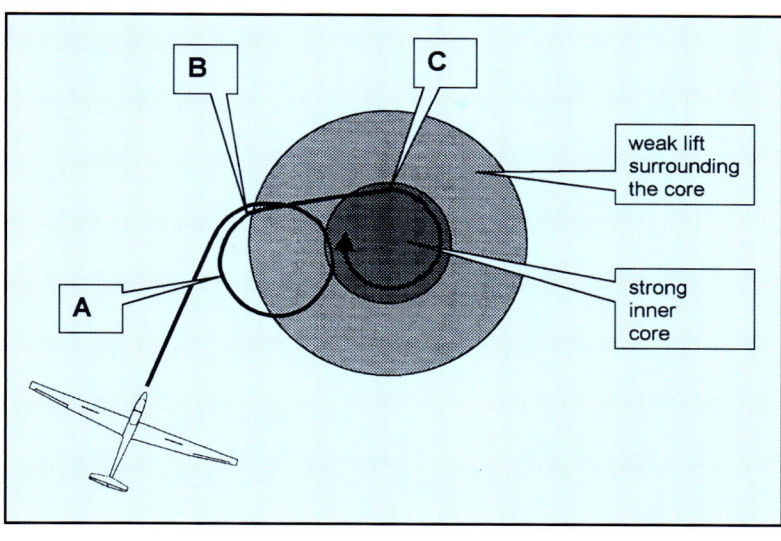

Figure 4: Worst Heading thermal centring method

The "Worst Heading" centring method requires that we make a mental note of our worst position in the thermal (Point "A") and wait for almost a quarter of a turn before we level our glider completely (Point "B"). After a short while we roll the glider back in the same direction (Point "C") and should now be positioned substantially closer to the core. Whatever levelling time we decide upon depends on the diameter of the thermal, our speed, and our distance from the core, but the manoeuvre needs to be repeated as long as subsequent turns are still partly in sink. A good indication of being in the core is an even and smooth climb relatively free of turbulence.

While flying at 50 kts we travel at a speed of 26 m/s, which means that levelling the wings for two seconds theoretically shifts our position by 50 metres. However, we also need to consider the distance covered while rolling out of and back into the turn that, depending on the roll rate of our glider and our speed, can easily account for the same distance again. A two-second levelling of the wings therefore results in a position change of approximately 100 metres. Significantly larger corrections are very rarely required unless we are dealing with a monster of a thermal or have drifted a fair distance away from the core.

The timing of our control inputs is just as important. Levelling our wings too early or too late makes the glider point in the wrong direction and possibly towards sink. For this reason, most experienced pilots use a reference point and form a mental picture of the thermal. The reference point may be the position of the sun or some feature on the ground. Personally I prefer the position of the sun, simply because it is useful even while flying over featureless terrain. It does not matter which reference point we use but it is of utmost importance to establish a mental picture of the lift distribution in the thermal.

By paying careful attention to the "feel" of the air we get useful clues about the location of the core. A short moment of smooth air should make us shift our position towards this smoother patch of air. Equally, sudden turbulence indicates a position close to the edge of the thermal and a need to move towards the opposite side of the circle. In other words, we must update our position in the core all the time using firm and precise control inputs.

Training in the vicinity of the home airfield

Let the fun begin

The more pilots we ask about their preferred method of thermal centring the more answers we get. This is not surprising given that thermal diameter and thermal characteristics vary considerably throughout the year and different parts of the world. What holds true for stronger and larger diameter thermals in the more arid parts of the globe doesn't necessary apply for Central Europe or more temperate areas. For smaller diameter thermals it often pays to tighten the turn when intercepting the core but remaining as close as possible to the best part of the lift is always of prime importance. (Refer to Section 1.9 below.)

The chosen method often comes down to personal preferences, thermal characteristics and the type of glider we fly. Some gliders are not as manoeuvrable as others, which brings control responsiveness into the equation as well. If a chosen method works well, stick with it; but if you are frequently left behind in a thermal, the above hints will be of some assistance. Finding and successfully working lift has little to do with good luck. Only your skill and your ability to get as close as possible to the centre of the lift will make the difference. When flying competitively, it's also important to get into the core as quickly as possible, but we will look at this closer in Chapters 5 and 6.

My advice is emphatic; WORK ON ONE PARTICULAR ASPECT OF THERMALLING ONLY AND TAKE ONE STEP AT A TIME. Finding thermals and centring them is difficult enough, and I suggest developing this particular skill before attempting to speed up the process.

1.4 Using other gliders as lift indicators

One of the best things that can happen is to be joined by another glider at roughly the same level, but only when both pilots know what to do and how to take advantage of the situation. If both gliders remain more or less opposite each other the pilots can compare their rates of climb and make precise observations regarding the strongest part of the thermal. However, both aircraft must remain in full view of the other pilot at all times. Then, and only then, the two gliders turn into first-class variometers. In fact they become the most effective varios imaginable by helping us to climb very efficiently simply by shifting the circle towards the most buoyant part of the lift.

As usual, theory and practice are far apart at times. Differences in glider performance and pilot skill result in different rates of climb. On top of this, we often operate our gliders at different wing loadings (the weight per square metre of wing), so it is not hard to see why we often see one glider catching up with another circling above.

The faster-climbing pilot can subsequently be forced to fly at the same angle of bank as the other pilot in order to maintain separation. If he decides to fly directly behind other gliders he not only creates a safety problem but also forfeits the advantages described above. It also becomes impossible for the pilot in the leading aircraft to see the other. This is far from ideal from a performance point of view because both gliders fly through the same air mass at roughly the same time and the pilots are therefore unable to gauge subtle differences in climb rate.

**A big gaggle
Photo:
André Becker**

To sum it up, flying in close proximity to other gliders allows us to use them not only as variometers but also as good indicators of the shape and the size of thermals.

In this context, a word or two on safety is needed. Sharing a thermal with other gliders can be very rewarding, not only because it offers the potential to improve the rate of climb, but because it gives us a perfect opportunity to observe these beautiful and graceful machines in their element and at relatively close proximity. For the experienced pilot it adds a satisfying degree of pleasure to the sport but it demands a high degree of responsibility.

Whether we like it or not, our beautiful sport can be dangerous. However, it is only as dangerous as we make it and the application of common sense can go a long way towards minimizing danger. The importance of a good lookout cannot be over-emphasised. Sharing a thermal with other gliders undoubtedly increases the risk of a collision, but this risk can be almost completely eliminated if we do our best never to lose sight of other gliders operating at roughly the same level. I'd be the first to admit that this is easier said than done and becomes more difficult once several gliders converge at the same altitude.

This can be a serious trap for less experienced pilots, because flying in close proximity to other gliders greatly increases the workload. As every instructor knows, lookout goes down

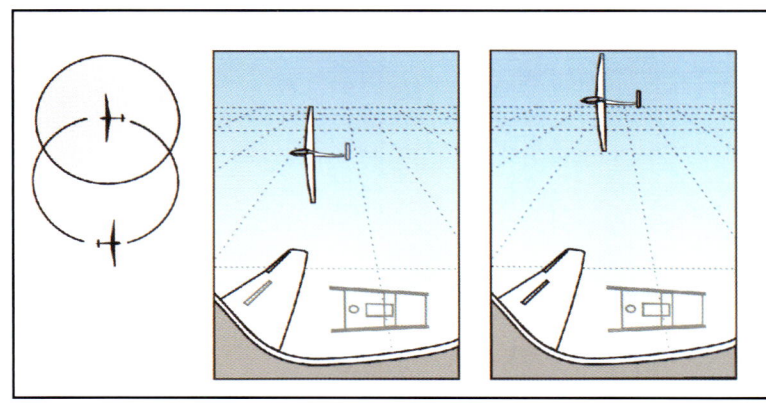

**Figure 5:
Using another glide as a lift indicator
(Courtesy of Jon Hall, UK)**

as workload goes up; a fact we should all remember when sharing thermals with less experienced pilots. But, even with the best intentions, we can't always remain in full view of each other. In such situations it is helpful to think of our co-pilot who goes by the name of Murphy. Remember, his Rule No.1 states that if things can go wrong they will. Relying on other pilots to maintain adequate separation invites Murphy to prove himself to be correct once again.

Safety must always take precedence over competitive advantage. This means that if we cannot out-climb the other glider and keep it in sight at the same time, we must choose between either leaving the thermal or accepting the rate of climb dictated by the other glider. I recommend a few extra knots of airspeed for safety and improved control responsiveness in a crowded thermal.

1.5 Thermalling at a steady rate of climb

Let us invest a minute or two on considering the importance of thermalling at a steady rate of climb. Although easy to write about, it is far more difficult to implement – especially on tricky days with broken and narrow thermals. In fact, climbing at a steady rate might almost be impossible under some conditions, but we are nevertheless well advised never to give up trying. New glider pilots in particular, and occasionally even quite seasoned ones, are often satisfied with an uneven climb rate in a thermal and tolerate it as long as there is a net gain in altitude. For example, a pilot might climb at four knots for part of a turn and find himself in only one knot just moments later. Experience indicates that, in such a situation, the pilot is in danger of losing the thermal altogether.

Let's trace the steps of a pilot about to fall out of a thermal. Initially his glider is a constant distance away from the centre of the thermal and the variometer indicates a fairly steady rate of climb. The pilot has managed to keep the core almost exactly opposite the inner wing and can at least momentarily relax in the knowledge that he can't do much better.

This ideal situation changes rapidly when the vario begins to indicate varying lift strength. Obviously, the glider's orbit is not centred on the core any longer. For part of the turn, the glider is near the centre, but for the reminder of the turn the glider is significantly further from the core. Without correction, the very next turn could well see the glider pass through the exact centre of the lift. Although the pilot would momentarily enjoy a greater rate of climb, he is likely to be in sink at the exact opposite part of the turn. If this happens, the alarm bells should ring because subsequent circles are likely to be displaced further, perhaps even to the extent that the outer wing moves through the centre of the lift. This has the unwanted effect of accelerating the glider away from the core directly into the heavy sink nearby. The glider can be thrown out of the thermal by the forces meant to lift it up.

As a result, the thermal is lost. Our pilot could have avoided this situation by taking corrective action as soon as the rate of climb started to fluctuate. Instead, he failed to shift his position early enough and this procrastination not only led to the complete loss of the thermal but also to contact with heavy sink. Experienced pilots make corrections as soon as the sound of their audio variometer changes. For them, climbing has become second-nature. They centre and re-centre their glider without really thinking about it. More often than not, their early response is a gentle variation in the angle of bank, just enough to steady the rate of climb again.

Having fun in early spring
Photo: Manfred Muench

1.6 Audio variometers

I am dismayed that some glider pilots make no use of audio variometers at all. Some gliders are not even equipped with audio varios and, where this is the case, clubs would be well advised to review their priorities. Even more disturbing are persistent rumors that some pilots simply turn the audio volume off. Their reasons appear to be quite plausible on the surface and include hindering of radio communication, unpleasant noise and some degree of distraction.

However, a serious problem occurs when audio systems are not used during basic training. It means that, from the very first day at the controls of a glider, a student has no choice but to look at the vario for indication of lift or sink. No wonder eyes become focused on the variometer and the instrument panel becomes a prime attraction. Sure, we always remind our student to scan the sky for other traffic. We also tell him never to keep his eyes in the cockpit at the expense of a good lookout and safety. While performing circuits, and while the instructor is watching closely from behind, this mistake can be corrected, but one day our student will become a solo pilot. Imagine that on one of his first solo flights our new pilot manages to find some weak lift. Working it without any help from the instructor is exciting and fills him with a great sense of achievement. He concentrates very hard indeed and is hell bent on not losing this thermal. But his eyes are stuck on the vario because this is the only lift / sink indicator our inexperienced aviator has been exposed to. Over the next few weeks our new pilot repeats this "successful" technique, not even realising that he is consolidating a bad habit.

It is no good blaming the new pilot – he is only doing what he did during pre-solo training – the only difference is that he will do it more often and for longer periods. The gentle reminders of the instructor are history; our post-solo pilot does what he believes is easiest and what comes naturally. In fact, we have given our new pilot little chance to avoid this potentially lethal trap.

Isn't it about time that we acknowledged the advantages of audio varios and train students in their correct use? Why not cover up the instruments for the first dozen flights or so? The law of primacy ensures that students will learn to judge airspeed by airflow noise as well as attitude and they will become much better and safer pilots as a result. Our sense of hearing lies partly dormant while soaring; a fact all top pilots have turned into a competitive advantage a long time ago. Audio systems make the job of finding and centring lift much easier as their use frees up time for scanning and detection of airmass movements. The ability to focus on valuable hints for lift from sources outside the cockpit is an additional bonus.

The sooner we get used to this kind of flying the better, as it not only greatly improves safety but also enhances the enjoyment to be gained from our sport.

1.7 Thermalling speeds

I'm sure that it will come as no surprise to anyone that the airspeed for minimum sink is best for thermalling. However, contrary to popular belief, the speed for minimum sink is NOT just above stalling speed. In fact, a significant penalty is paid for flying too slowly. Consider a typical polar curve of a two-seat trainer: (Figure 6)

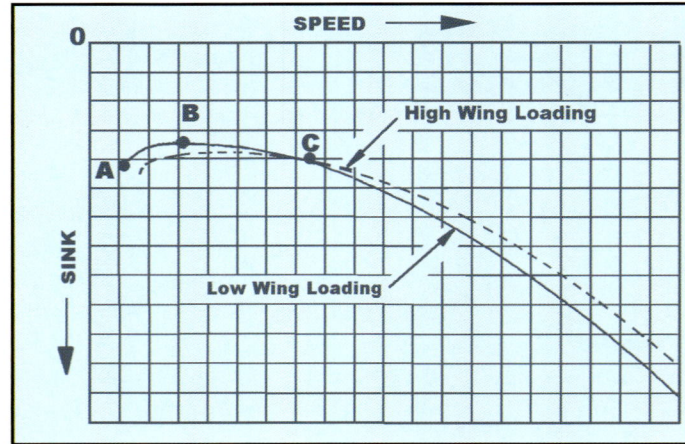

Figure 6:
The polar curve (Speed polar)

Point A corresponds to the minimum speed at which the glider will still fly. Any slower and the aircraft will stall.

Point B corresponds to the optimum speed if the aim is to sink as slowly as possible.

Point C corresponds to the speed for best glide ratio. While circling it is of no concern.

Flying at speeds between points A and B results in a higher than necessary sink rate. Also, circling just above the stall can be dangerous, uncomfortable and inefficient, and far from ideal from a performance point of view. Poor aileron control makes thermal finding and thermal centring difficult, unpleasant and tiring. Under no circumstances should the polar curve be consulted for determining optimum thermalling speeds. It is only valid for straight and level flight.

The question is one of how much extra speed is required in a steady turn. The mathematically minded among us can determine the speed by applying the knowledge that the stall speed increases with the square root of the g-force. The g-forces for steady turns at various bank angles are shown in Table 2 on page 25.

Example:

Say your glider stalls at 40 knots and you want to thermal at a 45° angle of bank (resulting in a g-force of 1.41 g). 40 knots times the square root of 1.41 (approx. 1.2) equals 48 knots.

After this short excursion into theory, let's look at the benefits of thermalling at higher than minimum speeds:

- Control response is much better, enabling us to manoeuvre the glider quickly, and effortlessly into the best part of the thermal.
- The nice feel and feedback a glider gives us if we fly at the right speed makes it so much easier to FEEL where the best part of the thermal is, thus decreasing our reliance on the instruments.
- Higher speeds increase safety margins. If we ever hit a severe gust or inadvertently wash off some airspeed, we are less likely to drop a wing or even enter a spin- a very important issue in a crowded thermal.

For a given bank angle, the radius of turn varies with the square of airspeed which demonstrates that it is important not to fly faster than necessary. If pilots need to keep an eye on the airspeed indicator while thermalling they are not yet ready to fly in close proximity to other gliders.

Experienced pilots only glance at their airspeed indicator from time to time, but take far more notice of attitude and airflow noise. By doing so they can observe the airspace around them, watch other gliders, soaring birds, dust devils etc.

Flying on ice and snow

1.8 The effect of different wing loadings

Increasing the weight of a glider can be an advantage on cross–country flights as it flattens the glide angle at higher speeds. In Chapter 4: "Extended Local Soaring" this is covered in detail. At this stage all we need to know that changing a glider's weight makes it behave differently. New pilots notice the effect when flying without an instructor for the first time. The reduced weight changes the characteristics of the two–seater as the aircraft can be flown slower without stalling or losing control responsiveness.

Because a lighter glider allows slower flying, it tends to float for longer on landing and, for this reason, I'm yet to see a first–solo flight that does not end up with a touch down much further down the strip than usual.

Quite the opposite happens when the glider carries water ballast. The dashed line in Figure 6 shows that the sink rate is higher at thermalling speeds and the stalling speed goes up. In contrast, the rate of sink at higher airspeeds is lower.

Needless to say, we have to adjust our thermalling speed to the weight of our glider. The heavier a glider becomes, the faster we need to thermal and the slower we climb. The radius of turn will also become larger, making it more difficult for us to climb in weak and narrow lift.

1.9 Angle of bank

The single most important factor in terms of extracting the maximum rate of climb from a given thermal is angle of bank. Thermals are strongest at their centres and the optimum bank angle is the one that maximises the glider's climb rate.

Circling at too shallow an angle of bank means that we will fly around the core and work very weak lift. On the other hand, an angle of bank too steep for our thermal is also detrimental to our rate of climb due to the significantly higher sink rate it causes.

> Perhaps at this point I should throw in a practical example and make mention of my first solo flights. In the days when many pilots were buying ASW 20's the sky around the biggest gliding field in Germany was full of them. My club's first solo aircraft was a Ka8, which features a big wooden wing weighing next to nothing. Although still very green, I never seemed to have any problem matching the climb rate of all the hot ships. I felt rather good about it and was beginning to think that I might make a half decent glider pilot until I realised that my featherweight Ka8 had a wing loading of roughly 1/3 of the ASW 20. As a result I was able to fly slow enough for other pilots to remark that this #@*! Ka8 was able to park right in the core of a thermal.
> The moral is obvious; a lighter glider allows slower thermalling speeds and a smaller radius of turn at a given bank angle. Although the Ka8 had a comparatively high sink rate, it could be flown very close to the strongest part of the thermal and hence match the climb rate of other pilots in "plastic fantastic" aircraft. Making it back to the airfield into a headwind was another story which I might return to some other time…..

The graph on the next page (Figure 7) is perhaps slightly too simplistic and not entirely representative of what happens in the real world. Still, let us assume we are approaching our thermal from left to right. At first we fly through neutral air with our total energy variometer showing a sink rate applicable to the current airspeed (Point A).

Next we notice some slight turbulence (Point B) and soon afterwards we experience

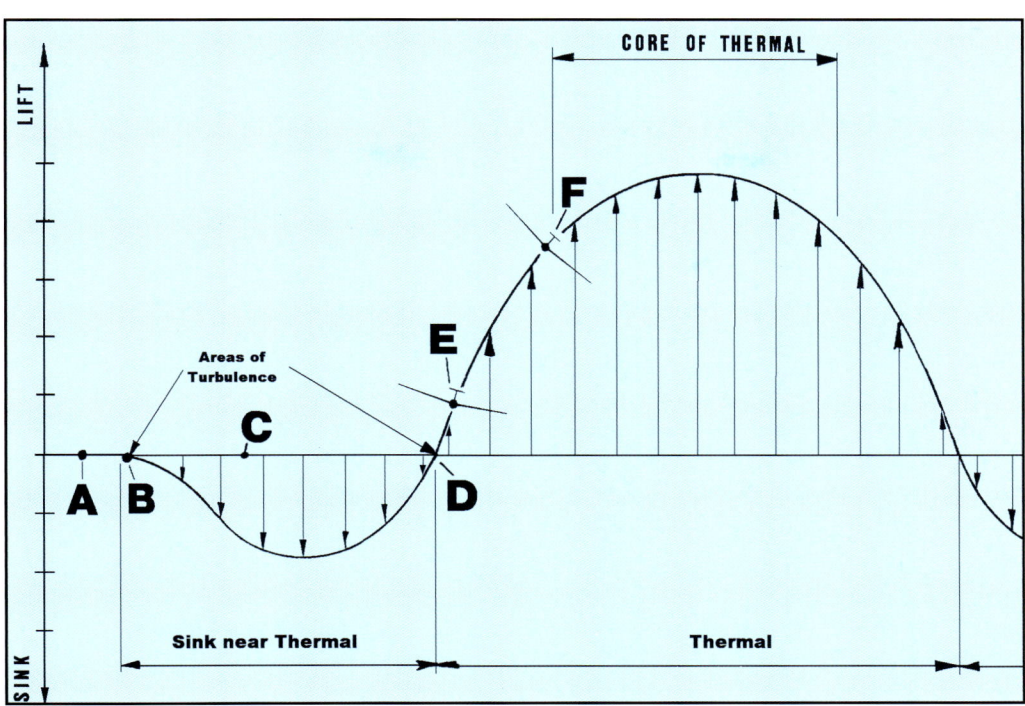

Figure 7: Vertical air movements (simplified)

an increased rate of sink (Point C). Now we have entered the area of sink normally encountered next to a thermal. Naturally, we would tend to fly faster here to cross this area quickly. Flying along and arriving at Point D we again feel some turbulence. More often than not it is more pronounced than at Point B. Friction between sinking and rising air is the culprit. On entering the lift we have to make decisions. Not only do we have to decide when (and in which direction) to turn but also what angle of bank to use. A small and comfortable angle of bank will result in a radius of turn that is more often than not too large to stay in lift. At best we will be flying near Point E. It means that we will not only climb in very weak lift but also get dangerously close to heavy sink.

Wouldn't it be better to increase our angle of bank and achieve a much smaller radius of turn? We would then fly near the core (Point F) and take advantage of lift at least twice as strong as near point E. Furthermore, we would still be in weak lift if we momentarily lose the core and we can then re-centre our thermal just by varying in the angle of bank.

This brings me to another often neglected thermalling aspect. Most pilots wrongly assume that they are in the best lift when they sense a strong vertical acceleration. However, glider pilots should not be interested in maximum acceleration, but maximum lift. A closer look at Figure 7 reveals that maximum acceleration occurs somewhere between Point E and F. If we centre our turn on this point we will constantly be in and out of the best lift.

Maximum lift only occurs in the core of the thermal. This means that we need to shift our circle towards the core where the vertical speed remains not only strong but also relatively constant. We can conclude that:

a We should delay turning on thermal entry for one or two seconds after the vertical acceleration has peaked; and

b) We need to consult the vario for an indication of vertical speed because our body can't sense vertical speed. (see Section 1.2 above.)

Unfortunately, we cannot ignore the fact that the tighter the turn, the higher our sink rate becomes. Just by way of an example, let us assume our glider's sink rate is 1.5 knots at a comfortable radius of turn. When we reduce the radius we must fly at a steeper angle of bank and accept a significant increase in our sink rate to approx. 4 knots.
If we now go back to Figure 7 we can do some simple arithmetic:

Point E   Flying through Point E we might get 1.5 knots of lift. However, as our glider's sink rate is also 1.5 knots, there is at best zero sink for us at this angle of bank.

Point F   If, in contrast, we thermal steeper and manage to fly near Point F, we will find lift of 5 knots. After subtracting our higher rate of sink (4 knots) we still go up at a rate of 1 knot.

This simple example serves to show that pilots prepared to fly a little faster and bank steeper will climb away while others will find themselves struggling or even back on the ground. The lesson is simple: Unless we bank according to the diameter of our thermal we will not achieve the maximum possible rate of climb.

That's all very well you might say, but the above arithmetic is based on assumptions and must be underpinned by conclusive evidence. Absolutely correct. We need to tackle the issue further and determine the optimum angle of bank for a given thermal.

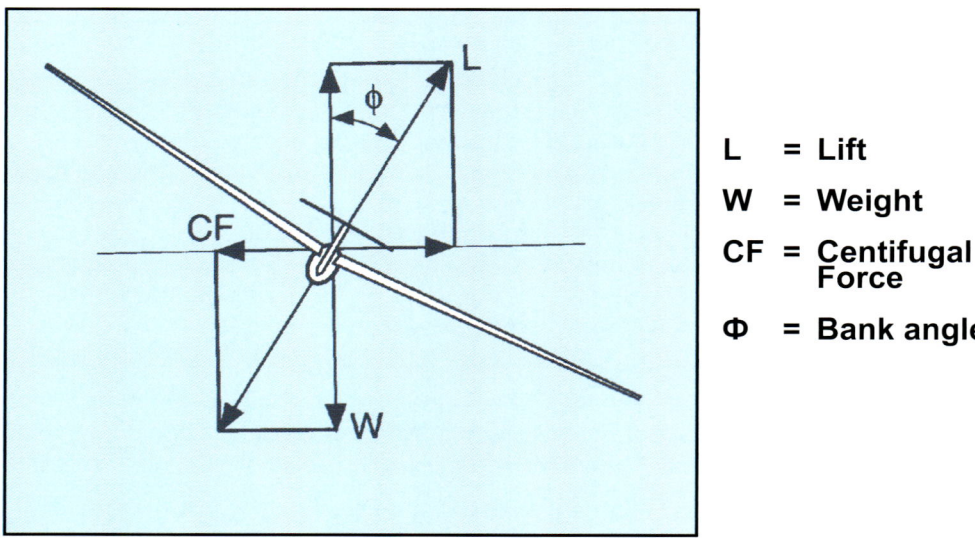

Figure 8: Equilibrium of forces in a turn

In level flight, the lift generated needs to be equal to the weight of the aircraft, but in circling flight, wings have to produce more lift to counter the additional centrifugal force. If anyone wants to do some number crunching, the formula is

Lift (L) = Weight (W) / cos Φ

At 30° angle of bank the required lift is 1.15 times the weight of the glider. If the angle of bank is increased to 45° the wings need to produce 1.41 times the amount of lift compared to level flight. In order to fly at an angle of bank of 60° we need to generate lift equal to twice the weight of the glider.

Table 1: Lift required and increase in stalling speed for given angles of bank

Angle of bank	Lift required (multiples of glider weight)	Approximate increase in stalling speed
0	1.0 times weight of glider	0
15°	1.04 times weight of glider	2%
30°	1.15 times weight of glider	8%
45°	1.41 times weight of glider	20%
60°	2.0 times weight of glider	40%

Table 1 indicates the approximate increase in stalling speed at various angles of bank and also provides information on the lift required. How do we generate the extra lift? Well, if flying a flapped glider, we can use positive flap to generate slightly more lift. This can contribute to solving the problem but, unfortunately, only to a relatively small extent.

Generation of the extra lift requires either a higher lift coefficient or a greater airspeed, or both. A higher lift coefficient might be obtained by increasing the angle of attack. On the other hand, if the airspeed is increased, the extra lift can be generated at the same angle of attack. In practice we usually increase both.

Now let us look into the effect various angles of bank have on the radius of turn and note the g-forces involved.

Table 2: Circle diameter in relation to angle of bank

Airspeed (kts)	CIRCLE DIAMETER IN METRES – Bank Angle in Degrees								
	20	25	30	35	40	45	50	55	60
40	237	185	150	123	103	86	72	60	50
45	300	234	189	156	130	109	92	76	63
50	371	289	234	193	161	135	113	94	78
55	448	350	283	233	194	163	137	114	94
60	534	416	336	277	231	194	163	136	112
65	626	489	395	326	272	228	191	160	132
g-force	1.06	1.10	1.15	1.22	1.31	1.41	1.56	1.74	2.00

Knowing the circle diameter at various airspeeds is useful, but it is more important to know the sink rate of a particular glider at a given radius of turn. Therefore we will look deeper into thermalling sink rates after we have considered drag.

1.10 Drag

Drag is the main foe of all glider pilots. Flying without drag is impossible, but we can minimise drag to some extent by the way we operate our glider. Below, a very useful chart not only lists the different types of drag acting on a glider but also shows how the percentages of the drag components change with different coefficients of lift. (Figure 9)

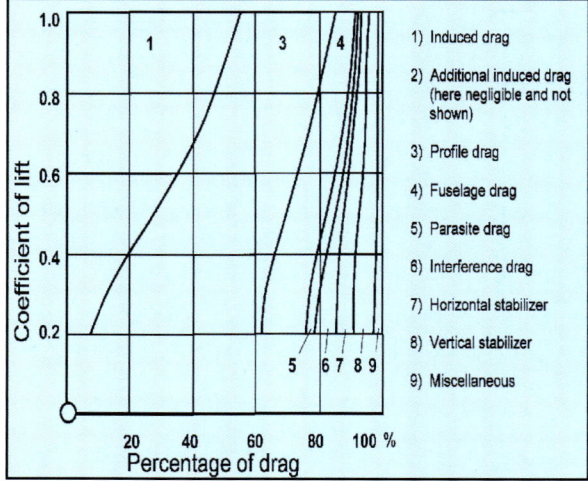

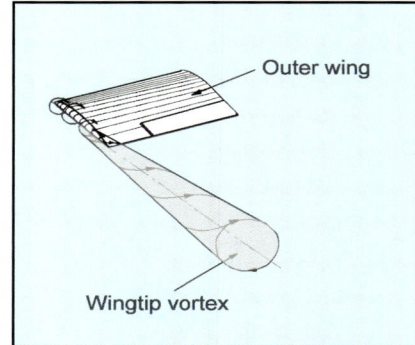

Figure 9: Typical breakdown of drag on a glider

Figure 10: Induced drag

While thermalling, wings operate close to a lift coefficient of 1.0 which has the nasty side effect of creating large amounts of induced drag. The pressure differential between the upper and lower surface of the wing makes the high-pressure air from below the wing curl around the wing tip upward into the low-pressure area above it. The resulting spiralling vortex is illustrated in Figure 10. High induced drag is the penalty we pay for creating lift; it accounts for over 50% of our total drag while flying slowly and near maximum lift coefficients. However, when flying fast, the lift coefficient drops to approx. 0.25, which in turn reduces the percentage of induced drag to only 10% or so. The other major culprit is the profile drag generated by the surface of the wing.

Showing the amount of drag as a function of lift coefficient is useful for theoretical purposes but of little practical value. Therefore Mr. A. Smith of Adelaide has converted the above diagram to show the sink rate contribution of various types of drag at different flying speeds. This is illustrated in Figure 11.

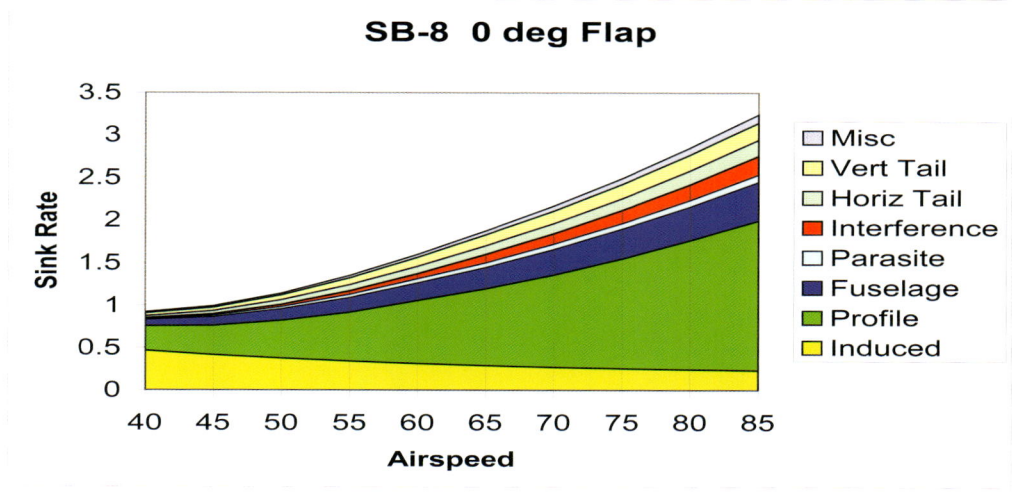

Figure 11: Sink rate breakdown with changing airspeed for SB 8 glider

So far, we have only considered drag in level flight, or as engineers would say, "at 1g". However, Table 2 shows that while banking steeply we operate our gliders at significantly higher g-forces. In fact a 45° angle of bank leads to a g-force increase of 41%. Higher g-forces demand higher lifting forces and even higher proportions of induced drag. This has a dramatic effect on the polar curve.

A diagram is needed showing the true rate of sink at any given diameter of turn. Such a diagram is called a circling polar. Figure 12 is based on the ASW 28-18. (The thick line is for a wing loading of 40 kg/m2 and the thin one is valid for 30 kg/m2)

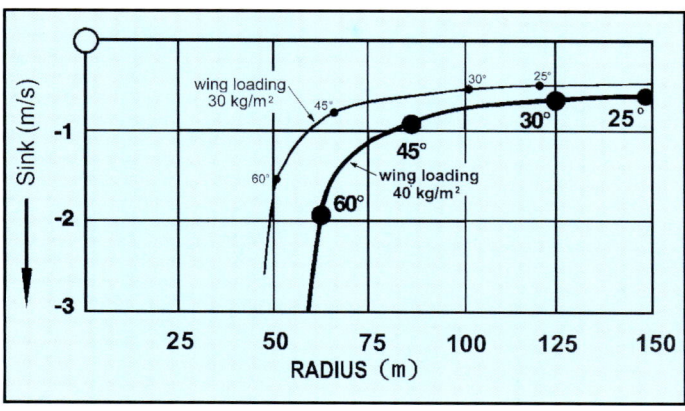

Figure 12: Circling polar curve for standard class glider ASW 28-18

A circling polar is compiled after obtaining minimum sink rates at various angles of bank. If we consider the 40 kg/m² wing loading we can see that a low minimum sink rate of 0.6 m/s (just over 1 kt) in level flight increases quite rapidly to 1 m/s (or 2 kts) when flying at a 45° angle of bank. Banking the glider at 60° increases the sink rate by a factor of three to almost 2 m/s.

The graph not only shows the increase in the rate of sink but also the radius of turn achieved at various bank angles. Again for 40 kg/m² it ranges from about 60 m at 60° angle of bank to almost 150 m at 25°. All these figures are valid for the minimum possible airspeed and indicate a 43% smaller circle diameter when banking 45° compared to 25°. Figure 13 illustrates the magnitude of the reduction in circle diameter.

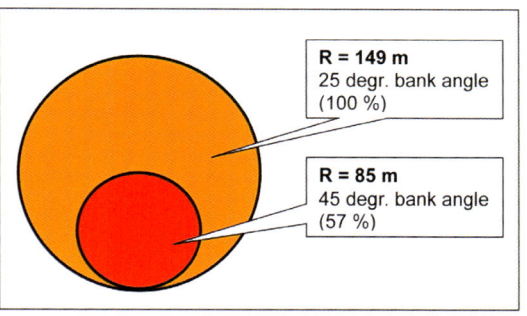

Figure 13: Comparison of circle diameters

If all thermals were of the same strength, had a similar diameter and an identical lift distribution, it would be easy to determine the optimum bank angle. Reality sees us in different thermals with different characteristics all the time, so for the purpose of bank angle optimisation we need to refer to known data on typical thermals.

German researchers have categorised thermals into four different combinations of various strength and diameter as per Figure 14. The resulting climb gradients allowed a mathematical tackling of the matter. In Figure 15 the circling polar is combined with a lift distribution diagram in graphical form. To remain consistent, a 40 kg/m² wing

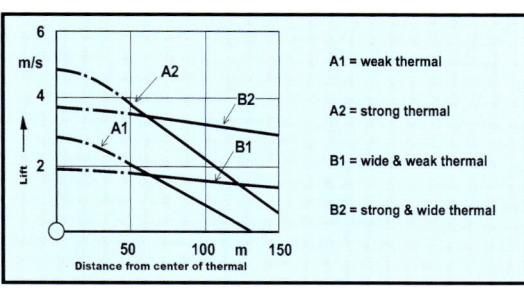

Figure 14: Horstmann thermal model

Training in the vicinity of the home airfield

loading was used. By subtracting the glider's sink rate from the thermal strength, a true picture of the possible rate of climb is obtained.

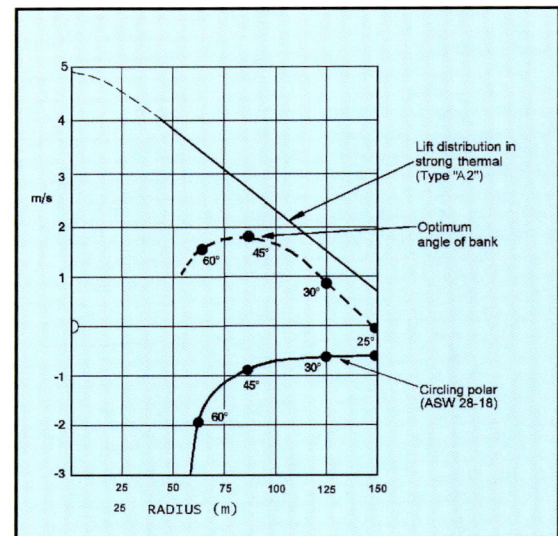

Figure 15: Optimum bank angle for "strong thermal" (Type A2)

For thermal type A2 (strong thermal), a bank angle of 45° is clearly best – a result no doubt anticipated by many pilots based on simple in-flight observations. Flying at higher or lower angles of bank has a detrimental effect on the achieved rate of climb. The diagram shows that circling at 45° achieves a climb rate of almost 2 m/s (or 4 kts). Banking the glider 30° makes for a climb rate of 1 m/s (or 2 kts) and a bank angle of a mere 25° will at best result in zero sink. Excessive banking of 60° is also far from ideal. It can only be justified when extremely narrow lift is encountered (e.g. at low altitudes) and a circling diameter of less than 70 m is necessary to climb at all.

**Flying in formation
Photo:
Siegfried Samson**

Now let us find out whether these findings hold true for a strong thermal with a rather large diameter.

As might be expected, wide thermals of type B2 tolerate flying at slightly shallower angles of bank without a detrimental effect on the rate of climb. In this particular case, a 40° angle of bank is close to the optimum although a bank angle of 30° provides only a slightly lower climb rate. The problem is that such thermals are very rare indeed and must therefore be regarded as exceptions. What we frequently find are narrow thermals at lower levels with diameters that slowly increase with altitude, although the diameter of the strongest part (the core) hardly changes at all.

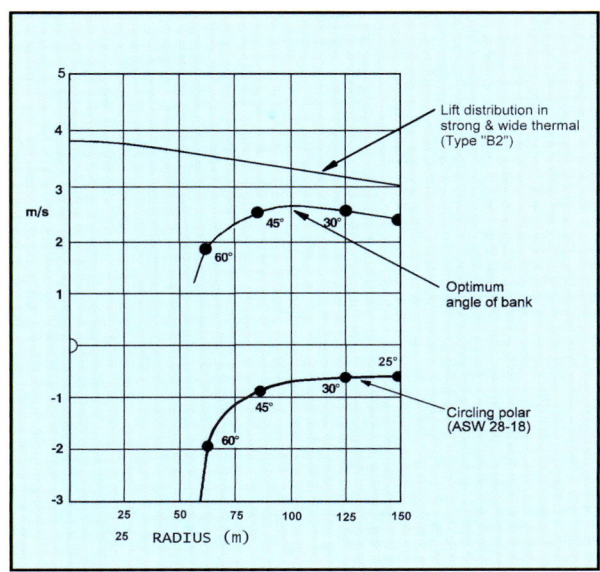

Figure 16: Optimum angle of bank for "strong & wide thermal" (Type B2)

If the thermals are weak, or even weak and narrow, it is vital to reduce the wing loading. A lighter glider with a more favourable circling polar usually provides an overall advantage in weak conditions. (Refer to Figure 12.)

The findings are conclusive; thermalling at approximately 45° angles of bank definitely offers an advantage. Sure, it requires higher levels of skill, produces higher g-forces, and makes thermalling generally less pleasant but pilots, especially performance-orientated ones, cannot ignore the benefits.

1.11 Practical hints

It is not easy to judge the angle of bank accurately. Most pilots thermal at a much shallower angle than they think. Experience suggests that newcomers in particular tend to circle at less than 30° when they think they are banking the glider 40° or even more. Here are three simple suggestions that can aid pilots in flying near the optimum bank angle.

The first hint is very easy to implement and probably even the most effective one although requiring nothing more than a piece of wire, a bit of plywood and some masking tape.

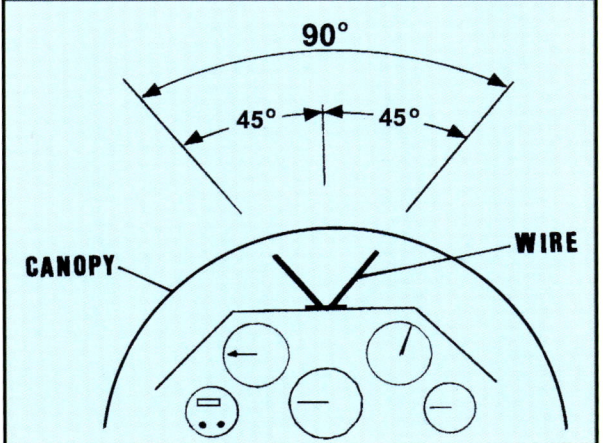

Figure 17: Angle of bank indicator

The wire is bent in accordance with the above sketch and is then permanently glued onto a piece of plywood of approximately 50 x 50 mm. This cheap gadget can easily be affixed to the top of the instrument panel with some masking tape. While circling at 45° angle of bank, one of the two ends of wire will stand perpendicular to the horizon. While checking the "nose/horizon attitude" it is easy to check whether we are still thermalling anywhere near our chosen 45° angle of bank. (Self adhesive strips of coloured tape on the inside of the canopy provide the same effect).

Another method is checking the time for a complete turn. The table below shows the circle time at various airspeeds and the corresponding angle of bank.

Table 3: Circle time in relation to bank angle

Speed	CIRCLE TIME IN SECONDS								
	Bank Angle in Degrees								
(kts)	20	25	30	35	40	45	50	55	60
40	36	28	23	19	16	13	11	9	8
45	41	32	26	21	18	15	12	10	9
50	45	35	29	24	20	16	14	12	10
55	50	39	31	26	22	18	15	13	10
60	54	42	34	28	24	20	17	14	11
65	59	46	37	31	26	21	18	15	12
g-force	1.06	1.10	1.15	1.22	1.31	1.41	1.56	1.74	2.00

Last but not least we can use a datalogger if available. Set at a 5 second recording interval, the trace shows a perfect square for a 20 second turn. Looking at Table 3 we can see that a bank angle of 45° and a speed of 60 kts correspond to 20 seconds for a full turn. I personally prefer using the first method shown in Figure 17 as it provides instant feedback.

1.12 Problems arising while thermalling steeply

Our wings travel at different airspeeds in a banking turn. This may sound a bit odd at first but becomes rather obvious when looking at Figure 18 below. While thermalling, the outer wing travels markedly further in the same amount of time and the resultant faster speed produces slightly more lift. The slower inner wing generates less lift and wants to drop. Having different amounts of lift on each wing is hardly noticeable at shallow bank angles, but becomes a complication when circling steeply. Without correcting control inputs, the outer wing keeps rising and the inner wing keeps going down. As a result,

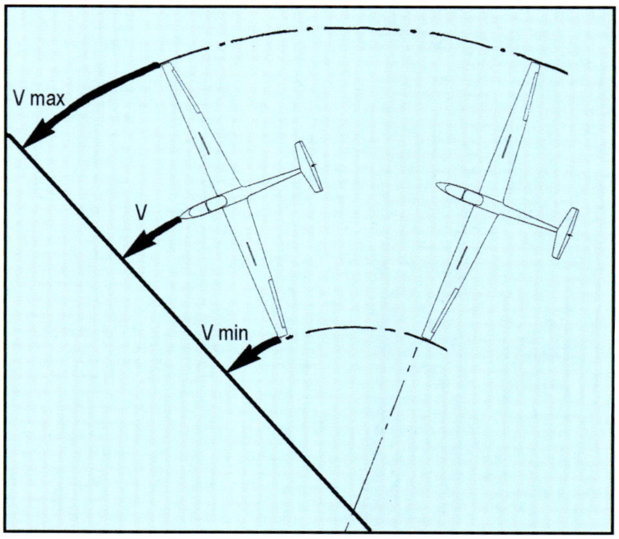

Figure 18: Speed difference between inner and outer wing

our angle of bank increases steadily and soon we find ourselves banking much more steeply than intended. The resulting higher g-loads quickly reach uncomfortable levels, the speed builds up rapidly and newer pilots get overloaded in more ways than one.

To prevent these unwanted effects we simply apply and hold a small amount of opposite aileron – just enough to ensure that our chosen angle of bank is maintained. In other words, we don't allow the bank angle to exceed a self-imposed limit that very much depends on our skill level and the handling characteristics of the glider. (We will come back to this subject under the heading "Advanced cross-country flying")

If you have ever wondered why you have trouble maintaining a steep angle of bank, you might have just discovered the reason. Therefore, I suggest you put the theory to the test and perform steep turns in neutral air when next the opportunity presents itself. Soon you will develop a pretty good feel for the amount of opposite aileron required. The exercise will be of tremendous help whenever confronted with narrow thermals in future.

1.13 Avoiding sink after releasing

An interesting article written by Norman Kennedy contains hints for beginners who are struggling when it comes to staying out of sink. It was published a few years ago, but as it is relevant in this context it is included in abbreviated and slightly modified form.

In no way is this article an attempt to teach how to thermal; rather it's a short analysis of what one might term "bad habits".

Possibly one of the worst habits of many pilots is not maintaining a positive line when flying from one place to another while seeking lift on the way.

Figure 19 shows that glider A flown on a steady course is likely to find a thermal within a reasonable distance. Several other courses held straight could also be productive and as a result the chances of hitting a thermal are much improved. The pilot of glider B allows his aircraft to be influenced by weak lift as it passes the fringes of thermals.

As a result it is turned away gently by the lift. Glider B not only misses all thermals but is also likely to encounter the heavy sink usually surrounding thermals. In such cases, the glider effectively remains in sink and the pilot is forced to join circuit before long.

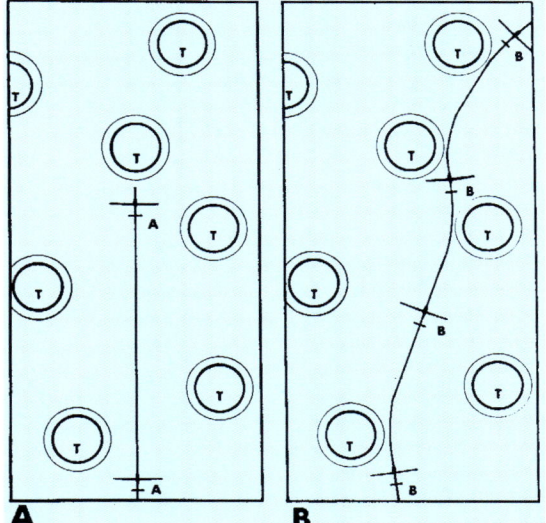

Figure 19: Two gliders cruising between thermals

Should the pilot fly with a heavy hand, watch the instruments, not take notice of air movements, or introduce unnecessary control inputs as he flies along, the lifting of one wing may well go unnoticed, unless it is quite exaggerated.

THIS IS A VERY COMMON HABIT WITH SOME PILOTS. THESE PILOTS DO NOT FLY THE GLIDER, BUT THE OPPOSITE IS TRUE, THE GLIDER FLIES THE PILOT.

Chapter 1
Training in the vicinity of the home airfield

In a thermal near Lake Benmore (New Zealand)

1.14 Structure of thermals

Thermals can be moody. One day they are strong, big, smooth and plentiful but on another day they are few and far between, weak, broken and narrow. What worked well for us one day will not necessarily work on another, and where we are finding regular lift today there might be heavy sink tomorrow. Different meteorological conditions result in different thermal behaviour and thermal characteristics. Useful research into the structure of thermals dates back to the fifties when R. S. Scorer began to experiment by releasing fluids of different density in a water tank. He sought to gain an insight of thermals by studying the motion within these "laboratory thermals". Assuming that the results of his experiments can be transferred to the free atmosphere, his work supported the concept of rising bubbles. As these bubbles rise through the atmosphere, they experience some resistance at their periphery. This drag is responsible for a flow pattern within the thermal that leads to significantly higher

Figure 20: Multicore thermal

upward flow at the centre compared to the perimeter. This is also known as the vortex ring theory.

Although this theory gained widespread acceptance for a while, glider pilots have thrown more and more doubt on it in recent years. Scorer's theory that thermals are short-lived entities is almost daily contradicted by glider pilots around the world. They often join a thermal a few thousand feet below another glider, and after having climbed several thousand feet, they regularly observe another glider commence thermalling quite some distance below. Obviously laboratory experiments bear little relationship to what is really happening in the atmosphere.

In the sixties, Russian scientists used powered aircraft and gliders to sample updrafts over Estonia. Their work pointed to single or multiple-core thermals, whereby multiple core thermals are prevalent if the vertical air temperature gradient in the lowest level of the atmosphere is above 0.8°C per 100 m (2.4 °C per 1000 ft). This very volatile and highly unstable layer is called the superadiabatic layer. It is normally as thin as 300 to 500 ft but can have a depth of several thousand feet over arid areas on days with intense heating and light winds. These findings relate very well to practical experience suggesting that, on days with low temperature gradients, thermals are not only small and weak but also usually confined to a single core. On the other hand, multiple-core thermals are frequently observed in strong conditions (higher temperature gradients) when we can often observe several gliders circling only a few hundred metres apart but enjoying very similar rates of climb.

Research has continued ever since – but particularly valuable work was conducted in the late eighties. It was performed over Eyre Peninsula in South Australia by Flinders University in South Australia using an instrumented Grob G109B motor glider with on-board sensitive instruments and a data acquisition and "real time" processing system.

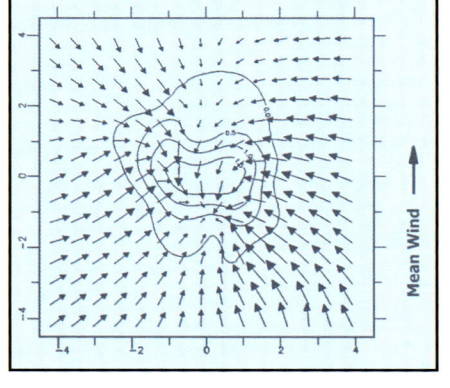

Figure 21:
Shape of updrought and direction of airflow at low levels

As well as helping to reveal the three-dimensional structure of thermals, the research program has recorded flow patterns near thermal updraughts that are of major interest to the gliding movement as a whole. Plotting the accumulated data as two-dimensional cross sections indicates strong inflows of air into thermals at lower levels and fairly irregular shaped updrafts. A typical horizontal cross section for a thermal within the superadiabatic layer is shown in Figure 21. The arrows indicate air velocity and direction of airflow, but please note that the mean wind vector has already been subtracted.

The horizontal cross section of a thermal well clear of the superadiabatic level looks rather different. Not only has the mean diameter increased by a significant amount, but the velocity of the airflow surrounding the thermal has also decreased significantly. These findings tend to underscore a widely held belief that gliders tend to drift towards the core when near the ground, while the same does not apply in well-established thermals at higher levels.

If the last two graphs aren't interesting enough, perhaps Figure 23 can create some

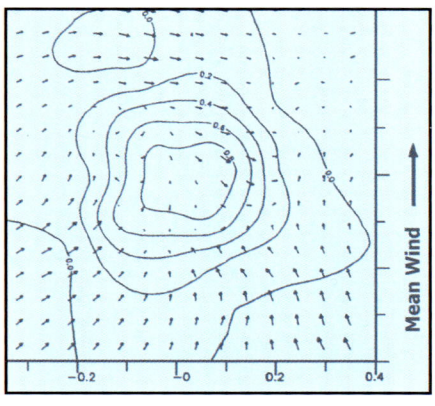

Figure 22:
Shape of updraught and direction of airflow at higher levels

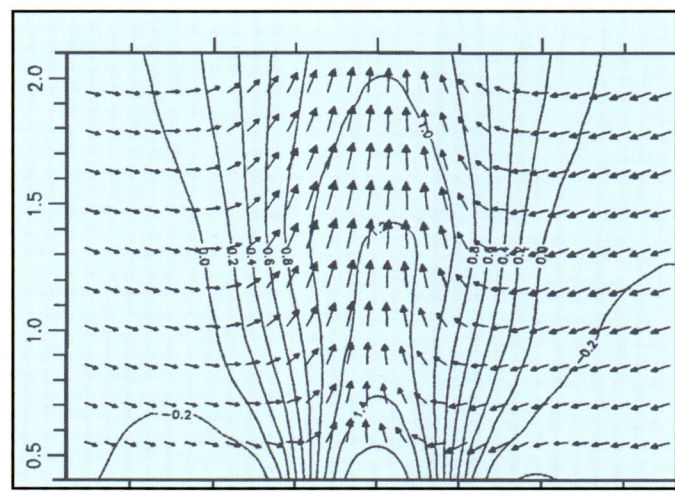

Figure 23: Vertical cross-section in the across-wind direction

excitement. It shows a vertical cross-section through a thermal, where weak sink surrounding the thermal gradually turns into strong lift near the core. Please note that the last three illustrations are not measurements of a single typical thermal, but are computer generated diagrams combining data from a large number of updrafts sampled over a single location in South Australia.

All measurements relate to a region of native mallee bushland with an average height of 2 to 4 metres and were compiled during the driest part of summer. We must therefore not assume that thermals are of a similar nature elsewhere or have identical characteristics all year round.

Further research conducted by Greenhut, Lenschow, Stephens, Khalsa, Crum and Young, based on conditional sampling of aircraft data, suggests that well defined up-drafts cover about 15 to 43% of the landscape while well defined downdrafts cover 20 to 55%. These findings appear to be in line with the day-to-day experiences of glider pilots. The question remains as to what constitutes a well defined up- or downdraught.

As far as glider pilots are concerned, only the strongest of thermal cores with the highest vertical airspeeds are of interest but, unfortunately, a percentage distribution of peak readings doesn't seem to be available. In 1986, Godowitch observed 36 to 40% updraughts and 49 to 52% downdraughts over both rural and urban sites, but concluded that thermals over urban sites had greater vertical speeds.

A contribution based on his flying experience of over 32 000 hours was made by four-times World Champion Ingo Renner. Working as a professional gliding instructor and coach in Europe as well as in Australia, Renner subscribes to the thermal model developed by Professor Heinz Fortak and Carsten Lindemann of the 'Free University of Berlin'. It is based on motorglider measurements and raises the really interesting concept of a narrowing of thermals just above the superadiabatic layer. Professor Fortak attributes this to the initial acceleration of air and the resulting Venturi effect. Inflow of air from all directions ensures that a glider circling just above the superadiabatic layer will slowly drift towards the core without any conscious control inputs by the pilot. As the thermal

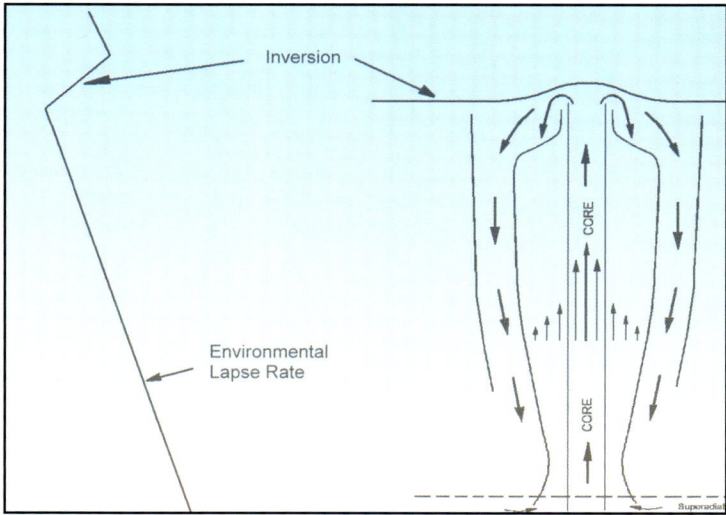

Figure 24: The Fortak thermal model

rises it encounters a falling ambient pressure, which ensures that the area of weaker lift around the thermal core increases. Scientific research and everyday practical experience clearly support such findings, although most top pilots seem to think that the diameter of the thermal core remains essentially unchanged. Renner concurs, and says that pilots thermalling steeply can remain in the core and climb high enough to get right into the inversion layer. In contrast, pilots thermalling with a shallow angle of bank will encounter sink well below the inversion. The reason becomes obvious when looking at Figure 24. The rising air of the thermal core is deflected straight off the inversion layer where it turns into heavy sink.

A field experiment with a difference was conducted by Noilhan and Benech in 1986. Using a total of 105 oil burners with a combined heat output of 1000 MW over an area of 15 000 m², they had little difficulty creating an artificial thermal. Upwind of the warm updraught, a cool downdraught was observed, while downwind a cool updraught was found. Most interesting of all, a pressure differential of about 0.1 kPa (1 mbar) was generated near the surface under the updraught, which induced strong horizontal convergence at the base of the updraught and might explain why thermals tend to collect all available warm air in the immediate vicinity.

Other studies have indicated that thermals start rising with a significant temperature advantage, but by the time the thermal arrived at inversion or convection level it was found to be cooler compared to the surrounding air. It is believed that these thermals gain most of their buoyancy from their moisture content. Readers interested in a detailed explanation of these phenomena are referred to Section 1.19.

1.15 Thermal formation and thermal behaviour on a calm day

The aforementioned research conducted by Flinders University suggests a rather chaotic situation within and around a hot air reservoir near the ground (Figure 25). Isolated plumes of warm air have been identified within and just above the main warm air reservoir. These plumes break away at irregular intervals and can fool glider pilots into believing that they have found steady lift. In reality they have found only a short-lived bubble likely to turn into heavy sink before the turn is completed.

Within the superadiabatic layer it is almost impossible to distinguish between a real thermal and temporarily separating bubbles. Instability within this lower layer allows an easy vertical displacement of air, which in turn makes any air movements almost totally unpredictable. It is assumed that low-level turbulence from vegetation or man-made structures also plays an important role. Therefore it is a good idea to resist the temptation to try and climb away from such low altitudes.

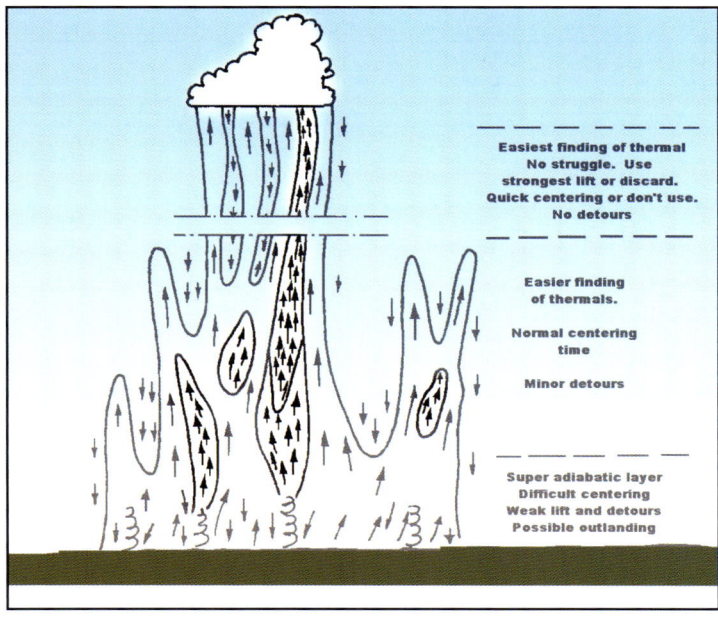

Figure 25: Thermal behaviour on a calm day

Training in the vicinity of the home airfield

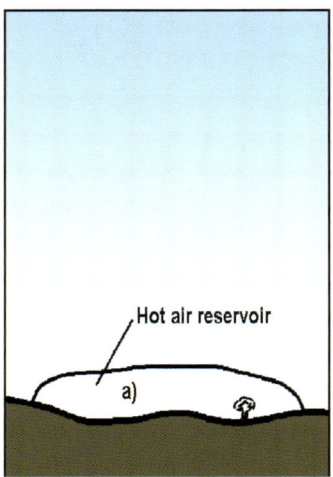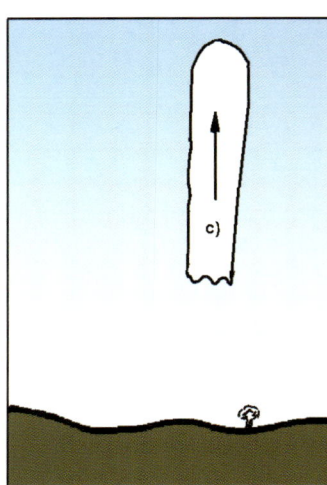

Figure 26: Formation of thermal and breaking away

The hot air reservoir grows bigger and bigger and eventually reaches a point where it can't grow any further. All this warm air escapes and breaks away to form a thermal. Once started, it behaves like a giant vacuum cleaner and drags in warm air from all sides. Personal observations point to steeply ascending single or multiple columns rather than an ascent as one huge bubble. (Refer Section 1.14.). Right under the centre of the thermal, swirling dust, debris, grass clippings etc. can often be observed. On days when farmers burn their stubble fields we often see well defined smoke thermals with a vertical extent amounting to many thousands of feet. Interestingly enough, they are anything but straight but rather tend to "snake about" with height.

Figure 26 shows that the rising air column maintains its momentum for as long as the supply of warm air continues. The lifecycle depends on the thickness of the superadiabatic layer, the size of the hot air reservoir, the intensity of the ongoing heating etc, but when the supply of hot air has run out the thermal will break away from the ground. Its remnants might continue to rise for a little while, but many glider pilots believe that it weakens quite significantly almost as soon as the warm air reservoir on the ground is exhausted. To me this theory has some credibility. Especially in gliding contests, we often observe gliders leaving thermals almost simultaneously regardless of altitude.

1.16 Finding thermals on blue days

Now let's look into more practical matters and work on finding thermals in the blue. Inexperienced pilots often rely on the analogous principle of eventually colliding with a tree while walking through a forest blindfolded.
No doubt, such tactics sometimes work, but they are not always appropriate. Remaining on track might be quite a good flying tactic within the upper third of our operating band because there is every chance of intercepting a good thermal by sheer luck. However, while operating closer to the ground such tactics are far from ideal. Lower down we must not rely on good luck but rather trust in good management. Locating areas of lift becomes much easier if we understand how thermals form and how they behave.
Contrary to popular belief, the air is not heated by the sun but by the ground. Almost all of the sun's short-wave radiation reaches the ground without warming the air in the process. After the ground has received heat energy from the sun it warms the air directly above and allows the formation of thermals. Ground that almost completely reflects the sun (e.g. snow) is never a good source of lift. Wet ground will also not experience much warming as the heat is transferred into deeper layers and the sun's energy is used for evaporation. The same applies to ground covered with thick and lush vegetation. Such

Training in the vicinity of the home airfield

vegetation requires water transpiration (evaporation from the leaves) for survival. The required energy is no longer available for heating the ground and as a consequence it remains cooler.

For this reason, glider pilots always need to identify which areas on the ground are absorbing heat energy. These are the hottest spots and the most likely thermal sources. It is essential that we assess the temperature difference of the terrain below. A few simple hints might be of help here:

1) Start to look at the ground during the launch or straight after release.
2) Imagine walking barefooted over the ground below.
3) Direct the flight path over and slightly downwind of areas assessed to be the hottest.

A dark, dry and bare paddock would be fairly warm (if not hot) after long periods of exposure to the sun. Heat is passed on to the air. It is not unusual for the temperature just above bare ground to be 4 to 5°C higher than a metre or so higher up. The density of the hotter air is relatively low so the air will eventually rise and form a thermal.

Getting ready for a good day of soaring

37

Therefore, direct your flight path over bare paddocks or sun-facing slopes rather than wet areas or fields covered with vegetation. The hot air closest to the ground mixes with the cooler air just above. Over a period of 10 to 20 minutes, this leads to a significant temperature increase within the superadiabatic layer. However, to start the thermal ascent, a trigger is needed. On a calm day, this trigger might be a moving vehicle; it might be a flock of birds, a winch launch, an aerotow or any other form of air disturbance. Thermal triggers on windy days are usually very different and will be looked at in Section 1.18.

1.17 Efficient centring of thermals in blue conditions

With some experience, we can recognise a blue thermal as we approach it by using such indicators as turbulence and increased rates of sink. The odds are clearly against us when it comes to encountering a thermal head on. Just as slim are our chances of getting an unmistakable indication of the correct direction of turn on thermal entry. What can we do if, after a quarter of a turn, we contact less buoyant air or even sink?

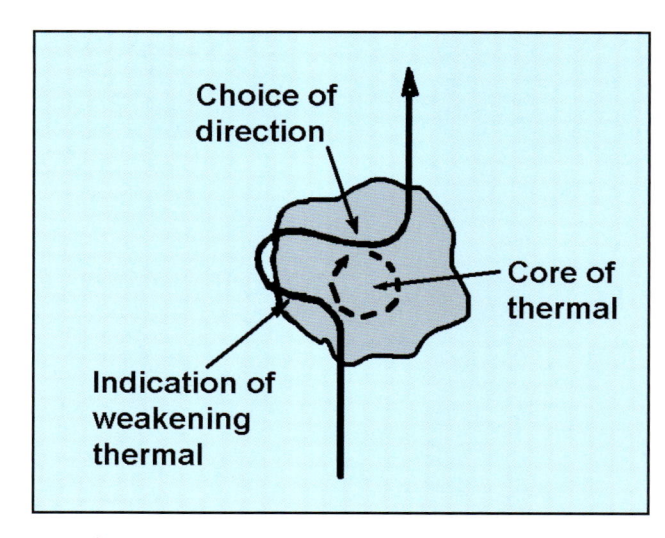

**Figure 27:
Searching for the core of the thermal**

Well, one possible solution is illustrated in Figure 27. If we have rolled the glider into a turn and realise that we have turned into sink, we must decide between continuing the full circle or changing the direction of turn. My advice is to perform a decisive 180° turn in the opposite direction and then wait until the audio variometer indicates strong lift again. If the lift is contacted, another decision regarding the direction of turn must be made, but if the rate of lift remains unsatisfactory, the glider is turned back onto the original course.

This tactic allows an effective search of either side of the original track without adding considerable distance. If, on the other hand, the initial turn is continued into sink, a significant amount of altitude can be lost.

1.18 Thermal behaviour on windy days

Light to moderate winds are beneficial for the formation of thermals. Strong winds, however, make soaring more difficult as they tend to break thermals up. Especially near the ground, it becomes very difficult to find any useful climbs. But even on windy days hot air reservoirs cling to the ground while the wind pushes them slowly downwind during the growing process. This continues until an obstacle is encountered, which causes the reservoir to break away from the surface. Plenty of observations suggest that such an obstacle could be a clump of trees, a house, a bordering patch of scrub, a road, an abrupt change of vegetation or a change of slope. Even a flock of birds can be the trigger and make the warm air separate from the ground.

Training in the vicinity of the home airfield

The warm air continues to be pushed along by the wind even after the thermal has fully established itself. Under its centre, a small area of lower pressure forms that has two welcome side effects. It causes more warm air to be sucked off the surface along the path of the slowly shrinking hot air reservoir, and by doing so it prolongs the useful life of thermals on windy days. Evidence of this can be found by studying the behaviour of dust devils. (Refer to Section 1.27.) This means that we may be wasting our time trying to locate a thermal by using tactics appropriate for calm days. Instead of finding lift directly over a promising field we must look for a thermal trigger downwind of it.

Although the travelling nature of a thermal is hardly under dispute over relative flat terrain, there are cases where – even on windy days – thermal source and trigger remain stationary. A mountain slope facing not only the sun but also the wind would be a prime example. In Section 5.12 we will look at mountain thermals more closely, but for now we can conclude that thermals break away from the ground at the top of the mountain where they can no longer draw in air from neighbouring terrain. Clearly we have a case of a stationary thermal source, but if we look at the cumulus cloud that may forme above we will see that it is anything but stationary. It always drifts away in the direction of the upper wind.

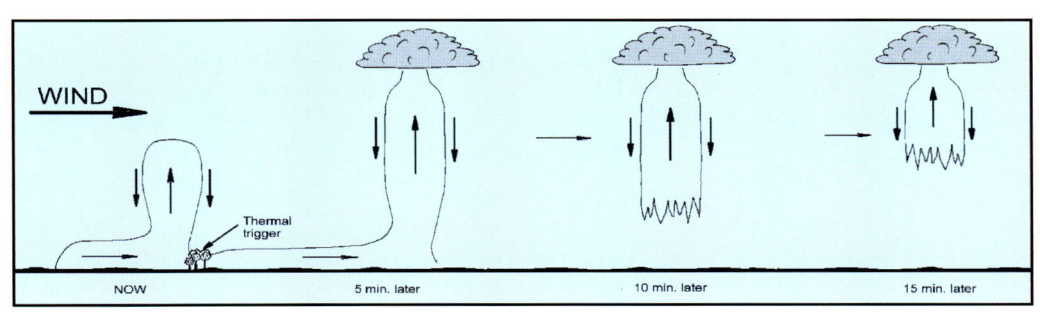

Figure 28: Thermal drifting downwind of trigger point

This raises an interesting question:

a) Does the thermal assume a progressively shallower slope as the cumulus cloud drifts further downwind, or

b) Do thermals still remain essentially vertical structures as per figure 28 above?

My practical experience and independent observations clearly support the latter. With stationary thermal sources new clouds tend to form in almost exactly the same position on a more or less regular basis. But this doesn't mean that older cumulus clouds further downwind instantly dissipate. Quite often these clouds are drawing in air from nearby decaying clouds (refer to Section 1.25) or still have

In close formation with an ASK 21

39

small residues of warm air feeding them. The self-stoking effect of cumulus clouds can also extend the useful life of downwind cumulus. (Refer to Section 1.26)

We can conclude that normal wind gradients seldom force thermals to adopt significant tilt angles. Ignoring their occasional bending (probably due to different wind strengths at various altitudes), it appears that updraughts have a tendency to align themselves in an almost vertical orientation. A lot of older (and even some newer) gliding literature seem to support the concept of leaning thermals and I'm happy to admit that this has greatly influenced my own thinking for quite some time. However, leading glider pilots are nowadays almost united in their opinion that a drifting thermal must not be confused with a leaning thermal.

Especially in top competitions, gliders are usually seen circling more or less directly above or below one another. This even applies when there is a moderate to strong wind and several thousand feet of vertical separation between circling gliders. Especially on windy days, it requires some practice to find updraughts at low level without wasting too much time in the process. For the purpose of learning, it is useful to identify thermal source and thermal trigger every time we are nicely established in an updraught. This is particularly valuable when lift is contacted below 2000 ft because at lower altitudes there is less ambiguity as to where it is coming from.

One soon gets into a habit of flying from one likely thermal source to another. We will also learn that it pays to tolerate small detours if we can remain over good thermal-producing ground. Such tactics must be adopted almost subconsciously and automatically, especially while flying low. As soon as they begin to work for us we develop a higher degree of confidence. As our success rate improves, so will our motivation and the enjoyment we get from our sport.

1.19 Lift towards the end of the day

Experienced glider pilots would confirm that, long after the usual thermal sources have quit their service for the day, smooth lift can often be found in the most unexpected places. In fact, lift is often found in areas synonymous with heavy sink earlier in the day. This is a good enough reason to investigate this strange phenomenon; you never know, it might get you across the line one day.

Thermals are parcels of air with a lower density compared to the surrounding air. Usually, the lower density is a result of a higher temperature, but it can also be a result of higher humidity. Water vapour molecules are lighter than those of dry air because they are of lower molecular weight. of hydrogen-oxygen molecules. If these displace some of the dry air's higher molecular weight nitrogen and oxygen molecules, buoyancy is added to a thermal. 100% saturated air has a significantly lower density compared to absolutely dry air at the same pressure and temperature, which explains the contribution of humidity to useful lift.

Consider an irrigated orchard next to a patch of dry and bare farmland. Both areas are exposed to the same amount of sunshine. Earlier in the day, the bare farmland heats up much quicker and the air above it is significantly warmer than over the orchard. Consequently a reliable and steady stream of good thermals is produced for as long as the sun maintains the heating process.

In contrast, the irrigated orchard remains relatively cool due to a high water content of the soil and the fact that the canopy of green leaves only allows the ground (and hence the air above it) to warm up slowly. The orchard is not at all a brilliant source of lift. On the contrary, is likely to be associated with heavy sink.

Training in the vicinity of the home airfield

When the sun is very low on the horizon, the farmland loses its ability to generate thermals, because the sun is hitting the ground at increasingly shallower angles. However, the orchard also had a full day of exposure to sunshine and, although the heating process was significantly retarded, a reservoir of warm air has slowly accumulated amongst the trees. Now the orchard air is warmer and this temperature difference generates a late but very welcome thermal.

But that is not all. Humidity is another good reason for the orchard to generate lift. The warm air trapped amongst the trees is relatively moist due to steady evaporation of water from the soil plus the many millions of leaves. We must remember that a single large tree can transpire up to 3000 litres of water on a day with intense sunshine. Hundreds of trees in close proximity can increase the humidity level considerably, which has the effect of lowering the air density and enhancing its buoyancy. A combination of the two effects of

a) residual heating; and
b) a local increase in humidity

can generate unexpectedly strong thermals, often surprisingly smooth and even quite large in diameter. However, this type of lift not only occurs very late in the day but also only once a day. As soon as the residual warm air has risen and is replaced by nearby cooler air, these late updraughts cease and glider pilots would be well advised to be on final glide by then.

Sharing the sky with dozens of hanggliders

If you think you can forget all about this phenomenon because there are no orchards near your gliding field, think again. Later in the day, plantation forests and even patches of dense scrub are likely to produce the same effect. There is never a guarantee of finding such lift on any given day, as other meteorological conditions also play an important role, but it happens often enough to deserve a mention.

Late lift can also be found along ridges or mountains with slopes facing west. Such slopes are subject to more intense heating while the sun is low on the horizon. Experienced pilots also know that final glide altitudes can often be gained from sources of lift that are independent of direct solar heating. Especially useful are wave lift, ridge lift, sea breeze fronts and convergence lines as a result of katabatic winds – subjects dealt with in later chapters.

1.20 Lift under cumulus clouds

The discussion on finding and working lift would not be complete without considering cumulus clouds. Thermals are colums of rising air which always contain some degree of moisture. As this moist air rises, it encounters reduced pressure at altitude. Lower pressure makes the air expand and cool down, and together with decreasing temperatures comes a lower moisture retention capacity. In other words, cooler air can hold less water vapour than warm air. As an example, 1 kg of air at 5°C can hold 5.5 grams of water vapour whereas at 20°C the maximum possible amount of retained water vapour increases almost threefold. At some temperature, known as the dew point, the air becomes saturated and some of the water vapour condenses into tiny water droplets to form a new cumulus cloud. (Refer to Section 2.7.)

Such clouds are loved by glider pilots as they advertise lift. However, no two cumulus clouds are the same. According to R. B. Stull, small and shallow cumuli (cumulus humilis) are likely to be fed by a single updraught. In spite of the latent heat release during condensation, (refer to Section 1.23), the clouds fail to develop vertically to any great extent. Air diverges from the centre towards the lateral edges and, in conditions of light wind shear, clouds often adopts the shape of a breaking wave. Updrafts are usually found on the upwind side and downdrafts are prominent downwind.

In contrast, cumulus clouds with a substantial vertical development (cumulus mediocris) are likely to be positively buoyant. This cloud forms when the rising thermal has enough inertia to overshoot the condensation level far enough for its temperature to rise to a point where it is again warmer than the environment. This greatly affects the cloud's evolution and allows it to draw in more air through its base. Such a cloud has a longer lifecycle than the thermal that first triggered it. Updraughts of varying strength are likely to be found along the entire base of the cloud and downdrafts are less common, as almost all the rising air is vented through the cloud and escapes sideways. Look for the darkest part of the cloud, because the strongest thermal is often located under the part of the cloud that features the greatest vertical development. Most of the sunlight is blocked under this part of the cloud and therefore it appears a fair bit darker from underneath. If we cannot detect such shade variations, it is advisable to try upwind or head for an area with a flat, even and clearly-defined base.

Regardless of whether a cloud is large or small, we have to keep in mind that a cumulus cloud is a secondary effect of a thermal. We sometimes encounter thermals that have not (yet) formed a cloud and clouds that have already lost their thermal. The presence of a cumulus cloud is not a guarantee of a thermal and the lack of a cloud does not guarantee that there are no thermals either.

Training in the vicinity of the home airfield

1.21 Finding the core under larger cumulus clouds.

Flying high on cumulus days requires a change in our thermal finding tactics. Instead of looking down for likely sources of lift, we look up to get our clues from the clouds above. After all, they are visible proof of the convection we are relying on. No more guesswork, no looking at the ground for likely thermal sources and no more searching for thermal triggers.

While not all cumulus clouds have good thermals under them, others – especially larger ones – might have several useful cores. Whether a particular cloud yields a strong thermal depends mainly on its lifecycle. Therefore it is very important to have a good understanding of cumulus clouds in order to intercept the core quickly. Relying on luck might work occasionally but only under relatively small clouds.

Therefore, a more careful study of all indicators is always the better option. While gliding towards a cumulus, we have ample time to search for clues and determine where the cloud is most "active". Under no circumstances should we waste such opportunities by looking at our instruments.

If the air is relatively dry (or exceptionally warm) the thermal will push into the base of the cloud leaving a dome, sometimes to a depth of several hundred feet. The best lift is found directly underneath the dome. If, on the other hand, the thermal carries relatively moist air aloft, some condensation will occur well below cloudbase.

Approaching Mt Brewster (NZ)
Photo:
Marty Taylor, Glide Omarama

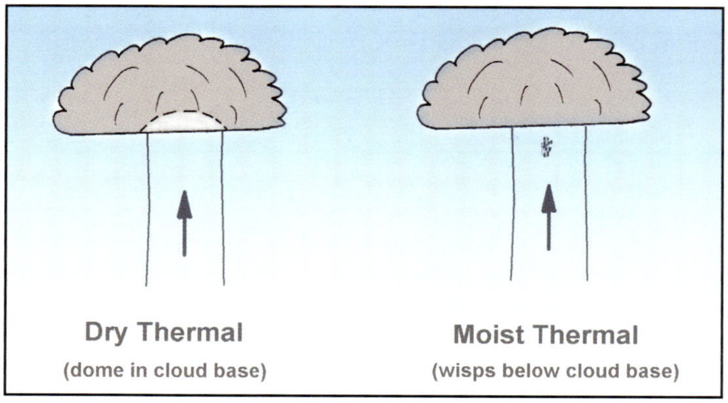

Training in the vicinity of the home airfield

**Figure 29:
The effect of different moisture levels in thermals**

Dry Thermal (dome in cloud base)

Moist Thermal (wisps below cloud base)

It means that small wisps of cloud form below the base are usually marking the core. We find the strongest lift by circling around them.

The size of the cloud can also have a major bearing on the search area underneath. Large clouds can produce considerable cloud shadows and the resulting lower ground temperatures usually depress new thermal activity. Finding the core quickly is certainly important, but it is just as crucial to avoid the heavy sink often associated with large clouds. For this reason it is important to watch the cloud shadow for an indication of the travelling direction and determine the likely thermal source on the ground. This helps us to approach the cloud from the right direction and minimises the risk of being caught in heavy sink.

On the other hand, large cumulus clouds promote instability within the cloud, prolonging convection and producing stronger climbs especially near cloud base (Section 1.26). If all else fails we can traverse the cloud in the direction of the wind at cloud level. Especially in strong wind situations the clouds tends to be elongated making it advantageous to traverse them in the direction of the wind (Figure 30). It improves our chances of intercepting buoyant air considerably and usually gives much better results than just following a straight line and hoping for the best.

Provided this manoeuvre is planned well before reaching the cloud the additional distance flown is almost negligible. Applying the same tactics on crosswind legs can also be successful. Such flying tactics have proved successful when approaching medium to large clouds. However, smaller and especially shallow cumulus clouds need to be treated differently, especially on days when their life-cycle is rather short. Flying towards promising-looking clouds can

**ASW 28 - 18 posing over grain terminal in Australia
Photo:
Paul Wiggins**

produce disappointing results, as the updraught might have completely stopped by the time we arrive underneath. In such short-cycle conditions, it usually proves best to head for developing wisps and fly towards the upwind edge of the cumulus cloud above. Remember, with a substantial vertical distance to the cloud and a strong wind the core is almost always located slightly upwind of the cloud.

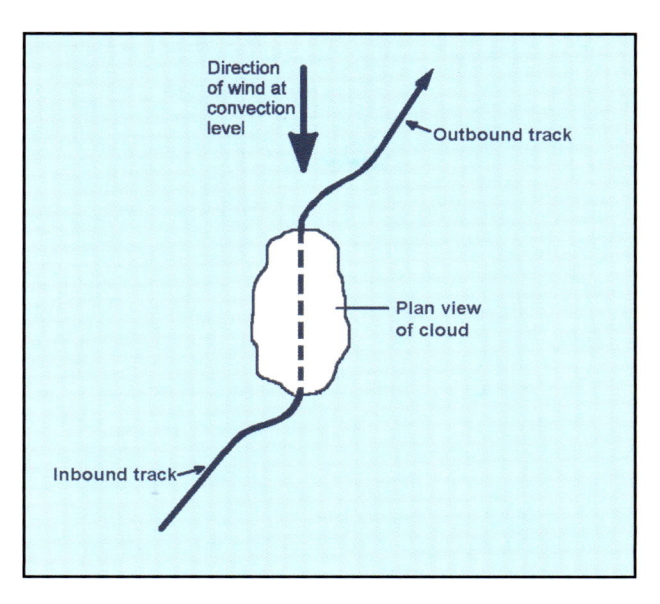

Figure 30: Traversing a large cloud in the direction of the wind at cloud level

1.22 Spacing of thermals

For reasons not yet fully understood, the distance between lift appears to be closely related to the depth of convection. As a rule of thumb, we can work on a thermal spacing of approximately 2.5 times convection depth. It is important to note that convection depth is defined as the distance between the ground and the top of the thermal (cloud top) – not the condensation level as many glider pilots believe.

If, for example, the top of the thermals reach 6500 ft (2000 m), we can expect these thermals to be approximately 5000 m or 5 km apart. The average life of a cumulus is only of the order of 20 minutes or so. However, this relatively short life span is a blessing in disguise for glider pilots as it makes it easier to draw valuable conclusions from a cloud's appearance and its growth pattern. To be more specific, look for signs of movement, curl-over, wisps of condensation etc. and try to form a mental picture of the location of the updraught underneath.

A cloud with an even base, billowing at the top and crisp with clearly defined edges is likely to be in its prime stage of development and almost certain to have a good thermal underneath. Looking for such clues is the best way to maximise chances of success.

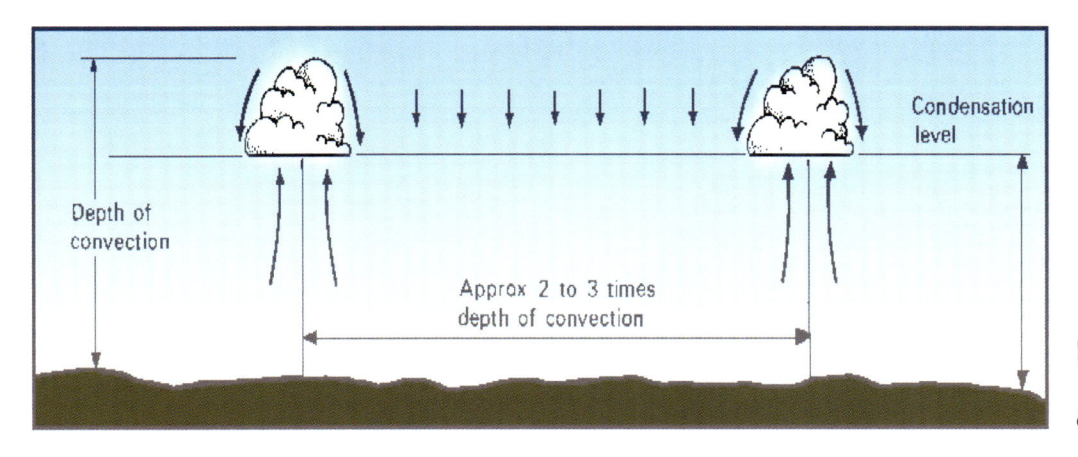

Figure 31: Spacing of thermals

1.23 Tactics just before and after launching

Glider pilots used to winch launching know only too well that a flight is rarely successful without putting some thought into it before getting into the cockpit and making some tactical decisions on the ground.

Picking a promising cloud shortly before the launch is always of advantage. It means that one less crucial decision needs to be made while airborne. At the top of the launch we check that our target cloud is still within reach and, if so, we keep flying towards it until we get there. In other words, we make a decision and stick to it unless safety considerations dictate a return to the airfield.

Remember, we have not only limited time but also limited height available. Therefore, we should think twice before we detour over promising ground below. It is also advisable to avoid throwing a turn if we are not very sure that we will finish up in good lift. We must simply keep flying towards our chosen cloud at a speed close to best L/D but stay ever mindful that we have to position ourselves upwind of it. The importance of contacting lift as soon as possible after release cannot be stressed too highly.

Much the same applies to aero-tow launching, although here we have the added advantage of being able to release as soon as we contact a thermal. A tow plane gaining altitude quickly is usually a good sign and gives the experienced pilot a hint of a thermal ahead. Usually this puts us straight into good lift but, in the event of a release away from a thermal, we head back to thermals identified while on tow. Remember, higher up, the thermal will have expanded in diameter making it easier for us to extract a reasonable climb.

In case we don't release in lift, we should head straight for the most promising cumulus cloud. Ideally, we pick one upwind of the airfield. While thermalling, the wind will ensure that we slowly drift back towards the airfield.

Our best chance of finding lift is to fly along a line between our suspected thermal trigger and our target cloud. At first glance, this might sound rather difficult to do, but it is much easier than expected when airborne. From the cockpit of a glider, travelling direction of clouds and wind speed can be assessed accurately simply by watching the shadows on the ground. Remember that wind direction and speed are usually different at cloud

A Grunau Baby ready for launch

and ground levels.

Only the wind at convection level matters when it comes to finding lift near the clouds. However, there are no hard and fast rules. Sometimes we find thermals under the sunlit part of the cloud, but on other days we might find it elsewhere. What tends to hold true though is that we usually find thermals in similar positions all day long. For this reason it is very advantageous to first determine where the lift is located in relation to the cloud – it makes subsequent thermal finding significantly easier.

The first thermal of the day doesn't have to be a boomer. In fact we are well advised to use weaker lift while still low even if we suspect that there are stronger thermals around. There are a number of good reasons for this. As the thermal is drifting along, it might momentarily draw in cooler air resulting in slightly weaker lift. However, when it collects air from hotter ground, the rate of climb will improve significantly.

Remember, a 4 kts (2 m/s) thermal will take 5 minutes to rise to 2000ft (600m) and better lift (as a result of warmer air) may only be a few turns away. Apart from that, it might be wise to get a feel for the day soon after releasing. Climbing away from down low is sometimes very difficult – especially for less experienced glider pilots. Therefore we are well advised to hang on to weaker lift until we have reached a more comfortable altitude. A costly and time-consuming second launch can spoil an otherwise perfect soaring day.

1.24 Over-development and cycling

Although more common in sub-tropical regions of the world, cumulus clouds can grow big enough and can become so numerous that they fill the sky completely. Even in central Europe, cumulus clouds can have a significantly longer lifecycle, as higher humidity levels slow down and delay the dissipation process considerably. It means that older clouds are very slow to disperse and, when new ones appear on a regular basis, a cloud blanket can form quickly. When this occurs we are faced with a phenomenon called "over-development." Needless to say, new convection is interrupted for as long as sunshine is unable to reach the ground. Only after the sun has burnt off some of the older clouds can it recommence heating the ground and, with a delay of approx. 20 to 30 minutes, the convection usually starts again. Sometimes this is called "cycling" in glider pilot's jargon; for a more detailed explanation please refer to Section 2.9.

1.25 Dissipating cumulus clouds

Because not every cloud is productive, we must be very selective to avoid wasting time and altitude under decaying cumulus. An almost completely dissipated cumulus cloud often has the same appearance as a newly forming one. Therefore, it is best to keep a close eye on doubtful wisps of clouds and only try them if they are clearly showing signs of life, activity and growth. Although this might seem easier said than done, there are quite a few clues that can help us avoid clouds that are developed past their prime.

Unless a cumulus cloud can draw in air horizontally, it usually begins to dissipate almost as soon as the updraught stops. This part of its lifecycle can be recognised by fading edges, uneven bases, fraying corners and an appearance of 'falling apart'. Compared to a developing and active cloud, the appearance is strikingly different. We are well advised to stay away from clouds looking a bit worse for wear, because there is usually nothing but sink under them.

Next time you wait for your turn to fly, attempt to identify active and decaying clouds. It will help provide valuable clues and you may find that cumulus cloud evaluation is not as difficult as first thought. It is good fun, especially if we involve other pilots on the ground. We may even find that our curiosity becomes contagious, which helps our fellow club members to become weatherwise as well.

At this juncture, a word of warning on the possible deceptiveness of cumulus clouds towards the end of a soaring day is appropriate. The temperature on the ground might have dropped by a few degrees only, and the clouds may still look as promising as ever. In reality however, the drop in temperature has either retarded or stopped the formation of new thermals, meaning that the appearance of the cumulus clouds is only kept up by the horizontal inflow of air from nearby decaying clouds, not from ground-based convection.

This does not mean that such clouds have outlived their usefulness altogether, because in the upper part of the convective layer reasonable lift can often still be found. Flying tactics must change though as we cannot get low and expect to find workable lift.

A well-known pilot was once asked how he managed to win a long-distance contest day when most of his competitors outlanded late afternoon. His answer was short and to the point: "At first", he said, "I stayed high and flew fast, but towards the end of the day I slowed down to remain in close contact with the clouds."

No wonder glider pilots often say: " There is no place like cloud base".

1.26 The self-stoking effect of cumulus clouds

Compared to a blue sky, we often experience much stronger lift and better gliding conditions under a sky full of cumulus clouds. At first sight, this seems far from logical, because a fair percentage of the ground is covered by cloud shadows. Therefore, one could be forgiven for thinking that the amount of heating is reduced, suppressing thermal activity and strength quite considerably. Practical experience, however, indicates that the opposite is true.

The reason is the release of latent heat at the moment of condensation. Your physics teacher probably explained that heat is required to change the state of water from liquid to vapour. There is always some moisture evaporated by the sun's heat, and that means that a certain quantity of water vapour is present in all thermals. This heat energy is not lost; it simply becomes trapped in the vapour as latent energy.

The sun's heat energy is released again when the process is reversed. In other words, when water vapour rises in a thermal and subsequently condenses at cloud level, we get a release of latent heat. Warming of the air enhances its buoyancy, which in turn increases the rate of lift. This effect is often quite noticeable just below cloud base.

1.27 Dust devils

Updraughts frequently become visible in the form of dust devils, especially during the dryer months of the year, Dry leaves, dust and other lightweight particles are whisked up by these rapidly rotating whirlwinds. Dust devils are also known to play havoc with gliders left unsecured and unattended on the ground.

The rotating motion of these updraughts of buoyant air immediately conjures pictures of hugely destructive tornadoes, even though dust devils are not directly related to tornadoes or water spouts. According to R.B. Stull ("An introduction to boundary layer meteorology"), the tangential velocity of dust devils is only in the order of 10 m/s, compared to 50 m/s for water spouts and 100 m/s for tornadoes. Average diameters of tens of metres and heights of about 100 m are typical, but over arid areas of the world dust devils can extend as high as six hundered metres (several thousand feet). In fact, Hans Werner Grosse has reported dust devils reaching 3000 m (10 000 ft) in central Australia.

Dust devil near Matamata Gliding Club (NZ)
Photo: Pam Gore

An independent field study was conducted by M.J. Hancy as far back as 1973. He concluded that dust devils are most prominent when the environmental lapse rate exceeds the dry adiabatic lapse rate. (See Chapter 2.)

Under such conditions, updraughts accelerate quite rapidly, which in turn seems to trigger their trademark swirling motion at ground level. As a logical consequence, dust devils are not only confined to patches of dusty ground. They can form over any thermal producing area but, if the surface is free of dust, the dust devils simply remain invisible.

Although dust devils usually stand out very well and are easily visible to the naked eye, we are normally hard-pressed to detect the less dusty centre from the ground. However, from the cockpit of an aircraft, this "eye" is often clearly visible. The dust-free centre is indicative of a downdraft with a vertical speed of

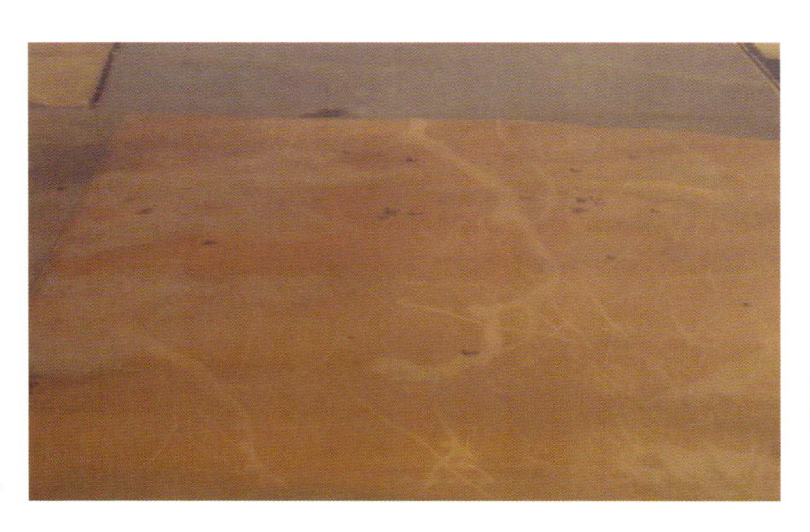

Trace of dust devils in stubble field
Photo: Mark Morgan

approximately 2 m/s. Consequently, we are faced with an outer updraft and an inner downdraft in very close proximity. No wonder glider pilots can sometimes get thrown around at lower levels!

The above comments have been confirmed by the experience of a fellow pilot from a neighbouring gliding club. He reported running towards a dust devil that was moving slowly across a stubble field. He goes on to write: "It was moving slowly enough that I could run after it and get inside of it. The wall of the thermal was very windy with stubble and dust flying around. The centre of the thermal was calm. Interestingly, the path of the thermal over the ground was irregular, i.e. it would stop, sometimes reverse or go sideways, but the general direction was with the prevailing wind."

The photo on the previous page confirms these observations. It shows several traces of dust devils in a drought-stricken field in South Australia and confirms a frequent change in the direction of travel. The photo cannot reflect the unpredictable speed variations, but it seems to confirm that dust devils seldom hover over the same patch of ground for more than a few seconds at a time. Field research also points to a ground tracks that on occasion can be almost perpendicular to the surface wind. The same studies also suggest travelling speeds faster than the surface wind. This is most likely due to a higher wind speed at altitude and the adaptation of the wind speed averaged over their entire height.

Contrary to popular belief, dust devils don't seem to have a favoured direction of rotation. Their rather short lifecycle and their relatively small scale do not allow Coriolis forces to take effect. It is assumed that the direction of rotation is often determined by smaller eddies generated when the wind is forced to flow around an obstacle on the ground. However, some authors have suggested a slight statistical bias favouring clockwise rotation south of the equator and anti clockwise rotation in the northern hemisphere. Glider pilots contacting dust devils at a low level are therefore well advised to circle in the opposite direction. The benefit is obvious – take advantage of the headwind component and hence reduce the circling diameter significantly. This comes in especially handy when battling a small diameter thermal relatively close to the ground.

The above comments might suggest that thermals are generally rotating. Recurrent articles in gliding magazines and frequent discussions in gliding circles indicate that this thought is entertained by a significant number of pilots. Some proponents of the idea have even thrown toilet roll streamers or confetti out of their glider to prove the point but so far nothing has been demonstrated convincingly. Undoubtedly thermals retain their initial rotation near ground level and field experiments by Noilhan and Benech (refer to Section 1.14) have established the presence of a pressure drop of 1 mbar in their centre. The resulting inflow of air creates a requirement for replacement, and the resulting convergent flow will bring about rotation just like it does for draining water around the plughole of a bathtub.

However, as the thermal rises above the superadiabatic layer, the rate of rotation most certainly diminishes significantly due to a reduction of pressure and the resulting lateral expansion of the rising air mass. Expanding air does the opposite of converging air. It causes any inherent rotation to fade; the friction created at the outer fringes is likely to reduce rotation to a point where it is almost unnoticeable to glider pilots. Mixing of rising air with surrounding air will also contribute to a swift diminishing of any initial rotation.

The above comments are applicable to the most common thermals in temperate regions. Observations by Hans Werner Grosse and other pilots suggest that dust devils in arid regions of the world carry dust to altitudes of 10 000 ft or so, but even these exceptionally strong thermals show little evidence of rotation at altitude. Even if a small degree of rotation is retained, it is hardly significant enough to justify reversing the

Training in the vicinity of the home airfield

direction of turn once properly established in a climb. My attempts to improve the rate of climb in exceptionally rough thermals by changing thermalling direction have only very seldom met with success.

1.28 The effect of a strong wind on thermals

Thermals are essentially vertical updrafts that tend to drift downwind as per Figure 27. On a calm day, the core of the thermal is located near the centre of the updraft, but on very windy days the situation is fundamentally different. A cross section through a thermal as per Figure 32 reveals an asymmetrical lift profile with stronger lift in the upwind quadrant of the circle – a notion very much supported by practical experience. The lift is strongest very close to heavy sink.

Figure 32: Core of thermal on windy days

Of course, in such conditions efficient thermalling is a very tricky, and sometimes frustrating, task. Moving only marginally further upwind could result in the loss of the core and drifting into very heavy sink, squandering altitude and hence valuable energy.

1.29 Thermal re-centring in windy conditions

Even very experienced pilots lose thermals. Loss of concentration, contacting a level with severe wind shear or a simple thermalling mistake are common reasons. This is not a problem as long as we have a fair idea of which direction we need to fly to find it again.

Although thermals drift with the wind, they seldom travel at wind speed, and hardly ever adopt the wind speed at altitude. By contrast, a circling glider tends to drift at the speed of the surrounding air. Consequently, it will move downwind faster than the thermal itself. Without the pilot taking corrective measures the thermal will be quickly lost.

To avoid losing the thermal, we need to adjust the angle of bank. This will result in an oval-shaped flight path, but this is exactly what we want in view of the situation illustrated in Figure 33. Depending on both the diameter of the lift and the strength of

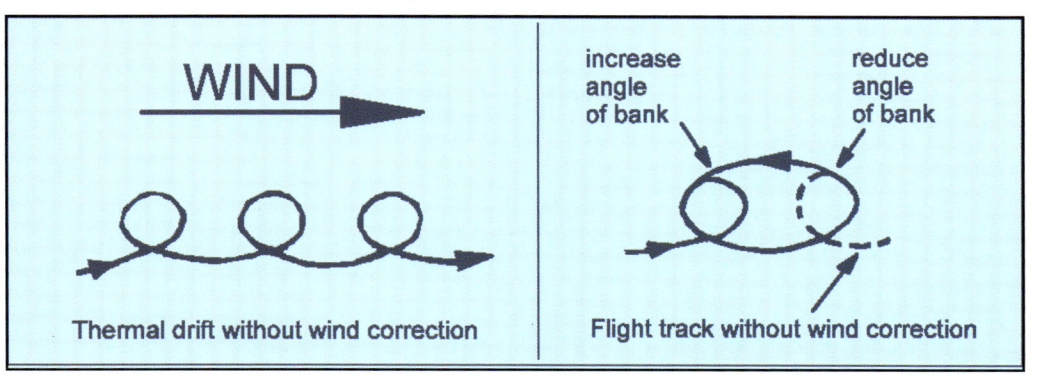

Figure 33: Flight path above ground with and without drift correction

the wind, the degree of re-positioning varies from a mild correction at every second turn to a major re-centring exercise at every circle. All of these manoeuvres have one thing in common - they require us to level the wings just before pointing into wind. Soon after we feel the vertical acceleration and just before our variometer shows the peak reading we roll into it again. If we wait until the vario peaks, it will be too late and we will have passed the core of the thermal. A good deal of anticipation is required, which needs to utilise sensitive nerve endings in our backside. Windy days with weak and broken lift provide ideal opportunities to acquire the skills for mastering these tricky soaring conditions.

1.30 The importance of flying accurately

I have saved the most important thermalling issue until the end of Chapter 1. All too often pilots work very hard to find these elusive thermals only to drop out of them soon afterwards. Obviously, getting into the core is one thing; staying there is quite another. If this story sounds familiar, the most likely question on your mind is: "How can I stay in the core of a thermal?"

The answer is surprisingly simple.

Fly accurately – very accurately, or better still, very very accurately indeed.

Flying accurately simply means maintaining airspeed and angle of bank appropriate for the current thermal. Not even minor inaccuracies can be tolerated if we want to hang on to the core – where we can extract the maximum rate of climb. However, as soon as we tolerate fluctuations of only 5 kts in airspeed and 5° in the angle of bank, we run a risk of losing the core, and the result is a struggle with the thermal's outer fringes.

For example, for half a turn a pilot is circling at 45° angle of bank while flying at 45 kts. For the other half of the turn our pilot allows the airspeed to increase to 50 kts while simultaneously reducing the angle of bank to only 40°. How far will the aircraft move away from the centre of its original circle? To get the answer to this question, go back to Section 1.9 of this book where we looked at circle diameters in relation to circling speed and angle of bank.

As we can see, a circle flown at 45 kts and 45° would result in a circle diameter of 109 metres, whereby a circle flown at 50 kts at a bank angle of 40° would increase the circle diameter to 161 metres. Not only has the pilot increased the circle diameter by 52 metre

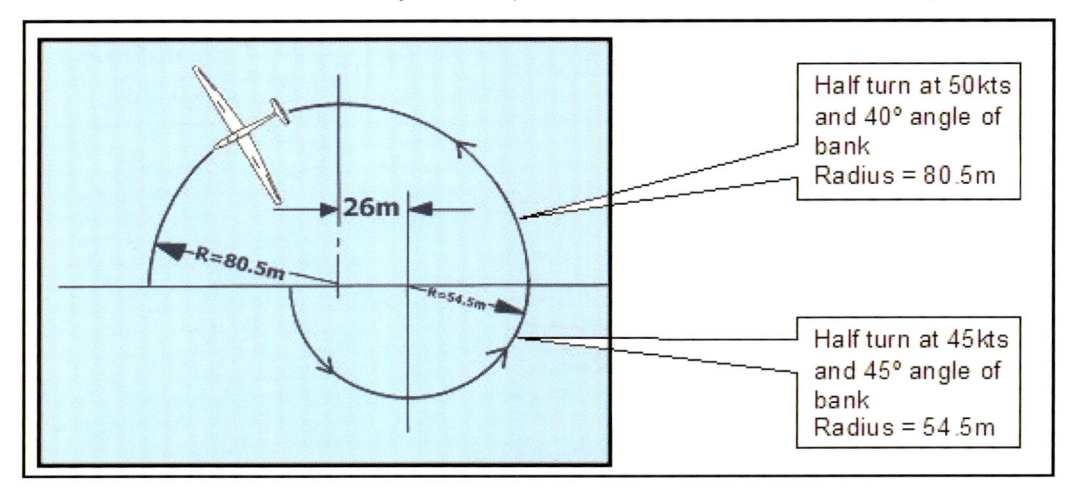

Figure 34: Re-positioning of glider as a result of inaccurate flying

Training in the vicinity of the home airfield

(or close to 50%), but he has also moved away from the centre of his original circle by as much as 26 metres.

In summary, flying accurately is vital in order to maintain our position in relation to the thermal core. Thermal behaviour is by no means an exact science and the many issues previously discussed are just too complex for detailed consideration in flight. On the other hand, a good grasp of the theoretical issues is very useful because it enables us to assess thermals much better and use them more efficiently. It also enhances our ability to predict soaring conditions accurately.

1.31 Other sources of energy

Apart from using conventional thermals, glider pilots can also gain energy from squall lines ahead of thunderstorms, convergence lines, ridge and wave lift and by dynamic soaring. Convergence lines are caused by the interaction of different air masses and are prevalent alongside mountain ranges.

Towards the end of the day, katabatic winds (refer to Section 10.6) usually create long lines of lift near the centres of valleys. Although such lift is seldom very strong, it allows for gentle climbs and extended glides in relatively smooth air.

The reality is that the vast majority of gliding sites are not located next to topography that allow such conditions to be explored. Therefore, many clubs resort to annual expeditions, allowing their members to experience a variety of different flying conditions. Newcomers as well as more experienced pilots are well advised to take advantage of such opportunities. However, prior to embarking on such expeditions, participants should acquire a sound understanding of the theory.

Successfully dealing with ridge lift and wave lift is not widely regarded as an absolutely necessary skill for glider pilots. Therefore an in-depth analysis of such types of lift (including dynamic soaring) is deferred to the end of the book.

A perfect day for ridge soaring Image: McCaw Media. (mccawmedia.co.nz)

Impressions of Europe from the air

Photo: Hiroshi Se...

Photo: Hiroshi Se...

Photo: Jean-Luc Colson

Photo: Fritz Brockmann

2 Weather and Gliding

2.1 Introduction

Keen glider pilots always strive to improve their knowledge and understanding of the multi-faceted gliding weather. By knowing how the atmosphere behaves pilots can get the most out of their flights and enjoy the sport to the fullest.

Making precious time available for gliding only to find that soaring conditions are unsuitable is what we dislike most. Still, it happens all too often – we rush to the airfield full of expectations but find ourselves struggling all day in very weak and broken lift. On another day it might appear very doubtful whether opening the hangar doors is at all worthwhile, but much to our surprise we experience excellent conditions all day long.

Fortunately, it isn't very difficult to assess the likely gliding conditions in advance as long as we have:

a) access to the Internet; and

b) a fairly rudimentary understanding of a temperature trace.

As most glider pilots have an Internet connection, we can collate the necessary weather data after only a few minutes. But let's put the Internet aside for the moment and instead look at some other sources of meteorological information. First, there is the weather news on TV and second, we can look up the forecasts in the local newspaper. These forecasts are not especially tailored for gliding operations, but they still contain some useful information for pilots who can read between the lines. The synoptic chart provides an overview of the positions of highs and lows and that gives a glider pilot a fairly good idea about broad soaring conditions, including wind direction and speed. In addition, the maximum temperatures are listed and that in itself is quite significant.

Don't forget to look outside. You never know, the forecasters might have got it wrong and a look out of the window in the morning could save a lot of frustration later in the day.

Okay, let's access the Internet now and collect some weather data. I personally prefer to visit http://slash.dotat.org/cgi-bin/atmos, a site established and maintained by a small group of very committed glider pilots from the Adelaide University Gliding Club. Apart from current satellite imagery, it provides upper-air temperature profiles for a large number of locations in Australia and diagrams that show the thermal height for various ground temperatures. For other valuable meteorological data, there are additional on line sources of information. For example, the Bureau of Meteorology distributes local area forecasts on www.bom.gov.au (accessible with user ID 'bomw007' and current password 'aviation'.) There are even specific and very up-to-date satellite images available at www.phys.unsw.edu.au and www.weatherzone.com.au.

The most exciting new gliding weather information is now available in the form of Boundry Layer Information Prediction MAP (BLIPMAP) forecasts. Their creator is US meteorologist Dr. John W. Glendening. (www.drjack.info/) BLIPMAPs predict soaring conditions in the lower part of the atmosphere which is not only affected by convection but also by other factors such as surface-based friction and terrain. For a prediction of soaring conditions outside the USA pilots can use RASP (Regional Atmospheric Soaring Prediction) BLIPMAPs. They are generally updated twice a day and have been proven to be accurate and reliable, although slightly on the conservative side. BLIPMAPs predict gliding conditions up to two days in advance. Everything glider pilots want to know, such as thermal height and strength, cloud base, wind strengths and directions, sea-breeze timing and strength, over-development, whether the thermals are going to be broken or smooth etc. is now available with a few clicks of the mouse. To say that glider pilots are excited is an understatement - our weather prediction tools are just getting better and better! An entire section of this boopk is reserved to discuss the prediction of soaring conditions in general and more specifically for Europe and Australia.

2.2 The sun hard at work

Before we go deeper into the subject, let's recap from the previous chapter where we learned that contrary to popular belief, the sun does not heat the air directly. Instead, the sun's short-wave radiation is partly absorbed by the ground, which in turn acts like a hotplate and returns the energy to the overlying air by long-wave radiation.

Therefore, the sun's aspect and apex play important roles in local ground temperatures, and so does the surface albedo. Albedo is equivalent to the fraction of solar radiation reflected from a surface. A high albedo means that much of the energy in incoming rays is reflected (for example snow and ice). A low albedo indicates that a large portion of the incoming radiation is absorbed and the chance of thermal activity is increased.

The percentage of reflected solar radiation for different surfaces are listed in 'Meteorology for glider pilots' by C. E. Wallington and are reproduced in Table 4.

Table 4: Energy wasted by reflection

Type of surface	Solar radiation wasted by reflection
Various cereal crops	3 -15%
Black mould	8 -14%
Patches of damp sand	10%
Bare ground	10 - 20%
Patches of dry sand	18%
Dry ploughed fields	20 - 25%
Various grass fields	14 - 37%
Deserts	24 - 28%
Snow or ice	46 - 86%

Thermal generation is also governed by meteorological and geographical factors. Meteorological aspects include the general synoptic situation and the stability of the air mass. Geographical features such as plains, hills, mountains ranges and, of course, moist valleys have to be taken into account as well, ie.the characteristics of the surface - dependent on soil humidity and type (sandy, loamy etc.) as well as predominant vegetation and its growing status - also affect thermal generation. Another factor is the distance of the place of interest from the sea and large pools of water such as lakes and rivers, and their moist floodplains.

Wallington sums it up by saying: "Of course, we could theorise on the combined effects [of the above] at great length, but since it is practically impossible to know how much of each effect applies to a particular place, such theorising is mainly inconclusive". I agree, and would like to add that a well-trained glider pilot can assess the suitability of the ground for thermal production reasonably well from the air.

The energy contained in a thermal depends on its size and strength. In a big and strong thermal, the power is enormous and can be as high as 1800 kW (2500 hp), although glider pilots can only extract a minute portion of it. Still, a glider of 500 kg climbing at a rate of 8 kts (4m/s) can extract as much as 20 kW (27 hp) from a thermal.

Lenticular clouds and Lake Pukaki, New Zealand, reflecting in the canopy
Photo: Gavin Wills, Glide Omarama

2.3 The upper air temperature profile

Competition pilots or pilots attempting long-distance flights usually study a temperature sounding taken near their home airfield. We are fortunate to have free-of-charge access to the results of meteorological balloon flights conducted at major meteorological centres twice a day. Along with other data, they transmit temperatures at various altitudes to ground-based recording stations. Sometimes the graphical representation of this data is called an "upper air temperature profile", but depending on the country we are in, it can also be referred to as a "temp. trace" or a "temperature – height diagram". Whatever the name almost all publications on the subject contain a lot of abbreviations and jargon. It is important that glider pilots make an effort to develop more than a very basic understanding of the "Temp. trace" in order to become sufficiently familiar with the complex properties of the lower atmosphere in which they spend so much time. Let's attempt to make the subject a bit more transparent and simplify matters as much as possible.

2.4 The importance of inversions

Usually, we experience a drop in air temperature with altitude. However, on occasions the exact opposite occurs. When the temperature increases with altitude we are either faced with a ground inversion or an inversion aloft. Ground inversions (or surface inversions) usually develop overnight due to nocturnal radiation. The air closest to the ground cools down more than the layers above. Fortunately, solar heating quickly reverses the situation, and after a few hours of morning sunshine thermal activity can start.

A common way for inversions to form aloft is through subsiding air associated with a high pressure system. (Refer to Section 2.11.1.) Other possibilities include warm air advection (horizontal movement of an air-mass) or the cooling of a lower layer by evaporation of clouds.

In other words, inversions cause stability of the air as a result of warming at altitude or by a cooling of air at ground level. Both scenarios have detrimental effects on gliding. Although heating at ground level is the main reason for instability, we can also get unstable air when cooler air slides into the upper levels.

2.5 The Dry Adiabatic Lapse Rate (DALR)

The air in a thermal theoretically cools at a rate of 3°C per 1000 ft (or 9.8°C for every 1000 m). This gradual drop in temperature is assumed constant over the entire thermal ascent. This is referred to as the Dry Adiabatic Lapse Rate (DALR) and exists as a result of the drop in ambient pressure with altitude. (When a reduction of pressure occurs, the air cools; when air is compressed it gets warmer.)

If we put all of this onto a diagram with the temperature on the horizontal axis and altitude on the vertical axis we get straight DALR lines running from the bottom right to the top left. For gliding purposes, a "Stüve" diagram as per Figure 35 is often used. If we know the current ground temperature, we can easily predict the temperature of an air parcel after it has risen to a certain altitude. For example, if air at 30°C ascends in a thermal to 6000 ft, it cools down by 6 x 3°C = 18°C, to a new temperature of 12°C.

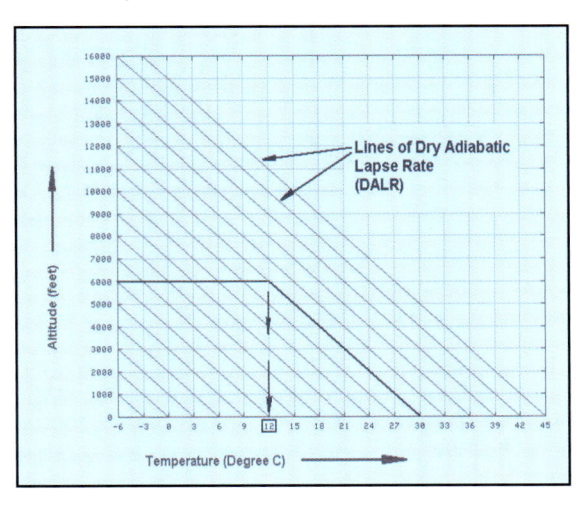

Figure 35: Dry Adiabatic Lapse Rate

2.6 The Environmental Lapse Rate (ELR)

The air outside of thermals (environmental air) also cools down with increasing altitude. On statistical average, this rate of cooling is about 2°C per 1000 ft. After all, this is the reason why glider pilots are very comfortable at altitude on days when their crews complain about scorching temperatures on the ground. However, the actual rate of cooling is anything but constant, partly due to changes during the course of the day as a result of the sun's heating. By plotting the early morning measurements onto the diagram as per Figure 36, we get an overview of the temperature at various altitudes at the time of recording.

The early morning Environmental Lapse Rate (ELR) changes in line with ongoing solar heating. For example, if we were to take another ELR after a few hours of sunshine, we would see that it tends to follow the DALR for the current temperature until intersecting with the early morning ELR.

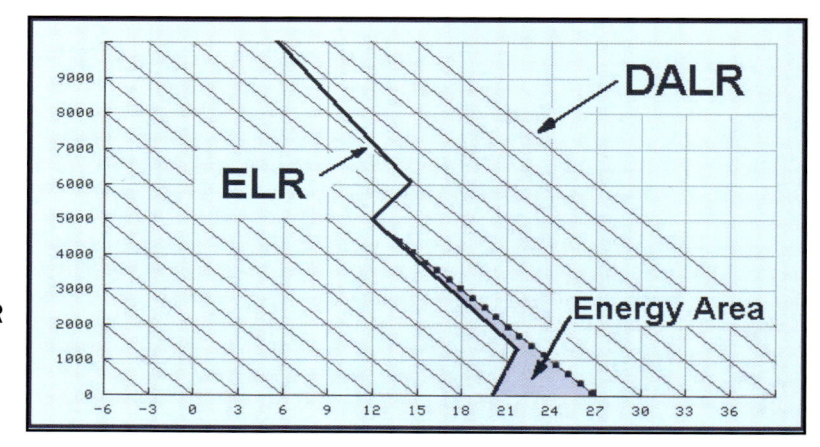

Figure 36: Changing of ELR by heating and energy area for 27°C

In the example (Figure 36) we have plotted the early morning ELR (thick line) as well as the ELR at the time the temperature has reached 27°C (dotted line). The ELR at 27°C runs parallel to the DALR up to a level of 4500 ft.

The shaded area of the diagram is a direct measure of the energy provided by the sun to raise the ground temperature to 27°C. Put another way, the area between the old and new temperature profile is a measure of the energy absorbed by the air mass. This is very important for an estimate of the time required for thermals to reach a certain level. We will come back to that subject later.

By having the early morning ELR and the DALR lines on the same diagram, the convection height can be determined easily. All we need to do is find the intersection of the early morning ELR with the ELR applicable for higher temperatures later in the day and read across to the vertical axis. At around this height the air stops rising, which means that a glider will not be able to climb any higher than this.

The air in a thermal loses its buoyancy when the temperature drops to the same level as the surrounding (environmental) air. However, once a thermal has picked up some speed, it has a tendency to continue for a little while past this point due to the momentum of the ascending air. As stated earlier, the mass of air in a thermal can amount to tens of thousands of tonnes, and it behaves just like a big train – it simply doesn't come to an abrupt stop.

Furthermore, thermals are known to entrain small amounts of air from their cooler surroundings, which results in a slightly accelerated cooling process. Some scientists believe that both effects cancel each other out, while others are of the opinion that thermals overshoot significantly and leave sizable domes or hummocks in the inversion layer. Practical experience supports this overshooting theory as we can often glide in very smooth air for several minutes after taking a strong thermal to the very top.

Scientists like Scorer, Deardorff and Stull are of the opinion that thermal tops rising deep into the inversion layer become negatively buoyant and eventually start to sink back into the convection layer. This may not only account for large areas of occasional strong sink, but may also explain the gradual erosion of the inversion layer (due to a mixing of air at inversion level) and subsequent increase in thermal height during the course of the day.

Weather and Gliding

A thunderstorm in the making
Photo: Mandy Temple

An everyday practical example

Let's assume we have an early morning temperature of 20°C at ground level that gradually increases to 22°C at 1200 ft. Between 1200 and 5000 ft a welcome reduction in temperature to 12°C occurs, but above this level we have a 1000 ft-thick layer of air in which the temperature increases to 14°C. Higher up the temperature drops evenly to 2.5°C at 11 500 ft and from there on it cools down to -2.5°C at 16 000 ft.

If we assume that at 10am the temperature reaches 21°C, and climbs at 3°C per hour up to a maximum of 36°C at 3pm, we can evaluate the maximum attainable altitude hour by hour.

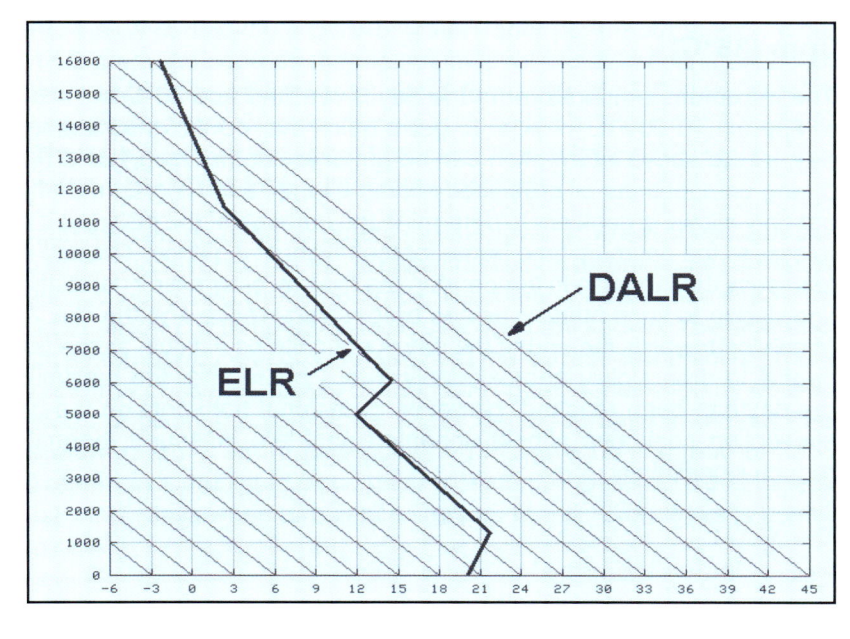

Figure 37: Temperature trace as per example above

Weather and Gliding

**Don't forget the undercarriage
Photo:
Manfred Muench**

Let's now predict cloud base by using the temp. trace. It is best to use aerological diagram paper with dew point lines. These due point lines lean back (approximately 0.5°C per 1000 ft) and run all over the diagram, but in the interests of clarity, only two dew point lines are shown in the example below.

A precondition for cumulus cloud to form is that convection reaches this level in the first place. For the determination of cloud base, only the dew point at ground level matters because mainly ground level air ascends in a thermal and consequently determines whether cumulus clouds form or not. Dew point readings at altitude are largely irrelevant for the purpose of this exercise. The relevant question is where the DALR intersects the dew point line. The intersection needs to occur to the right of the ELR, but with a dew point of 6°C, a ground temperature of 45°C is needed for cumulus cloud to form. As 36°C is the maximum temperature of the day, this does not occur. We can soar, but the air is simply too dry for cumulus clouds to form. We have to find thermals in the blue.

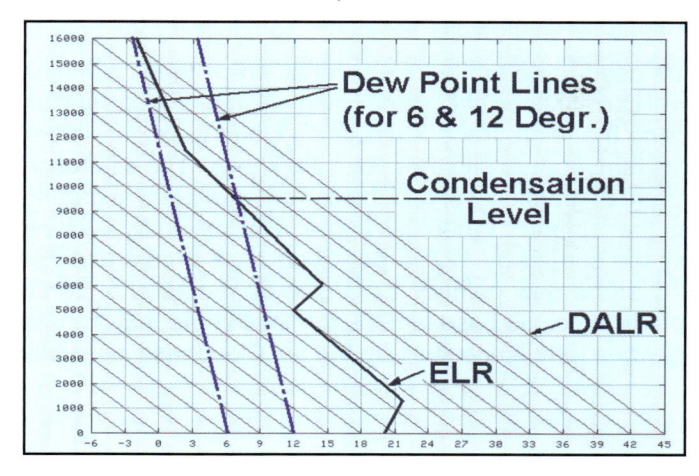

Figure 39: Effect of different dew points

Now let's repeat the procedure for a dew point of

12°C. The 12°C dew point line now intersects the ELR below the maximum convection level. When the ground temperature reaches 35°C, the thermals ascend to 9200 ft, where the temperature is 7°C and the relative humidity is 100%. Almost instantly all the water vapour condenses, ensuring a rapid development of cumulus clouds. The enormous amount of energy released by condensation causes the air to rise even further and faster. Of course, there is no guarantee that such cumulus cloud development will go on all day. An inflow of dryer air, for example, will lower the dew point and causes cumulus clouds to gradually dissipate.

Attentive readers would have noticed that the formation of cumulus clouds has deprived pilots of approx. 800 ft of possible altitude (in countries where cloud flying is illegal). While 10 000 ft thermals are possible in the blue, the higher dew point of 12°C results in cumulus with bases at "only" 9200 ft. Referring back to Figure 39, we can now predict the appearance of cumulus clouds and the time for it. (Refer to insert of Figure 38.)

2.8 Prediction of thunderstorms

Unfortunately for this section to make sense we have to get used to another bit of jargon. After talking a lot about the Dry Adiabatic Lapse Rate (DALR), let me now introduce the Saturated Adiabatic Lapse Rate (SALR). When a rising parcel of air reaches condensation level, its rate of cooling slows down significantly and from there on we have to apply the SALR to assess its temperature. While the DALR is a constant 3°C per 1000 ft, the same can't be said for the SALR, because it is very much dependent on the prevailing temperature. For example, at a temperature of 0°C, the SALR is just under 2°C per 1000 ft ,whereas it is just over 1°C per 1000 ft at a temperature of 30°C. If that sounds complicated, it probably is, but it becomes much clearer when we look at a typical example using the temp. trace.

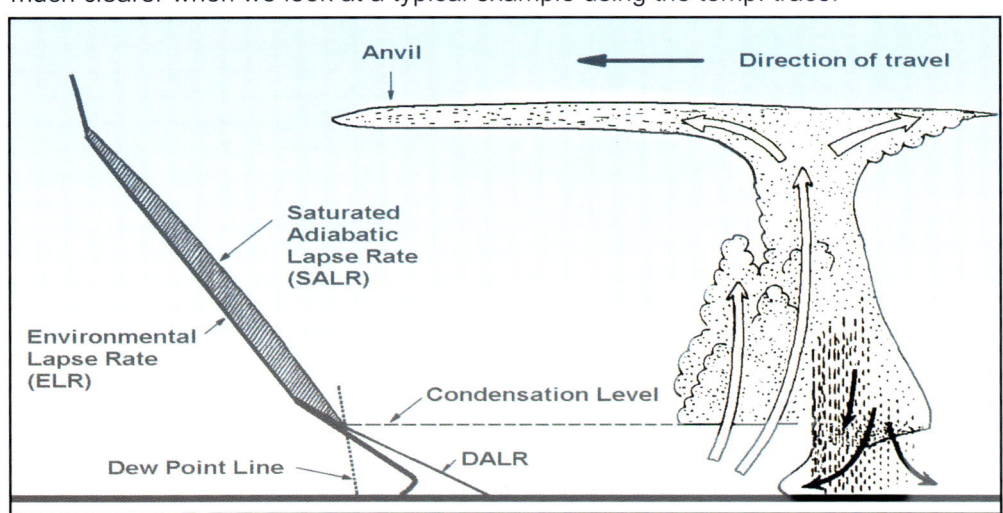

Figure 40: Thunderstorm development

The above sketch (Figure 40) shows a much steeper SALR compared to the DALR. The intersection of the ELR with the SALR occurs well above freezing level. When the inflow of moist air from nearby cumulus clouds couples with the self-stoking effect described in Chapter 1, we have all the ingredients for a thunderstorm. Storms are not predictable in behaviour or travel direction and are to be avoided.

Storms usually depress thermal activity nearby and can have severe wind gusts preceding them by up to 20 km. Give them a very wide berth and make sure your glider is safely sheltered well before you expect a storm to affect the area. A mature

**Tropical thunderstorm
Photo:
Dr Joerg Hacker**

storm can leave a trail of "dead" air for 50 km or more. Because the SALR varies with temperature, reliable and accurate assessments can only be made with proper aerological diagram paper (or with a corresponding computer program), therefore it is best left to weather forecasters. In general terms however, if the air above the convection level is unstable to a great height and the vertical development of clouds can continue unabated, conditions are right for thunderstorms. Glider pilots are well advised to take thunderstorm forecasts seriously and avoid flying anywhere near active cells. Severe downdrafts can combine with heavy rain or hail, which presents a real danger for aircraft of any kind. Especially, gliders should be on the ground well ahead of any squall lines – these are known to precede thunderstorms and habitualy turn unsecured light aircraft and gliders upside down. Even airliners and military aircraft respectfully avoid thunderstorms despite being properly equipped with blind-flying instruments.

2.9 Over-development of cumulus clouds

We have already touched on the subject earlier and briefly discussed the slowing of cloud evaporation in an environment of high humidity. Under such circumstances ,rapidly appearing new cumulus quickly turn the sky into a tight blanket of clouds.

There are good gliding forecasts available that predict such over-development. They might state: "Cloud cover increasing to seven octa". An octa (also spelt okta) is equivalent to a cloud cover over 1/8 of the sky and is simply a unit of measurement. Open sky can be reported in terms of how many eighths of the sky are obscured by cloud, ranging from completely clear (0 octas) through to completely overcast (8 octas). An alternative way of describing the amount of sky obscured by clouds is for example, "7/8 cloud cover", but in any case, this measure does not specify cloud type or thickness.

Needless to say, solid cloud cover greatly diminishes the sun's ability to heat the ground and thermal activity may be terminated. Airborne glider pilots should head for the last remaining sunlit patches of ground and work any available lift until enough clouds have dissipated for normal thermal activity to recommence. More often than not such a cycle passes reasonably quickly and things are back to normal within 30 minutes or so. However, on occasions heating is stopped for longer — too long for a glider pilot to remain airborne.

But the reasons for over–development are not always as straight forward as high humidity. Sometimes the sky can rapidly fill up with stratocumulus (SC) for two reasons:

a)   We have an inversion above convection level as per Figure 41 and

b)   The relative humidity is too high for older cumulus clouds to dissipate quickly enough, as discussed above.

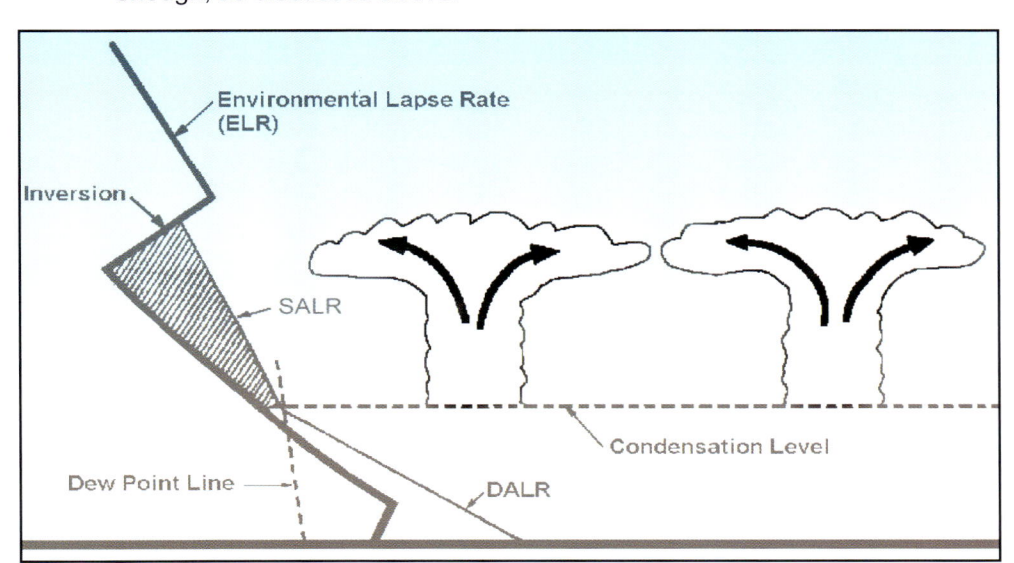

Figure 41: Spreading of cumulus clouds caused by an inversion

In the above example the dew point is high enough to allow the formation of cumulus clouds. Just because the ascending air has reached condensation level (for all practical purposes, cloud base), it does not mean that its ascent will cease. On the contrary, the release of latent heat makes the air even more buoyant and further ascent along the SALR will be more rapid. However, once the growing clouds push against the inversion, their ascent is abruptly halted. The inversion acts like a lid and the clouds have little choice but to spread out. If this spreading occurs over a large part of the sky, it results in a blanketing of the ground below. The resultant temperature drop is likely to stop convection and, in turn, will usually force glider pilots to land. However, known hot spots on the ground might take some time to cool and could allow weaker and lower thermals to form, despite the lack of direct sunlight.

2.10 Strength of thermal activity

A lengthy study conducted in Australia has established that the slope of the ELR greatly determines the characteristics and workability of thermals. This work was initiated by professional weather forecaster M.J. Hancy as far back as the early seventies. In exchange for providing gliding forecasts, he asked pilots for feedback on the actual conditions encountered. Although the reported climb rates were partly dependent on the skill levels of the pilots concerned, a clear picture emerged after analysing a total of 2470 cross-country flights. It confirmed that the buoyancy equation first developed by Priestley (1953) for buoyant motions in thunderstorms can sometimes be used with sufficient accuracy to predict thermal strength:

$$\text{Thermal acceleration} = g \times \frac{\text{Temp. of thermal} - \text{Temp. of environment}}{\text{Average temp. of convective layer}}$$

Buoyancy equation

Because the above formula ignores such important factors as friction and the total volume of the ascending air parcel, it is not sufficiently reliable for everyday thermal strength forecasts. However, it often equates reasonably well with practical experience, since it indicates that (for DALR conditions) the strength of the lift amounts to approximately 1 kt for every 1000 ft of convection height. However, when the ELR exhibits more stable layers, the strength of the thermals may vary considerably.

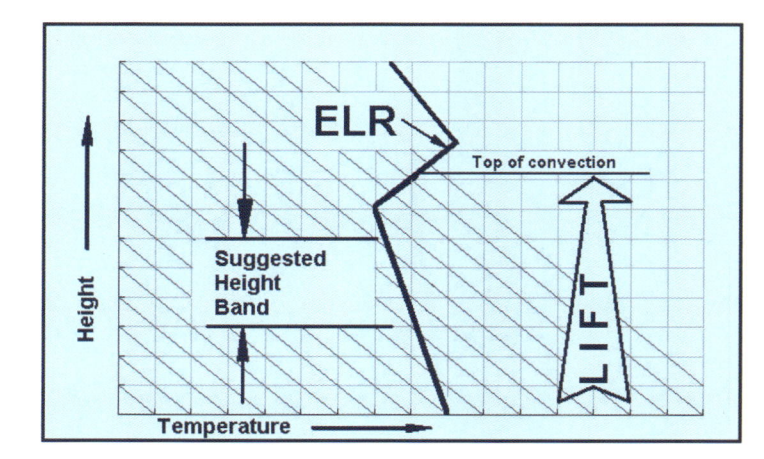

Examples of stable and unstable conditions are shown in Figures 42 and 43 respectively. Stable conditions exist when the ELR displays a steeper gradient than the DALR, and an unstable air mass is characterised by an ELR shallower than the DALR.

Figure 42: Strength of lift in stable conditions

Please note that the extreme stability and instability as per Figures 42 and 43 is never encountered in practice. It is deliberately exaggerated in both examples to point glider pilots towards the appropriate height band for different meteorological conditions. For example, in stable conditions we can expect a weakening of lift with increasing altitudes. In such conditions, it is rather difficult to find the right compromise between a reasonably safe height band on one hand and weakening thermals on the other. A suitable operating level for efficient cross-country flying might be near the middle of the available convection band. Operating lower down is bound to provide stronger climbs, but leaves little margin for error. Stable conditions are generally suitable for cross-country flying, but it is important to select only the very best of thermals as weaker lift might not even reach convection or inversion level.

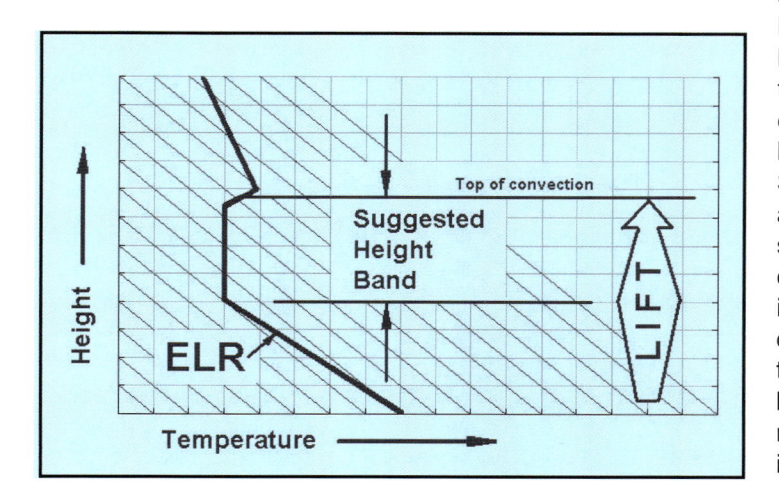

Figure 43: Strength of lift in unstable conditions

Weather and Gliding

In unstable conditions (Figure 43), thermals usually improve with height and accelerate. In the example above, we can expect a strengthening of the updraught until the isothermal layer is reached (a layer where the temperature does not change with height). Within the isothermal layer, the lift might even weaken, but assuming that the lift strength is not affected significantly it seems prudent to utilise the middle to upper height band.

**Ready to land
Photo:
Manfred Muench**

2.11 Highs, lows, troughs and ridges

Flying conditions are continuously influenced by high and low pressure systems including fronts, troughs and ridges. We will now look at these phenomena purely from a glider pilot's point of view and primarily for a band between about 30 to 40 degrees latitude around the earth.

Solar radiation and hence warming is greatest near the equator which causes a large scale rising of the air within a band of low pressure. Near the top of the troposphere (at an altitude of about 14 kilometres), the air begins to flow horizontally to the North and South Poles. When the air descends again near 30° north and south, a band of high pressure is created. Flow from this band back to the equator is modified by Coriolis forces to create the trade winds, an easterly airflow that generally affects northern

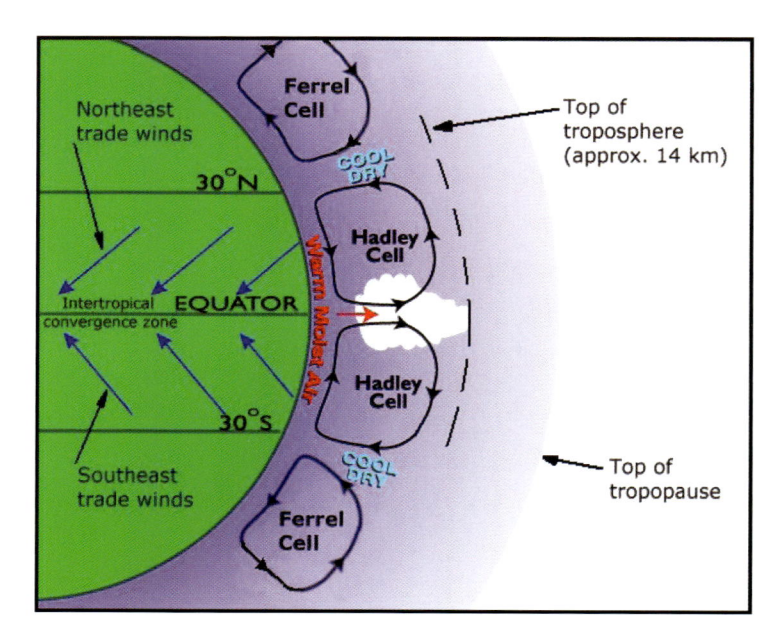

Figure 44:
Trade winds in equatorial regions.

Australia. Southerly airflow from this high pressure band causes the "roaring forties", with a mostly westerly stream affecting southern Australia. There is a band of low pressure at around 60° south. Turbulence within these airstreams and continental land masses cause disturbances that result in alternating highs and lows.

2.11.1 Highs

High pressure systems (or anticyclones) are characterised by slowly subsiding air which, in the southern hemisphere, circles in an anti clockwise direction. (North of the equator the direction of flow is reversed.) The subsiding air is compressed and the resultant warming increases the ability of the air to absorb moisture. Clouds usually dissipate in line with a decreasing relative humidity, which often makes for fair weather with little or no clouds. When the air is subsiding it forms an inversion layer that is generally most pronounced in the north-eastern quarter of the high pressure system.

According to C. E. Wallington (Meteorology for glider pilots), the rate of subsidence in a well-developed high is of the order of 90 metre per hour (300 ft/h) at an altitude of 10 000 ft above mean sea level. At first glance this appears to be rather insignificant, but assuming that the air is not saturated (and hence changes temperature at the dry adiabatic rate of 3°C per 1000 ft), it results in a warming of 9°C over a period of 10 hours. This is usually more than enough heating to depress gliding conditions due to the formation of subsidence inversions, which can even occur at several levels. Thermals still exist, but near the centre of the high they are often narrow, broken and difficult to work. On days influenced by a high pressure system, thermals usually start well after midday. However, even in the middle of a high pressure system the afternoons can be quite soarable although generally blue.

2.11.2 Lows

The reverse process occurs in a low pressure system (or depression). In the southern hemisphere, the air circles around the low in a clockwise direction and ascends. Ascending air expands and cools; an increase in relative humidity is responsible for the formation of clouds. These clouds can have a substantial vertical development, especially near the centre of the low pressure system. A low cloud base is often associated with drizzle or rain, which generally depresses gliding conditions or stops convection altogether. Away from the centre of the low, good gliding conditions can be expected as long as there is no blanketing of the ground by substantial cloud cover.

2.11.3 Troughs

Provided relative humidity is not too high, troughs (of low pressure) enhance gliding conditions and often provide ideal weather patterns for record attempts and long distance flights. A trough is an elongated extension of isobars away from a low pressure centre. On weather charts it is depicted as a dashed line (refer to Figures 45 & 46) which is usually - but not always - moving from west to east and, in Australia, is generally orientated in a north/south direction. Very different soaring conditions can be experienced depending on which side of the trough line gliding operations occur. One of the reasons is vorticity, which is generated when the air flows around the trough axis and changes direction.

We will first consider an easterly trough in the southern hemisphere. An easterly trough exists if the inflow into the trough is from east to west (Figure 45), typical in areas governed by the easterly trade winds. It generally travels from west to east in accordance with the general movement of the highs. The situation becomes clear when we become conscious of the fact that colder maritime air approaching the trough receives additional warming due to trough compression. While this process is taking place, the approaching air undercuts the warmer continental air and forces it to rise. The effect on convection is dramatic. On the eastern side of the trough axis, the thermals are not only smoother but also much stronger and may even reach greater heights.

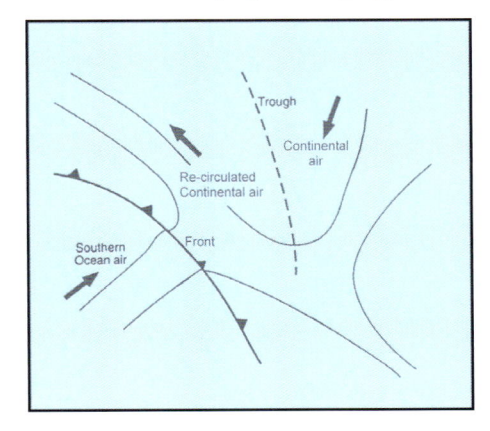

Figure 45: Prefrontal easterly trough in the Australian and New Zealand region

However, on the other side of the trough axis the situation is very different. The air subsides making thermals broken, weak and sometimes difficult to work. This explains why soaring conditions differ greatly in the vicinity of a trough, and why the

Cumulus congestus marking trough axis over Japan. Photo: Yuji Higuchi

trough axis is often marked by increasing amounts of cumulus congestus (clumps of large billowing cumulus growing rapidly) and especially altocumulus castellanus (altocumulus with cumulus tops) under which excellent streeting can be found. A continuous lift band of varying strength is only sporadically interrupted by small areas of sink. Often this allows high speed cruising near cloud base without thermalling – a glider pilot's delight. It is also not hard to see why a trough of low pressure sometimes leads to the development of a low pressure system and is frequently associated with thunderstorm activity.

For a westerly trough in the Southern Hemisphere as per Figure 46 the same fundamentals hold true. The general airflow around the trough axis is from west to east and the best soaring conditions can again be found on the eastern side of the trough axis. The situation described above is primarily applicable to continental areas in sub-tropical regions of the Southern Hemisphere. Prime examples are the world famous gliding regions in Southern Africa, South America and Australia. Please note that the situation is different in the northern hemisphere. Due to a reversed airflow direction, and a host of other influences soaring conditions in the area of a trough need to be assessed, not withstanding the above discussion.

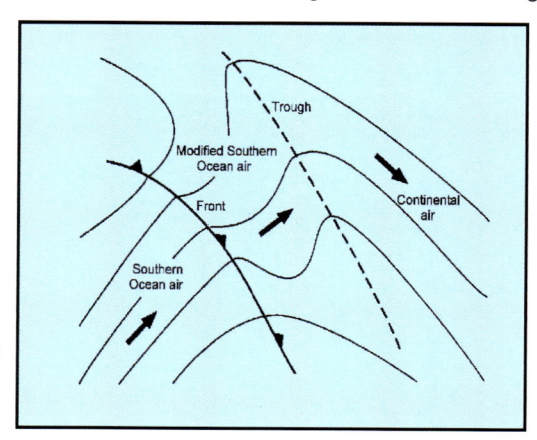

Figure 46: Prefrontal westerly trough in the Southern Hemisphere

2.11.4 Ridges

The opposite of a trough of low pressure is a ridge of high pressure. A ridge is an elongated extension of isobars away from a high pressure system. The points discussed under 2.11.1 remain valid, but as a ridge is usually located a fair distance away from the centre of a high pressure system, gliding conditions aren't nearly as difficult.

2.11.5 Frontal systems

a) Warm front

A warm front indicates to the knowledgeable aviator that there they will find cold air closely followed by warm air with a tendency to overtake the cold air. As cold air possesses a higher density, it remains on the ground and the warm air has no choice but to flow up its invisible sloping surface. This slope is shallow enough to create clouds at 20 000 to 30 000 ft as far away as 600 km from the warm front. At this altitude, the water vapour condenses to ice crystals rather than liquid water drops, resulting in the formation of wispy white clouds with elongated comma shapes. They are commonly called cirrus clouds and are known to herald the approach of a frontal system.

As the front gets closer, thicker cirrostratus develop followed by altocumulus with a cloud base at around 20 000 ft. Glider pilots should know that altocumulus is not the result of ground-based convection, but the upward motion of frontal air. After the arrival of altostratus, cloud base drops rapidly and the sun becomes barely visible behind a gradually thickening cloud layer. Occasionally light rain might develop which may or may not reach the ground. However, heavier rain is most likely when nimbostratus arrives just ahead of the warm front. The wind gradually increases in speed and cloud base often drops to less than 2000 ft. After the passage of the front, the surface wind 'backs' * (or 'veers'in the northern hemisphere), temperature and dew point increase and the rain may ease off or be replaced by drizzle.

Cirrus clouds heralding the approach of a frontal system

b) Cold front

Cold fronts are more common in Australia by far. Here the cold air overtakes the warmer air. Cold fronts are marked on the weather chart by a spiked line with the spikes pointing towards the warm air. (Refer to Figures 45 & 46.) The line denotes the boundary between warm air and a following cold air mass.

Compared to a warm front, the frontal surface of a cold front is considerably steeper. Convective currents may interweave with the broad scale lifting of the warm air. Due to its higher density, the approaching cold air acts like a wedge. It is prising up the warm air and is causing condensation. In the southern parts of Australia, the upper part of a cold front often has the same characteristics of a typical warm front, with high cirrus clouds appearing approximately 24 hours ahead of the lower level front. Altostratus forms up to 100 km ahead of the front, whereas altocumulus and nimbostratus clouds can be found in relatively close proximity to the front. Rain is usually heaviest during the passage of the cold front. In the southern hemisphere the wind backs just behind the front, which is accompanied by a decreased temperature and dew point. Soon after the cold front has passed, the cloud cover breaks up and – at least in the lowest layer - the instability of the air increases. Precipitation ceases, the wind usually abates rapidly, visibility improves and after only minimal solar heating low convection can be expected again. As a rule of thumb, air pockets need to be 2 – 3°C warmer than the surrounding air to restart convection. Often this can be expected approximately 4 hours after the passing of a cold front with rain, or much earlier if no evaporation of moisture slows down the heating process. If the front arrives in the late afternoon convection may not restart again.

It is worth noting that the cold air coming in behind the front is usually unstable and the temperature profile is often parallel to the adiabatic lapse rate up to inversion level. The day after the passage of the front, thermals often start much earlier compared to the previous day. However, thermal height in the southern parts of Australia is limited to 6000 ft or even lower in this situation.

* (The wind "backs" when it changes in an anticlockwise direction and "veers" when it changes direction clockwise)

2.12 Weather patterns in Australia

As Australia is a major destination for international glider pilots for record attempts and long distance flying, a short section on the typical weather patterns is given here. So far we have only considered the prediction of gliding conditions for the day ahead, but when glider pilots want to know how the weather is shaping up two or even three days in advance they need to keep an eye on the long-term outlook. Fortunately we now have very valuable sources of information in the form of 4-day forecasts and the like.

However, to make good use of all this information, a proper interpretation of these data is required as well as some basic knowledge on airflows around high and low-pressure systems. One feature of the Australian climate is a rather regular weather pattern dominated by high-pressure systems. During the summer months, these high-pressure systems bypass the continent to the south, while they move almost through the centre of mainland Australia during the winter season.

2.12.1 Winter weather patterns

In order to get a better idea about weather patterns in Australia, let's first look at a typical weather map for a 4-day winter period. It becomes rather obvious that regular low-pressure troughs and cold fronts sweep across the southern parts of the continent in relatively quick succession, continually replacing the air mass. Although only the most severe of cold fronts produce any substantial rain, it is important to note that even the tail end of weaker fronts direct moist and unstable air into the southern coastal regions. This is good news for glider pilots, as a moist onshore wind usually results in cumulus clouds with a cloud base between 4000 and 5000 ft. Due to the relative instability of the air, useful thermal activity often commences after only a few degrees of heating. Moderate winds with closely-spaced thermals favour conditions for streeting. However, due to a relatively short convective period, such flights are usually limited to distances of 300 km although 500 km flights are not unheard of.

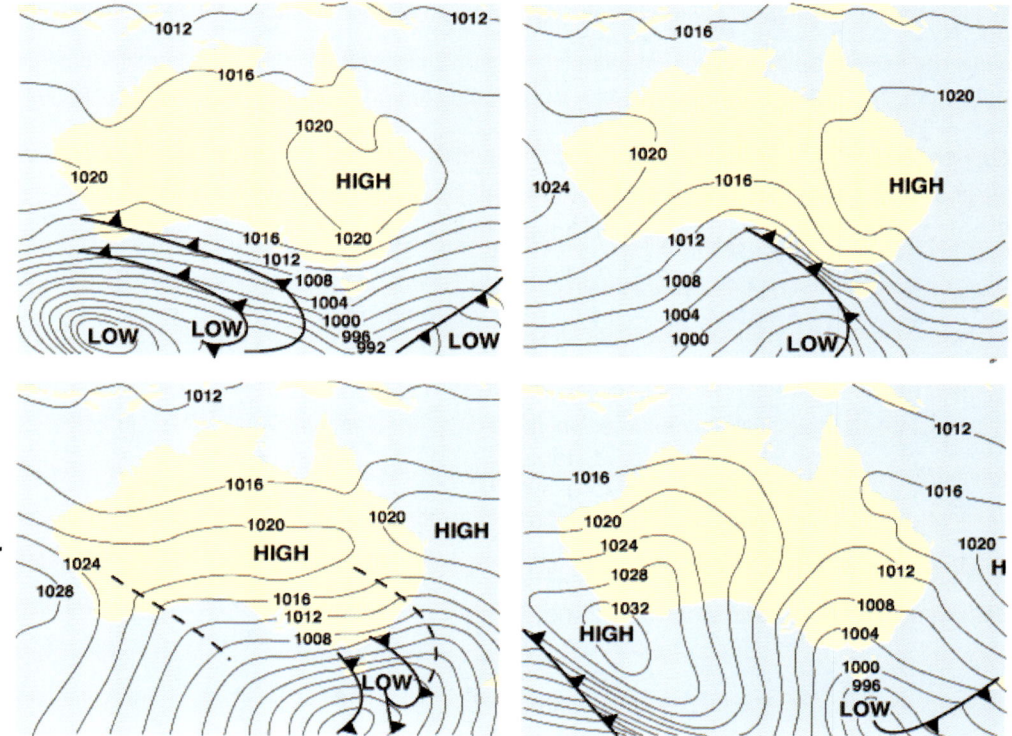

Figure 47: Typical winter weather pattern (Graphic courtesy BoM)

2.12.2 Summer weather patterns

In contrast, a typical summer weather pattern consists of a 7-day cycle. The high-pressure regions (usually bypassing the continent to the south) are often separated by weak frontal systems that feed relatively cold air from Antarctic regions into the southern parts of the continent. These "cool changes" flush out the warmer and relatively stable air and herald the beginning of a new weather cycle. Convection is initially limited to about 5000 ft or so after the passage of a frontal system but the higher moisture content of a new air mass raises the chances of cumulus cloud development.

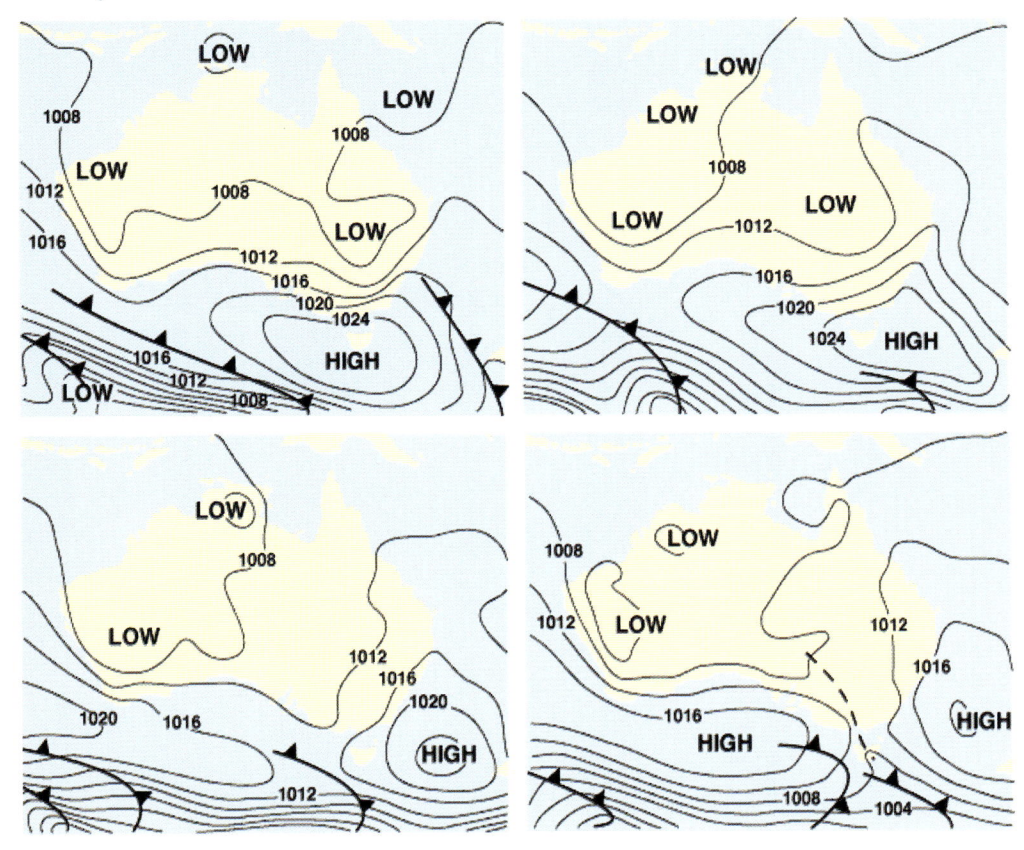

Figure 48: Typical summer weather pattern (Graphic courtesy BoM)

To predict the weather a few days in advance, we need to remember that:
a) South of the equator the winds rotate around high pressure systems in an anti clockwise direction;
b) The wind direction close to the ground is more or less parallel to the isobars; and
c) High usually move east at an average speed of approx. 500 km a day.

With these three basic principles in mind, it becomes easier to understand why we always experience a very predictable change in wind direction in line with the changing position of a high-pressure system. Just after the passage of a front, a strong south-westerly airflow is the dominant feature which usually changes to a southerly within half a day or so. As soon as the wind has an easterly component, it tends to abate and maximum daytime temperatures tend to rise quite rapidly. Eventually winds swing to the east and, within a day or two, via northeast to north. The northerly air stream reaching the southern regions of Australia has travelled a very long distance over the hot inland regions. The heating received is responsible for high temperatures in the southern states.

Weather and Gliding

Conditions for gliding in the southern part of the continent are usually best just a day ahead of the arrival of a new cold front. High temperatures associated with a northerly or north-westerly air stream and the diminishing effects of subsidence inversions often make for quite unstable air to great altitudes.

Glider pilots are well advised to look for such synoptic situations as they offer by far the greatest chances for successful long-distance flights. Of course, the above comments only represent a general overview and are mainly applicable for the

**ASH 26 E taking off
Photo:
David Marchon
(L'Express)**

southern part of the continent. They need to be refined by incorporating a detailed knowledge of the local climate. Especially with changes in topography, weather characteristics can vary significantly. Typical examples are regions sheltered by mountain ranges or coastal areas affected by sea breezes.

2.13 Soaring weather in Central Europe

The following section was contributed by Carsten Lindemann, a meteorological scientist and lecturer of Meteorology at the "Freie Universitaet von Berlin". Carsten is a well known competition pilot and has served various German national teams as meteorological advisor at several world championships.

2.13.1 General observations

Thermal convection heavily depends on favoured weather patterns, which vary considerably around the world. In subtropical regions, statements such as, "Hot weather is good soaring weather," hold true most of the time. However, humidity and the proximity to tropical troughs play an equally important role and determine the extent of blue sky or over-development.

The previous section describes typical weather patterns for drier and more arid parts of the globe. However, European patterns differ quite a lot due to Europe's different hemispheric position. Being outside the subtropics and inside the belt of cyclonic activity (with warm and cold fronts and troughs passing) means that weather pattern change far more frequently. Up to 160 fronts pass Europe per year. Days with very good soaring conditions are limited and, as a consequence, the number of consecutive good soaring days are quite rare indeed. However, during the last few years, long lasting and almost stationary high pressure systems over Scandinavia produced superb soaring weather in Northern Germany and Poland for several weeks at a time. (This was especially noticeable in May 2008 and April 2007.)

The soaring season in central Europe usually stretches from the beginning of March to early October. During the European winter there is very limited convection activity due to the predominantly stable air mass and rather windy conditions. Relatively high humidity levels lead to a high degree of cloud coverage, which in turn limits the amount of radiation that can reach the ground. On the other hand, windy conditions favour other kinds of updrafts such as slope lift and lee waves (Chapter 11 & 12) that can extend the soaring season in areas of suitable topography.

2.13.2 Air-mass behaviour based on different curvatures of isobars

Figure 50 represents the most important meteorological features for the mainly flat or moderately hilly countryside of Central Europe. They are presented firstly without an underlying map just to show the isobar curvature in principle. (Isobars indicate lines of identical pressure.) Regardless of whether we are looking at high or low pressure systems (or whether we are north or south of the equator), the air above the surface friction layer (about 1000 m above ground level) is generally flowing parallel to the isobars. Within the friction layer, the air flows out of the high and into the low at angles between 15° and 40° to the isobars. In the northern hemisphere, the airflow in a cyclonic weather system (area of low pressure) rotates in an anti-clockwise direction, while in an anti-cyclonic weather system (high pressure cell) the air circulates clockwise.

In the Southern Hemisphere the exact opposite holds true. Here the air rotates in a clockwise direction in a low pressure system and anti clockwise in a high pressure system.

The curvature of the isobars indicates the general vertical movement of the atmosphere and is more important than the pressure value of each isobar. If it is cyclonic, the air moves upwards (only a few cm/sec, not relevant for soaring). However, there is more cloud compared to parts of the same isobar with anti-cyclonic curvature. The most rapid upward motion of a low pressure system is found along the frontline which can sometimes reach into the high pressure cell while it loses activity. If it is anti-cyclonic, its general motion is downward, leading to cloud break-up or perhaps even a cloudless sky. In a dry atmosphere, cyclonic curvature of isobars

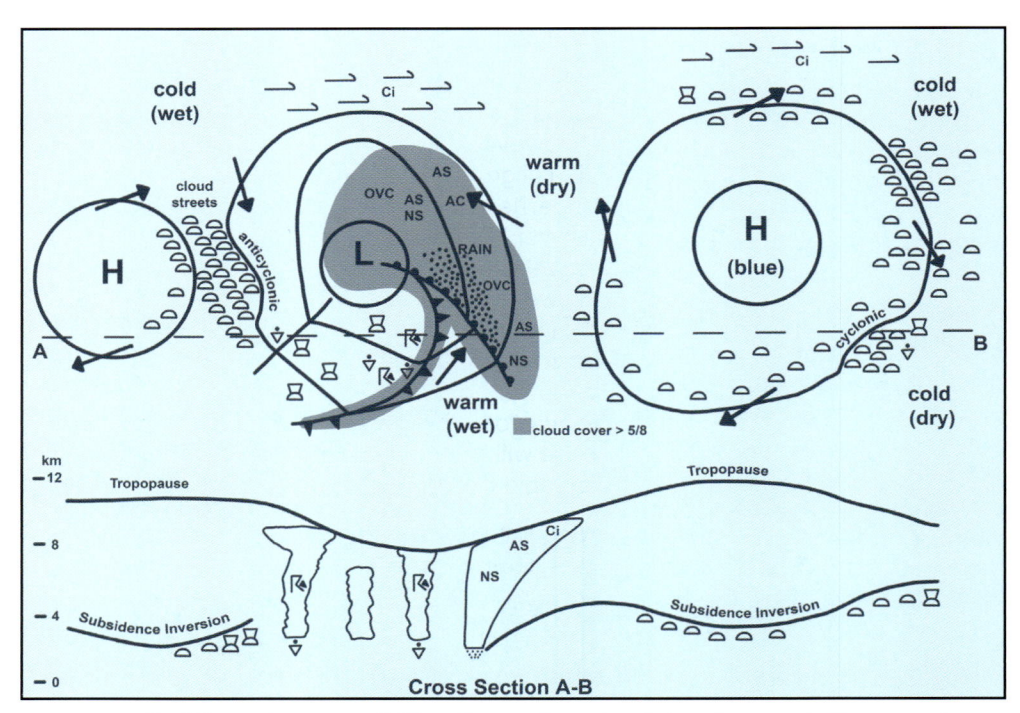

Figure 49: General European meteorological situation

can mean that there is a possibility of cumulus cloud development. Conversely, an anti-cyclonic curvature (and a wet atmosphere) means that there is a good chance of a break-up in the cloud cover.

The possible areas of more than 5/8 cloud cover (in and near the centre of the low) are indicated by the dark region in Figure 49. At the eastern side of a low and at the western side of a high, air masses are usually warm and either wet or dry - although they are often a little dryer towards the centre of a high. The area between highs and lows is often governed by warm southerly air advection and warm fronts that become less active at shorter distances from the centre of a high. The NW to N airflow at the western side of the low is normally cold and often wet. Soaring conditions are very favourable where the curvature of the isobars becomes anti-cyclonic.

At the northern and eastern part of a high, which can again be considered as the western part of the next low to the east, cold air advection is present. This cold air (being anti-cyclonic and thus in a region with less cloud cover) usually results in good and strong convection after only little heating. Another very favourable area is the southern side of a high pressure system. Air passes through NE to SE direction, which is normally dry and potentially warm in summer. This often happens over Great Britain or Scandinavia when a high pressure system is located near the western or northern parts of these countries. This also makes

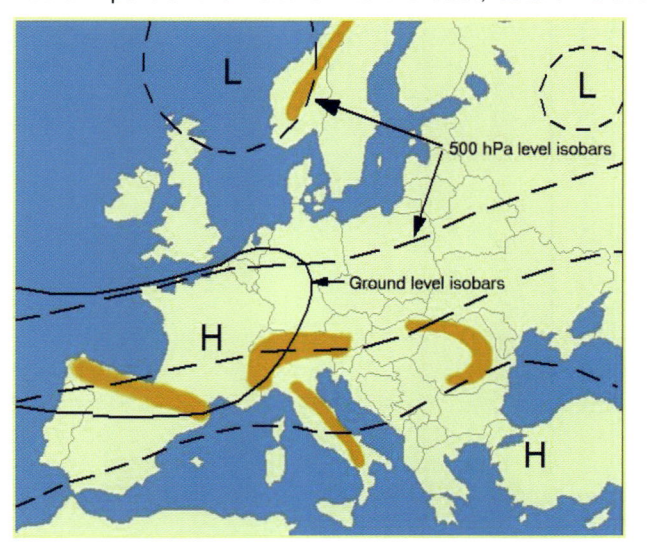

Figure 50: Examples of different pressure distributions at ground and 500 hPa level

Weather and Gliding

for good to excellent soaring conditions from Northern France to Poland.

By applying Figure 49 above (after an assessment of a temperature trace and the wind), we can determine where the best soaring conditions can be found in relation to high and low pressure systems. However, a standard synoptic chart only provides information on the pressure distribution at ground level, and therefore only allows a short term weather assessment. For a longer term weather forecast, we must consider the pressure distribution at the 500 hPa level. This equates to approximately 5500 metres or 18 000 ft (also known as 'Flight Level 180' or 'FL 180') and glider pilots can refer to these published figures. With a strong westerly airflow at this level (exemplified in Figure 50), we can expect conditions to change quickly. Such a situation will normally last for a day or two, or at least until the upper air flow provides new characteristics for surface air and pressure systems. Upper and lower pressure systems do not act independently of each other - this makes meteorological forecasting even more complicated. However, a high pressure system hovering above will provide good conditions for several days or even longer. Let's look at some favourable European weather patterns now.

Figure 51 depicts an example of favourable soaring conditions over the Alps at the end of April. The high pressure system is located east of the Alps and at the 500 hPa level, it stretches into southern Scandinavia and the Baltic Sea.

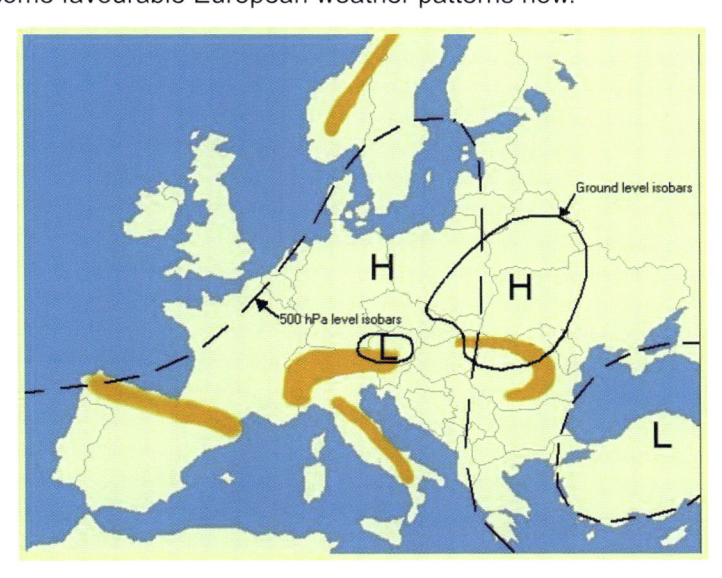

Figure 51: Favourable soaring conditions with a high over eastern Europe

Another favourable situation for the month of May is shown in Figure 52. Here the high pressure systems at ground level and 500 hPa are located over northern Germany/ Denmark and are only marginally displaced. Over the Alps we find a weak heat low (due to a greater warming of the mountain area). Conditions are less favourable in northern Germany as a result of the subsidence inversion near the centre of the high. (Refer to Section 2.11.1.)

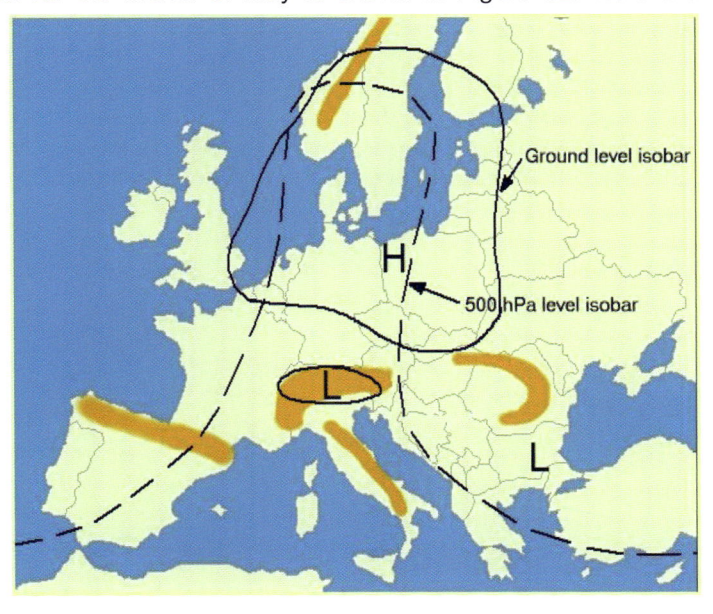

Figure 52: Favourable soaring conditions with a high over Scandinavia

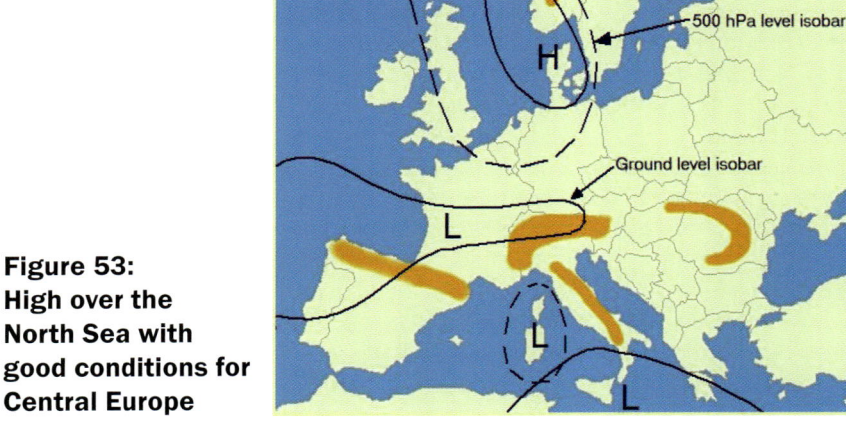

Weather and Gliding

Figure 53 shows a weather pattern with a high pressure system over the North Sea and an elongated low over the Atlantic coast of France and Spain. Good to very good conditions can not only be expected over the Alps, but also in Germany and surrounding countries.

**Figure 53:
High over the North Sea with good conditions for Central Europe**

The final example of a good soaring weather pattern for Central Europe is shown in Figure 54. The upper level high over the UK/Denmark and the weaker surface high over Central Europe provide for excellent gliding conditions. Even better soaring can be expected when the high is stationed further north between Great Britain and Scandinavia. The resulting weather pattern is conducive to easterly airstreams and can delight glider pilots in the Benelux countries, eastern France, Poland, Germany, Czech Republic and Slovakia for long periods – sometimes even weeks. However, soaring in the Alps can be negatively affected when different air-masses mix. The resulting instabilities can lead to extensive cloud cover.

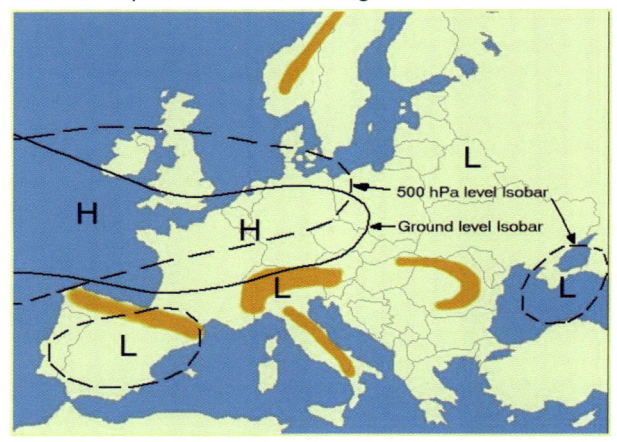

**Figure 54:
High over the Benelux countries with good conditions for Central Europe**

To sum it up with a more general statement, the position of the surface high has a major bearing on the ideal location for good thermal activity, whereas speed and direction of the upper air mass dictate the duration of suitable weather patterns. The upper air mass also impacts on thermal strength and convection height.

2.13.3 Soaring conditions in the European Alps

The first general observations of Alpine soaring weather were recorded by Jochen von Kalkreuth in the 1970's. He divided the Alps into four zones of differing weather patterns and suggested different flying tactics depending on the season and the general synoptic situation. Even today his recommendations are still valid, but with knowledge gained during some fantastic Alpine long range flights, more detailed and up-to-date information is now available. Typical thermally induced circulations in Alpine regions (under the general influence of a high pressure system) are shown in Figure 56. Generally, good soaring conditions are encountered from early April until June. Later in the season the area to the south of the Alps is influenced by warm and

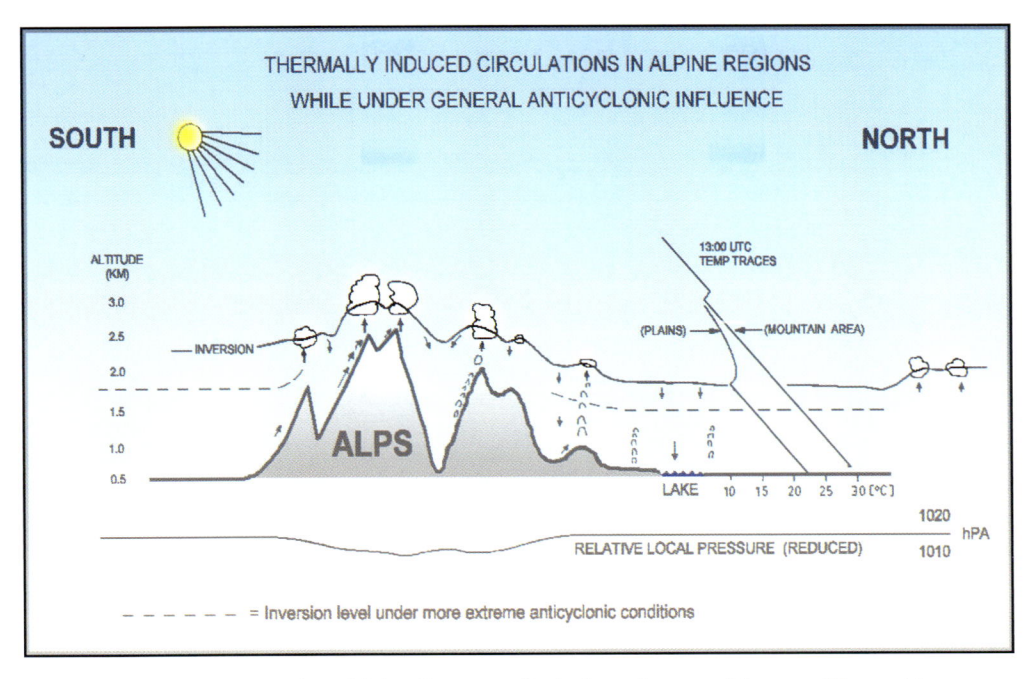

Figure 55: Convection currents in Alpine reasons

THERMALLY INDUCED CIRCULATIONS IN ALPINE REGIONS WHILE UNDER GENERAL ANTICYCLONIC INFLUENCE

humid Mediterranean air, which often results in less favourable conditions. However, the western Alpine region and Provence are better protected from the Mediterranean air and usually offer good soaring conditions even during the latter part of the season.

Excitement pure
Photo:
Gavin Wills
Glide Omarama

Chapter 2

Weather and Gliding

A nice day in the mountains
Photo: Michael Laykau

Experience shows that a high pressure system at surface level (with higher heating rates in the mountains) can lead to a slight drop in air pressure over the Alps as a result of the strong daytime thermal activity in the region. This is sometimes referred to as a heat low. A similar situation can be observed in other subtropical European regions such as Spain and Italy. Gliding conditions can be particularly favourable if such areas are blanketed by a weak high level westerly airflow.

In this context it should be noted that excellent Mediterranean soaring conditions are frequently encountered when Central Europe is plagued by successive low pressure systems. Equally, good gliding weather in Central Europe (especially when there is a high pressure system over Scandinavia) often goes hand in hand with less reliable soaring conditions in Mediterranean countries.

2.13.4 Seasonal soaring in the Provence region of France

Even as early as March, fantastic gliding conditions can be encountered in the Provence region of France. Being protected by mountains, the area warms to the east and northeast due to the sheltering effect of the Alps and the Massif Central. Northerly to north westerly cyclonic airflows usually leave their moisture in the mountains. Lee waves are a regular occurrence and thermal soaring conditions are marvellous in low to moderate wind speed situations. The Alps lose their winter snow first in Provence, and if a mistral (local wind) is persistent and strong it produces lee waves until a low forms in the Golf of Lyon region. Once a low is formed, a south easterly to south westerly warm and wet airflow governs this region with a period and rain falls for about a week. This happens quite often during early April.

2.13.5 Central European soaring conditions

The Central European soaring season usually commences at the end of March or in early April. Good soaring conditions start in the west and later extend to the east in line with spring vegetation development. At this time of year there is a good probability of first class gliding conditions especially in France, the Netherlands, Belgium, and Luxembourg. At the end of April, favourable weather patterns can be found in the whole of Central Europe and in the Alpine region. Later in the year, warm air advection can become detrimental to gliding conditions further west. Pilots need to pay more attention to soil characteristics and vegetation if this is the case.

2.13.6 Soaring conditions in Spain

Special attention should be given to soaring conditions in Spain, which can be the best of all Europe especially from mid June to mid August. Sometimes cold fronts from the W to NW pass over Spain and reduce the quality of thermals below that of Central Europe. After days of heating (or in a relative warm air mass), conditions improve and can then be rated good to excellent. The situation is typically governed by a westerly airflow at the 500 hPa level and a heat low at the surface. This creates a daily pressure variation - high at night and low during the day due to surface heating.

Quite often convergence lines develop over mountain ranges, especially the Sierra de Guadarrama. Here the convergence line(s) can be directly above the mountains or to the North of the range and can extend hundreds of kilometres. These convergence lines are a result of elevated heating effects and wind profiles. They provide for one of the most exciting thermal flying experiences in Europe.

2.13.7 Duration of thermal activity

The timing of the beginning and the end of the convection process is governed by the vertical temperature profile (temp. trace), intensity of radiation, degree of moisture evaporation and vegetation characteristics. In Central Europe the first thermals may start as early as two to three hours after sunrise (after cold air advection). More accurate predictions can be computed by a model such as Gold's if soil characteristics are taken into account.

Cessation of thermal activity can be computed in a similar way. However, general observations in different countries/climatic regions suggest the following timing:

Central Europe – lush vegetation -	2 hours before sunset
Central Spain – arid vegetation -	1 hour before sunset
Namibia – arid to desert vegetation -	<1/2 hour before sunset
Australia – arid vegetation -	1 hour before sunset

Other factors governing the end of thermal activity are sun aspect, sun apex and time of year. However, the vegetation and its evaporation/transpiration characteristics are the most decisive. (Refer to Section 1.19.)

Figure 56 shows some general features relating to the duration of thermals for three of the above mentioned regions. For clarity, thermal duration is shown in relation to local summer time. The time of thermal commencement only differs a little but the duration of sunshine differs a lot due to latitude factors. The hours of sunshine are greatest in Central Europe, resulting in the longest thermal duration, although even excellent soaring days only provide average climb rates of less than 2 m/s (4 kts). Thermal strength and convection height, seldom reach figures regarded as normal in Central Spain, Namibia, western USA or Australia.

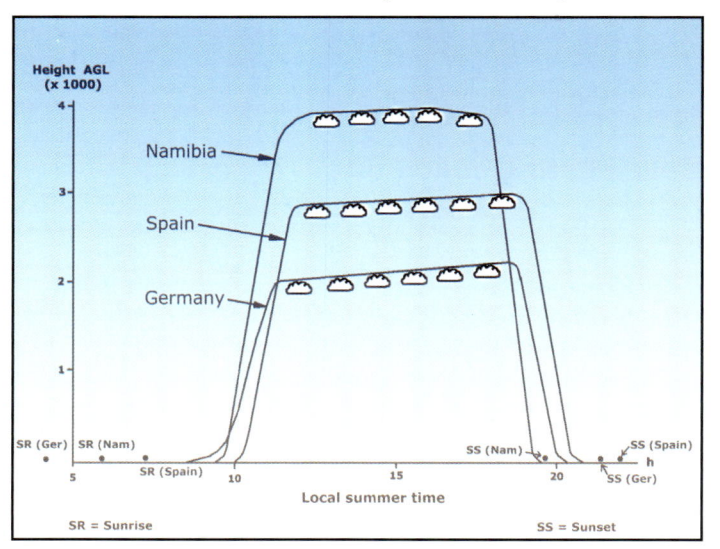

Figure 56: Thermal duration and heights in Namibia, Spain and Germany

In these regions, we find thermals that provide average climb rates of almost 3 m/s (6 kts) for the soaring day. This leads to higher average speeds, which compensates for the longer duration of thermal activity in Central Europe. However, stronger thermals do not entirely explain the much higher average speeds. The much deeper convection layer allows cruising at higher altitudes which brings the effect of density altitude into the equation. On average, the mean cruising altitude is more than 1500 m (5000 ft) higher in the world's most famous gliding regions.

Consequently, the longest flights in Germany and France are just over 1100 km while the best flights in Namibia, South Africa, and Australia approach 1500 km. It must be pointed out in this connection that western USA also offers superb summer thermal soaring. The number of days for long distance flights of more than 1000 km is about 1 to 5 per spring/summer in Germany, about 6 to 10 in Spain, and even more than 15 in South Africa/Namibia. Good conditions for long soaring flights in the Alps can be found for up to 10 days each year, mostly in spring and early summer.

2.14 Sea breeze fronts

A large number of gliding sites are affected by sea breezes. Pilots regularly flying under these conditions get used to it and see it as a challenge rather than a problem. However, a strong sea breeze certainly has all the potential to ruin an otherwise good soaring day.

Sea breeze fronts develop due to surface heating over inland regions and subsequent thermal activity. These thermals not only lift inland air to higher altitude, but also lead to a slightly lower pressure over land. At ground level, colder and moister maritime air rushes in to equalise the pressure while at altitude the air moves towards the sea where it slowly descends. This process sets up a circulation that usually causes enough stability to stop thermal activity in costal regions. However, in rare cases weak lift can reappear after a few hours of intense heating. Sea breezes are known to penetrate far inland, therefore it seems appropriate to consider the various meteorological conditions that assist or hinder their development.

2.14.1 Factors that influence a sea breeze

A very strong offshore wind, for example, will not only delay the arrival of a sea breeze but may even prevent it from penetrating more than just a few kilometres inland. If, on the other hand, the general wind direction is almost parallel to the coastline a sea breeze is more likely. The strength and intensity of a sea breeze is mainly determined by inland convection. Relatively stable air combined with a low convection level makes it unlikely for a sea breeze circulation to develop properly. A deep convection layer also makes it unlikely for a sea breeze to reach very far inland, but a medium depth of convection clearly favours a strong and vigorous sea breeze.

Lower sea breeze convection compared to cumulus clouds in foreground

As might be expected, the difference between land and sea temperatures also plays a major role. A relatively high water temperature, or generally speaking a small temperature differential between ocean and land, tends to reduce the likelihood of a strong sea breeze. This explains why relatively high water temperatures in autumn and lower land temperatures in winter account for weaker sea breezes.

This requirement for a high temperature differential might also explain why sea breezes reach hundreds of kilometres inland on very hot days in Australia whereas in more temperate climates (or during the colder times of the year) we seldom hear about sea breezes penetrating more than about 50 km or so inland.

One of the most indicative characteristics of a sea breeze is a gradual change of wind direction. While it initially comes in at right angles to the coastline, the breeze tends to changes direction once the Coriolis force takes effect. Therefore, in the Southern Hemisphere we see a slow deflection to the left after only a few hours. Put simply, if we stand with our back to the sea breeze we can expect the wind to blow from further on our right later in the afternoon, and it should not be surprising if we feel it come even further around towards the evening. Of course, north of the equator the opposite holds true and the wind veers to the right.

Another fairly indicative feature is its varying speed of penetration. Often we see a sea breeze rushing in for quite some distance only to realise shortly afterwards that it has suddenly come to a halt. After taking a rest for quite some time, it then moves on further and often faster than before. This pulsing type of behaviour has caught many glider pilots (including myself) by surprise and has been responsible for quite a few outlandings.

The shape of the coastline also seems to have a major influence. Personally, I'm lucky enough to fly from an airfield only about 30 km away from Yorke Peninsula in South Australia where there are plenty of opportunities to take advantage of a sea breeze coming in from both coasts. In such a scenario, a convergence line tends to form roughly over the middle of the peninsula, allowing flights of 100 km or so without thermalling. On rare occasions, thermal wave forms in front of such convergence lines, allowing breathtaking soaring with splendid views of both coastlines. In other parts of the world there are similar convergence lines for knowledgeable pilots to explore.

When it comes to the speed of sea breeze penetration, all of the above comments need to be taken into account. In a low-wind scenario a sea breeze front penetrates inland at a speed of approx. 10 to 15 km/h, but can reach more than twice this speed on occasion. This makes it not only difficult to determine the time of arrival at a particular gliding site, but difficult to estimate its depth of penetration. Needless to say that it presents an outlanding risk for cross-country pilots.

2.14.2 The mechanics of a sea breeze

Before we progress further we first need to understand the mechanics of a sea breeze front. Most pilots know that approaching maritime air replaces warmer and dryer inland air and that a sea breeze does not represent a new mass of air with a different character. In fact, a sea breeze is typically only a 500 to 1000 ft layer of cooler and moister air that acts like the thin end of a wedge as it sowly creeps in from a lake or the ocean. On many occasions, I have returned from a cross-country flight and kept an eye on the temperature. As the electric variometer in my ASH 25 features an outside temperature readout, it is easy to determine when the descent into the sea breeze air occurs. More often than not, a rather sudden temperature drop amounting to 5°C or more over a few seconds occurs somewhere within the 500 to 1000 ft level.

This might explain why a sea breeze is even more difficult to deal with in mountainous areas. It can sneak in through valleys or passes and completely kill any convection generated by the valley floor. However, because it does not reach the higher parts of the mountains, thermal activity continues unabated from the sunlit parts of the slopes. In such terrain, it is useful to think of a sea breeze as a large amount of water slowly flooding the low-lying areas.

Because cooler air is always denser, it remains close to the ground and gradually creeps under the warmer inland air. Therefore it is not hard to imagine why a sea breeze is the best thermal trigger known to glider pilots. Along a broad line, this miniature front of maritime air separates all the warm air from the ground and produces a line of good lift along its leading edge. Once the sea breeze air engulfs a particular flatland gliding site, flying is usually confined to circuits. However, there are occasions when the relatively thin layer of maritime air receives sufficient heating to restart the normal convection process. This is an exception to the rule and can't be relied on.

2.14.3 Flying tactics

A sea breeze can only develop if and when convection occurs. This means that even gliding clubs located relatively close to the sea get a few hours of early soaring before the arrival of maritime air. These early thermals may initially prove to be weak, but they are usually quite workable. Provided we get our first climb during this period, we can move further inland and enjoy a perfectly normal day of soaring. In other words, if we want to beat the sea breeze we should not waste any time in the morning.

A lot of inexperienced glider pilots are very concerned about sea breezes for fear they might not make it back to the airfield later in the day. Although this is a well known problem in a competition environment, it is usually less of a problem for pilots free to select and change their task. Provided some local knowledge is applied, a return into a sea breeze usually presents no major issue with today's modern gliders. Assuming we take a high enough climb near the incoming sea breeze front, we are usually able to penetrate into the strong headwinds that are almost always associated with a return to the home airfield. Such aircraft as the world-class glider or older wooden ships struggle on occasions, but a sea breeze is not the demon it used to be in the old days of aircraft with poor glide ratios and an even worse ability to penetrate into a headwind.

Curtain (or Veil) Cloud (Photo: Gavin Wills, GlideOmarama.com)

2.14.4 Visual indications

In conditions of very high humidity, a sea breeze often leaves unmistakable signs of its position in the form of cumulus clouds. These clouds are often of a very diffuse shape, but to the trained eye they reveal what is happening in the atmosphere. Figure 57 illustrates the basic airflow pattern and points to the reason for the convergence line.

Research dating back to 1987 indicates that the leading edge of a sea breeze front can have about twice the depth of the trailing flow. It was also discovered that the speed of the trailing flow is faster than the propagation speed of the front, which might explain the reason for the pulsing behaviour and the varying speed of penetration. Where the cool and moist ocean air meets the warm and dry inland air, we have a collision between two masses of air. The only way for the air to go is up. The moister sea air condenses at a fairly low level and as a result we get cumulus clouds with a low base. In contrast, the warmer and dryer inland air condenses much later resulting in cumulus clouds at a significantly higher level. A cluster of clouds with vastly different cloud bases develops.

But not only that - in conditions of very high humidity we can also get wisps of clouds seemingly suspended from the lower cumulus. In Europe the term "curtain

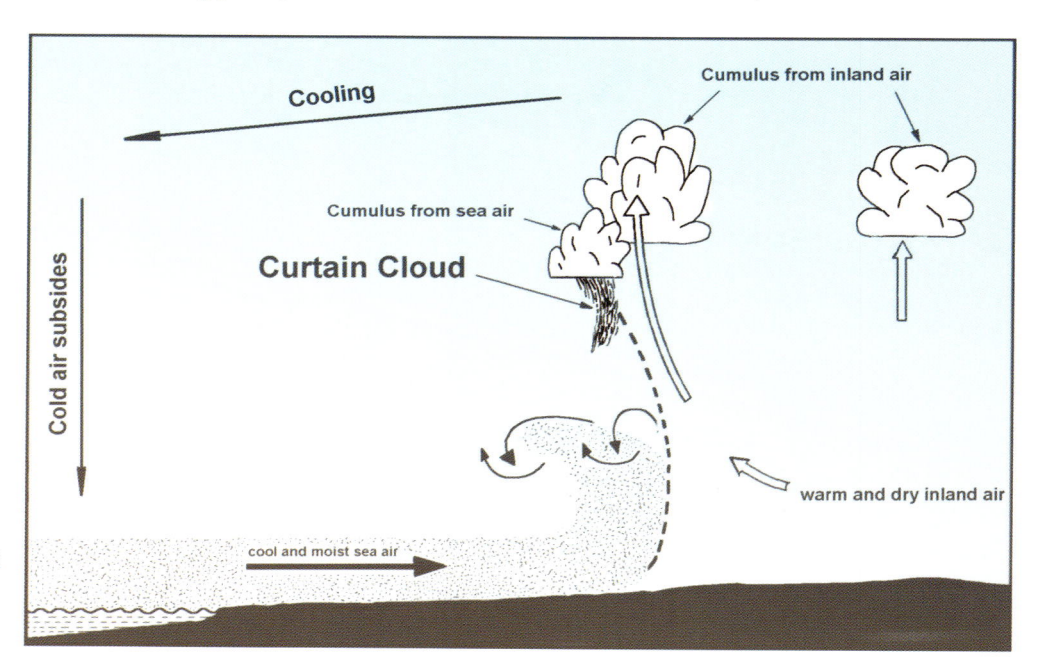

Figure 57: Airflow along a sea breeze front

cloud" or "veil cloud" is used to describe the phenomenon. These clouds mark the place where the moist sea air meets the dryer inland air at cloud level. The best lift is found just to the landward side of these clouds and slightly towards the higher cumulus.

Although it is fair to assume that the behaviour of the air along the leading edge of every sea breeze is more or less identical, it does not mean that the process can always be detected by the naked eye. Only a relatively high amount of moisture in the air makes these processes visible and it should go without saying that different amounts of moisture will result in very different cloud appearances.

Weather and Gliding

**Cumulus clouds over the Olivine Ice Plateau (NZ)
Photo:
G. Dale
GlideOmarama.com**

A low inland air humidity level, for example, deprives us of inland cumulus clouds and, if the air off the ocean is also relatively dry, we won't see any clouds at all. Particularly when a sea breeze front is marked by clouds, there is a good chance of getting some first-hand experience and a feel for the air along a convergence line. Being weatherwise, reading the sky more effectively and having a better understanding of sea breeze behaviour is bound to be of huge advantage whenever we fly on those tricky sea breeze days in the future.

Even without any clouds we can get some visual clues. Onshore winds are almost always characterised by higher levels of humidity, and when this slightly hazier (and salt laden) air moves slowly inland it often marks the depth of maritime air penetration quite clearly.

Especially from the cockpit of a glider, we can often detect this slight variation in visibility and that should give the switched-on pilot more than enough warning. But, especially in relative dry climates like Australia's, dust is often kicked up by the leading edge of a sea breeze in a similar fashion to squall lines ahead of thunderstorms. Again, if such signs are noticed and acted upon, the chances of being brought down by a sea breeze are much reduced.

Last but not least, we should make mention of man-made early warning systems. Many gliding clubs broadcast a warning to their cross-country pilots within minutes of a sea breeze´s arrival. My club is no exception and I'm sure that this excellent service has saved a lot of pilots from a possible outlanding over the years. In cases where such a service doesn't exist, there is nothing to stop pilots from requesting wind direction and strength over the radio before embarking on a final glide back to the home airfield. It is preferable to hang on to a thermal for a little longer than to land in a paddock a few kilometres from home or to get high blood pressure during the last part of the final glide.

2.14.5 Taking advantage of sea breeze fronts

I'm sure many readers have made a mental note about my earlier comments on flying a sea breeze convergence line over Yorke Peninsula on the south coast of South Australia. Of course, such flights clearly fall into the category of sightseeing, although they are hugely educational and provide firstclass opportunities to assess the meteorological forces at work. Comparing the location of the convergence line for different wind directions, for example, or observing the change in cloud base in line with a variation in ambient temperatures is most enlightening and very interesting at the same time.

For readers unfamiliar with the area a map of Yorke Peninsula is reproduced (Figure 58). It might be shaped not unlike the Italian Peninsula, but its average width amounts to only 40 km and its length is in the order of 150 km. Although the sea breeze convergence line is usually located near its centre, there have been occasions where the best lift was found along the western coastline and, on rare occasions (with a very strong easterly airflow), even a few kilometres out to sea.

A strong sea breeze front over the open sea is by no means an isolated occurrence in this part of South Australia. The local geography is dominated by a coastline aligned in a north – south direction, resulting in some extremely interesting weather phenomena in easterly airstreams.

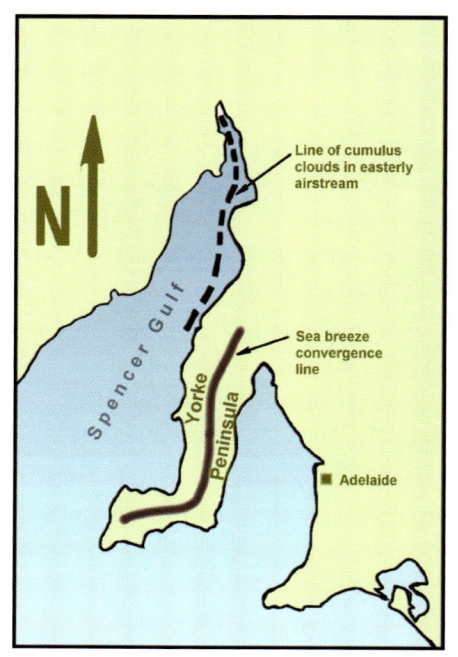

Figure 58: Coastline around Yorke Peninsula

On days of a high convection, there have been numerous cases where there have been blue thermals over land in conjunction with a distinct line of high cumulus cloud over Spencer Gulf. I have explored this unusual phenomenon not only with powered aircraft, but also in gliders and have come to the conclusion that we are dealing with standard sea breeze fronts. The only difference from Figure 57 is that the very high convection in combination with a strong easterly wind forces the sea breeze air back over the sea. When this moist air condenses between 8000 and 12 000 ft. it forms a picture postcard cloud street with excellent soaring conditions underneath. I'm happy to admit that cruising under a cloud street as far as 5 km out to sea feels a bit strange at first, but when it works really well it serves as another unforgettable experience for a glider pilot.

It is possible to take advantage of a sea breeze on cross-country flights along most coastlines of the world. In the final analysis, it all comes down to good planning. When a task is selected that provides an opportunity to fly at least one leg along a sea breeze front, we not only increase our chances of a successful completion but we should be able to achieve a much higher speed.

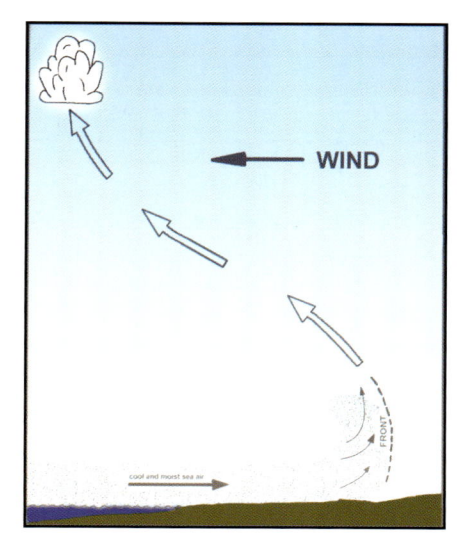

Figure: 59 Seabreeze convection pushed out to sea

To underline these comments let me report on a recent flight with my club's CFI. We shared the pleasure of flying an ASH 25 until we were about 10 km short of the second turn point and approx. 170 km away from home. Keen to demonstrate the high-speed performance of the glider, I took over and announced that it was my intention not to thermal on the way back. The reply was as short as it was to the point: "I want to see that." During a minor deviation (to align the flight path with some cumulus clouds on track), we picked up enough height to cruise home at 100 kts or so. Just as we got ready for a fast final glide we noticed a line of clouds in the distance. As both of us suspected that these clouds marked the leading edge of the sea breeze front, we decided to extend our flight and add another turn point in order to take full advantage of this convergence line. But even before we arrived anywhere near the clouds, our instruments showed very strong lift. In fact, the pointer of the netto variometer was often hard against the stop for more than a minute at a time. Although our airspeed now approached 120 kts and the GPS indicated a ground speed of over 250 km/h our biggest problem was getting down to the 8500 ft maximum altitude overhead our home airfield. As neither of us wanted to open the airbrakes, we decided to add one more turn point, but even after rounding it we still had the same problem. Because my friend in the back seat was overdue for some check flights we changed tactics and went for an additional turn point approx. 40 km within the sea breeze-affected area. When we finally landed, we noted we had not done a single turn over a distance of 236 km, which we covered in 76 minutes for an average speed of 183 km/h.

That says it all. As much as glider pilots generally dislike sea breezes, they can provide fantastic soaring conditions if only we manage to be in the right spot at the right time.

2.14.6 Pseudo sea breezes

The subject would not be covered properly without a quick mention of pseudo sea breeze fronts. In the case of a conventional sea breeze, the supply of cold and moist air comes from the sea; when a part of the country lies under a thick blanket of low-level cloud while an adjacent area receives ample solar heating, a temperature differential develops that produces a circulation very similar to a conventional sea breeze.

Air from a cloudy and colder region flows towards the warmer sunlit areas. Where the cool air collides with the warmer air we can again expect a classic sea breeze like front. Especially when we fly near large areas of fog or thick layers of low level stratus clouds, we need to be very alert and remember to apply the flying tactics described previously.

In closing this section, I would like to encourage readers to learn more about this fascinating subject called "Weather". We are very fortunate that top meteorologists such as the late Tom Bradbury (Meteorology and flight) and Wally Wallington (Meterorology for glider pilots) were glider pilots themselves and have

Low level cloud conducive to a pseudo sea breeze

published excellent books on the subject. More scientifically orientated readers might want to study "An introduction to boundary layer meteorology" by Ronald B. Stull, with all its advanced maths.

All of these books are highly recommended for the serious glider pilot.

2.15 A clue from the clouds above

Clouds not only rank among the most fascinating of all weather spectacles, but can also provide useful information. Knowledgeable glider pilots can often assess the day's soaring conditions without a lengthy study of forecasts or satellite images; they merely look at the sky and observe the clouds. The layer of the atmosphere where almost all cloud exists is the troposphere, although the tops of some severe thunderstorms can occasionally pierce the tropopause. (Refer to Section 2.8.)

Clouds provide telltale signs of air movement in the troposphere and can therefore greatly help enhance performance, enjoyment and safety in gliding. All clouds originate from water that continually evaporates from oceans, lakes and rivers etc. and transpires from plant life. Water can either be present in asolid form (ice/snow), in liquid form (rain/drizzle) or as invisible water vapour contained in the air.

Air can hold only a certain amount of water vapour (dependent on temperature). When the air reaches its maximum water content it is at the dew point (refer to Section 2.7) and instant condensation occurs. The invisible water vapour turns into tiny but visible water droplets. At or near ground level we call this fog but at altitude we refer to this as cloud.

Meteorologists rank clouds according to their height and shape. Let's first try to classify the different types of cloud and as a second step, determine what types of cloud are associated with particular weather systems.

1. High-level clouds

High-level clouds form above 20 000 feet (6000 metres) where temperatures are so low that these clouds are primarily composed of ice crystals. High-level clouds are typically thin and white in appearance, but can appear to exhibit many different colours especially when the sun is low on the horizon. The three main types of high level cloud are cirrus, cirrostratus and cirrocumulus.

2. Middle-level clouds

Middle-level clouds appear typically between 6500 to 20 000 feet (2000 to 6000 metres). Examples are altocumulus, altostratus and nimbostratus clouds. They are composed primarily of tiny water droplets, but can be made up of of ice crystals when temperatures are low enough.

3. Low-level clouds

Low-level clouds are also mostly composed of water droplets, since their bases generally lie below 6500 feet (2000 metres). Examples are cumulus, stratocumulus and stratus clouds. They may also contain ice particles and snow provided ambient temperatures are low enough.

In addition there are four primary cloud groups:
- Cirrus - Latin for 'curl of hair'; to describe a wispy cloud
- Stratus - Latin for 'layer'; to describe a sheet-like cloud
- Cumulus - Latin for 'heap'; to describe a puffy cloud with vertical development
- Nimbus - Latin for 'violent rain'; to describe a rain cloud.

Other clouds can be described by combining these basic terms. For example, nimbostratus is a rain cloud that occurs in layers, whereas cumulonimbus is a rain cloud with pronounced vertical development. Cirrostratus is a wispy, sheet-like cloud, and stratocumulus is a layer cloud with some cumulus features.

Sample photos of the different cloud types are shown below. The sequence is in line with the typical cloud progression for an approaching frontal system.

Cirrus clouds are thin, often wispy, high-level clouds. They are found at mean heights above ground of 42 000 to 16 000 feet (13 to 5 km) and as such, always form above freezing level. Precipitation is never to be expected from cirrus clouds. Made of small ice crystals, they seldom affect gliding conditions in any major way unless they become thick and dense enough to reduce the amount of heating at ground level.

Cirrus heralding the approach of a frontal system

Altocumulus are greyish-white middle-level clouds and are about 3000 ft (1 km) thick. They are not created by ground-based convection but are usually part of an approaching frontal system. Altocumulus develop when an expanding layer of air rises or when turbulence occurs within an unstable layer of middle-level cloud. If altocumulus clouds thicken, precipitation is likely. The appearance of altocumulus clouds in a warm and humid environment frequently leads to thunderstorm activity later in the day.

**Altocumulus clouds
Photo:
Michael Bath
http://
Australiasevereweather.
com**

Weather and Gliding

Altostratus cloud cover

Altostratus belongs to the group of middle level clouds (2000 - 6000 m). An altostratus cloud usually forms ahead of rain-bearing fronts, but little or no rain falls from it. Altostratus usually covers large sections of the sky and has a grey or blue-grey appearance. The sun might shine through altostratus in thinner places and will make the cloud appear watery or fuzzy. If heavy rain sets in, we are usually dealing with nimbostratus.

Virga at dusk

Virga (Latin for 'twig' or 'branch') is highly relevant to gliding operations. It does not occur in conjunction with every frontal system and is not technically cloud; in fact it is observable rain falling from cloud. All virga precipitation evaporates before reaching the ground – something very common in dry climates during the summer period. As the precipitation evaporates (changes from liquid to vapour) it briskly cools the surrounding air and the resulting higher density air descends very rapidly. Often the descend rate is high enough to create a dry microburst – a localised column of rapidly sinking air. The scale and suddenness of a microburst makes it a great danger to all types of aircraft, including gliders. Especially at low-level wind shear and gust fronts can play havoc with aircraft and have contributed to several fatal crashes.

The above types of cloud rank amongst the most interesting and relevant to gliding operations. Additional formations such as cumulonimbus (Cb) and Mamatus clouds are described and pictured in Section 4.12. Details on pileus and lenticular clouds can be found in Chapter 12.

Finally, back to our most favourable type of clouds - cumulus. They often dominate the sky for several days soon after the passage of a frontal system. These vertically-developed clouds and are often referred to as 'fair weather cumulus'. They are

Evenly spread thin cumulus clouds (Cumulus humilis)

cauliflower-shaped low to mid-level clouds with dark bases and bright tops and have the appearance of floating cotton balls. Their lifespan is between 5 and 40 minutes. As long as they retain their flat bases (and slight vertical growth with distinct outlines), they point us to active updraughts. The cloud tops indicate the extent of the rising air but given suitable conditions, harmless fair weather cumulus can develop into towering cumulonimbus clouds, which are often associated with powerful thunderstorms. When observing cumulus, we are actually observing the condensation process of rising thermals.

Weather and Gliding

2.16 The "Skew T - Log P diagram"

Earlier in this chapter we had a detailed look at the "Stüve" diagram. It certainly presents the easiest, but by no means the only method of determining gliding conditions in advance. Especially in North America, but also in some other countries, a different aerological diagram called a "Skew T - Log P diagram", (or "F160"), is often used. Therefore we will now explore the major differences.

On a 'Stüve' diagram, height above sea level is shown on the vertical axis and temperature is plotted on the horizontal axis. In other words, the isobars (lines of equal pressure) are straight horizontal lines. The isotherms (lines of equal temperature) are straight vertical lines and the dry adiabats are straight lines running from the bottom right to the top left.

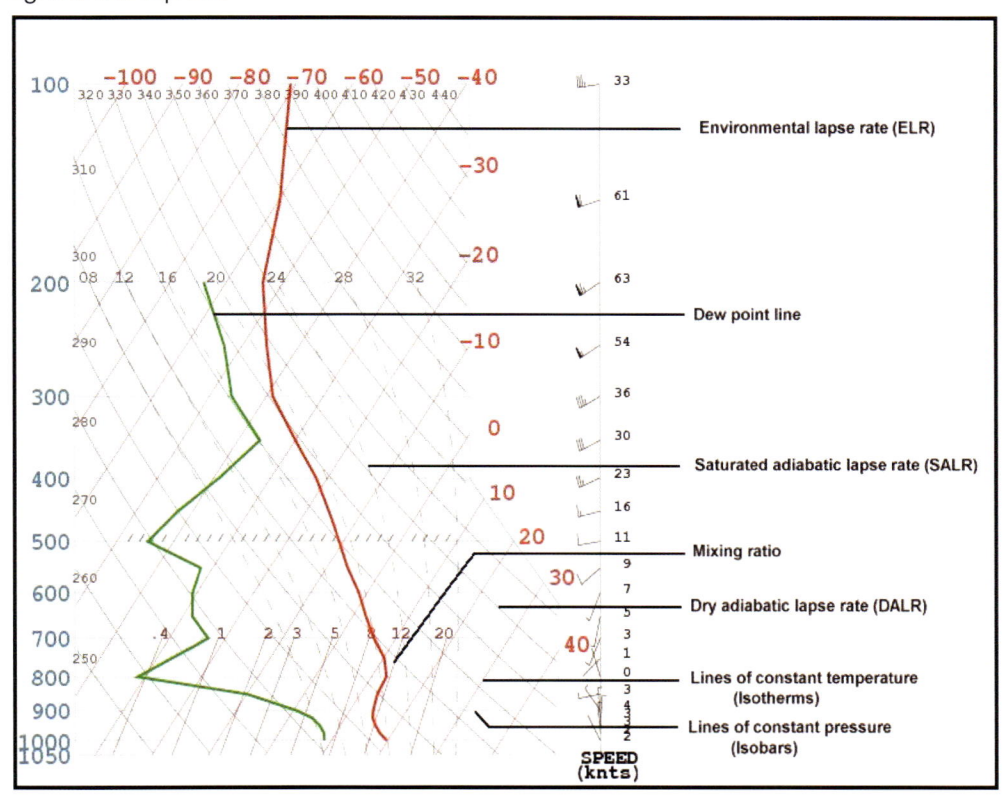

Figure 60: Skew T - Log P diagram with key to chart lines

On a "Skew T - Log P diagram" we have skewed temperature lines and a logarithmic pressure scale. Pressure (instead of height above sea level) is shown on the left vertical scale and the isobars are maintained as straight horizontal lines. As ambient pressure varies from day to day, we cannot assign an altitude to a particular pressure. However, for our purpose we can work with a pressure drop of about 1 millibar per 30 ft of altitude. If we deal with the standard atmosphere, sea level pressure is 1013.2 mb 3000 ft is about 900 mb 5000 ft is about 850 mb, 10 000 ft is about 700 mb and 18 000 ft is about 500 mb.

Temperature values are shown on the right vertical axis, but the isotherms are not vertical but run from the top right to the bottom left. This, and the fact that both dry and wet adiabats are curved, makes the "Skew T - Log P diagram" slightly more difficult to interpret. Still, it seems to be preferred by meteorologists and most military forces. Unfortunately the standard forms extend to an altitude of 53 000 ft and the lower altitudes (which are of special interest to glider pilots) are shown right at the very bottom at a rather compressed scale.

Weather and Gliding

Figure 61: Examples of wind speed & direction symbols

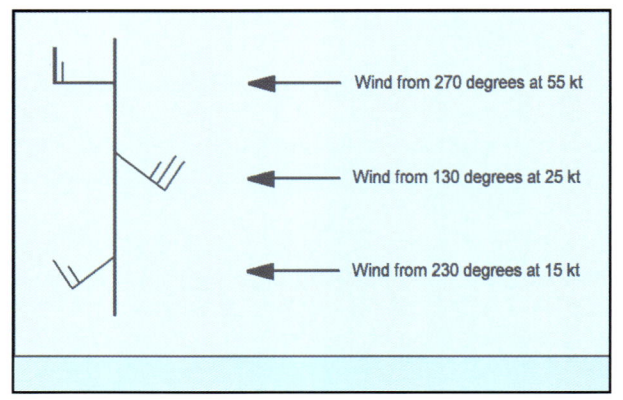

Wind from 270 degrees at 55 kt
Wind from 130 degrees at 25 kt
Wind from 230 degrees at 15 kt

A welcome indication of wind strength and direction is given by the symbols on the far right of the diagram. The orientation of each line that originates from the vertical axis indicates the wind direction (the direction the wind is blowing from) at the corresponding pressure level. The shorter perpendicular lines signify the wind strength as follows: Full bold line = 50 kts; full normal line = 10 kts; half normal line = 5 kts

In weather reports for the general public only wind speeds at ground level are routinely forecast. Still, they provide a reasonable assessment of wind strength for gliding purposes and are based on the Beaufort scale below:

Table 5: Beaufort wind strength classification

Description	Speed (kts)	Mean speed (kts)	Speed (km/h)	Beaufort classification	Forecast for general public
Calm	<1	0	0	0	Calm
Light air	1-3	2	3-4	1	Light
Light breeze	4-6	5	7-11	2	Light
Gentle breeze	7-10	9	13-18	3	Light
Moderate br.	11-16	13	20-30	4	Moderate
Fresh breeze	17-21	19	31-39	5	Fresh
Strong breeze	22-27	24	40-50	6	Strong
Moderate gale	28-33	30	51-61	7	Strong
Fresh gale	34-40	37	63-74	8	Gale
Strong gale	41-47	44	75-87	9	Storm
Whole gale	48-55	52	88-102	10	Storm
Storm	56-63	60	103-117	11	Storm
Hurricane	64-71	68	118-131	12	Storm

2.17 The tephigram.

A third type of aerological diagram is a tephigram. Meteorologists often use the letter T to denote temperature and the Greek symbol Φ (phi) for the potential heat energy of the air. Therefore it is easy to see how the name T-Φ gram (or tephigram) came about.

On a tephigram we also have pressure altitude instead of height above sea level. Temperature is still shown on the horizontal axis and the isotherms are straight vertical lines. In contrast, isobars run from the bottom left to the top right and dry adiabatic lines are straight horizontal lines.

Again, both dry and wet adiabats are curved, which makes the tephigram slightly more difficult to interpret than the "Stüve" diagram. However, the principles covered above still apply. Glider pilots keen to use tephigrams for their convection predictions should be able to extract the relevant information after only a short period of adaptation.

Chapter 2 — Weather and Gliding

ASW 28 ridge flying
in New Zealand
Image: McCaw Media.
(mccawmedia.co.nz)

Chapter 2

Weather and Gliding

Top technology and
nature in perfect harmony
Image: McCaw Media.
(mccawmedia.co.nz)

Weather and Gliding

Chapter 2

3 Preparing for cross-country flying

3.1 Getting ready for road retrieves

For absolute peace of mind, cross-country pilots do not only need a dependable crew, but also access to a reliable and serviceable trailer. An outlanding is not the time to discover that one of the trailer lights misbehaves or that tyres and brakes need attention. Time spent on preparation and trailer maintenance always pays off and also provides a psychological advantage.

Modern glider trailers usually come with the latest ground handling gear and hence allow retrieves by a single person. However, on windy days, it is always advisable to take a second person along. A crew of three people is certainly preferable when retrieving an open-class glider or two-seater. If a verified GPS position is not available after an outlanding, or a handheld GPS receiver is not at hand, it is vital to obtain precise directions from the pilot before leaving base. Too many retrieve crews have failed to find their pilot for quite some time because the directions were either inadequate or the crew neglected to write them down. Mobile phones may not always work in remote areas, and relying on memory after spending quite some time on the road is inviting trouble - unless it was arranged to meet the pilot at a place known to at least one member of the retrieve crew.

Pilots can make a major contribution towards a quick and trouble free retrieve. As an example, the pilot can find the gate to the field or ask the farmer for permission to retrieve the glider while waiting for the crew. This is not only a matter of courtesy, but is highly advisable as many of today's modern vehicles fitted with catalytic converters. These exhausts get extremely hot and are known to start fires in long and dry vegetation. Under such circumstances, it might be wise to use another car or move the glider to the gate and leave car and trailer parked on the road.

As the pilot knows his aircraft best, he is preferably put in charge of de-rigging. Every aircraft has its peculiarities and, as long as the job is coordinated by a single person with an in-depth knowledge of the type, there is a much reduced likelihood of finger pointing later. Before driving off, we should check that all items are properly secured and also surge the area thoroughly for smaller items temporarily placed on the ground. Nothing but our footprints should be left behind – not even the smallest bit of sealing tape.

3.2 A partnership with your crew

Pilot and crew need to work together closely. Of course, when an outlanding occurs, the crew is there to get the pilot back, but we must remember that nothing is more demoralising than being relegated to mere standby personnel for retrieves. Finding a good crew is becoming more and more difficult. Perhaps the increasing popularity of engine-equipped gliders is partly due to the problem of finding a suitable crew for the duration of a competition.

The club pilot aiming for a badge flight, for example, usually relies on a fellow club member for retrieves. Prior to the flight, crew and pilot ensure that all fittings are inside the trailer, but there is generally little need for a close bond between pilot and crew. However, any bond can be severely strained if the pilot takes the retrieve car keys along with him on the flight!

Preparing for cross-country flying

An open-class trailer dwarfed by a "road train" in Australia

The situation is fundamentally different in a competition environment. A top crew can contribute a great deal to competition success and in such circumstances it is vital for pilot and crew to work as a harmonious team. The key is the involvement of the whole crew in the daily preparation of the glider; a report on the flight at the end of the day is just as important. This sharing of information is not only vital for unconditional support, but also helps to create a relaxed atmosphere amongst team members.

Treating the crew as equals, and leaving them in no doubt about the importance of their contribution, ensures successful and enjoyable cooperation. Of course, a good crew member must be highly dependable but does not necessarily have to be a pilot. A conscientious nature and a determination to help the pilot, not only with the daily chores but also with moral support when needed, is what matters most. Conversations between team members should be kept positive during the entire contest. Ensuring that the pilot is not unduly distracted is just as important. Especially close to launch and when the pilot is already sitting in the cockpit, a good crew will intercept spectators and answer questions on behalf of the pilot. A top competition pilot needs to be a good psychologist but exactly the same can be said for a first-class crew member.

3.3 Preparing for longer flights

"Listen mate, I think today's conditions are good enough for a 5 hour flight. I suggest you claim an aircraft and give it a go", says the duty instructor.

That is only one possible scenario. If you are known to strive for badges, or even diamond flights, the club coach could say something like this:

"Today it's your turn my friend - get ready and prepare yourself for your 300 km flight, but let me know where you want to go and who is crewing for you".

Hopefully, this is music to your ears and is the green light you have been waiting for. The conditions are right, an aircraft is available, the instructor or coach wants to see you go; the big question is:"Are you ready?" Are you adequately prepared to achieve your goal? You need more than just a glider and a tug or a winch. If you want to succeed, you need to look at:

   a)   your personal wellbeing; and

   b)   equipment necessary.

Preparing for cross-country flying

PILOT WELLBEING

For a pilot with limited experience, even a relatively short distance flight can become a very demanding endurance event. The same holds true for a 5 hour duration flight. Countless such flights have been unsuccessful simply because the pilot was inadequately prepared, did not have the stamina, or returned without completing the task because he or she got sick. The majority of such flights could have been successful and far more enjoyable if the pilot had taken a few basic matters into consideration. Here they are!

Comfort

It is a well known fact that successful pilots take steps to ensure they will be comfortable towards the end of a very long day in the cockpit. This is easier said than done. In fact, for taller and larger pilots it may even be impossible to achieve with some of today's narrow fuselage designs. On average people grow taller and bigger by two or three centimetres per generation, and pilots are certainly no exception. However, this fact seems to have gone unnoticed when considering various recent cockpit designs. Some designers try to squeeze better performance out of their models by reducing the fuselage size and in turn expect pilots to squeeze themselves into ridiculously narrow cockpits with hardly any room to move. As a result, the pilot's performance is likely to suffer over time and a marginally better performing aircraft can turn into a distinct disadvantage for anyone but the smallest of pilots.

Cockpit noises from poorly sealed canopies or air vents are an equally important issue. Noise can not only be highly distracting but can result in a fatigue issue with all its known safety implications. Even a seemingly small wallet left in the back pocket may cause discomfort on a longer flight. It can literally turn into "a pain in the butt" and is best left behind. Only a few notes in the back pocket are needed for "piece of mind".

We can conclude that performance, safety and enjoyment depend to a very large extent on the "feel good factor". Adaptable backrests or adjustable rudder pedals are often not quite enough to ensure comfort for flights lasting more than just an hour or two. We all come in different shapes and sizes and therefore need to put considerable effort into seating comfort. What was reasonably comfortable on a

Flying over remote parts of Australia

quick one hour flight might result in a sore back or even worse after a flight lasting five hours or more. Parachute owners can have their chute repacked for improved comfort, but for other pilots inflatable seat cushions or foam of different density might help to improve comfort. By far the best material seems to be Dynafoam as its energy absorbing ability improves safety, although some softer material may be placed on top for additional comfort. Whatever you do, just make sure you can comfortably reach all the controls and can adjust all instruments without stretching.

Drinking water

Performance deteriorates rapidly as soon as the body starts to suffer from dehydration. Only very mild dehydration severely degrades the logical processes of the brain. It is a very insidious deterioation and almost impossible to detect for yourself. If we only drink when we feel thirsty we are certainly not drinking enough, because the feeling of thirst is a lagging indicator of dehydration. It is necessary to drink prior to, and during the flight to compensate for the large amounts of water lost through perspiration and urination.

Urine is also an excellent indicator of hydration level but, as with thirst, it is very much a lagging one. As a rule of thumb, if urine has a distinct yellow appearance or a pungent smell we are likely to be dehydrated already. Consuming water in sufficient quantities will give urine a colour not unlike a glass of Riesling. Physical activity on a hot day sees an average adult male lose up to 10–12 litres of fluid. It is possible to perspire almost two litres of water in the time it takes to check the glider, prepare for the flight and move the glider onto the strip.

Imagine that the pilot doesn't get away on the first launch. Pushing the aircraft back and waiting for another launch in temperatures of 35°C or more means that the pilot is almost certainly dehydrated before he even finds a thermal that gets him into cooler air. Although we notice when our body is sweating profusely on the ground, we may not be aware of it at higher altitudes. Perspiration disappears without a trace in the cool air from cockpit ventilation.

The big problem with dehydration is that it is difficult to realise when the body is affected by it. It is extremely insidious and, as a result, we carry on with activities while becoming tired, inefficient, forgetful, tense and sometimes even oblivious to safety matters. According to an article recently published in a CASA flight safety magazine, severe dehydration can lead to heat stress, resulting in lightheadedness, nausea and even blurred vision. The author goes on to say that the human body is about 70% water. Our bodies use water for just about everything: temperature regulation, the elimination of waste, digestion and the transport of nutrients.

Perspiration is one of the body's main temperature regulation mechanisms and is a large consumer of fluid reserves. Sweat cools the surface of the skin when it evaporates. At the same time, the rate of blood flow to the skin increases as the blood vessels dilate. The skin acts like a car radiator, cooling the blood to be returned to the rest of the body. It is important to note that the cooling action of sweat can only work where the sweat can evaporate. Tight clothing, particularly when made of synthetic material, will hinder evaporation and hence reduce the rate of cooling. Further, when perspiration is wiped away or drips off its cooling action is lost.

After a water loss of about 2% of body weight we start to get thirsty. At the 4–5% mark we get sluggish and tired, maybe even nauseated and irritable. This is a very dangerous condition for pilots to be in, and marks the time when mental faculties begin t to be affected. In practical terms, if a pilot loses more than 3% of body weight, in water mental performance reduces by as much as 20%. In our mentally demanding sport the impact on performance and safety is very significant.

Fluid replacement is especially important for older pilots. Their diminished thermoregulatory function makes them less responsive to thirst and therefore less likely to replenish their fluids in time.

The lesson from this is clear. Commence your fluid intake as soon as possible in the morning and continue right until take-off. From then on, drink small amounts of water at short intervals. The body accepts water more readily in small but regular doses rather than in large quantities. The easiest way to facilitate this is to insert a tube into an on-board water container, secure it to the microphone boom and suck on it every few minutes or so. If you have to reach to access fluids, you are likely to delay having a drink, which heightens the risk of dehydration. Remember, you can't drink too much.

Lately there have been discussions about the use of 'sports drinks' in gliding. These rather expensive drinks contain a large variety of substances including sugar and electrolytes. If consumed straight out of their container they do not pose any problems; pouring them into an on-board water container that you reuse increases the risk of bacterial growth inside your container. Electrolytes undoubtedly speed up the body's water absorption rate, but the same effect can be achieved by mixing small amounts of apple juice into drinking water for example. In any case, using anything but plain water in your reusable on-board drinking container necessitates very thorough cleaning, which can be next to impossible due to small openings and restricted access.

An efficient system for fluid elimination is vital. Some pilots wrongly curb their water intake for fear of having to pass water. Admittedly, it is anything but easy in the tight cockpit of a modern glider. It requires a fair bit of concentration and, dare I say it, practice. However, it needs to be mastered in order to maintain a reasonable level of comfort. Too many long flights have resulted in totally unnecessary failures or outlandings. At best, a full bladder spoils an otherwise enjoyable flight, but at worst it can lead to bladder infections. Let's face it, a pilot in severe discomfort is unlikely to perform well and will probably think twice before he undertakes another long flight. What a pity!!!

Some private owners have solved the problem by installing urine draining systems, but as few club gliders have the same luxury, we often have to resort to readily available medical incontinence equipment from surgical supply houses. They require little pre-flight preparation and are also available for females. Alternatively, men can resort to trusty old plastic bags. Don't just buy the cheapest ones around, - go for medium-sized extra heavy-duty freezer bags (Ziploc type plastic bags). They are not likely to fail or leak and can be disposed of without risk of spillage. Some pilots play it extra safe and put the pad of a cheap disposable nappy into their plastic bag. It absorbs the fluid and forms a solid lump.

Sun protection

Adequate protection from the sun is another important consideration. The UV levels on days with good gliding conditions are extreme. Generous amounts of sunscreen must be applied to exposed skin. Take care to avoid getting sun lotion near the eyes, because any sweating will result in eye irritation, which can be dangerous and even very painful in flight. Always wear a hat with a broad brim, a long-sleeve shirt and long trousers. Appropriate clothing is not only important for sun protection – it can

Preparing for cross-country flying

Entering the sierra Wave
Photo:
Gavin Wills
Glide Omarama

also aid pilot comfort on days where we find ourselves at 12 000 ft (4000 m) or even higher. At such altitudes, the temperature is approximately 25°C cooler and circling in the shadow of a large cumulus cloud surely makes false teeth chatter before long. This holds true especially if the pilot is sitting there almost motionless wearing only a T-shirt and shorts.

Wearing a set of quality sunglasses is important for a number of reasons. They not only significantly improve your ability to spot haze domes on blue days (refer to Section 5.9) but they also protect your eyes and are very beneficial when it comes to spotting other aircraft. Make sure you select sunglasses that block out light wavelengths under 500 nanometres. (billionths of a metre) Such frequency-selective glasses have excellent UV filter characteristics and eliminate essentially all the blue light wavelengths. (That's why they are often referred to as "blue blockers".) At the same time, the green, yellow and red wavelengths are attenuated by about 10%. This not only provides excellent eye protection and lessens the strain on your eyes, but it also creates a much sharper image.

Fortunately, glider canopies also absorb some UV, but pilots need to consider the increase in UV intensity with altitude. At a mere 5000 ft (1500 m), there is twice as much UV radiation as there is at ground level.

Blue-blocker sunglasses also offer increased cloud contrast and improved haze penetration. Highlighting bright colours is a welcome side-effect as it helps us spot our predominantly white gliders much easier. However, for the protection of your eyes, even low-cost sunglasses are beneficial – something I would like to stress in case there are pilots who think they don't need them.

Preparing for cross-country flying

ture and quite normal, but if we want to make progress we are well advised to change such habits. The question is: "How?"

The key to improvement is practice. We seem to know that - but do we really know how to go about it or do we confuse plain flying with practicing? A well-proven method that encourages us to practice asks us to write ourselves a note and stick it on a vacant spot in the cockpit as a permanent reminder to focus on improving a particular skill, or eliminating a bad habit. The secret to ongoing improvement is to practice under-developed skills one at a time. In other words, practice must be channelled

**Dawn flight over rice paddies in Japan
Photo:
Hiroshi Seo**

towards a particular problem or weakness. Only when we are entirely happy with the results should we move on and tackle something else. Remember - amateurs train until they get it right; professionals train until they can't get it wrong.

Part of the process is to set aside a few minutes after every flight to score ourselves and analyse our strengths and weaknesses. Work out what went well and how our training can be improved. A logbook entry is an excellent reminder that we need to apply a systematic approach to training and to ask yourself the following questions:

- What went well today?
- What didn't go well today?
- How can I improve on today's performance?

Let me give you another example. During my early flying career, I tensed up easily, which manifested as excessive pressure on the rudder pedals. It was very annoying because it was not only tiring but it also made much harder to feel the air. The solution was straightforward: I wrote "Relax rudder pressure" on my cockpit note and focused on eliminating this bad habit over time. Because it was deeply engrained it took almost a full year to drive out - but it worked!

PERSISTENCE is the key word here. Don't expect miracles and make sure you tackle only one area of weakness at a time. We are all creatures of habit. Eliminating a bad habit is one of the hardest things to do. It requires a departure from a deeply ingrained and familiar way of doing things. None of us likes that very much, but it is essential to persist if we strive for improvement.

3.7 Checklist for taking a glider away

Stories of pilots towing a glider hundreds of kilometres only to discover that a vital item was forgotten are plentiful. A main pin left behind at the club or a forgotten tailplane bolt has certainly all the potential to ruin a good gliding holiday.

The solution is straightforward and only calls for a simple checklist:

- Battery
- Battery charger
- Main pin(s) and bolt for tailplane
- Insurance papers
- Pilot's logbook
- Maintenance release
- Grease and tape remover
- Spare roll of sealing tape
- Parachute
- Ballast for C of G adjustments
- Tie-down kit
- Canopy cover
- Drink container
- Maps and charts with airspace information
- Datalogger
- Barograph
- Tail dolly and wingtip wheel
- Towing device
- Bucket and chamois
- On-board urinal
- Sun lotion and sunglasses
- Wide-brimmed hat and gloves

Of course, the above list may have to be extended for specific gliders and can therefore not be regarded as exhaustive. However, it can serve as a starting point for your own checklist, which one day might save a lot of anguish, frustration and heartache.

4 Extended local soaring

4.1 Introduction

The first chapter of this book dealt with the art of finding lift and working it in an efficient manner. Ideally, you acquired this skill during stage one of your learning process when you were still heavily dependant on your instructor and a mere participant in your own training. Now things have changed. You are a solo pilot and have moved on to stage two. From now on you are taking a growing responsibility for your own training and hopefully moving quickly towards ever increasing independence.

Let me give you a bit of good news and encouragement to begin with. If you can soar efficiently you have already accumulated the vast majority of skills necessary for extended local soaring. Successful flying away from your home airfield is not much more than the proper application of theoretical knowledge and the implementation of good soaring skills. However, before you venture out beyond the gliding range of your aircraft, you must first obtain some outlanding training and apply for your-cross country rating. Different countries have different rules and while only a corresponding logbook endorsement is required in some countries, a full glider pilot's licence is required in others.

Knowledge   **Understanding**

In any case, it is best to develop a guide that will pave the way for a smooth transition from local soaring to cross-country flying. By embedding any previously acquired knowledge into closely related issues we will not only gain a much deeper understanding but also develop the confidence to fly beyond the gliding range of our home airfield. This is what Chapters 4 and 5 are all about. It will show pilots how to soar not only in the strongest of summer thermals but also on days when the meteorological conditions are far from ideal.

4.2 Stepping out of your comfort zone

Most new pilots face a mild case of anxiety or "butterflies" prior to venturing beyond the gliding range of their home airfield for the first time. The reasons are plentiful, understandable and plausible. Often these butterflies stem from the bother of a possible retrieve or they may be due to concerns about perceived navigation problems. But this is normal and as old as the sport of gliding. Severe reservations prior to leaving the vicinity of the airfield for the first time can't be bandaged or surgically repaired but must be gradually removed by ongoing soaring near the very edge of the gliding range of our home airfield.

Such training will gradually provide a reasonable level of comfort which is absolutely crucial for making quick progress and for becoming a safe pilot. However, a very large number of glider pilots keep operating within their comfort zone for much too long after having gone solo. Sure, no two students are the same, and while some are very keen to experiment, others need strong encouragement to push themselves beyond familiar limits first established during basic training. In other words, some pilots have a reluctance to do anything that hasn't been done with an instructor or coach and as a result fail to make real progress in terms of their cross country flying.

If you think you fall into this category here are a few suggestions for you.

- Why not talk to your duty instructor and request permission to perform a right hand circuit onto the runway that you have so far only used for left hand circuits. (or vice versa)
- Have you ever considered performing a voluntary outlanding? Again, talk to your instructor first because this subject is covered later in this book. The outlanding can be made in a field only a few kilometres down the road. A nearby airstrip is also suitable, but either way, it provides a first class chance to get out of that comfort zone again.
- If you belong to a group of pilots who like to return to the circuit area with at least 1000 ft to spare I suggest you make an attempt to get out of this habit and deliberately put yourself into a position where you have to fly accurately, efficiently and cleanly to make it back to the airfield with just enough height for a normal circuit. (Only advisable for airfields with outlanding options along the approach path)

Accepting such challenges tends to focus your mind wonderfully and the reward for operating at the limit of your comfort zone is a vastly increased level of proficiency and competency. Apart from that, it also allows you to get a much better feel for the true performance of your aircraft and it enables you to confidently judge what is safe and what is not – an essential skill for cross-country flying.

Whatever you do, make sure you do it safely and never let your aircraft take you to places your brain hasn't been to a few minutes earlier.

4.3 Dealing with fear

Sports scientists claim, with evidence, that progress in sport can only be expected when participants constantly seek to extend themselves by training outside their comfort zone.

For quick and efficient learning we need to be challenged. Moving away from the comfort zone gets us into an area of increased discomfort but this is where learning happens fast and efficiently. Too far out from comfort, however, can arouse fear. The book 'Move Closer – Stay Longer' by Dr. Stephanie Burns is about the nature of fear. When we sense danger we respond with fear which, under control, ensures that we are vigilant; it makes us more disciplined; protects us from injury and even loss of life. As such, fear is important and essential.

Extended local soaring

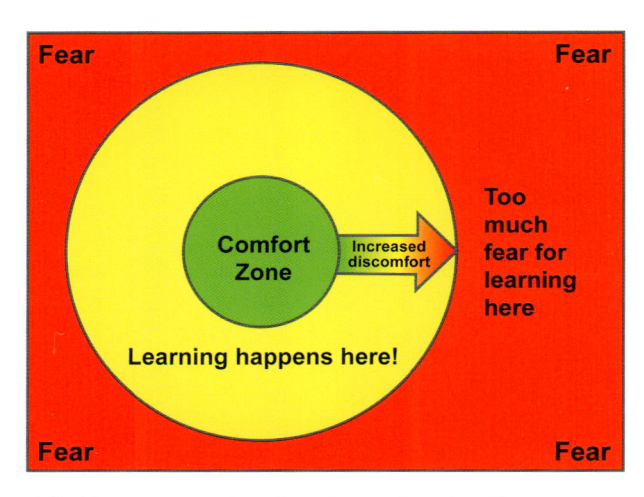

Figure 63: Comfort and fear zone

[Diagram showing concentric zones: "Comfort Zone" (green center), surrounded by yellow zone labeled "Learning happens here!", with arrow "Increased discomfort" pointing to "Too much fear for learning here", all surrounded by red "Fear" zone on all four corners.]

But fear can also be irrational and based on wrong information, obsessive or phobic. Fear of this kind interferes with useful, positive action, replacing it with panic and useless, counter-productive action or no action at all. As a result we prematurely quit before we have any chance to learn.

For instance, if we have the goal of soaring beyond the gliding range of the home airfield, we may develop fear of outlanding at a strange place. This may cause us to avoid the new challenge and to procrastinate. Willingly engaging in a frightening activity is not easy. What can we do about it? The issues revolving around outlanding can be resolved by refresher training with an instructor or coach. The fear can also be removed by practice under supervision.

As an example let me report on some of my ridge soaring flights with 'flatland' pilots. My co-pilots were initially apprehensive but after just an hour or so they were quite happy to take the controls and fly close to steep and rather rugged mountains. Activities initially seen as scary become by far less frightening after a prolonged and controlled exposure.

Another efficient method of overcoming nervousness in novice cross-country pilots is to fly in pairs. This provides a feeling of enhanced security. A possible outlanding seems less daunting with a fellow pilot in the vicinity. Uneasiness about navigational matters also evaporates. Experience is pooled and decision making, including such matters as whether to press on with the task or to turn back in the face of serious difficulties, is shared.

Let's sum it up now. To have fear is human, to overcome it requires a strategy, and to laugh is what we do when the blips on the fear radar gradually disappear. Every action we take, no matter how small, is one step closer to our goal and another step we never have to take again. These steps might be difficult but the rewards far outweigh the early sacrifices.

4.4 Training

Amateurs train until they get it right, but professionals train until they can't get it wrong. Only when ongoing training and practice is combined with the implementation of newly-gained theoretical knowledge do we have the key ingredients for success. Less ambitious pilots often confuse practicing with a joy flight in the vicinity of the home airfield, but there comes a time when you want to stretch the envelope a bit. Serious training must be channelled towards specific problems. Even the best of us have weaknesses that are worth eliminating. Let's take a closer look at training and regard it as a long-term investment into our gliding future.

To begin with, let's briefly consider mental aspects and physical fitness. Athletes spend countless hours conditioning their bodies but, in contrast, glider pilots mainly use their intellect for performance enhancement. This does not mean that we pilots

Extended local soaring

ASH 31 Mi on its maiden flight
Photo:
Manfred Muench

can afford to ignore physical fitness altogether. On the contrary – it plays a very important role, but the fact remains that mental fitness ranks higher in our sport than physical fitness. That is good news indeed – at least we can go on flying quite well long after all these celebrated athletes have gone into retirement with aching joints.

What can we do to improve our practical skills and how can we turn a weekend joy flight into one that enhances our cross-country skills?

Here are a few hints.

- On a day with, say, 5000 ft convection leave every thermal at 3000 ft and find another updraught elsewhere.
- Set yourself a limit as far as thermal strength is concerned. Leave every thermal that doesn't provide a pre-determined rate of climb after centring.
- "Don't fly through the same 'bad air' twice" is another rules that comes to mind.
- Climb to a predetermined height and then glide back to the airfield, noting your arrival altitude. If you get back to the airfield at more than 500 ft above standard circuit entry level adjust your final glide distance or final glide height on the next attempt.
- Try to practice such final glide runs at various airspeeds and take notice of the difference in height loss.
- Try to do the same in crosswind, headwind and tailwind situations.
- Fly with a coach in a two seater glider and take notice of his or her flying techniques.
- Take turns at flying a two seater and encourage your fellow pilot to

- comment on your flying and your decision making.
- Use your airbrake to lose height and climb in another thermal as quickly and as efficiently as possible.
- Start your landing approach deliberately a little high or a little low as practice for future outlandings. (check with your instructor first)
- Practice thermalling on a weak lift day and try to stay airborne as long as possible towards the end of a soaring day.
- While thermalling, keep your bank angle at 45 degrees and try to complete each orbit in 20 seconds.
- Try to encourage your fellow club members to undertake similar training activities enabling you to compare performances at the end of the day.
- Make every landing a spot landing.
- Fly at a site other than your home airfield.
- Fly under a wide variety of weather conditions.
- On marginal days attempt a small task around your local airfield while staying within glide range, e.g. fly a square route with four 10 km legs (centred on the home airfield) a number of times and try to decrease the time taken for each 40 km round trip.

We must resist the temptation to confine our training to days with easy soaring conditions and learn to remain airborne safely for an extended period when our fellow pilots don't even want to open the hangar doors. Competition pilots know only too well that championships are won and lost on weak days. The message is clear; unless we fly whenever practical we will never encounter the full spectrum of soaring conditions and we will make little progress in terms of our cross-country ambitions.

Finally, a famous quote from four-time world champion Ingo Renner. When asked why he won so many championships he replied that it was sheer luck: "However," he said: "the more I practiced the luckier I got".

4.5 Getting help from a coach

Undoubtedly, efficient thermalling is one of the more difficult skills to learn, but we need to master it. Let's not forget that our instructors normally share the cockpit with us only for a short time. Consequently, they can only work on the basics with us, demonstrating their preferred thermalling technique, giving us some guidance on thermal recognition and thermal entry procedures and helping us with thermal centring. Very good instructors might even deliberately fly the glider out of a thermal and then boost the student's confidence by helping him or her to find it again. However, due to various constraints, instructors usually focus on safety, consistency and basic skills. Coaching is different. There is room for individual preferences and different ideas and coaches are only too happy to help when it comes to the fine-tuning or refining of specific skills. Diversity is encouraged and nurtured and differences are accepted. However it is very helpful to remember my own instructor's standard line: "The mind is like a parachute – it doesn't function until it's open".

Suggesting to a coach to come for a flight in a two-seater is not something that immediately springs to mind for most pilots. After all, flying with an instructor is compulsory, but flying with a coach is voluntary. Understandably pleased that they have banned the instructor from the back seat most new pilots are usually reluctant to invite a coach to take his place, but learning a bit more has never done anyone harm and skill refinements have never been a disadvantage.

A few flights with a coach are very likely to get us on a steeper learning curve. They allow us to benefit from the coach's years of experience and enable us to compare our technique with the one our coach uses. Remember, we won't live long enough to make all the mistakes ourselves, so we might as well pick the brains of others and save ourselves some time, some money and frustration.

Old but still beautiful

My advice could not be more emphatic – go and grab a coach every time the opportunity presents itself. The long-term benefits are plentiful. We have every chance of finding better ways of doing things, we increase our chances of success the next time we are on our own and we are bound to get more enjoyment from our flying in future.

However, to gain maximum benefit from our coaching flight we need to put some effort into preparation. Information needs to flow in both directions for coaching to be most effective. Coaches aren't instructors who teach very basic flying skills. Coaches are consultants who provide help in specific areas but they are usually poor mind readers. Therefore it is always a good idea to tell them what aspect of our flying we hope to improve. Such pre-flight briefings usually pay big dividends as the subject can be discussed in a relaxed manner prior to the flight. It also gives student and coach time to think about suitable preparatory reading material and the best possible method of implementation.

The benefits gained by watching our coach on a dual flight are also plentiful. Such flights allow students to steal with their eyes, a practice not at all in conflict with the law. Just by watching and trying to understand the reasoning behind certain control inputs a lot can be learned and absorbed. This holds especially true in the area of decision making, a subject we will cover in detail at a later stage.

Having said all that, it needs to be stressed that dual coaching flights only provide lasting benefits if the student is observing the coach very closely. It is a good idea to take notes during the flight as it stimulates a debriefing and further discussion in a more comfortable place at the end of the day. In between coaching sessions we should use every opportunity to work on the skill needing further development. Especially if our coach has suggested concentrating on a particular aspect of our flying, we'd be wise to accept his advice. However, as solo pilots we are also free to implement the many hints and suggestions found in good soaring literature.

Experimenting is part of the learning process and invariably leads to a better understanding of such important issues as thermal structures and thermal behaviour.

Extended local soaring

Even top pilots are still learning some sort of lesson on every flight and strive to improve their thermalling skills at every possible opportunity. What is good enough for them should be good enough for us, but even if we have no ambition to rank amongst the top pilots we cannot afford to stop learning after going solo. The opposite is what we should be aiming for – going solo should be regarded as a license to learn.

All pilots have a few areas of weakness. Some grin and bear it while others smile and change it. The smartest amongst us change it by enrolling with a coach.

4.6 Lead & follow coaching

As an alternative to coaching in a two-seater, we will now look more closely at lead & follow coaching. The idea is for a coach to guide a cross-country student around a suitable task in gliders of similar performance and with roughly the same wing loading. Lead & follow coaching is not to be confused with pair flying (or team flying) but it can serve as preparation for future flights of this nature.

Moving out of gliding range of the home airfield for the first time is very daunting for most new solo pilots. However, with help from a competent pilot, a reluctance to step outside of our comfort zone can be overcome and an initial apprehension can be turned into eager anticipation. Proper lead & follow coaching not only provides fun and enjoyment for both pilots involved but it is also bound to enhance confidence and it greatly increases the chances of a successful outcome.

Lead & follow coaching can be positive and motivating but getting it wrong can lead to much frustration, compromised safety and very little learning. What are the proven methods and how can we ensure safety at all times?

As always, a little planning and a pre-flight briefing is all that's needed to ensure success. Matters like frequency on task, break-off height, procedures when getting low, weather, task, and turn point sequence should be discussed beforehand and summarised on a little task sheet. Good radio communication is vital, and to avoid annoying other radio users, it is advisable to select a discrete frequency for use on task.

For a good start to the coaching flight it is highly advisable that both pilots get airborne around the same time and come together as soon as possible in the same source of lift. Otherwise considerable time can be lost looking for each other and

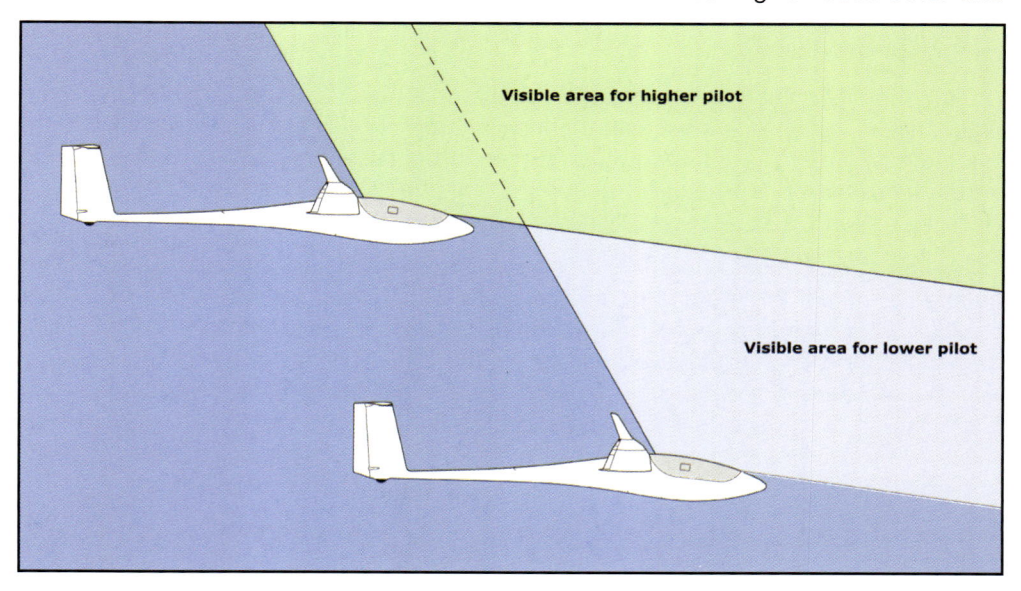

Figure 65: Double blind situation.

Extended local soaring

establishing contact. On busy days it might become necessary to call on the launch frequency to get together and then utilise the same thermal for the initial climb or as soon as possible after. Once visual contact is established, it is highly advisable to stay in the same thermal and allow the lower glider to catch up.

A decision to go on task can be made jointly but to get the maximum benefit for the student, the coach should leave first, allowing the student to follow slightly behind and approximately 500 metres to one side. (Refer to Figure 64.)

Figure 64: Horizontal separation in cruise

There are numerous advantages. Firstly, it allows both pilots to keep an eye on each other. It also enables the follower to observe the coach and study his dolphin flying technique and decision making. But such a separation is also important from a safety point of view. If the leading aircraft commences a turn towards the follower there is no risk of a collision - even if both pilots momentarily lose sight of each other.

But that's not all. Apart from observing the coach's flying style from relatively close quarters the student can monitor his thermal selection criteria and examine proven thermal centring techniques. After one full turn the coach should announce the average climb rate and indicate whether the thermal is worth taking. If appropriate, the follower can top-up but should try to join the thermal by arriving at the opposite side of the circle. For a novice cross-country pilot this is easier said than done but it is worth aiming for and will become easier with practice. Proper and efficient thermalling at the correct speed and with the optimum angle of bank can be observed by the student provided the vertical separation is not more than a few hundred feet.

Try to copy the coach's flying and aim to remain roughly opposite. If the coach straightens out and then rolls back into the turn it demonstrates how adjustments are made to stay in the strongest lift. Just follow the coach and refrain from trying to locate the core independently. This can easily lead to a double blind situation which is another term for an in-flight situation where neither pilot can see the other (Figure 65). This is highly dangerous with insufficient vertical separation and has led to a number of mid-air collisions in the past. Needless to say that it must be avoided at all costs. Flying in relatively close proximity

Together on task

121

Team flying in progress

Photo: Jörg Strub

might make a novice cross-country pilot feel uneasy at first but with a little practice it will soon become comfortable and enhance the fun and enjoyment. Doing it with a competent coach will most certainly make for an extremely enlightening experience.

In case a significant altitude difference develops between coach and student the coach needs to deploy the airbrakes and continue the flight with an extended undercarriage or an incorrect flap setting. Dumping water ballast is the least preferred option. Different wing loadings make for vastly different thermalling behaviour and diminish the student's learning effect.

On leaving the thermal the highest glider should transmit: "Alpha, Bravo, Charlie - leaving" and possibly add: "Cruising 75? kts". This allows the follower to anticipate the lead aircraft's likely position and prepare for the next cruise. The response should simply be: "Following at 75 kts". This is vital if the coaching flight is to be of value as only one more turn by the follower results in a separation of about one kilometre. If the follower adds another turn the visual contact is almost certainly lost. Lengthy radio communications usually follow which is distracting to both pilots. It also leads to inefficient flying and in turn makes the coaching less effective. For additional standard phrases and radio procedures please refer to Section 10.8.

Slowing down just to maintain the same height as the leader is also highly detrimental to lead & follow coaching. Unless the follower is getting very low, he or she should cruise at the same speed and make up the height difference in the next thermal. Usually the leader requires a turn or two before finding the strongest part of the thermal and by the time the follower reaches the updraught the core should already be well marked.

A horizontal separation of about 500 metres is also beneficial in cruise. Apart from sampling a much wider area of the sky (and enhancing the chances of finding above average lift) the follower can easily move closer if the leader is in a more buoyant part of the sky. Conversely they can move further apart when the leader is experiencing significant sink. Although such tactics add a bit of flying distance they usually allow the follower to stay in touch with a more experienced pilot or a higher performance glider.

Another welcome consequence is the identification and efficient use of streeting; and this holds especially true on blue days. We will deal with thermal streets in section 5.7 but by observing each other in cruise we get valuable information on the best energy lines in the sky. Glide angles can often be doubled and the chances of finding the strongest updraughts are greatly increased. It is heart-warming for the coach and confidence-building for the student to realise that for a considerable distance only very little altitude was lost. Just think of the pleasure when a plan comes together.

Finally word on the use of radio during lead & follow flights. Top glider pilots tend to keep the chat down and instead focus on "feeling the air". But when these pilots act as coaches the situation needs to change. The coach becomes a teacher and needs to make use of his or her communication skills. Any messages need to be tailored to the momentary mental state of the student but equally important is that the student's skill level is taken into account. Bombarding the student with information or even instructions can be highly detrimental. Providing too little advice means that teaching opportunities are being wasted.

Let us not forget that early cross-country pilots have to pay more attention to basic flying and are usually tense while operating well outside of their comfort zone. They often find it hard to absorb and implement even the best of advice – especially while in the bottom half of the available height band.

Periods of relaxation are crucial and need to be built into any coaching flights. The best time for this is after climbing back to the convection ceiling and can be as simple as suggesting that the time has come for a drink or an apple. Pointing out a certain feature on the ground and using this for navigation can also aid relaxation. While approaching a turn point the coach should indicate the sector and possibly remind the follower to maintain vigilance and a good look-out around these usually congested airspaces. This helps to direct the student's attention away from navigation instruments and improves lookout which in turn enhances safety on future (competition) flights.

There should be only one follower on lead & follow flights. After having participated in lead & follow flights as one of many followers (and after evaluating the learning results as well as the safety implications) I strongly favour this approach unless all the participants are of a very high standard indeed.

4.7 Team flying

The best thing that can possibly happen to a group of like-minded pilots is access to gliders with comparable performance. But, even when the performance is not closely matched, training can be made easier and more effective if jealousy and envy is replaced by a spirit of sportsmanship and co-operation.

Extended local soaring

Let's look at a number of options for team flying.

- We can agree on a triangle and fly the task independently (but in the shortest possible time).
- We can start on a predetermined task at the same time and at roughly the same height to allow participants to compare techniques and decision making.
- We can fly as many laps as possible around a short task.
- We can fly a mutually agreed task and time competitors from lift off to the end of ground run.
- We can set off on an "out and return" flight with the aim to go as far into wind as possible without outlanding on the way home.

All of these little exercises foster a spirit of friendly competition and should greatly contribute to an enhancement of camaraderie amongst pilots. But it is important to conduct a debriefing at the end of the day and to compare notes with other pilots. Only by freely exchanging information on positive as well as negative aspects of the flight can we expect to learn valuable lessons from such mini contests.

To keep distracting radio communications to an absolute minimum (and to avoid any misunderstandings) the following standard phrases have proven quite sufficient. Experience shows that pilots soon recognise their voices which even allows the elimination of call signs but to eliminate any inconvenience for other aviators any such radio communications should be conducted on a descrete gliding frequency.

Table 6: Abbreviated team flying communications.

Flight segment	Phrase	Meaning
Entering thermal	Turning	I'm going to sample this thermal
	3,4,5 etc.	Instantanious climb rate
	Yes or good	I'm talking this climb
	No	I'm disregarding this thermal
	Not sure	I haven't found a strong core yet
	4 point 8	Average climb rate
	Building	The thermal is improving
	Dropping off	The thermal is weakening
Climbing	Ready? (Question)	Are you ready to leave?
	Ready! (Statement)	I'm ready to leave
	OK	I'm ready too
	Not ready	I want to climb more
	Leaving	Setting off on track
	Leaving on (210)	My departure track is 210 Degr.
Cruising	Better Left/Right	To assist leading glider
	Good air	To assist trailing glider
	Bad air	To assist trailing glider

4.8 Flying with water ballast

Although we have briefly touched on flying with water ballast in Chapter 1, we will now look at it more closely in the context of cross-country flying.

Essentially water ballast shifts the gliders polar curve down the line of the best glide slope but your best glide ratio remains the same, regardless of the glider's weight. With todays gliders we can almost double the weight by adding water ballast. The speed at which we achieve the best glide ratio is now 1.414 (the square root of 2) times the best empty glide ratio. For example, if we achieve 50:1 at 55 kts empty, we would still achieve 50:1 but at a speed of 77.8 kts. The sink rate is also magnified by the same factor. At 55 kts and empty, the sink rate might be 1.1 kts but with twice the wing loading, the sink rate is now 1.56 kts at a speed of 77.8 kts.

With twice the wing loading, we will be thermalling at 1.414 times the empty speed and because our turn radius is proportional to the square of our speed we are now circling at twice the radius. We know that thermals are weaker as we move further away from the core and this means that not only are we climbing more slowly due to the glider's higher sink rate, but we are also flying in the weaker outer part of the thermal.

So flying with water ballast becomes a compromise between our cruise performance and our ability to climb. Our ability to climb is not only dependant on the strength of the thermal, but the thermals radius as well. And it is the radius of the thermal which is the most important factor and the least regarded.

Researchers around Professor Fred Thomas have determined the effect of thermal characteristics on achievable cross-country speed by using the same thermal model already shown in Chapter 1. For reasons of convenience it is reproduced below. (Figure 66). It defines the strength and diameter of four different types of thermals and allows a mathematical evaluation of optimum wing loadings for the purpose of cross-country flying.

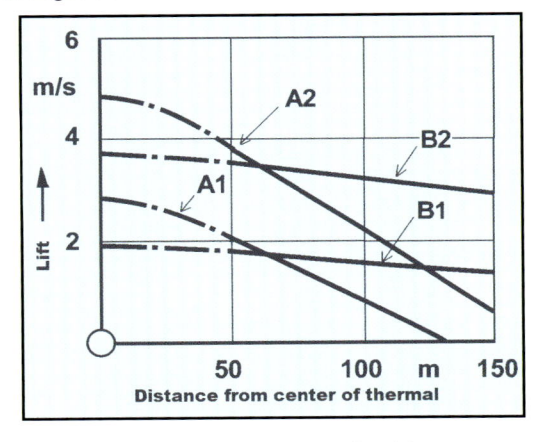

Figure 66: Horstmann thermal model

The achievable cross-country speeds for a standard class glider (in this case an ASW 15) and the four different types of thermals are shown in figure 67. Only in a thermal of type B2 (strong and wide) can we expect to increase speed by carrying water ballast. Please note that the graph is based on one of the very first fibreglass gliders with limited water carrying capability. Mr. A. Smith of Adelaide University Gliding Club has investigated whether the same holds true for today's modern gliders. He has inserted the achievable cross country speeds for an ASG 29 into the graph of figure 67 and the results are shown in Figure 68. An investigation of thermal type A1 was omitted as the findings for thermal type B1 speak for themselves.

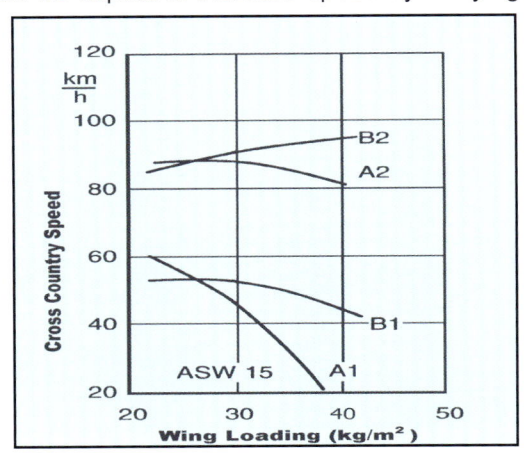

Figure 67: Average cross-country speed of an ASW 15 as a function of wing loading and thermal model

Extended local soaring

Figure 68: Comparison of achievable cross country speeds between ASW 15 and ASG 29

- - - - Achievable cross-country speeds of ASW 15
——— Achievable cross-country speeds of ASG 29

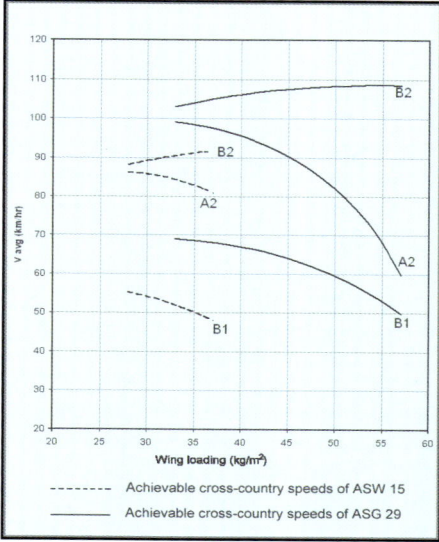

The comparison is not entirely fair because the ASW 15 is a 15 m wingspan standard class glider and the ASG 29 is the most modern flapped glider with 18 m wingspan. However, figure 68 highlights the advances in sailplane technology rather well. In line with a rather steep increase in wing loadings (from approx 37kg/m² to 57kg/m²) we can see that modern gliders allow significantly higher cross country speeds regardless whether they are flown with or without water ballast. Figure 68 also confirms the findings of Professor Thomas. Only on days with strong and wide lift can a heavy glider provide an advantage. The graphs make it also abundantly clear that ballast is detrimental when (for whatever reason) we have to be content with a slow rate of climb.

For this reason, keen competition pilots often launch with maximum ballast on board but dump some (or all) of the water after they have sampled a few thermals and assessed the conditions of the day. After returning from a flight, they are interested in comparing their wing-loadings. As different types of gliders have different wing areas, this is the only way of conducting a fair comparison.

After these rather theoretical considerations let's look into practical matters again. Less experienced pilots often carry more than the optimum amount of water and think that water ballast is beneficial when thermals are 4 kts or stronger. How true is this assessment in light of the above findings? Wouldn't it be fair to say that the diameter of the thermal plays an equally important role? After all, what matters most is the achieved rate of climb compared to an unballasted glider. While flying large circles the aerodynamic losses are relatively small but when a heavy glider needs to circle very steeply we see a disproportional increase in sink rate. Put differently, if the ballasted glider can climb without a significant penalty in large-diameter thermals it might be worthwhile to carry water ballast even if the strength of the thermals is nothing to write home about.

An even more important issue is the question of thermal streeting on track. Water ballast is very beneficial as long as energy can be extracted in a straight glide and the amount of thermalling is kept to a minimum. If we don't need to thermal and if we gain height in cruise, we don't need to be concerned about the drawbacks in circling flight.

In this context, a message to pilots who believe that water ballast will do wonders to their cross-country speeds even though their thermalling skills are far from polished. Water ballast is likely to have the effect of depressing the achieved rate of climb further, and it becomes almost

A rush to the finish line. Photo: Hiroshi Seo

impossible to make up for this loss of time while cruising. The lesson is simple, work on your thermalling skills and get used to banking the glider steeply before you expect to increase speed by using water ballast. As water ballast is mainly carried in the wing, the glider will display a much reduced rate of roll due to the increased inertia. The resulting sluggish aileron response must be anticipated by the pilot, especially when operating in close proximity to other gliders. While thermalling, the glider will leave the pilot in no doubt that it wants to be flown faster and the important thing is to let it do so. For a typical 50% increase of wing loading due to water ballast an 8 – 10 kts (15 – 18 km/h) increase in thermalling speed is fairly close to the mark. This will partly overcome the reduced aileron response mentioned earlier. Pilots new to water ballast should realise that partly ballasted gliders tend to create problems on take-off due to sloshing of water. For this reason it might be a good idea to increase the amount of water in small increments and slowly get used to the new behaviour of the glider. Only then should we think about going to the maximum legal limit.

Exceeding the limit is not only risking the structural integrity of the glider but will also carry a severe penalty in competitions where the organisers have arranged spot weighing checks.

Flying in close formation under a textbook sky

On return to the airfield we had better take into account that it will take several minutes to jettison the water. Opening the dump valve only on arrival in the circuit area increases the chances of landing with a fair amount of water on board, making it more difficult to dissipate all the energy. The ground run will be significantly longer and, especially if the airfield is rough, we might strain our glider unnecessarily. Therefore my recommendation is emphatic: Always jettison the water ballast early enough and never intentionally land a glider with water ballast on board.

Finally let's consider the optimum amount of water for long-distance flying on one hand and competition flying on the other. Because a typical race in a competition lasts for approximately three hours, the pilots will only be on task during the very best part of the day. It does not matter what rates of climb are achieved prior to the start of the race as long as the wing loading is close to optimum when it really matters. In contrast, a long-distance pilot will usually start on his task soon after the first weak lift has set in and might return after the last thermal of the day. Climbing in weak and narrow lift during the early part of the day might be impossible with a full load of water on board. The decision is therefore to postpone launching until the thermals have picked up strength or, alternatively, embark on the task with a lighter glider. The latter is usually the better option for flights of around 1000 km or for 750 km flights with older generation gliders. It is very difficult to make up for time lost earlier in the day especially in view of the fact that a 15 percent lower wing loading usually results in a relatively small performance penalty. What we lose in high-speed performance we gain in maneuverability, enhanced handling, and better feedback from the glider, not to mention the improved rate of climb.

To sum it up, higher wing loadings provide a competitive advantage on days with strong and large diameter thermals. The same applies on days with good streeting on track. However, on days with weak or narrow thermals water ballast is certain to slow down progress – far from being beneficial, it becomes a hindrance.

4.9 Looking for lift when low

What constitutes low? An early solo pilot will most certainly view it differently compared to a seasoned cross-country pilot. An altitude of 2000 ft (600 m) on a day with 3000 ft (900 m) convection can not be considered very low but when thermals go to 12 000 ft (3600 m) we should be rightly concerned when the altimeter is approaching 2000 ft. The reason is, of course, that thermal spacing and convection height form a close relationship which means that on days with rather low thermals we can expect to run into lift every few kilometres or so. (Section 1.22.)

But whatever our level of experience, for a variety of reasons we sometimes find ourselves too low for comfort. The pressure is on to find some lift and if it is not found quickly an outlanding could follow sooner rather than later. What can we do to keep the glider airborne and what tactics should be employed to return to a more comfortable level?

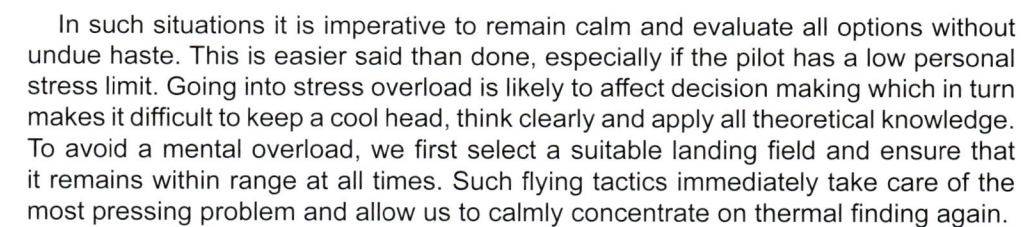

In such situations it is imperative to remain calm and evaluate all options without undue haste. This is easier said than done, especially if the pilot has a low personal stress limit. Going into stress overload is likely to affect decision making which in turn makes it difficult to keep a cool head, think clearly and apply all theoretical knowledge. To avoid a mental overload, we first select a suitable landing field and ensure that it remains within range at all times. Such flying tactics immediately take care of the most pressing problem and allow us to calmly concentrate on thermal finding again.

The following clues might prove helpful.

- Look for soaring birds or rising dust triggered by moving stock or farm equipment.
- Any form of smoke raises our suspicion especially when two or more ground based indicators point to different wind directions. The smoke trail usually travels towards a nearby thermal.
- Dust devils within reach are good thermal indicators and if possible should be circled in the opposite direction to the vortex rotation in order to minimize our diameter of turn.
- Tractors ploughing dry paddocks are almost always worth a little detour as they sometimes trigger small thermals in quick succession.

Other gliders might provide useful clues and with a bit of luck fellow pilots might even direct you into nearby lift by radio. (Make sure you return the favour one day.)

More than ever we look for thermal sources and thermal triggers and search slightly downwind of potential areas of lift. If necessary we circle in zero sink for a while. You might be circling over a hot-air reservoir on the ground ready to release a thermal.

Ignoring clouds when low is almost always a mistake as they usually provide the best indication of lift. Try to fly from under the cloud directly into wind and if you find weak lift hang on to it as it might be the top of a bubble starting to rise. With a bit of luck the weak bubble will turn into a reasonable thermal. A random search on dropping below our comfort zone is rarely productive. Because thermal spacing and convection height form a close relationship, we must fly on until we reach an area where buoyant air is evident. Only then does it make sense to perform a series of "S" turns, fly a figure 8 pattern or even conduct a fully blown clover leaf search pattern.

While we are still airborne we have every chance of getting clues for lift and finding a saving updraught. The closer we get to the ground the earlier we will accept a thermal that we wouldn't have considered strong enough only a few minutes earlier. Now we are well advised to make a real effort to keep concentrating and put all our efforts into efficient thermalling. It is all too easy to breathe a sigh of relief on finding lift and promptly fall out of the updraught. If we lose the thermal before we get high enough to continue on track, it is usually best to fly into wind and go back to the area where the thermal was first encountered.

But whatever you do, you must not fall into the trap of hanging on to this sub-standard thermal for longer than necessary. Beginners often cling to such "lifesavers" for far too long and milk them for everything they are worth. However, more experienced pilots know that "being low means being slow" and leave weaker thermals as soon as they are reasonably confident of finding stronger lift on track.

Now let's look at the safety aspect of flying low. Assume you are on a cross-country flight and the altimeter and your own assessment of altitude give ample reason for concern. Imagine you are about to enter the circuit when you feel a surge. Decision time has come – do you turn or land?

My recommendation is quite simple. If you can afford to lose 200 ft and still perform a safe circuit go ahead and initiate a turn – if not, you had better proceed with the circuit. Why 200 ft, you might ask? Well, if you turn in the wrong direction and you strike 6 kts of sink for a full 20 second turn you are likely to lose about 200 ft. Remember, down low thermals are usually narrow and even if you turn the right way you are unlikely to climb all the way around. In fact, you will probably struggle to hold your own for a while.

On occasions like this it is important to tap the altimeter from time to time and make sure that all your hard work is paying off. Especially with a sticky altimeter it is all too easy to find yourself slowly descending and hence eroding any remaining safety margin.

4.10 Wind shear

A gradual change in wind speed is usually referred to as a wind gradient, but a more abrupt change in wind speed or wind direction – especially at a specific level – is what pilots generally call wind shear.

A wind shear often occurs around the level of a weak inversion. Above the inversion the wind is usually not only stronger but also comes from a different direction. This wind change always distorts a thermal and if the pilot does not re-centre promptly the thermal can be quickly lost. At windshear level the climb rate usually drops off (at least temporarily) and the core tends to shift to another side. A good weather briefing

Extended local soaring

**A textbook wave cloud over Mt. Cook (NZ)
Photo:
Bill Verco**

Figure 69: Illustration of wind shear

is very helpful. Knowing the wind direction above the inversion provides a definite clue and makes re-centring less time consuming.

Having managed to climb above wind-shear level it is usually best to adopt slightly more conservative flying tactics in an attempt to remain high. Experience shows that the slow climb rates at windshear level can reduce the average rate of climb considerably. Repeatedly dropping below the shear level usually equates to an ongoing struggle with the wind shear and can reduce the achieved cross-country speed substantially.

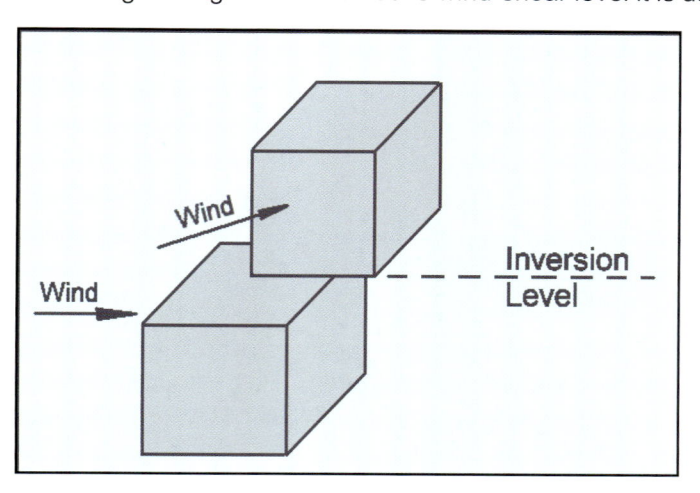

Extended local soaring

4.11 Influence of airflow above the convection level

Let's be honest – we have all experienced buoyant air with pockets of good lift for miles on end which rather unexpectedly turns into never ending sink. It seems like someone has flicked a switch, replacing easy soaring conditions by unworkable lift with large patches of heavy sink in between. Our adrenalin levels increase in direct proportion to the unwinding of the altimeter and we ask ourselves: "What on earth is going on?"

If we have not experienced such conditions, we almost certainly will in the future. Perhaps we think of streeting first, but on second thoughts this appears rather unlikely. But what is it that puts us off on days like these? The answer is: "Probably it is the airflow above the convection level" or put another way: "the influence of waves aloft".

Most glider pilots know that the basic ingredients of wave flow are a strengthening of wind with height and a stable layer of air above the convection level. If these conditions are met and there is some sort of upwind undulation in the ground there is a good chance of upper level wave. (Refer to Figure 70.)

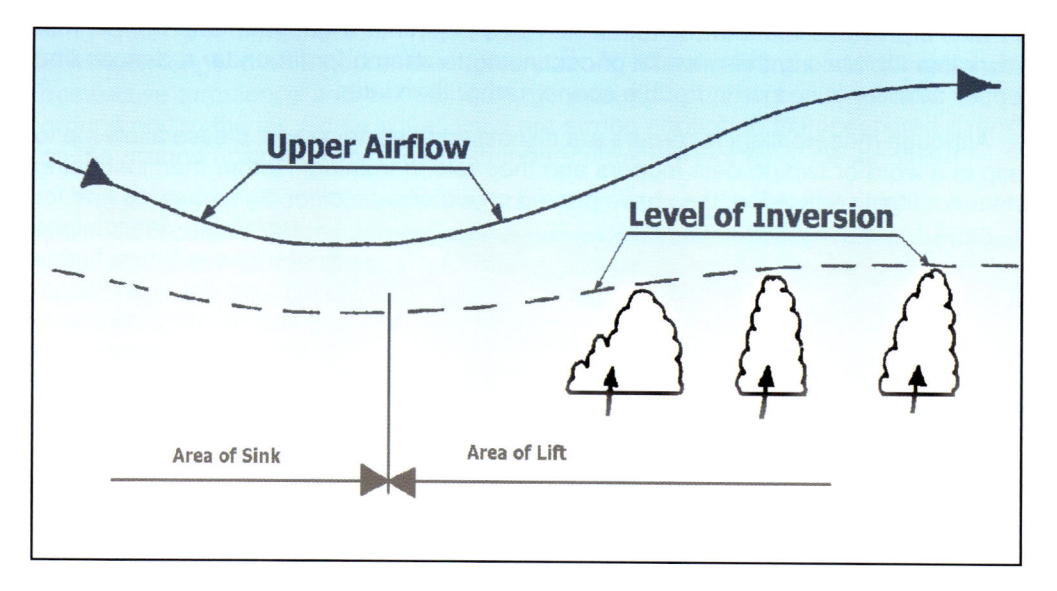

Figure 70: Influence of airflow above the convection level

Just because the above illustration does not show a penetration of wave motion into the convective layer, it doesn't mean that it is not affecting the lower levels. On the contrary – what happens aloft has a significant effect on thermal activity below. Wave-like upper airflow not only tends to boost thermals but it can also provide larger-scale buoyancy. On the other hand, it has the potential for greatly suppressing lift in other areas, to the extent that thermals can become very broken or even completely unworkable.

Four times World Champion Ingo Renner is of the opinion that such conditions exist far more frequently than expected. In fact, he believes that in some parts of the world wave inter-related thermals are found on 50% of all flying days and that upwind hills or mountains trigger thermals which in turn increase the size of the obstacle for the wave flow. The subsequent primary and secondary wave downstream of the mountains de-stabilise the air below their crest and encourage cumulus type wave clouds to form. These cumulus clouds, with their thermals below them, enhance the wave flow, with the result that it continues well into the plains for a long distance.

Extended local soaring

4.14.1 FAI Badges

After having earned the certificates of your national gliding body and after having learned a few lessons while conducting extended local soaring you might want to aim for badges issued by FAI – the international governing body for sports aviation. These FAI badges are international standards of achievement which are not required to be renewed. Flights qualifying for badges are controlled in accordance with the requirements of Section 3 of the FAI Sporting Code.

The soaring performances required to qualify for the FAI badge standards of achievement are:

Silver Badge: The Silver badge is achieved on completing the following three soaring performances:

a. SILVER DISTANCE a flight on a straight course of at least 50 kilometres. Any leg of 50 kilometres or more of a longer predeclared course may qualify, subject to the requirements of 4.4.2 of the FAI Sporting Code Section 3, on altitude difference applied to the whole course flown. The Silver distance flight should be flown without navigational or other assistance given over the radio (other than permission to land on an airfield) or help or guidance from another aircraft.

b. SILVER DURATION a duration flight of at least 5 hours.

c. SILVER HEIGHT a gain of height of at least 1000 metres.

Gold Badge: The Gold badge is achieved on completing the following three soaring performances:

a. GOLD DISTANCE a distance flight of at least 300 kilometres,

b. GOLD DURATION a duration flight of at least 5 hours,

c. GOLD HEIGHT a gain of height of at least 3000 metres.

Diamonds: There are three Diamonds, each of which may be worn on the Silver, Gold, and the badges for flights of 1000 kilometres or more.

a. DIAMOND DISTANCE a distance flight of at least 500 kilometres.

b. DIAMOND GOAL a goal flight of at least 300 kilometres over an out-and return or triangular course.

c. DIAMOND HEIGHT a gain of height of at least 5000 metres.

Distance Flights: Badges and Diplomas for flights of 1000 kilometres and more.

These are a family of badges that are achieved on completing a distance flight of 1000 kilometres or more, in increments of 250 kilometres (ie. 1000 km, 1250 km, 1500 km, etc.). One badge is awarded per flight, for the incremental distance immediately less than the distance flown.

One of the many good things about our sport is that there is an almost endless list of goals and achievements. The fact that gliding only requires minimum physical effort means that we can work on achieving these goals over decades of active involvement. Also, women can compete with men on an equal footing which is only possible in very few other sports.

Extended local soaring

Chapter 4

A modern glider on the ground and in the air

141

Flying in the Australian outback

(Flinders Ranges National Park)

5 Advanced cross-country flying

5.1 Introduction

You are now firmly on the way to a successful cross-country pilot and you will find that your level of enjoyment will grow with every successfully completed flight – regardless of the distance involved. If my own experience is anything to go by you will find that your confidence grows rapidly; you know that you have the basic skills and you feel that it is just a matter of accumulating the necessary experience in order to be able to match it with the hot-shots.

However, there is one small area of concern. You have accumulated the vast majority of skills necessary for cross-country flying, but when you compare your speed with your fellow cross-country pilots you realise that they are a fair bit faster. Obviously there is a difference between flying cross-country and racing and perhaps there is something that these pilots know you don't. But what is it? How can others consistently beat you home and are at least 10 to 15 km/h faster?

Well, there are probably a good number of reasons but before we look into practical matters we need to consider the pilot's mindset. Unless you can clear your mind of the fear of landing out you will always be a great deal slower. Only your confidence in finding a good source of lift will make you press on and allow you to focus on maximising the rate of climb.

Within a wingspan of the mountain

5.2 Getting the speed up

When it comes to practical matters, it is important to note that just talking about your flight does very little to reveal the real reasons for the performance difference. Regardless whether we strive to improve our performance for competitions, for badge flying or for the 'On Line Contest' (OLC) we need to ask some serious questions and compare barograph traces or datalogger recordings.

5.2.1 Are we using too many thermals?

If we are looking at a large number of climbs of only 1000 ft or so on a day with say 8000 ft convection there is every chance that we are wasting a lot of time centring lift for only a small gain of altitude. Wouldn't it much better to glide through most of these thermals at a slightly reduced speed, gain a little height in the process and only circle in a thermal when we have descended to approximately 2/3 of the maximum altitude of the day? I know, it's much easier said than done, we all prefer to be as high as possible and we just don't want to be low. However, if we want to get faster we need to shake off this habit. Unless we consistently manage to place the first circle right in the core of the thermal we may be wasting valuable time. The initial thermal centring procedures are very time consuming and have a major impact on the achieved crosscountry speed. The fewer thermals we use the better, but I hasten to add that it always pays dividends to top up in exceptionally strong thermals – even if the possible height gain is limited.

Of course, the altitude at which you decide to top up needs to be reviewed in line with your experience and the prevailing conditions. Not only does your ability to find another thermal play an important role, but also the height band at which the thermals are at their strongest. For example, if thermals are notoriously weak and narrow down low it pays to avoid lower altitudes at all costs. Under such circumstances even the occasional average climb is preferable to a "low safe and a slow climb".

5.2.2 Are we hanging on to a thermal for too long?

Thermals often weaken towards the top. There can be a number of reasons for that. For example, their strength can suffer when the updraft approaches the inversion level. In conditions like this, a lot of time can be saved if we don't try to milk every thermal for everything it is worth. It pays to keep track of the maximum strength of the thermal and leave in search of something better the moment the climb rate drops noticeably. I have heard pilots say that they are leaving the moment the lift drops to approx. 2/3 of the maximum climb rate, but my recommendation is to leave a thermal as soon as we are confident that the achievable average rate of climb in the next thermal will be equal or better than the rate of climb in the current thermal.

However, a decision to leave a thermal also depends on the time of the day. (Refer to Sections 1.19 and 1.25.)

5.2.3 Are we centring a thermal quickly enough?

Getting the glider right into the core of a thermal on the first turn is easier said than done, but it is most definitely something we should aim for. Time spent centring a thermal is time wasted and if only part of the first turn is in sink it can halve the average rate of climb straight away.

At this point I would like to insert a little table. It assumes that it takes a pilot two minutes to centre a thermal and then calculates the actual climb rate for various height gains. As we can see, the actual climb rate suffers disproportionately for stronger thermals, and for smaller height gains. Therefore, it is a crucial piece of flying strategy to keep thermal centring time down to an absolute minimum. Don't be afraid to use full control deflections and discard the thermal after a quarter of the turn if you can feel that you have missed the core. This way you will have performed a small S-shaped manoeuvre in lift, which is preferable to dropping into sink for the remainder of the turn.

Advanced cross-country flying

Table 7: Actual climb rates if it takes 2 minutes to centre a thermal

Height gain in feet	Thermal strength in knots			
	1	2	3	4
500	0.7	1.1	1.5	1.8
1000	0.8	1.4	2.2	2.7
2000	0.9	1.7	2.9	3.8
5000	1	1.9	3.4	4.8

Completing the turn will take another 15 seconds or so and even if we assume that the turn resulted in no altitude loss it means that we have wasted 15 valuable seconds. If we have dropped into heavy sink the loss of time could easily amount to a minute or two.

The above table raises the question of whether we tend to over-estimate our average climb rate by looking at the averager during the best part of the thermal and then draw conclusions about the average rate of climb. Averagers usually display a 20-second average climb rate and not the rate of climb for the whole thermal. Therefore it is up to the pilot to assess the average rate of climb correctly. We will come back to this issue and look at it more closely under the heading "Speed to fly".

Small weaknesses in our thermal entry procedures and a poor thermalling technique can have a major detrimental effect on our achieved rate of climb. For fast cross-country flights, it is of utmost importance to spend as little time as possible thermalling. We only cover distance while cruising and therefore we need to keep the climb/cruise ratio as low as possible. Pilots who spend the least amount of time in thermals are usually the winners of a glider race unless, of course, they have made some other blunders.

5.2.4 Are we thermalling efficiently enough?

Although we have dealt with basic thermalling earlier we will now look at some refinements under the heading: "Advanced cross-country flying". It is sound advice for a pilot under training to apply opposite aileron to prevent the glider from overbanking while circling. However, this doesn't mean that this type of thermalling is efficient.

Aileron deflections not only increase the amount of drag but also make the airfoil less efficient. The net result is a negative impact on the maximum possible rate of climb.

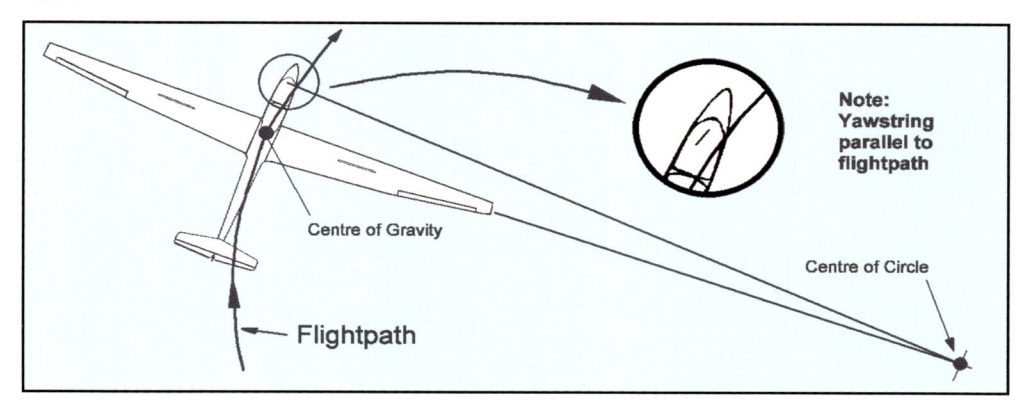

Figure 72: Yawstring displacement for optimum thermalling performance

Advanced cross-country flying

Because a glider's yawstring is mounted well ahead of the aircraft's centre, the air striking the yawstring arrives slightly from one side of the aircraft's nose (Figure 72). This not only induces a mild sideslip and increases drag but it also makes speed control more difficult. Therefore, more advanced pilots do not keep the yawstring centred and instead apply a small amount of top rudder which puts the yawstring a few degrees towards the outer wing.

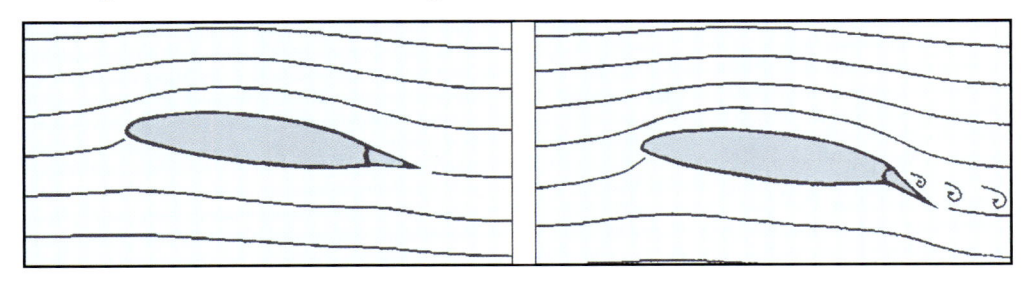

Figure : 73 Disturbance of airflow with aileron deflection

Provided top rudder is applied sensibly (the yawstring should never point more than 10 degrees on the high side of the turn) it can improve the rate of climb due to the fact that the ailerons can remain centred for minimum drag. I also feel that this technique allows a slightly lower thermalling speed and hence a smaller radius of turn. Never fly with the yawstring on the low side of the turn because this requires too much opposite aileron deflection to prevent over-banking.

5.2.5 Yawstring corrections

Many pilots only know about the use of rudder for yawstring corrections but more advanced pilots also use the ailerons. Let us assume we are in a right hand turn in a thermal when we notice our yawstring moving out to the left. We all know that applying right rudder will fix the problem straight away. However, in a situation like this right rudder also tightens our turn. Tightening our turn might not be desired or warranted at the time as it might move us away from the core of the thermal.

In situations like this, we can apply left aileron to produce the same effect. It will put the yawstring in the centre almost as quickly as the use of right rudder. The resulting shallower angle of bank often comes handy for position changes within the thermal. Whether we use ailerons or rudder is entirely up to us. What we do depends on our assessment whether a tighter or wider turn is the preferred option at the time.

To sum up I have put the options for yawstring corrections during a right hand turn together.

RIGHT TURN / YAWSTRING OUT TO THE LEFT
Use right rudder for tighter turn OR use left aileron for wider turn

RIGHT TURN / YAWSTRING OUT TO THE RIGHT
Use left rudder for wider turn OR use right aileron for tighter turn

May I suggest that you invest a minute or two working out what control deflections are required for yawstring corrections in a left turn? Completing this exercise will ensure a proper understanding of the matter and will also enable you to apply it properly next time you fly.

5.2.6 Is our meteorological navigation up to scratch?

Successful cross-country pilots select a track through the air which is often referred to as "the energy path". Their route through the air coincides with the path of maximum atmospheric energy – a path that is most certainly not a straight line but always the route that maximizes time in lift.

Flying in a straight line on a cross-country flight on a day with cumulus clouds will not only see us intercept a thermal on rare occasions but we will also lose a lot of altitude between areas of lift. However, if we are prepared to divert slightly and cruise through the lift marked by clouds, we will greatly improve our energy extraction and, just as importantly, stay away from sink. If we also slightly reduce our speed while in lift, we further increase our efficiency.

Under a blue sky we are deprived of visible clues for lift. However, we still have the option of assessing the ground for likely hot spots and to select our route to intercept as many likely thermal sources as possible. In hilly parts of the country we should favour slopes facing the sun and the prevailing wind. This will give us the best chance of intercepting good thermals because we have two things working in our favour. Also we take advantage of stronger and higher thermals (Section 5.10). Tactics like these increase our chances of remaining in buoyant air for longer. The more time we spend in buoyant air the lower the likelihood of running into areas of sink. This more than compensates for small detours.

If streeting is marked by cumulus clouds it pays to make substantial detours to remain in lift. Leaving the street close to cloud base allows us to cross areas of sink in between the cloud streets easily. Streeting in the blue is just as common but admittedly, under those conditions, it is far harder to find the best path through the air. It is still possible though, as our top pilots demonstrate time and time again.

5.2.7 Is our thermal selection good enough?

When early solo pilots practice around the home airfield, they are usually grateful for any updraught and are often seen to circle in the outer fringes of thermals. They are happy to have found any lift and even happier when the altimeter shows a net gain of altitude – gaining altitude quickly is not very high on their list of priorities.

However, when we make the transition to cross-country flying even efficient thermalling is not good enough any more. We need to work on finding only the strongest of thermals because, more than anything else, this is what makes us fast and what leads to competition success.

To underline the statement let's look at an example of two pilots flying the same 100 km triangle with two identical gliders. Pilot 1 works thermals of 6 kts average for a total height gain of 10 000ft but Pilot 2 accepts only one weaker thermal and, as a result, only manages to average 5 kts for the same height gain. How much faster would Pilot 1 be?

Pilot 1 would spend three minutes less time gaining the 10 000 ft needed to get around the task, but because he can afford to cruise a little faster, he would manage to shave another minute or so off the total time. If Pilot 1 completes the task in 1 hour and Pilot 2 needs an additional 5 minutes the speed of Pilot 1 would be 100 km/h but the speed of Pilot 2 would drop to 92.5 km/h.

Remember that Pilot 2 accepted only one weaker thermal, that's all it took to be left behind by 7.5 km/h. The message is clear, if we want to get our speed up, we must use only the strongest of thermals.

Advanced cross-country flying

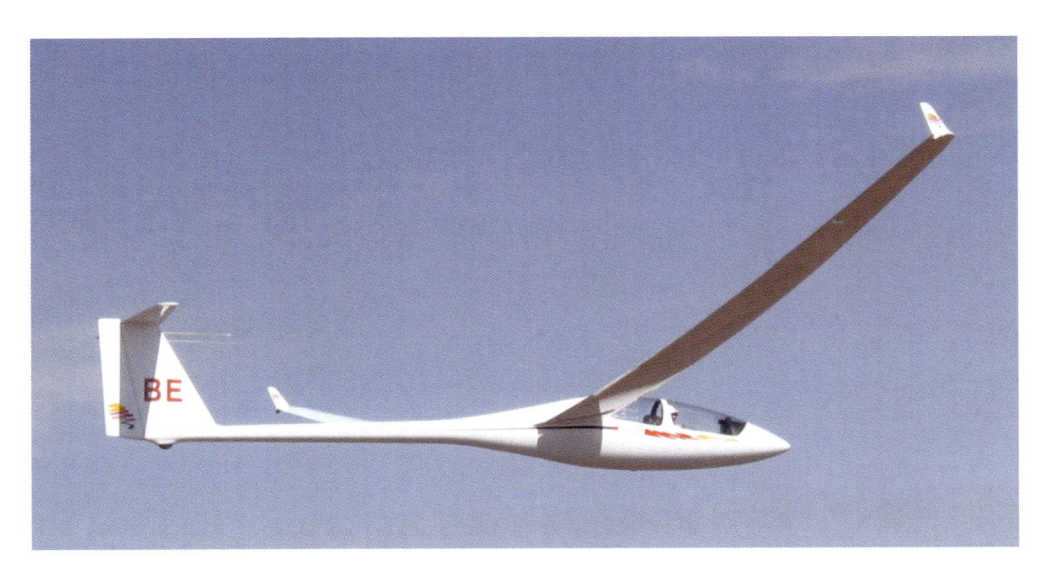

Cruising along

5.3 The effect of detours

Flying an additional distance to pass through areas of good lift is all very well but there comes a point where the increase in travelling distance will wipe out any gains made by flying through areas of good lift. So when does it pay to perform detours and when is it better to remain on track?

Assume that three identical gliders fly from point A to point B – a distance of 100 km. Pilot 1 travels in a straight line but Pilot 2 decides on a detour in order to contact good lift about 20 km to one side, (a mountain range or a few promising cumulus clouds for example) roughly half way down the track. Pilot 3 wants to keep his options open. Initially he tracks straight towards his goal, but half way down the track he decides to detour for better lift. To start with, let's find out what the additional travelling distance of Pilot 2 and Pilot 3 amounts to.

The additional travelling distance of Pilot 2 is a mere 7.7 km although he went 20 km off track. Pilot 3 delayed changing course until abeam the lift area. His late decision results in a 23.85 km increase of distance. If the decision to divert is made early the additional travelling distance is minimal. If, on the other hand, procrastination is allowed to get the upper hand a significant penalty is paid.

Taking the example one step further, assume that, as a result of their detours, Pilots 2 and 3 manage an average climb rate of 4 kts (2 m/s) compared to Pilot 1 who only averages 3 kts (1.5 m/s). Let's also assume that Pilot 1 needs to climb 10 000 ft to cruise at 80 kts (150 km/h). The question is which pilot

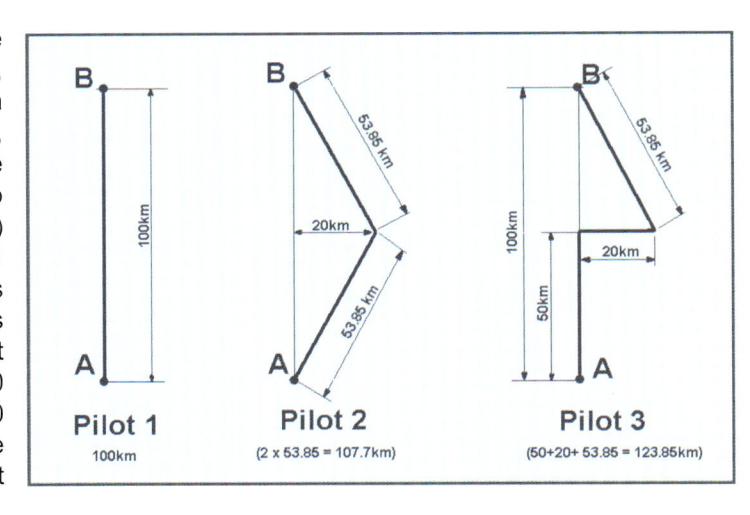

Figure 74: Additional distance through detours

Pilot 1
100km

Pilot 2
(2 x 53.85 = 107.7km)

Pilot 3
(50+20+ 53.85 = 123.85km)

149

Advanced cross-country flying

made the better decision? Obviously Pilot 1 travels a shorter distance, but Pilots 2 and 3 find stronger lift. If pilot 1 needs to climb 10 000 ft, Pilots 2 and 3 would need to climb 10 770 ft and 12 396 ft respectively because of their longer track distance. Now we have a situation where:

- Pilot 1 spends 32.92 minutes to gain 10 000 ft for a distance of 100 km,
- Pilot 2 spends 26.59 minutes to gain 10 770 ft for a distance of 107.7 km, and
- Pilot 3 spends 30.61 minutes to gain 12 396 ft for a distance of 123.96 km.

To calculate the speeds we need to allow for the cruising time as well.

- Pilot 1 spends 40.00 minutes cruising 100 km at 80 kts,
- Pilot 2 spends 43.08 minutes cruising 107.7 km at 80 kts, and
- Pilot 3 spends 49.58 minutes cruising 123.96 km at 80 kts.

Although our three pilots have flown a different distance all of them get credited with 100 km only. The resulting speeds are as follows:

- Pilot 1 averages a speed of 82.3 km/h.
- Pilot 2 averages a speed of 86.1 km/h.
- Pilot 3 averages a speed of 74.8 km/h.

Pilot 2 is the clear winner of the race. He is a very impressive 4 km/h faster than Pilot 1 and almost 12 km/h faster than Pilot 3.

These simple calculations are based on a zero wind situation. Upwind detours positively affect the cross-country speed but downwind detours have a very negative impact as section 4.13 explains. Therefore upwind detours should always be given strong priority over downwind ones.

If a pilot flies from A to D but detours via a cumulus cloud at C the additional distance can be calculate as shown below:

$$AC = \frac{AB}{\cos \alpha}$$

$$B1C = AC - AB$$

Figure 75: Additional distance calculations

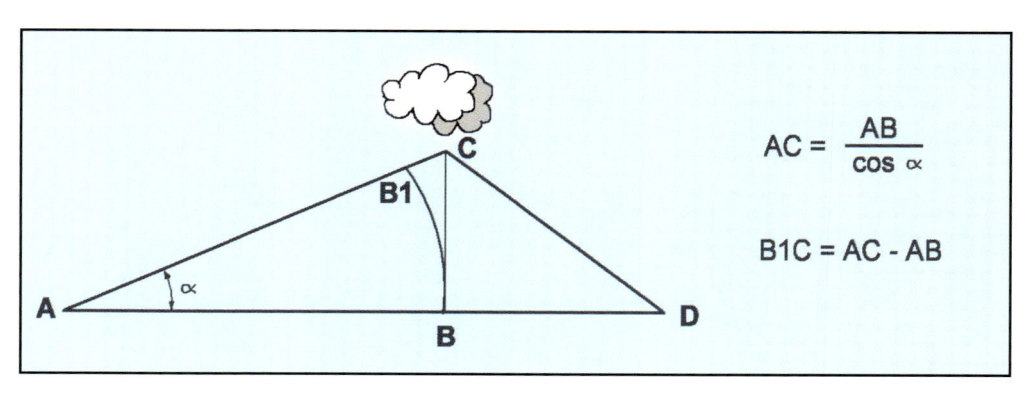

The table below lists the increase in travelling distance. The centre column shows the percentage increase for various diversion angles but to get back on track the same distance needs to be added again. Therefore the total percentage increase is shown in the column on the far right.

It is now evident that small diversions can almost be neglected and even going off course by 15° has a minimal impact on the distance flown. It follows that detours made in the name of better climb rates are almost always certain to pay big dividends. Detours leading to conditions of streeting are worth taking even if the streets are off

Advanced cross-country flying

track by as much as 40 degrees. In fact diversions of up to 30° are justifiable as long as they are made early and as long as there is a significant difference in lift strength. It follows that it is best to get back on track with as shallow an angle as possible. Just as important is to remain close to your track (or upwind of it) while approaching your turn point. And finally, the better the performance of our aircraft the smaller the penalty of an additional distance becomes.

Table 8: Increase in distance due to diversions

Percentage increase in distance due to diversions		
Degrees off track	Percentage increase	Return to track
0	0	0
5	0.36	0.72
10	1.54	3.08
15	3.53	7.06
20	6.42	12.84
25	10.34	20.68
30	15.47	30.94
35	22.08	44.16
40	30.54	61.08
45	41.42	82.84
50	55.57	111.14
55	74.34	148.68
60	100	200

ASG 29 in weak thermal wave
Photo: Manfred Muench

Advanced cross-country flying

5.4 Speed to fly

Ever since gliders have been flying cross-country the question of the optimum cruising speed has occupied the mind of pilots. Because modern gliders feature a permissible speed range of about 40 kts to 150 kts it is not hard to see why the correct cruising speed can make a significant difference. However, when theoretically optimising the speed to fly we must first of all distinguish between:

a) optimum cruising speed to maximise glide distance, and

b) optimum cruising speed to maximise average cross-country speed.

5.4.1 Maximizing glide distance

A typical scenario would be a return from a cross-country flight into dead air and the pilot deciding to glide as far as possible to shorten the retrieve. In other words, speed has become irrelevant – all that matters now is maximum distance. As far as his cruising speed is concerned, the pilot has the three following options:

a) he could fly at the speed of best glide angle (best L/D),

b) he could fly a little faster, or

c) he could fly a little slower.

What is his best option and what speed would get him the furthest? The answer is not as simple as you might think – in fact the correct answer can only be given if the strength of a headwind or tailwind is known. Only in a zero wind situation (and without any lift or sink on track) the speed of best L/D is clearly best.

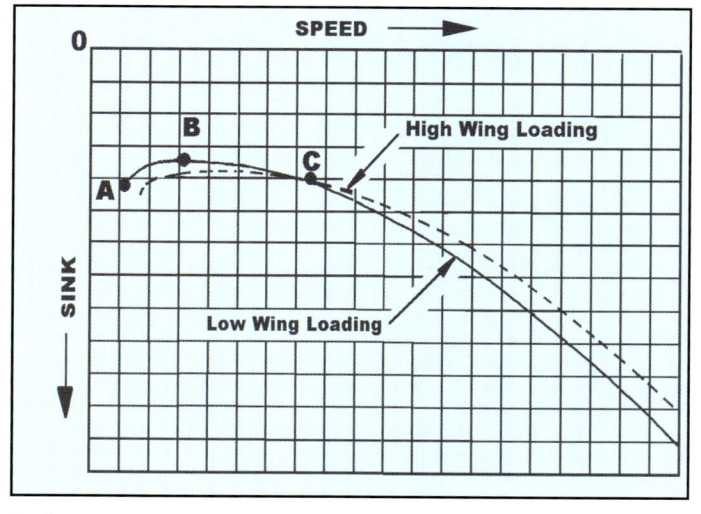

In Chapter 1 we had a brief look at a polar curve and discovered that the speed of minimum sink is significantly lower than the speed of best L/D. For ease of reference, a typical polar curve of a training aircraft is reproduced below. Points A, B, and C represent the speeds of stall, minimum sink and best L/D respectively.

Figure 76: Typical polar curve of a sailplane

Before we go any further, let's use our imagination to determine the best flying tactics in a tailwind situation. By flying a little slower, we will stay airborne a little longer (due to a lower rate of sink) and the tailwind will have more time to blow us towards our goal. As expected, we benefit nicely from the tailwind and by flying a little slower we benefit even longer.

If that makes good sense let's consider a headwind and determine the exact optimum speed to fly for a specific wind strength. In order to find the answer, we will resort to the polar curve of a modern ASH 26 sailplane and play a little with graphics. All we need to know beforehand is that the speed of best L/D is found by drawing a straight line from the zero speed point onto the polar curve and where the line touches the polar curve is the speed of best L/D.

In the above example, this exercise has already been done for you (based on a wing loading of 45 kg/m²) and as you can see best L/D of 50:1 occurs at a speed of approximately 60 kts. If we want to find the optimum speed for a 20 kts tailwind we need to shift the vertical axis back by 20 kts and draw another straight line intersecting the polar curve to arrive at an optimum speed of 54 kts.

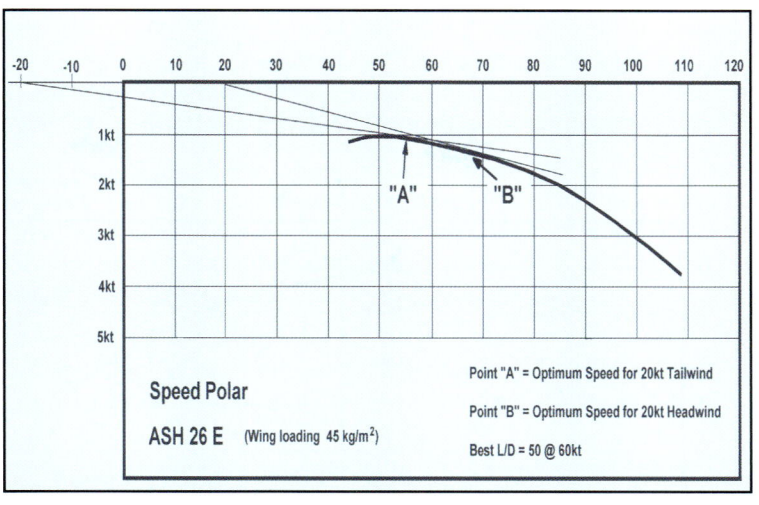

Figure 77: Determining optimum speeds for head- and tailwind glides

The same procedures would apply for a headwind situation, but in this case the vertical axis would need to be shifted to the right resulting in an optimum speed of approx. 68 kts. When flying into a headwind, we need to be a little faster in order to maximise the distance. This gives the headwind less time to hinder our progress.

The same method can be used to determine the correct speeds for any other glider. Before we go on to the next subject, I would like to pass on a rule of thumb which says: Add 1/3 of the headwind component to the speed of best L/D to obtain the optimum speed for maximum distance and subtract 1/3 of the tailwind component for maximum glide distance in a tailwind situation. You will find that this rule is sufficiently accurate for modern high-performance gliders or medium performance aircraft with water ballast. However, for lower performance gliders, we should add or subtract 1/4 of the tailwind component.

These days most gliders used for cross-country flying are equipped with flight computers which display the best speed for final glides into a head- or tailwind. However, the computer can only display the appropriate speed as long as the pilot has entered the correct settings for the prevailing conditions.

The point to keep in mind though is that (in my opinion) these gadgets distract pilots too much from looking out for other traffic. For this reason I personally go by the above rule of thumb – a more precise indication is hardly necessary especially with the very flat polar curves of modern gliders.

5.4.2 Maximizing average cross-country speed

Maximising distance on a final glide is one thing, but optimising the average speed on a cross country flight is quite another. Flying competitively or attempting long distance cross country flights requires us to get into racing mode.

The question is:" What is the optimum cruising speed?" We don't want to waste time by flying too slow and we don't want to waste altitude by flying too fast. Any wasted altitude needs to be regained in thermals and thermalling is just like unnecessary stops for a car at a fuel station – it only adds to our trip time. It also means that we are flying backwards half the time. Mathematically-minded glider pilots did the work for us a long time ago and today their work is known as the "MacCready Theory". It works fine,

Chapter 5

Advanced cross-country flying

Thermalling over a desert resort in central Australia

Not thermalling unless the lift comes up to our pre-determined strength is perhaps the biggest lesson to be learned from the MacCready theory. Multiple world record holder Hans Werner Grosse puts it differently! He says: "If in doubt, climb straight ahead!" These six words are excellent advice and say it all. But there is an exception to every rule — if we are in danger of outlanding, we top up in weaker lift. However, as soon as we are confident of finding a stronger thermal somewhere down the track we should head off again.

5.5 How important is cruising at optimum speed?

To assess the overall impact of the optimum speed to fly on our average cross-country speed, let's use the example of a pilot misjudging his climb rate by as much as 25% and investigate what effect a wrong inter–thermal cruising speed has on the speed around the task.

The answer might surprise you because the reduction in average speed is less than one percent. A 1% penalty is comparatively small but can be devastating in a high-level competition. The early cross-country pilot, however, might be well advised to concentrate on other areas of flying such as efficient thermalling, meteorological navigation and proper decision making when striving for major improvements in cross-country speed.

Having said that, I hasten to add that I do not advocate complacency in terms of inter-thermal cruising speed. In fact an incorrect assessment of more than 25% in climb rate, and subsequent selection of an inappropriate cruising speed, leads to a much higher reduction in average speed. For example, cruising at the speed of best L/D when lift of 4 kts can be found reduces the possible average speed by as much as 22%. Needless to say, such an economy cruise should only be done if we can't otherwise reach areas of thermal activity or if we want to stretch our glide as far as possible.

5.6 Flying tactics on track and height bands

Relatively new cross country pilots often have little or no plan other than a determination to get home at the end of the day. By contrast, the majority of performance–oriented pilots have a predetermined course of action for various eventualities. It minimizes decision making while on task, reduces the mental workload in tricky situations and frees up resources for efficient flying.

For example, by knowing that any searches for lift are always associated with a loss of time it makes good sense to apply different flying tactics depending on the current height above ground. For flying in rather uniform soaring conditions over relatively flat or moderately hilly terrain Figure 79 might provide some useful guidance. For flying in mountainous terrain different tactics apply.

Generally speaking it is useful to divide the maximum operating height into three equal bands and predetermine tactics based on the pilot's level of experience and the

Cloud base or top of convection

	Blue Sky	Cumulous Sky	MacCready
1/3	Stay on track	Intercept all active cumulus clouds within 15 to 20 degrees on either side of track	Set to expected average climb rate in next thermal
1/3	Consider small track deviations to align track with likely thermal sources.	As above but include clouds further off track. Accept average lift.	As above
1/3	As above but accept greater track deviations	Look for lift upwind of cloud and accept average lift to get up again	Reduce MacCready setting to extend range

Figure 79: Suggested height bands

aircraft's performance. This can reduce the mental workload considerably and free up valuable time for other tasks.

The most appropriate tactic while in the uppermost height band would be to remain on track and fly towards the next turn point with a minimum of interruptions or time wasting. Of course this does not mean that we ignore a good thermal and it is certainly no justification for neglecting meteorological navigation but while cruising at such a comfortable altitude we will not be tempted to circle in average lift or fly more than very minor deviations. The plan is to find a strong thermal on track and select the cruising speed based on the better climb rates of the day.

On dropping into the middle level height band our flying tactics would change slightly. Here we begin to actively vary our track in order to intercept many likely sources of lift even though these small detours add a little to our track distance. Perhaps even an "S" turn in an area of buoyant air might be performed in an attempt to find the core of a strong thermal. If this is unsuccessful, we will simply press on. If appropriate, we will circle in average lift to stay clear of trouble and to get back into the upper height band.

Down in the lower half of the middle level band we might even invest in a gentle exploratory 360° turn as long as we are confident that some useful lift is likely to be found. Unless we are sure to contact strong lift very soon we reduce our cruising speed by some 20% or so.

In the lowest height band we might want to adopt a slightly more conservative approach. That doesn't mean that we immediately switch to survival mode but it does dictate that we further reduce our cruising speed in order to widen our search area. It also means that we invest in more than a single searching turn if we are confident of a reasonable thermal in the vicinity. A below–average thermal might be taken (at least for a little while) and even short off–track headings are considered if they are likely to lead to areas of better soaring conditions. This could involve a dash to a ridge or a slow glide towards known thermal sources.

Every gliding coach will confirm that the implementation of such flying tactics by relative newcomers is a very different matter. Seemingly endless searches for another thermal within a few hundred feet of maximum altitude are commonplace although such mistakes are readily recognized and acknowledged during debriefing at the end of the day. Obviously we all like to be high rather than low, but if we want to improve our cross country speed we are well advised to eradicate such habits. By contrast, more experienced cross country pilots develop and apply self–imposed flying tactics and benefit greatly from a strict application of their own rules in flight.

But let's consider a few other aspects affecting our selection of cruise speed. Thermals seldom have the same strength all the way up. In fact they are often weaker down low or near the top of convection (refer to Section 2.10). To remain in the optimum height band for the day it is advisable to adjust the cruising speed just to avoid dropping out of the strongest band of lift. We also need to consider tactical matters and look at the conditions ahead. If, for example, we have to cross an irrigated area (or any patch of ground unlikely to produce good lift) we would be well advised to slow down regardless of what the speed to fly instrument indicates.

If, on the other hand, we spot some promising cumulus clouds appearing on track (and within reach) we can confidently speed up and take advantage of stronger lift ahead. However, if we descend into the bottom third of our available working height (or we drop below a level we are comfortable with), our flying tactics should change and with it our decision on the appropriate cruising speed. In a nutshell, the speed to fly is not only determined by the MacCready Theory but is to a large extend dictated by flying tactics and by what the pilot perceives as his best option at the time.

Okay, let's briefly summarise the most crucial points.

Advanced cross-country flying

- Try to minimise the number of thermals in order to avoid time losses associated with thermal centring.
- Transition smoothly between cruise and climb in order to reduce entry losses and avoid wasting time.
- Leave the lift as soon as you are confident of achieving a better rate of climb in the next thermal on track.
- Maximise the rate of climb from every thermal and try to improve the climb rate by applying a bit of 'top rudder'.
- Pay particular attention to meteorological navigation.
- Climb only in the strongest thermals unless you drop into the bottom height band and run the risk of an outlanding.
- Detours can be of advantage if they lead to better areas of lift. Going off track by up to 20° attracts a relatively small penalty in terms of distance travelled. Upwind detours are recommended. Downwind detours should be avoided at all costs.
- Avoid abrupt elevator movements to minimise aerodynamic losses.
- Minor deviations from the optimum cruising speed result only in minute reductions in average speed around the task.
- Stay in the hight band of the strongest lift even if it reduces the available working height.
- An energy efficient transition between climb and cruise is just as crucial as the correct entering of thermals.

Sharing the fun is twice the fun
Photo:
Jean-Luc Colson

Advanced cross-country flying

5.7 Thermal Streets

Provided the prevailing meteorological conditions are favourable, convection over relatively flat terrain is often organised into streets running parallel to the wind at convection or inversion level.

Research has confirmed that contra-rotating vortices generate long rows of lift with lines of sink in between (refer to Figure 80). Very interesting laboratory experiments conducted by French scientist Bénard have provided glider pilots with an insight into convection behaviour below an inversion layer.

Bénard used a flat dish containing a shallow layer of liquid covering its bottom. Evenly heating the dish over the entire bottom resulted in a temperature gradient which in turn encouraged the warm liquid to rise and the cooler liquid to sink to the bottom. A film placed on top of the liquid was pulled slowly across the upper surface and caused the convection to align itself into pairs of elongated parallel rolls rotating in opposite direction.

The atmosphere behaves similarly. Research meteorologists believe that in conditions of moderate to strong winds the convection layer is organised in a like manner. The wind above the inversion layer acts in a similar way as a film pulled across the top surface of a heated pool of liquid. Here is a list of "favourable conditions" for future reference:

a) The convection must be capped by an inversion

b) Only small changes in wind direction occur within the convective layer and

c) The speed of the wind increases with height but ideally has its maximum within the convective layer

Glider pilots enthusiastically refer to such conditions as 'streeting'. It is probably fair to say that there is almost always some 'streeting' effect even though it might not always be apparent. Thermals under these streets of lift seem to be greatly enhanced but completely absent in the clear air in between. Sometimes streets of lift don't even seem to require hot spots on the ground — evidence can often be found over oceans, thousands of kilometres away from land. The greater the depth of the convection the wider the gap in between these streets becomes. As a rule of thumb, the distance between lines of lift amounts to approximately three times the depth of convection.

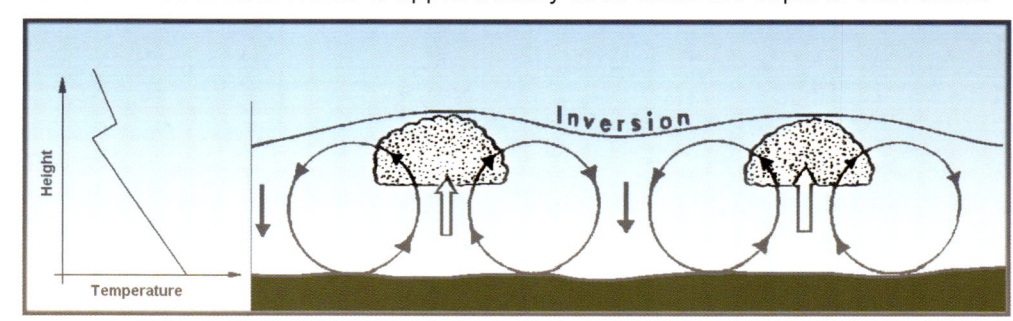

Figure 80: Streeting

From the air it is often easier to recognise 'streeting' by looking at the cloud shadows on the ground than by looking at the clouds themselves. If cloud streets are present we are well advised to get underneath one of those as quickly as practicable. These streets not only enable us to pick the most energy-efficient route, but they also increase our chances of finding a strong thermal. Look for wisps of cloud hanging down just below cloud base because they usually point towards areas of strong lift.

Keeping a light hand on the control stick also helps to find an efficient path through the air as long as the pilot promptly, but gently, changes the heading towards the lifting

Advanced cross-country flying

wing. Cross–country pilots often fly for distances of 100 km or more without stopping in a thermal but by following the right track through the air. Cloud streets often provide enough energy to maintain altitude even at relatively high cruising speeds. Some phenomenal cross–country speeds and distances have been recorded by pilots taking full advantage of such conditions. Flying either downwind or directly into wind and just "jumping across" to an adjacent street when necessary makes for some extremely fast and enjoyable cross–country flying indeed.

It must also be mentioned that streeting is common even on cloudless days although under such conditions it becomes more difficult to detect and follow these invisible energy highways. It is possible though and extremely satisfying when we manage to stay in good air for long glides on blue days. However, it is more important than ever to be in the right spot at the right time and if we find ourselves in sink for any length of time we might be flying along a street of sink. Only changing our heading promptly (I suggest by approx.45°) will get us out of sink and back into lift again.

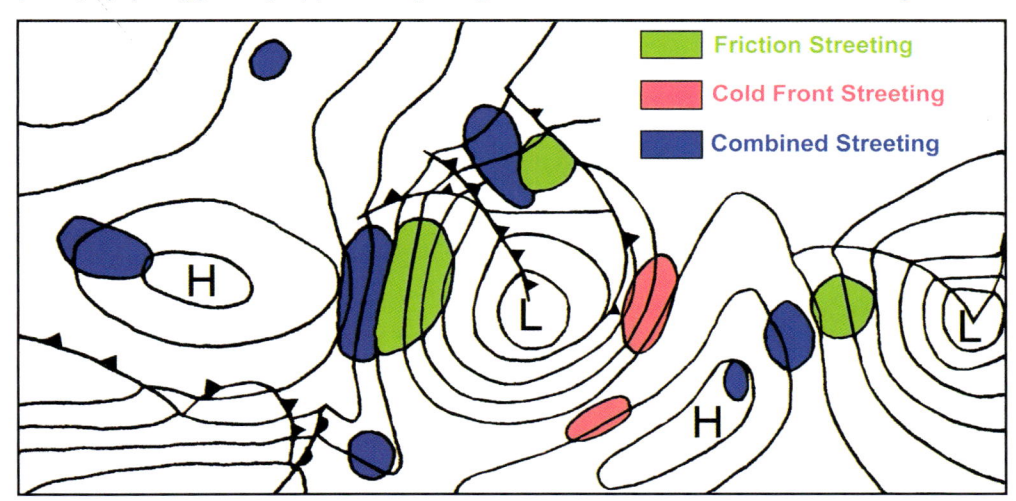

Figure 81: Schematic weather map showing areas where cloud streets may be expected in relation to highs and lows.

Figure 81 shows a typical meteorological situation for the southern half of the Australian continent without an underlying map. It was adapted for the southern hemisphere by M. J. Hancy after D. Muller, D. Elting, Ch. Kottmeier and R. Roth in 1985. As the weather systems move slowly across the continent, the likely areas of wind shear and thermal streets also shift in line with the main meteorological features.

Kuettner was the first to develop the theory of cloud street development and according to Carsten Lindemann (Free University of Berlin) Kuettner's theory is still valid. Lindemann believes that in reality we observe more cloud streets than can be forecast by the theory. We know that a curved vertical wind profile with a maximum wind speed at, or just below, the convection layer is ideal for cloud street development. We also know that further wind speed increases just above convection level are detrimental. Especially in the morning and prior to the onset of thermal convection, we observe a lot of curved wind profiles as a result of low-level jet streams.

Even linear increases of wind speed tend to form cloud streets. In all cases the reason is an alignment due to friction forces acting on

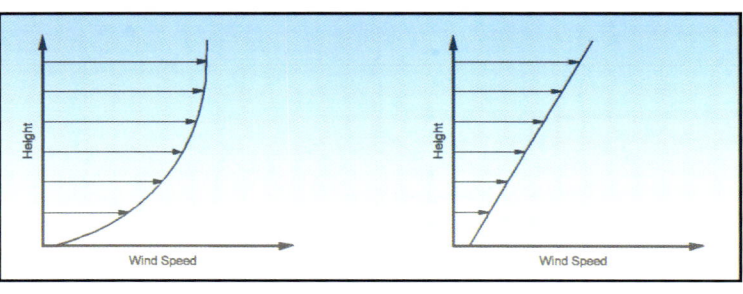

Figure 82: Examples of curved and linear vertical wind speed profiles

161

Advanced cross-country flying

Textbook streeting conditions in northern USA

all parts of the thermal. The surrounding air mass is pushed aside by an upward movement of the rising thermal. If the upward movement can align, only the forces perpendicular to the alignment are acting. But the alignment must be supported by forces near the surface to encourage the flow perpendicular to main airflow.

Friction streeting.

The most favourable locations are those between the high pressure and low pressure centres. When the winds are from the same direction throughout the convection layer, then cumulus clouds and thermals tend to align themselves as described above. This is particularly true in the SE to NE Trade wind belt associated with sub-tropical highs and ridges. They form under a subsidence inversion associated with the proximity of a high pressure system.

Cold front streeting

The closer cloud streets are to an active low pressure system, then the more likely they are to also form cross-wind bands. These are associated with wave formations under an inversion in moderate to strong wind conditions. They typically occur following the passage of cold fronts, in SW airstreams' (refer to Sections 12.14 and 12.15). The lateral movement of cross-wind bands causes alternate periods of enhanced and depressed lift, due to wave activity. These conditions are said to be "cycling."

The time period for one complete cycle varies with the strength of the wind and the height of the inversion. It is usually of the order of 10 to 20 minutes. Cross-wind bands also occur with thermals on blue days. Hauf T. et al referred to these as cold front shear streets, so called because they are associated with a frontal inversion.

The cross-wind bands are more dominant than down-wind cloud streets under these conditions. The above explains cloud street formation for reasons of wind profile alone. But cloud streets are also formed for orographic reasons and can often be observed

Advanced cross-country flying

in mountainous regions. Especially when exposed rock faces of a mountain range are receiving intense heat, we can expect nicely aligned lift along the entire spine of the mountain range. The same applies in flat terrain if strong thermal sources are well-aligned with the prevailing surface wind.

Sometimes thermal streets are formed near the end of the day due to katabatic wind effects in mountains (refer to Section 11.6). Weak, but large, diameter thermals are plentiful over the valleys providing pleasant soaring and allow knowledgeable and experienced pilots to extend their glide ratio considerably. These alignments are also found on the plains. Sometimes sink lines are discovered where good lift was encountered earlier in the day and vice versa. More research is needed to explain the phenomenon.

A cloud street in southern Australia

So far we have mainly considered the theory behind streeting without looking deeper into practical aspects. Due to the close proximity of lift and sink, proper energy management is absolutely critical for optimum energy extraction. The MacCready Theory discussed in section 5.4.2 remains valid but we have to remember that a glider's optimum performance is achieved when the airspeed is equal to the speed of best L/D multiplied by the current g-load. In principle this dictates the most efficient flying style and the optimum g loading. Energy is gained when the lift vectors and the vertical movement of the glider point in the same direction. In other words, by pulling on the stick in lift we will have an efficient energy exchange with the atmosphere. However, it is very important to be gentle and always maintain momentum and rhythm. Coarse elevator movements will result in aerodynamic losses and are not only known to spoil our energy balance but are also adding significantly to the distance travelled.

Please note that in theory we can even extract energy from the atmosphere in sink by pushing forward on the stick and achieving negative g-loads. However, sailplane airfoils do not work efficiently at negative g-loads and the resulting aerodynamic losses make a practical energy gain very doubtful.

In contrast, large amounts of energy are lost when the lift/sink vectors and the vertical movement of our glider point in the opposite direction. By pushing on the stick in lift and by pulling on the stick in sink we will experience a severe energy loss and make our total energy variometer drop deeply into negative territory – the cardinal sin of dolphin flying!!!

Advanced cross-country flying

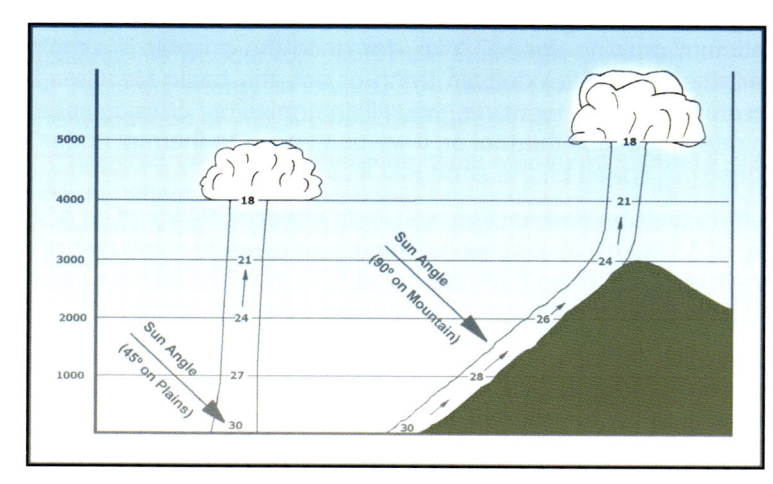

Figure 83: Mountain Thermal

When comparing a flatland thermal with one over mountainous terrain, it becomes obvious that the degree of cooling is different. A thermal originating from the plains experiences a cooling of 3° C per 1000 ft and, given the conditions as per the above example, forms a cumulus cloud at 4000 ft.

Theoretically, the same cooling should apply to the mountain-generated thermal, but it doesn't because the air continues to warm while ascending still close to the ground and along the mountain slope. Also, heating is more intense due to the fact that the sun is striking the ground at almost right angles. By the time the thermal separates from the top of the slope, it has picked up an additional 3° C in temperature. This not only pushes the thermal to a height of 5000 ft but also makes for much stronger lift beneath the cloud. In fact, thermals over relatively bare mountains might go thousands of feet higher than over the plains.

However, heavily wooded mountain faces tend to suppress the effect significantly. The thermal energy otherwise available is absorbed via evaporation of moisture from the vegetation. For a more detailed explanation please refer to Section 1.16.

What does all that mean for everyday practical mountain flying? To start with it means that on light wind days thermals originate from the bottom of the mountain and rise up on the sunlit mountain flanks as narrow curtains of warm air (refer to Section 11.6 – Katabatic & anabatic winds). The air flowing up the highest peaks warms the

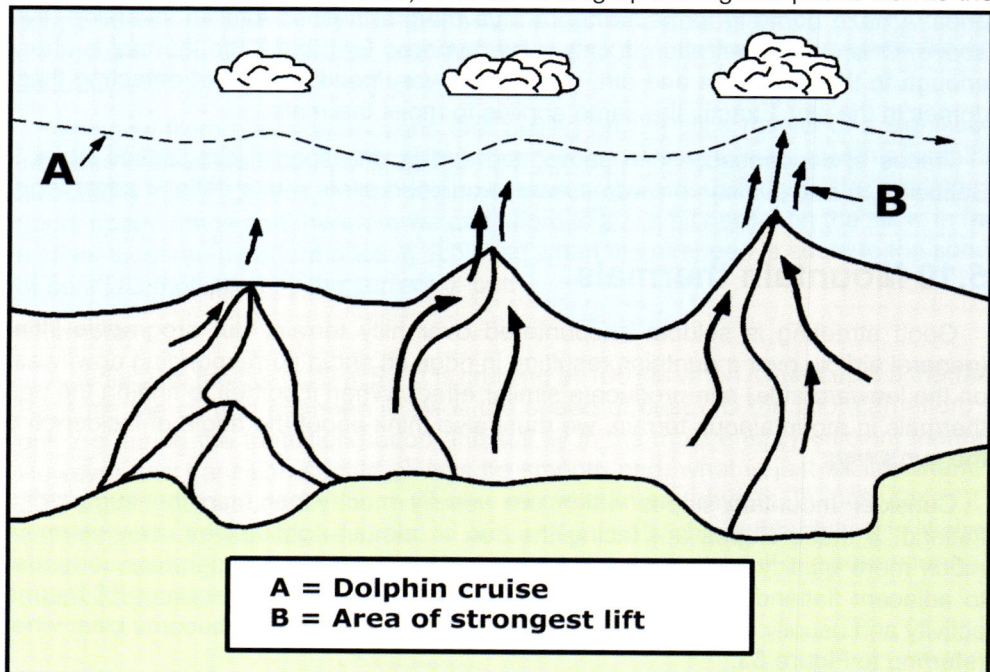

Figure 84: Thermal sources in mountainous terrain

A = Dolphin cruise
B = Area of strongest lift

air which most often results in thermals of exceptional strength. Below ridge top level we best apply the slope soaring techniques described in Chapter 11. As soon as sufficient clearance from the mountain is achieved we can resume using standard thermalling methods.

Along the spine of the mountain we often find a line of cumulus clouds which might allow dolphin flying techniques for rapid progress on cross-country flights. On such occasions pilots are well advised to identify the sources of the best thermals to practice locating strong lift on future blue days.

Soaring amongst mountains is exciting and challenging at the same time. Flatland flying experience is of some advantage but accounts for little in an environment where it is all too easy to become distracted by the spectacular views and gorgeous panoramas. Good familiarity with the terrain and an ability to handle the glider without conscious control inputs are preconditions for safe flying in mountainous regions where outlanding options are usually few and far between.

5.10.1 Ground inversions in mountainous terrain

Glider pilots can often encounter a very strong ground inversion as a result of nocturnal radiation. The effect is especially noticeable when cool and humid air resides over airfields located in mountain valleys (refer to Section 2.4). Often the top of this inversion is close to 1000 ft (approx. 300 m) above ground and can therefore only be expected to disperse after prolonged and intense heating. In fact, the inversion might never be broken if a large part of the valley floor remains in the shadow of the surrounding mountains for the best part of a mild day, such as in autumn.

In spite of this, there is still some convection occurring nearby which certainly doesn't stop us from soaring. Mountain slopes towering above the inversion can still produce thermals - especially when facing the sun. As long as we get launched high enough and only release after contacting lift above the top of the inversion we have every chance of a good soaring flight. In fact, we might even get well into a planned cross-country flight before the ground inversion is finally broken by the effect of rising temperature . At that point, our fellow glider pilots will be able to utilise convection originating from the valley floor.

**Approaching Mt. Cook (NZ)
Photo:
Gavin Wills, Glide Omarama.com**

What we must avoid at all costs though is to drop below the inversion level for as long as it persists. The inversion's lack of lift will inevitably lead to an outlanding unless we are in reach of a suitable slope and the wind is strong enough to lift us above the inversion layer again.

Advanced cross-country flying

Finally, some advice on the optimum cruising altitude. In a modern glider and on days when cumulus clouds are nicely aligned it is usually advantageous to cruise significantly below cloud-base. Such tactics allows us to observe the clouds from a near optimum angle. This provides clues on the location of the strongest lift and hence the best track through the air. If, in contrast, we remain in close proximity of the clouds we are depriving us of these visual clues and have little chance of following the optimum track in terms of meteorological navigation (refer to Section 5.2.6).

5.11 Exiting a thermal

After gaining altitude in a thermal we need to ensure that the energy is put to good use. Exiting thermals badly is just as wasteful as entering them inefficiently. The recreational pilot is usually keen to retain the energy for soaring whereas the competitively minded one is interested in converting height into distance. Both pilots have one thing in common; they want to leave the thermal in the most efficient manner that is leaving it through the centre and speeding up in the process.

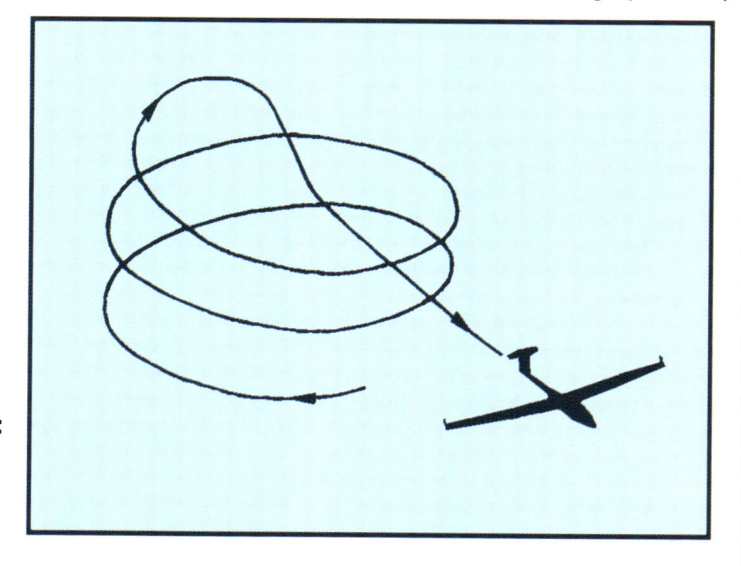

Figure 85: Efficient exiting of a thermal

Lift and sink belong together; they can always be found alongside each other. Departing lift means that we have to cross an area of descending air. A lot of energy can be lost by leaving the thermal carelessly and on the wrong heading. On very windy days especially, thermals tend to have an elongated shape and for this reason it is often a good strategy to leave the thermal on the wind line (Section 1.21 and 1.28). There, and only there, can we expect to transit some buoyant air which can only be good news in terms of our energy retention strategy.

Before we exit a thermal, we ensure that we roll out on the right heading but still aim to extract the maximum energy on the last turn. My preferred method is to tighten the final turn in order to cross the core and smoothly accelerate almost immediately afterwards to avoid being slow in the sinking air surrounding the thermal.

An example:

A 500 metre wide patch of bad air (sinking at a rate of 2.5 m/s) is crossed by two identical gliders. Pilot 1 (let us call him "Mr. Slow") flies through it at just 50 kts relying on a low glider sink rate of 0.6 m/s.

His friend Pilot 2 ("Mr. Fast") is in a hurry and shoots through at 90 kts knowing full well that at this speed his aircraft is coming down at a rate of 1.6 m/s. Who is better off when they both arrive at the far side of the bad area?

Pilot "Slow":

At 50 kts it takes just under 20 seconds to cross the sink. Descending at 0.6 m/s but adding the additional 2.5 m/s of sink gives a total sink rate of 3.1 m/s. Consequently after 20 seconds a total altitude of 62 metres or 200 ft has been lost.

Pilot "Fast":

At 90 kts it takes just 11 sec. to cross the sink. However the total sink rate is 4.1 m/s (1.6 m/s + 2.5 m/s) giving an altitude loss of 45 metres or 145 ft.

It's obvious that pilot "Mr. Fast" truly deserves his name. He spent a minimum amount of time in bad air and arrives at the end of the sink 55 ft higher and 9 seconds ahead. Best of all, he is now already cruising 40 knots faster and his friend will lose sight of him before much longer. The conclusion is to speed up early enough to cross any sink at an increased speed. Not doing so will result in wasting altitude unnecessarily.

Now let's look at the last and most exciting part of any cross-country flight.

5.12 Final glide

The days when we had to make primitive final glide calculators from discs of cardboard are gone forever and, as this book goes to press, most gliders are equipped with some form of final glide computer or modern GPS unit. As long as we feed these gadgets with the correct parameters (e.g. wing loading and performance deterioration from turbulence created by bugs on the leading edge of the wings) they allow us to adjust the airspeed in order to arrive with a suitable altitude margin over our home airfield.

Trusting your final glide computer is perhaps the hardest thing to do with today's high performance gliders but repeated safe final glides will soon instil the necessary degree of confidence in these modern wonders.

We are aiming for a glide home with enough height to perform a safe circuit. Sure, returning to base at maximum speed is quite impressive from a spectator's point of view, but for insiders it only proves that the pilot badly misjudged the final glide. Time was wasted because the altitude required for the spectacular homecoming first had to be gained in a thermal.

But what is the correct speed on final glide? As we have learned in Section 5.4.2, the optimum cruise speed depends on the expected rate of climb in the next thermal and that creates a problem straight away. After final glide, there is no thermal – only a landing.

We clearly have a special case here, but the predicament can be solved by feeding our on–board computer with the achieved rate of climb in the final thermal. Based on this data, the computer will display the required altitude. However, as soon as we have attained this height we leave the thermal in the knowledge that we get back in the most efficient manner and in the absolute minimum amount of time.

But this doesn't mean that we can afford to put our brain in neutral. Even on final glide we need to be alert and deviate slightly to transit as much buoyant air as possible. In the end we mightn't need it, but such tactics have the potential of allowing us to speed up the final glide considerably. But the dangers of getting it wrong cannot be over-emphasised. It is all too easy to encounter long distances of above average sink and this risk is by far greater the closer we get to the ground. All too often this can turn a reasonably safe final glide into a nail biting one.

Humans are reluctant to abandon their goal the closer they get to it and too many glider pilots have continued on a very marginal final glide although in hindsight an outlanding would have been the only safe option. Let's resist the temptation to compromise safety if and when it arises. Too many accidents near the end of a marginal final glide should serve as a warning to all of us.

My advice to early cross-country pilots is to start the final glide about 5 kts slower and gradually speed up when an excess altitude over the destination is the likely result. To my way of thinking a few seconds delay in the arrival time is by far preferable to a nail biting finish and a nagging feeling of stupidity for days or even weeks to come. Competition pilots might not agree and advocate a more aggressive approach but I doubt whether the associated risks outweigh the advantages in the long term.

5.13 Low-level finishes

We have all seen it and possibly even enjoyed it. Returning from a competition flight, gliders often approach the airfield rather low but near top speed. What is normal practice at competitions is now becoming part of a training routine for performance-orientated pilots at the end of a cross-country flight.

Such finishes are illegal in some parts of the world but are allowed in other countries. Where permitted, this practice ensures that suitably qualified pilots remain current in the art of energy management. Low and fast finishes undoubtedly add an element of fun to the sport but require a high degree of responsibility in the interest of safety.

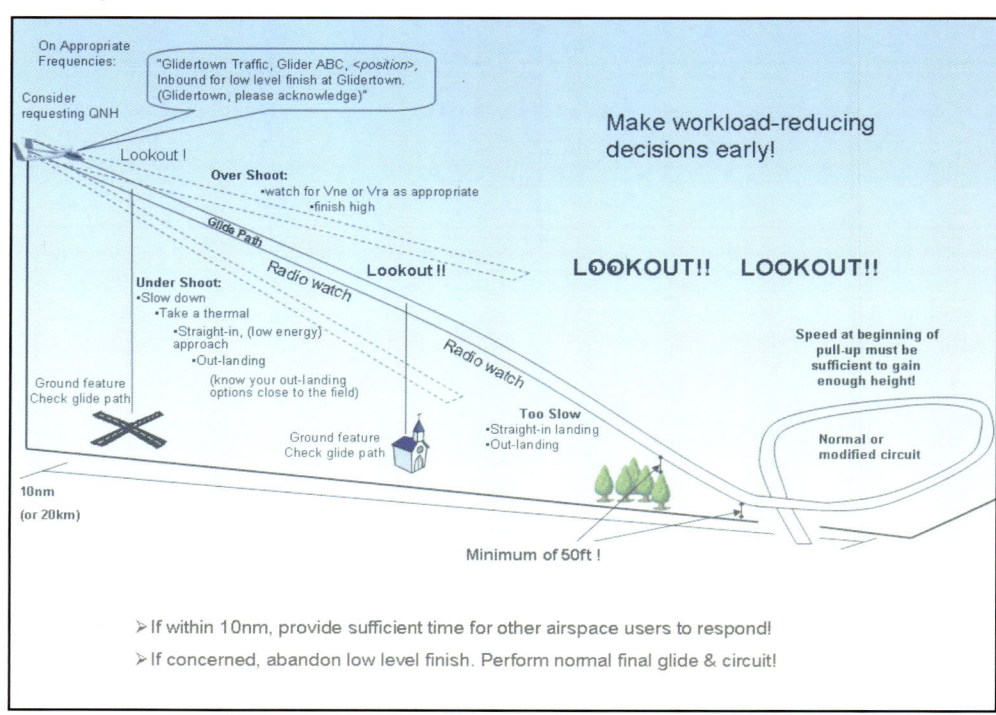

Figure 86: Graphic illustration of low level finish. (Courtesy of Ulrich & Colin Stauss)

Preconditions for a low-level finish include a working radio, a prior logbook endorsement, a familiarity with the airfield and an inbound call about 10 nm (approx. 20 km) away from the airfield. An acknowledgement from base must be received and the pilot must remain on frequency. Another inbound radio call a 5 nm away from the circuit area is mandatory and so is a circuit entry call on long final. The higher traffic density around airfields demands a first-class lookout and if another aircraft is spotted in the circuit the low-level finish should be abandoned.

Advanced cross-country flying

As always in gliding, pre-planning is everything and this must include some emergency options. Figure 86 shows the most important steps and also recommends options for under- or overshoot situations. A late decision on an alternative finishing procedure increases the workload and often causes attention narrowing. A proper 'Plan B' eliminates these stresses and helps to avoid 'pushonitis' due to a lack of alternatives.

A self launching glider sharing the tarmac with some passenger jets

Advanced cross-country flying

Low-level finishes are all about proper energy management and converting kinetic energy (Velocity) into potential energy (Height). Looking closer at the mathematics and ignoring aerodynamic losses we find that:

a) kinetic energy can be expresses as: $E_k = \frac{1}{2} \times m \times v^2$ and

b) potential energy is: $E_p = m \times g^* \times h$

Energy is proportional to the square of the entry speed making it obvious that speed is the most important factor for regaining height during the pull-up. Mathematically this can be expressed as:

$$\text{Gain of height} = (V_{initial}^2 - V_{final}^2) / 2g$$

To save readers crunching the numbers here are a few examples.

Example 1:

Entry speed @50 ft = 140 kts and speed at the top of the pull-up is 60 kts

Height (AGL) at top of pull-up is:

50 ft initial plus 690 ft height gain is 740 ft (Enough for a safe circuit.)

Example 2:

Entry speed @50 ft = 100 kts and speed on top of pull-up is 60 kts

Height (AGL) at top of pull-up is:

50 ft initial plus 270 ft height gain is ~320 ft (**NOT** sufficient for a normal circuit!)

Special care needs to be taken not to descent below 50 ft and not to exceed Vne or Vra. (max. speed and max. rough air speed). Especially on days with turbulent air (and with modern slippery gliders) it is very easy to exceed these speeds inadvertently. Make sure the pull-up is gentle and always double check whether the airspace above you is still clear of other traffic.

* "g" is the load factor on the aircraft whereby 1 g is the normal state of an aircraft in straight and level flight. Any increase of g loading, (e.g. pulling back on the stick at high speed), makes pilot (and aircraft) feel heavier. At 2 g the pilot and aircraft are effectively twice their normal weights, and so on. Negative g is the opposite, when the stick is pushed forward pilot and aircraft are becoming effectively lighter and the stalling speed decreases.

5.14 Flight analysis

Isn't it great to live in the electronic age and to utilise modern GPS based avionics as well as data recorder (datalogger) technology for flight verification? We have touched on the subject before but now it's time to look a little deeper into the options. Pilots keen on improving their performance can use self-teaching methods to great effect and the following comments provide guidance.

At first we need to download information from the datalogger onto a personal computer for subsequent flight analysis with suitable software programs. Although there are competing flight analysis programs on the market we will use **See You** for the following discussion and it is assumed that readers not only have access to this software but also an elementary understanding of it. To start with let's look at the flight window - the main page of See You. We arrange the windows in such a way that 3D view, route and barograph trace are displayed simultaneously. (Window > Desktops > 3D+Route+Barogram)

Advanced cross-country flying

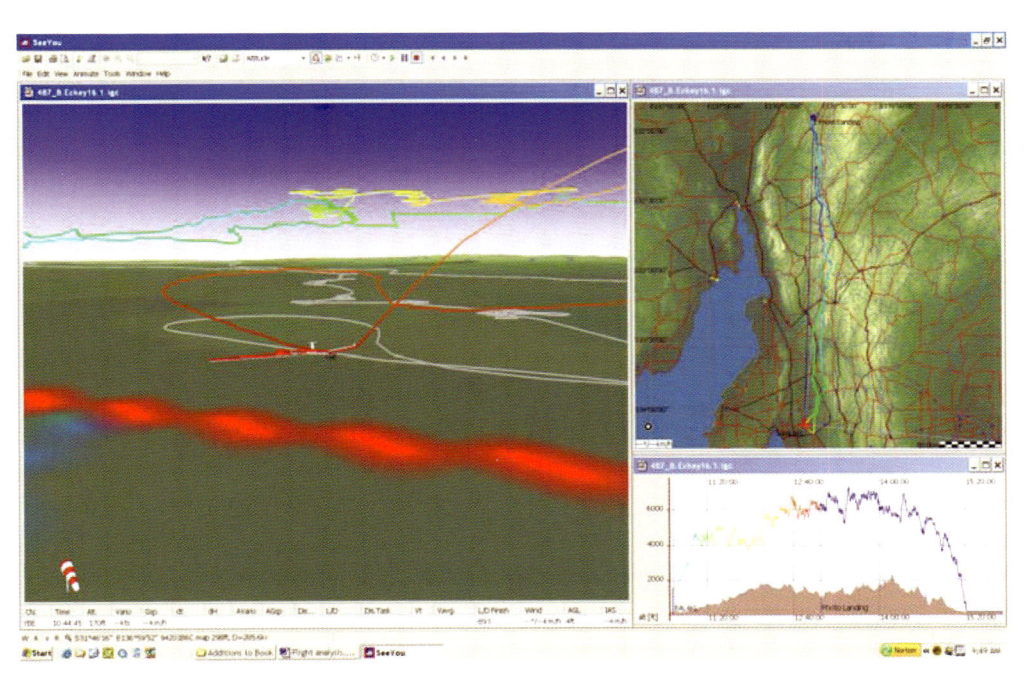

Figure 87: Main Page of See You

Let's start with an analysis of the climbs. This is where the early solo pilot can expect the biggest gain in performance. The first step is to set the datalogger recording interval to 4 seconds. The reason is that a full 360° circle (flown at a speed of 50 kts and 45° angle of bank) will take 16 seconds (refer to Table 3). This will put 4 fixes on the route trace and leaves us with an almost perfect square for every full circle.

(The same principle applies for gliders with higher wing loadings and faster thermalling speeds. At a speed of 60 kts, for example, a full 45° angle of bank circle takes approx. 20 seconds. Using a recording interval of 5 seconds will provide 4 fixes and the preferred squares again.) Never use recording intervals of more than 5 seconds as it will smooth out the trace and make any subsequent flight analysis significantly more difficult.

Analysing a climb and finding mainly squares on the trace points to consistent flying at the optimum angle of bank and speed. If, however, the shape of the trace changes from a hexagon to a square and back to a pentagon, the pilot flew erratically. Poor speed control or variations in bank angle will have, in all likelihood, contributed to an inferior climb rate. Examples of perfect and less than perfect thermalling are shown in Figure 88.

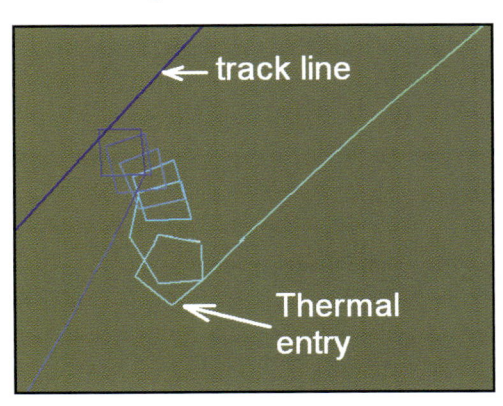

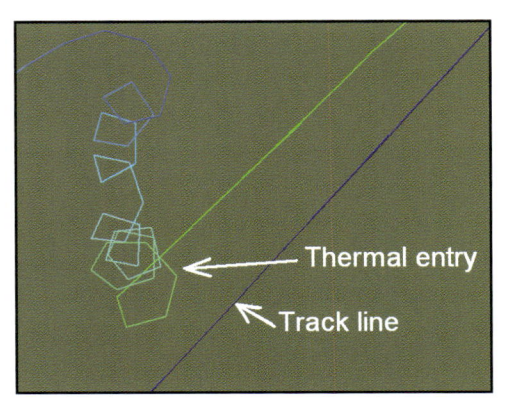

Figure 88: Consistent and erratic thermalling

Advanced cross-country flying

An even more comprehensive assessment can be performed by dividing the time of the entire climb by the number of turns. If the average circle time is higher than 20 seconds per turn the angle of bank is nowhere near the optimum 45°. Imperfect thermalling techniques also show up during a detailed review of the barograph trace. Going back to the main page (Figure 87) and double clicking on the blue bar on top of the barograph window will enlarge the barograph trace. Now we can stretch the trace by repeatedly clicking on the magnifying glass.

Figure 89: Stretching the barograph trace.

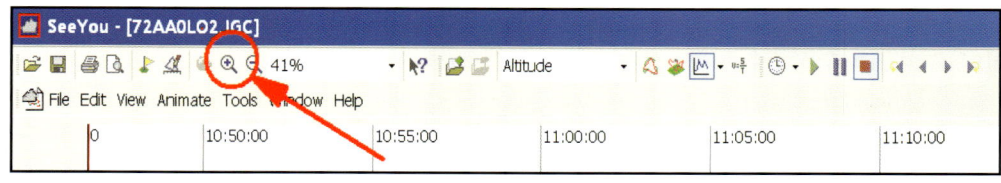

What might appear as a smooth climb at first sight can suddenly look very different. Dropping out of the thermal for only a few seconds will leave a small step on the trace. When this is happening repeatedly and consistently pilots need to work on polishing their thermal centring skills. Some hints can be found in Sections 1.3 to 1.7.

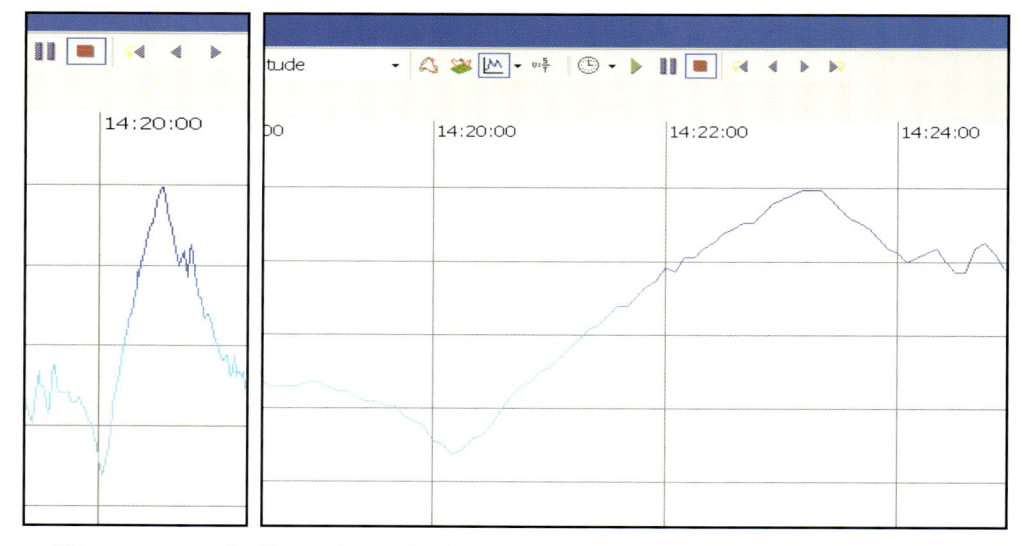

Figure 90: The same climb before and after stretching.

Other common faults such as clinging to a thermal and trying to squeeze everything out of weakening lift are highlighted as well. In the excitement of a flight such habits are less obvious to the pilot and may arise from the wish to operate at the highest possible altitude. During flight analysis on a computer screen these flaws stand out extremely well. The examples below highlight the importance of climb rate monitoring as well as proper thermal entry and exiting techniques.

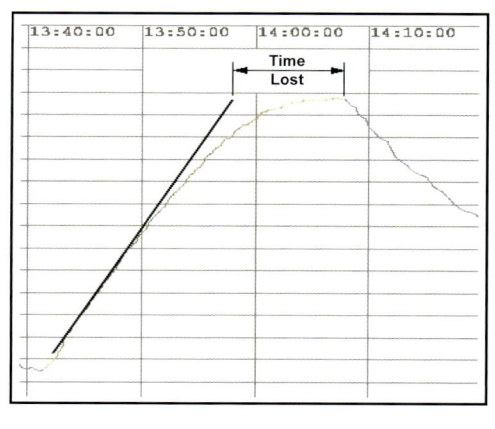

Figure 91: Hanging on to a weakening thermal

Dissect the first half of the barograph trace in figure 90. The thermal was centered quickly and the energy was extracted very efficiently. The pilot did well. It appears that the thermal maintained its full strength for about 80 percent of the climb. However, drawing a straight line on the trace reveals that the thermal was beginning to weaken half way up. The pilot can be forgiven for continuing to use it if the climb rate remained at or above the average for the day.

But what about the last 20 percent of the climb? Should the pilot have left the thermal earlier? Probably yes, unless there was reason to believe that this thermal was the last of the day, perhaps the only way to get to final glide height. The decision to hang on was then justified. The same would be true if the pilot was drifting towards his goal with a strong tailwind prior to crossing a large area of non-landable terrain.

By drawing a straight line on the trace the pilot can quickly determine the accumulated time loss. Cross-country pilots are often surprised when they conduct this exercise and realize the huge impact on the achieved speed. The same applies for poor thermal centring techniques and for taking a long time to get into the core.

Another method of assessing the rate of climb is via the statistics page. (View > Statistics > Phases)

SeeYou - [6B4A0LO2.IGC]

Altitude

File Edit View Animate Tools Window Help

Flight | Task | Selection | Phases

Phase	Begin	End	Duration	Start Alt.	End Alt.	dH	AVario	Netto	AGsp	Avg.IAS	DisDone	D/H
Straight (Tow)	11:09:35	11:10:15	00:00:40	170ft	1377ft	1207ft	17.9kts	18.9kts	83km/h	108km/h	0.9km	-2.5
Straight	11:10:15	11:11:40	00:01:25	1377ft	1157ft	-220ft	-1.5kts	-0.6kts	84km/h	97km/h	2.0km	30
Circling - Mixed	11:11:35	11:16:35	00:05:00	1210ft	1945ft	735ft	1.5kts	2.3kts		95km/h		
Straight	11:16:30	11:17:20	00:00:50	1938ft	1892ft	-46ft	-0.5kts	0.4kts	110km/h	105km/h	1.5km	109
Circling - Right	11:17:15	11:18:35	00:01:20	1886ft	2132ft	246ft	1.8kts	2.8kts		102km/h		
Straight	11:18:30	11:19:20	00:00:50	2145ft	2132ft	-13ft	-0.2kts	0.8kts	112km/h	102km/h	1.6km	388
Circling - Right	11:19:15	11:21:10	00:01:55	2086ft	2424ft	338ft	1.7kts	2.7kts		102km/h		
Straight	11:21:05	11:22:20	00:01:15	2424ft	2309ft	-115ft	-0.9kts	0.3kts	102km/h	122km/h	2.1km	61
Circling - Left	11:22:15	11:23:15	00:01:00	2332ft	2355ft	23ft	0.2kts	1.2kts		107km/h		
Straight	11:23:10	11:25:20	00:02:10	2394ft	2292ft	-102ft	-0.5kts	0.7kts	115km/h	118km/h	4.1km	133
Circling - Right	11:25:15	11:28:10	00:02:55	2302ft	2975ft	673ft	2.3kts	3.2kts		97km/h		
Straight	11:28:05	11:35:32	00:07:27	2975ft	2161ft	-814ft	-1.1kts	0.0kts	116km/h	117km/h	14.4km	58
Circling - Mixed	11:35:27	11:40:47	00:05:20	2092ft	2542ft	449ft	0.8kts	1.8kts		103km/h		
Straight	11:40:42	11:43:58	00:03:16	2558ft	1869ft	-689ft	-2.1kts	-0.9kts	121km/h	124km/h	6.6km	31
Circling - Mixed	11:43:52	11:46:27	00:02:35	1817ft	1899ft	82ft	0.3kts	1.2kts		102km/h		
Straight	11:46:22	11:47:32	00:01:10	1954ft	1794ft	-161ft	-1.4kts	-0.1kts	122km/h	125km/h	2.4km	49
Circling - Left	11:47:28	11:49:18	00:01:50	1764ft	1994ft	230ft	1.2kts	2.1kts		100km/h		
Straight	11:49:12	11:49:32	00:00:20	1968ft	1994ft	26ft	0.8kts	1.8kts	75km/h	109km/h	0.4km	-52
Circling - Right	11:49:27	11:53:52	00:04:25	2017ft	2998ft	981ft	2.2kts	3.1kts		101km/h		

Figure 92: Phases

Here we find not only the average rate of climb for every thermal but also the overall height gain for every climb. Many short climbs near the upper limit of convection require many thermal centring processes. As we seldom place the entire first turn in the core of the thermal this equates to wasting valuable time. A more efficient method of cross-country flying is to use dolphin soaring extracting energy from average lift and circling only in the strongest thermals for a much greater height gain. Put simply, climb in one good thermal instead of three average ones. Tactics like these reduce the thermalling time significantly and hence contribute to more efficient cross-country flying. Pilots who extract the energy in the most effective way are usually the fastest in a competition. (See sections 5.2.2 and 5.2.3).

The statistics page also reveals whether the pilot has a preferred thermalling direction and whether he or she has developed a habit of always turning the same way. If, for example, most turns are to the right the pilot should correct this. The inefficiency of this practice and a proven rectification method were discussed in Section 1.3.

Flight analysis should also be extended to the cruising part of the flight. This is

Advanced cross-country flying

possible as long as we are conscious of the fact that any compelling conclusions can be drawn only after a comparison of several flights performed at the same time and over the same area. SeeYou allows such simultaneous reviews by showing different gliders in different colors and with their altitudes displayed. By synchronizing all the traces to start at the same time (irrespective of their actual start times), less experienced pilots can quickly learn why different decisions or tactics result in vastly different outcomes or speeds.

Even the review of a single flight record can provide a great deal of feedback and lead to better decision making in future. The main topics are meteorological navigation, flight tactics and diversions. Meteorological navigation has already been discussed in section 5.2.6 but modern flight analysis software allows us to determine retrospectively what impact a tactical decision has made on the speed between two points. If, for example, in flight we decided to follow an off-track cloud street we can set a marker on the trace at the beginning and the end of our diversion and obtain the speed for this section of the flight as follows:

1) press & hold 'Shift'.

2) click on the track at the beginning of the diversion.

3) click on the track at the end of the diversion. (A blue and a red dot appear marking the beginning and the end of the flight track under review)

4) Click on View > Statistics > Selection

A statistics page like this will appear.

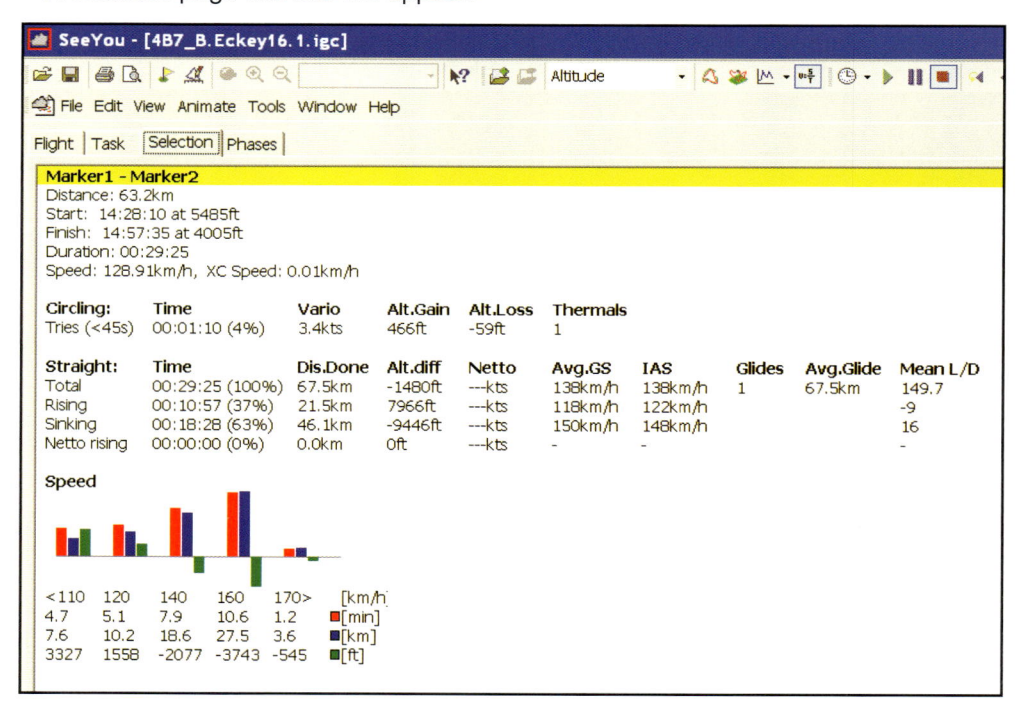

Figure 93: Statistics

Now we are utilizing ready made statistics for a detailed analysis of the flight track between the two markers. The distance between the markers and the achieved speed are displayed in the top left of the window. (Due to the diversion the pilot covered a much greater distance but the speed is calculated for the shortest distance between the markers.)

Was the pilot's decision to follow the cloud street worthwhile or should he have flown to the second marker in a straight line? The answer depends on the strength of the thermal which gets the pilot back to the same altitude. Assume the pilot cruises strictly in accordance with the MacCready theory and manages to remain in neutral air between the two markers. The achieved cross-country speeds for a fully ballasted ASW 28-18 would be as follows:

Table 10: Achieved cross-country speeds and L/Ds for ASW 28-18

Climb rate (kts)	Climb rate (m/s)	Cruise speed (kts)	L/D at this speed	Achieved cross-country speed (km/h)
2	1.0	81	42	76
3	1.5	88	38	92
4	2.1	95	34	104
5	2.6	100	32	113
6	3.1	105	29	122
7	3.6	109	27	129
8	4.1	114	25	141
9	4.6	114	25	142
10	5.1	115	25	144

Now we can see where the break-even point is and which tactical decision proved best. Conducting an exercise like this allows us to draw valuable conclusions and will provide greater confidence for similar tactical decisions in future. (However, a diversion is sometimes necessary just to avoid an outlanding.)

The options for flight analysis between thermals don't end here.

We can also review our cruising performance via the statistics page (See Fig. 93). The D/H column on the far right is a valuable tool. This represents the achieved L/D between thermals and two columns further left we find the average speed for this flight segment. (Avg. IAS = Average Indicated Air Speed).

To determine whether we have been successful in extracting atmospheric energy in cruise we need to compare the achieved L/D with the theoretical L/D of our glider at the same speed. Table 7 shows the L/D figures of a modern Standard Class glider at various speeds. Every foot of altitude not lost in cruise is a foot of altitude that doesn't have to be regained in a thermal and at the expense of time. A negative figure is reason for celebration – it indicates that the pilot gained altitude during the cruise.

To sum it all up, the use of datalogger technology and detailed flight analysis allows pilots to become their own coaches and accelerate their learning.

On final over Lake Keepit
Photo: Geraldine Clark

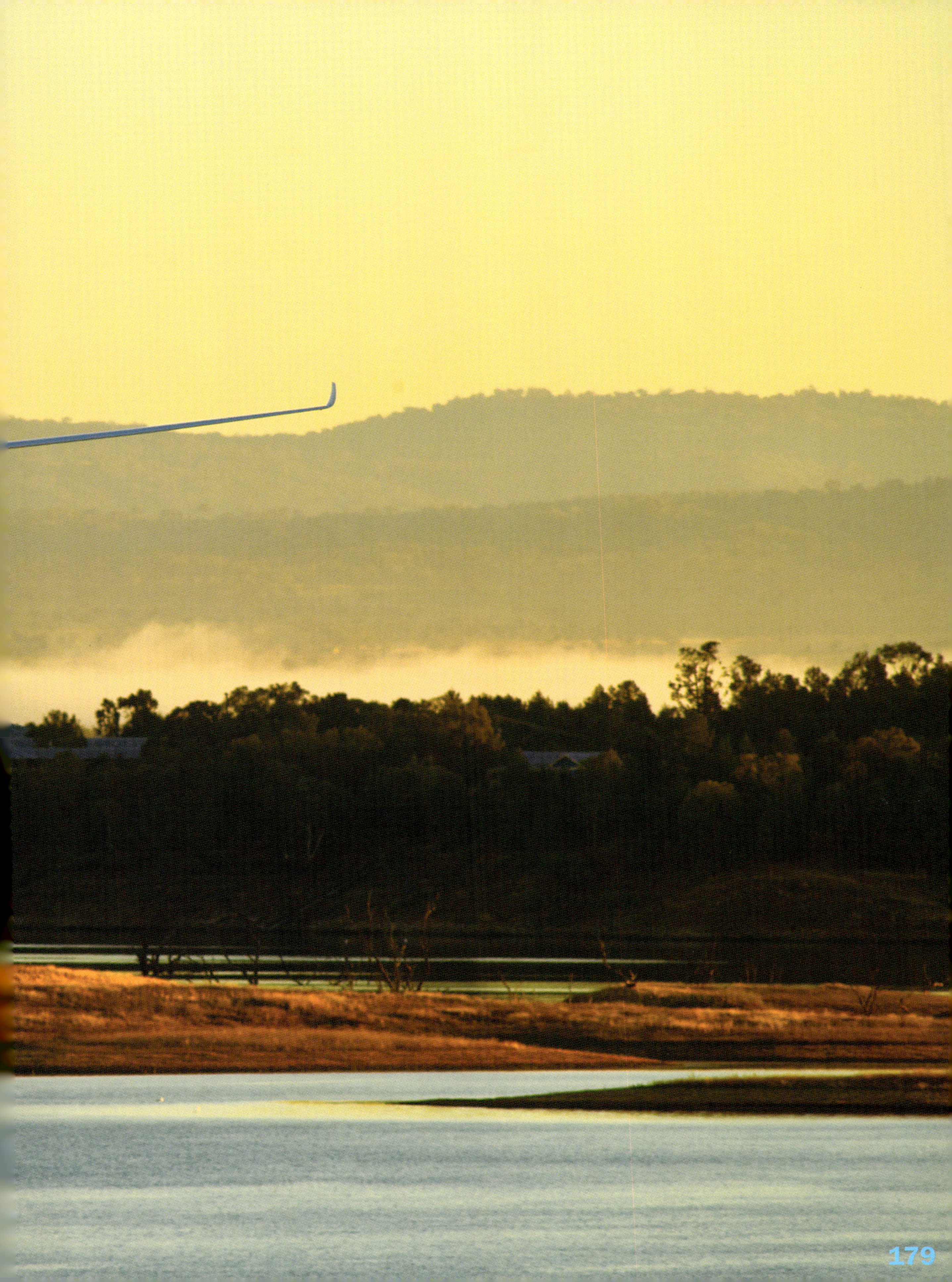

6 Winning the mental game

6.1 Planning.

"**M**ake sure you stay on top of the mental game" said the coach to a novice competition pilot at the beginning of his first regional championship. "Did I hear that right?" you might say, "sport psychology might be the key to success for our much celebrated top athletes, but does it really apply to gliding?" Well, I have news for you! If you think that the mental game is only important in other sports, or if you think that it only applies to top level competition flying, think again!

Flying gliders requires only minimal physical strength, but few other sports demand such lengthy and uninterrupted mental effort. Regardless of whether we are flying cross-country for fun or we are competing in a top level championship we always need to be one step ahead mentally. Sport psychology is just as important as practical skills – especially in difficult or stressful situations. Therefore we will now learn how to master our thought processes, emotions and feelings!

Glider pilots never plan to fail but it is a well known fact that some of them fail to plan. If it is true that the difference between a dream and a goal is a plan then we need to consider some form of planning for an individual pilot and assist with the development of a tailor made plan. In other words, first plan your work and then work your plan. Success is by far more likely if planned and individualised training programs replace haphazard and ad-hoc coaching sessions. Our seasonal sport combined with the uncertainties of gliding weather and the infrequent availability of gliding coaches require very careful medium to long term planning.

Let's consider the case of an ambitious early solo pilot who is exhibiting some weakness (or problems) with soaring. The coach should put together a training plan aimed at further improving the pilot's skill and theoretical knowledge. Developed in close co-operation with the student, the plan must revolve around the various constraints of both student and coach. It should also include suggestions for practising particular skills and a timeframe for future coaching flight(s).

Why is it necessary to go through all this trouble? Well here are some very good reasons for it:

a) A plan puts a goal clearly in front of both student and coach.
b) It will create a performance enhancing environment
c) It allows the student to gauge his or her progress.
d) It sets a realistic time frame for the achievements of goals.
e) It fosters self-satisfaction and confidence.
f) It allows an easy adaptation if unforeseen circumstances develop or a poor soaring season is encountered.

Putting the plan on paper is of prime importance and should be the very next step. But rather than placing it in a drawer it is best kept in a prominent place. There it can be reviewed on a regular, if not daily, basis where it constantly reminds the pilot of his or her goal and the preparations necessary for achieving it.

Not surprisingly there are standard training programs and detailed plans for performance enhancement available for almost all sports - except gliding. The three year training plan on the opposite page is an attempt to change this.

Three year training plan

Name of Pilot:

Time frame	Year 1		Year 2		Year 3	
	Intermediate step	Date of completion	Intermediate step	Date of completion	Intermediate step	Date of completion
Quarter season						
Mid season						
3/4 season						
START HERE	Goal for 1st season:		Goal for 2nd season:		Goal for 3rd season:	

Let's look at the plan in detail. The first step is to insert the pilot's goal for each soaring season at the bottom of the plan. Please note that it is the coached person who determines the goal and not the coach. Financial constraints, family commitments and other limitations on the available time can best be assessed by the trainee pilot and although the coach's recommendations should take a trainee's possible under- or overconfidence into account they are just that – mere recommendations.

The next step is to insert the "stepping stones" for achieving the season's goals. This is where the coach's input is most valuable. Based on the skill level of the pilot in question the coach should provide guidance not only on the timing but if possible also on the sequence of the various intermediate goals. After all that is done student and coach have a blueprint for the pilot's continued development with direction and focus. Now we only need to implement the tailor made training program, monitor it and modify it if and when changing circumstances dictate it.

6.2 Positive thinking

Avoiding success is simple; all we need to do is to allow ourselves to slip into a negative frame of mind. When we find ourselves in a difficult situation and decide that it is all too hard, or that the challenge ahead is far too great, we are on the fast track to failure. Fear of failure impedes the realisation of our potential. If deep down we fear defeat, we have already lost before we have even started. The misery is self-inflicted – we have succumbed to the power of negative thinking.

As with any other endeavour, a negative frame of mind must be turned into a positive one and this holds especially true if you want to have success in gliding, because a negative or defeatist attitude and poor performance go hand in hand.

But let's not dwell on negative thinking for too long – we don't want to waste time. And anyhow, all of this does not apply to you – you are the fortunate type of person with a positive mental attitude. If this is the case, let me congratulate you. You are made for success and you can just skip over this chapter.

**A self launch into a murky Japanese sky
Photo:
Hiroshi Seo**

Winning the mental game

Only if on occasions you slip into a negative frame of mind, feel free to read on. A negative frame of mind can be turned into a positive one with a plan; with a good dose of willpower and with determination. Provided you do it properly, and provided you are realistic, you will not only improve your gliding but also change your life for the better. Yes, the right mindset will have benefits far beyond your chosen sport and will impact positively on many other aspects of everyday life. Surely, that's enough incentive to give it a go, but the question is where do you start?

Well, the first step is to be realistic when it comes to motivating yourself. You can't expect to break a world record on your very next attempt or become the next world gliding champion overnight. It's just not reasonable and therefore bound to end in disappointment. Be more realistic and set yourself an achievable goal. An early solo pilot, for example, can aim for a one-hour soaring flight but for a more advanced pilot a sensible goal might be a 500 km badge. But whatever you do, you must believe in your abilities and you must be determined to become an achiever. I know, it's easier said than done, but success is not achieved by settling into familiar patterns of behaviour. To climb the ladder of success, a negative mindset must be turned around. Sure, we all get discouraged from time to time, but how we deal with it is what matters most. We need to get our mind into a winning mode and redirect it towards success. Every time a negative thought enters your mind respond with a positive one.

Concentrate on achievements and focus on successful outcomes. That is what positive thinking is all about. By adopting positive thinking, you not only motivate yourself but, simultaneously, others around you. A totally new atmosphere is created, one that breeds success, one of accomplishments and one that fellow pilots will want to embrace.

Positive thinking must be combined with problem-solving skills and the knowledge that the solution to the great majority of problems is to break them down into smaller ones. Put simply, overcome one small obstacle at a time and think of what you have learned while reading this book. You have no excuse any longer – it contains all you need to know.

If you hit any obstacle, it is just a matter of remembering the relevant hints or suggestions and then implementing the solutions. If you are facing in the right direction, all you have to do is keep walking. If the solution to your problem doesn't come to mind straight away, read the relevant section of this book again but, whatever you do just do not give up on positive thinking.

Talk to yourself and reaffirm that you will manage this challenge and pass the test with flying colours. Practising positive self-talk isn't a lot of hot air – it is essential for gaining the frame of mind necessary for success. Replace negative thoughts with positive ones on every possible occasion. While flying locally, believe in your knowledge and your ability to find a thermal and successfully work the lift. When flying cross-country, have the willpower and determination to make it around the task even in the most demanding of conditions. Not once, not twice, but every time you step into a glider.

6.3 Making decisions

Everything a glider pilot does must be done for a reason. There is no exception to this rule. Doing something for no particular reason is relying on good fortune rather than good management. Smart decision making, followed by prompt implementation, usually makes the difference between success and disappointment. But in our sport the choices are seldom clear cut, necessitating that benefits and consequences are weighted up carefully.

Winning the mental game

In cruise over the Australian outback

Have you ever noticed that switched on glider pilots are continually gathering information? The reason is simple and doesn't need much elaboration! If we don't want to rely on good luck our decision making must be underpinned by first class observation and a careful evaluation of all available information. It goes without saying that prompt implementation is a logical conclusion. Procrastination must never be allowed to get the upper hand in gliding.

The advantages of information gathering also extend to the subconscious level. With growing experience hundreds of additional and seemingly insignificant items are noticed and stored subconsciously. Far from useless, they greatly assist our intuition – our 'gut feeling' so to speak. Heavily relying on intuition when rational thinking doesn't dictate a clear path of action is a trademark of thriving people and is particularly common amongst successful glider pilots.

Even the greatest minds of all times freely admit that rational thinking was accompanied by intuition for some of history's greatest discoveries or breakthroughs. Be careful though – never let intuition overrule facts and logical thinking and don't confuse intuition with impulsive decisions. They are often taken in haste and stem from anger due to a lack of alternatives.

How does all of this apply to a pilot preparing for local soaring? Observing a few launches and closely watching other gliders, smoke or soaring birds is just as much part of the observation process as noticing areas of lift or strong sink. Indications like these are vital and must be memorised.

Other equally important clues are provided by the windsock, the vegetation and the topography. This is especially so if the wind's strength and direction have a strong effect on local sources of lift and known thermal triggers. Every possible hint is taken into account and that includes drawing on local knowledge and past experiences. The more observations, the better!

Decision making in a competition environment takes on a totally different meaning. Observations must become broader by an order of magnitude and this includes an assessment of flying conditions as far as 50 km ahead. Only pilots who keep their eyes out of the cockpit can evaluate weather and terrain correctly and stand a chance to adapt their flying tactics accordingly. Well before arriving anywhere near a turn point we should consider the flying conditions on the next leg and include a good cloud assessment in this process. Concentration must be at peak level, especially when tactical considerations enter the fray. Sound knowledge and experience make the job easier but intense concentration for 5 or 6 hours per day over a two-week period is very hard work indeed. No wonder that even experienced cross-country pilots buckle under the pressure and often come apart under competition stress. Pressure may be part and parcel of competition flying but it must not lead to greatly diminished observations and reduced decision making. If it does, it is very easy to confuse bad luck with bad judgement.

Observations and fact finding also extends to pilot briefings – and weather briefings in particular. Especially at high level competitions the interpretation of weather data is often left to the pilot. Therefore, a study of synoptic charts with an independent assessment of possible changes to soaring conditions should become part of every pilot's pre take-off weather observation process.

Considerations like these dictate the time frame for the best soaring conditions and have a strong bearing on the optimum time for a start. (Refer to Section 7.4.) A frequent reassessment of decisions is just as vital. Top pilots continually evaluate previous actions regardless of whether they have proven successful or not. Here are a few examples for the thermalling part of a flight:

- Adjust the angle of bank
- Correct nose/horizon attitude
- Use more (or less) rudder
- Adjust airspeed
- Check flap setting (if applicable)
- Re-evaluate thermal strength
- Decide when to leave the thermal

If we don't reassess our decisions every 15 seconds or so while thermalling we are likely to be left behind. The winner of a race (or a whole competition for that matter) is usually the pilot who spends the least amount of time circling.

Conducting a similar exercise for the cruising part of the flight, the list we would include such things as:

- Heading changes to ensure better extraction of atmospheric energy
- Circumnavigating areas of over-development
- Speed adjustments in areas of lift or sink
- Detours to sample areas marked by soaring birds
- Bypassing irrigation areas
- Cruise speed variations in view of improving or deteriorating conditions

Of course, we can't expect all our decisions to be right. But if we want to improve we had better keep working on this aspect of our flying and aim for as high a percentage of correct decisions as possible.

The quality of the equipment and the skills of our top pilots are almost identical these days, but even at world championship level we see a significant point spread on the score sheet at the end of a contest. It is therefore fair to surmise that smart decision making is the deciding factor. Lady luck may favour a pilot on occasions but have you ever noticed that the same pilots usually have all the luck? The more decisions they make the better their chances of getting things right - and the luckier they get! And finally a word of wisdom! Making no decision is the worst decision a glider pilot can ever make.

6.4 Thinking ahead

When we learned to fly, our instructors undoubtedly told us to expect the unexpected. Another aircraft appearing out of the blue, changing weather conditions, a tailwind springing up on short final, just to mention a few. If we are prepared for the unexpected we can cope much better when difficult situations arise.

Take the matter one step further and always mentally prepare for the next stage of the flight or the next decision to be made. This thinking ahead is absolutely essential for safe and successful soaring. The sooner we start thinking about the next decision, the better are our chances of getting it right. Being mentally "one step ahead" often makes the difference between success and failure.

Excitement in Patagonia Photo: Dr. Rick Agnew

As an example, say that we are in a strong climb under a cumulus cloud and are approaching cloud base rapidly. We have only a few seconds before we must leave the thermal and we have to decide on our next course of action. We have deprived ourselves of the opportunity to make a calculated and balanced choice on the options available to us because we have left the decision rather late.

If, on the other hand, we start our decision-making process well before we reach cloud base we are much better off. We can pick the most promising cloud and have a much better chance of finding the next strong thermal without delay. Further, we can take into account matters relating to navigation and the optimum track across the ground.

Few rushed "ad hoc" decisions are likely to be good ones just as split-second decisions are unlikely to be perfect.

6.5 Concentration and relaxation

Concentration is the art of focussing on the right thing at the right time. Few other areas are as important. The very safety of a flight depends to a large degree on the ability of the pilot to concentrate until the aircraft is back on the ground or, better still, back in the hangar. On some flights, we can't relax for a single minute, while on others we can afford to sit back and admire the view. The need to concentrate fully also depends on whether we fly competitively or whether we conduct local soaring and fly just for the fun of it. This statement doesn't imply disrespect for pilots conducting local soaring, but local soaring requires nowhere near as much concentration as a cross-country flight. The necessary level of concentration also depends very much on the various stages of the flight. Apart from takeoff and landing, our utmost concentration is required while low and in need of a thermal. Maintaining such a high level of concentration is hardly possible over a long period. For this reason, it becomes important to regulate concentration and arousal levels especially during long-distance flights.

Most of us have little trouble concentrating while the task on hand is progressing as expected. We run on automatic – in "cruise control" so to speak. Our mind is clear to focus on the broader issues and we feel relaxed in the knowledge that we have the situation nicely under control. Scientists call this the 'Ideal Performance State' (IPS). In other words, as long as everything is running smoothly, humans are in a frame of mind which ensures that an appropriate level of concentration is maintained. This occurs without any great input on the part of the individual.

But things can change rapidly when we get distracted or stressed. External distractions from other people, the environment, equipment problems, incomplete preparation etc. are just as detrimental as internal distractions from our own mind such as emotions, mental baggage and the like. As soon as our arousal level changes (or we get very nervous or feel particularly anxious) we move away from our IPS. Things get even worse when stress – our greatest enemy – takes over. Understanding what causes stress is vital when it comes to coping with it and successfully managing it.

Stress occurs in two stages.

Stage 1 – Trigger.

The trigger to stress is our reaction to something. The examples in gliding are plentiful. If, for example, we experience very strong sink and get alarmingly close to an outlanding (perhaps even over difficult terrain) stage 2 will be triggered automatically.

Stage 2 – Arousal.

Our body reacts instantly by releasing a complex combination of stress hormones. They ensure that all available blood is directed towards our muscles and our body gets ready for an inherent 'fight or flight' response. Little blood is left for the brain which means that our mental capacity and our concentration levels become mismatched to the task on hand. We become overloaded and as a result we usually experience a highly significant drop in performance. (Refer to Section 7.7).

All individuals have their own concentration styles or characteristic ways of focussing on the job at hand. For example, some pilots function well under pressure while others don't handle high situational demands very well and become easily confused or overloaded. Overload situations occur when too many things are going on at the same time and pilots are unsure what their priorities should be. Countless thoughts are rushing through their heads and there are just too many points to think about. For an inexperienced pilot task prioritisation can easily become too complex and it is common for old, bad habits to creep back in or for mistakes to occur. However, experienced pilots are less likely to suffer from overload situations. They can ignore irrelevant information and block out distractions while executing proven solutions learned during similar situations in the past.

Some exceptional pilots have acquired the ability to switch to a narrow type of concentration and focus on nothing but an answer to a specific predicament. Analytical thinking and the ability to come up with alternative solutions is a very important skill in gliding and comes handy in situations where our attention needs to be directed towards critical operational demands. After a particular crisis has been satisfactorily resolved these pilots can switch back to a broader type of focus again. Needless to say that people possessing the technique to adapt their concentration levels as required greatly increase their chances of a superior performance.

6.5.1 Adjusting concentration levels to specific in-flight situations.

Experienced pilots know that even long phases of brilliance can never make up for short periods of poor concentration. They also know that peak concentration is neither possible nor required at all times. After a good climb back to a comfortable altitude, or when conditions ahead give no reason for concern, we can and should relax a little. In situations like these we can reaffirm to ourselves that we have the situation nicely under control. After re-trimming the glider we can eat an apple, take a bite from a sandwich, have a drink, or simply find time for a position report.

The situation is fundamentally different when we are in any form of tricky in-flight situation. Because high levels of concentration are required in these circumstances we must employ thought control techniques and arousal control skills as discussed below.

6.5.2 Relaxation

What can we do to avoid excessive tension build-up and how can we relax or remain relaxed during critical in-flight situations? One of the first things to happen to our body in a stressful situation is a tensioning of muscles in preparation to a 'fight or flight' response. At the same time there is a release of adrenalin and an increase in the rate of breathing to meet the extra demand for oxygen. Although these are automatic body responses we must direct our attention towards these functions. Two proven methods are described below.

A) Controlling our breathing.

This is of great value in relaxation. People at ease with themselves and the world breathe slowly, deeply and rhythmically. Fortunately we can control our breathing and therefore we can, at least for a short time, override our automatic body functions and take conscious control of it by inhaling deeply and slowly through the nose. We concentrate on the movement of our chest and inhale very deeply indeed, but unforced and unhurried. Whilst slowly breathing in, we count to four or five and when the inhalation is complete we pause for about two seconds. As we exhale very slowly through the nose we count to four or five again. Exhalation should take at least as long as inhalation.

Of course, we need to repeat the exercise a few times and when we feel the first positive results it is helpful to say to ourselves that our breathing has become calm, deep and regular. Intrusive thoughts might periodically come into our mind to interrupt the smooth flow of this technique. This is quite normal. We just refocus on our slow breathing (and counting) as we resume the exercise and carry on where we left off. Only after a short period of time we will find that we markedly unwind and significantly reduce our level of tension.

B) Progressive muscle relaxation.

Again, the objective is to relax on cue but this method is less suitable for use in an aircraft as it takes longer and could therefore become a safety issue. For this reason it should only be undertaken prior to a flight or in a two-seater. The technique requires a deliberate tensioning of muscle groups for as long as it takes to feel the tension generated. After about 6-8 seconds we clearly notice how that feels. Now we relax this particular muscle group while paying attention to the contrasting feeling. Repeating the exercise several times and doing the same thing to other parts of the body (especially tense shoulders or neck muscles) is bound to lead to mental relaxation which in turn allows us to regulate concentration and arousal levels.

As for any other skill, these techniques need to be practiced and rehearsed to benefit from, if and when the going gets tough. Without prior practicing on the ground, pilots will find it hard to implement these suggestions properly and might not get the desired results. However, I want to assure you that the results will be worth the effort for the patient and committed glider pilot.

Gliding is all about information gathering, drawing the correct conclusions and implementing appropriate decisions. Being able to deal with a large number of inputs at one time is of vital importance for performance enhancement. A pilot who is able to concentrate in a focussed way while blocking out distractions is well prepared for success and safety. One reason why a five-hour flight remains part of the Silver C certificate is to test mental stamina. If glider pilots think of things other than the job at hand they are not concentrating enough. Fluctuations in concentration can often be traced back to unsuitable nutrition or dehydration, so be sure to attend to this first. (Refer to Section 3.3.)

Duo Discus near Mt. Cook (NZ)
Photo: Bill Verco

6.6 Learn how to learn

When you are really in love with an inspiring sport like gliding you will develop an almost insatiable appetite for increasing your knowledge of the subject. The more you know about gliding the more you want to learn about it and an upward spiral of understanding develops. Some pilots learn best by reading, detailed explanation and coaching while others learn mainly by practice. Regardless of the method, the acquired knowledge is necessary and vital for success.

After you have attained an advanced level you can learn without instructors or coaches. You are no longer dependant on others and by mastering the art of self-education you find success. The road to success is never straight and often full of potholes. Failure is an element of learning and bouncing back is critically important. There is nothing wrong with making the odd mistake as long as we admit it, learn from it, and strive for future improvement. No glider pilot has made it to the top without persistence and a string of failures along the way. And one more point for consideration. If you are socialising with achievers you will become an achiever by adopting the attitude of achievers.

6.7 Confidence and over-confidence

Unshakable confidence in your own skills is undoubtedly of utmost importance for success in any sport but when it comes to gliding it is of particular relevance. Regardless of whether we look at the sport from a competition aspect or just from a recreational perspective it shows time and time again that success and a healthy dose of confidence go hand in hand.

That said, I'm quick to add that we can only expect pilots to be confident if their ability matches the task at hand. An early solo pilot lacking confidence in his or her own soaring skills is unlikely to keep a glider up for any length of time. Equally, a cross-country pilot with insufficient confidence will either turn around at the first sign of trouble or outland frequently. But confidence only develops with repeated and regular successes. Unfortunately this psychological aspect of our sport is often under-estimated. How can low-confidence pilots get on the road to success? Here are a few suggestions for the early solo pilot.

- Choose to fly when the conditions are not too difficult – nothing is more disheartening than performing three consecutive circuits only to see your fellow club member climb into the same glider during the better part of the day and disappear for a lengthy flight.
- Ask your coach (or a pilot with proven soaring skills) to fly with you in a two-seater, share the flying and copy soaring techniques which have proven successful.
- When flying single seaters, follow a pilot with proven soaring skills and take mental notes on where he locates the lift and how he centres the thermal.

For budding cross country pilots the following suggestions might prove to be confidence boosters.

- Deliberately move just beyond the gliding range of your airfield. Making it back is bound to make a profound contribution to increased levels of confidence. Making it back easily will instil a real sense of achievement and hopefully encourage you to repeat such a success at the very next available opportunity.

Winning the mental game

- **Fly on days when other pilots choose to spend the afternoon in the clubhouse. Successfully keeping the glider airborne will boost your confidence levels and you will be better able to rely on your own skill and judgement.**

- **Never make the same mistake twice. It's not only the dumbest think one can ever do but it is also a frequent reason for disappointment and a consequent lack of confidence.**

- **Analyse less successful flights even more thoroughly than successful ones in a bid to avoid the decisions which have lead to an undesirable outcome.**

Now let's briefly turn our attention to over-confidence. There are pilots who, after a successful flight or two, seem to think they know it all. In their own minds, they are ready for long-distance flying and believe that records are no longer safe as soon as they get access to a competitive glider.

These pilots need just as much help as their more timid counterparts. Disappointment is waiting around the corner and may lead them to drop out of the sport very early without the successes they imagined. When over-confidence is paired with disregard for safety, the alarm bells must ring. An attitude such as "Regulations are for others to adhere to" and "I'm too good, an accident won't happen to me!" is a sure recipe for disaster.

Coming home at sunset. Photo: Courtesy of Diamond Aircraft

A confident pilot can properly assess his own abilities and limitations, and may sometimes say "NO" in a marginal situation. This is by no means equivalent to an admission of inadequacy, but points to a realistic, responsible and mature attitude.

6.8 Mental rehearsals

If we ask men or women occupying the top rankings in their respective sports they are usually adamant that winning happens almost exclusively in the head. Many of us wrongly interpret such comments as a reflection on the individual's intelligence and some of us immediately throw in the towel thinking that their intellect is not on par with these famous and highly celebrated athletes. In reality, however, intelligence plays only a minor roll. What really matters is that (parallel to the necessary physical skills) athletes have worked on their brain or, more precisely, on the processing capabilities of it. The result is an almost automatic implementation of appropriate responses through well established neuro-muscular pathways.

This can be applied to gliding and in particular to competition soaring. For example, daily winners of gliding competitions usually report on a very harmonious and effortless flight which turned out, for them, to be surprisingly easy and straight forward. They have made a thorough flight preparation incorporating a prior visualisation of the flight. These pilots have repeatedly performed the task with all its possible challenges and opportunities well before stepping into their glider.

What works well for competition pilots should be good enough for the rest of us. Practising gliding skills doesn't have to come to an end when we step out of a glider. On the contrary, all skills can (and should) be mentally refined and rehearsed between training flights. Such practice can be fitted into the busiest daily schedule and can be done more often than we think. If we are honest, we have numerous daily opportunities for practicing mental rehearsals.

Mental rehearsal is building successful repetitions of a performance segment by constructive use of your imagination. The first step is to select a quiet place and eliminate all possible distractions. Make yourself comfortable and close your eyes before you concentrate on visualising a specific flight situation. This can be achieved by imagining a scenario as seen through our eyes, as felt through our limbs, and as heard through our ears. For maximum benefit use your hands and feet to simulate moving stick and rudder!

Most pilots have a tendency of refining skills that they are already good at and they dislike practicing things in which they are less proficient. However, bad habits need more work. Implementing the new response mentally is part of your mental rehearsal process. Keep repeating the exercise and use every opportunity to perfect the skill in your own mind. The more positive repetitions you have completed, the better you will cope with a situation when it next arises

**Not a UFO but a spectacular wave cloud in South America
Photo:
Dr. Rick Agnew**

6.9 Commitment

We are spoilt for choice when it comes to aviation activities, but for very good reasons we have decided on gliding. But gliding is a time-consuming sport and family or friends often apply pressure to spend more time with them, or on other non-gliding activities. Unfortunately, spare time is often in short supply and therefore we are often forced into a delicate balancing act. However, especially during post-solo training it is absolutely essential to place gliding on top of our list of priorities until a level of proficiency is reached which allows a quick and trouble-free return to our sport if and when desired.

Failing to draw on our commitment to the sport and failing to prioritise in favour of gliding is all too often the reason for slow progress or even drop-outs. Making two steps forward and one step back is undesirable in any sport, but in gliding it is especially counterproductive. We must be quick to capitalise on opportunities for skill enhancement – a critically important issue during the early part of our gliding careers. Every now and then we must take ourselves aside and investigate whether our commitment is as high as it should be.

Commitment to achievement and progress is influenced by external and internal sources. Role models, coaches, friends, team mates and a host of other people are prime examples of external influences. If we socialise with dedicated glider pilots we are putting ourselves into an environment which is likely to lift our level of commitment. Mixing with top achievers will further benefit our level of commitment and will provide additional learning opportunities. Positive experiences or unexpected success can also energise us and become extremely powerful motivators. Meeting a gliding hero in person and learning from him or her is also sure to positively influence our commitment to gliding.

When it comes to internal sources for commitment, we have to draw on our own inner being. Usually the strongest and most consistent form of motivation and commitment comes from within us. Commitment is something personal and is related to what an individual would desperately like to achieve. Therefore our internal 'fire and drive' is a much better motivator than any of the above external sources.

If we keep the 'big picture' first and foremost in our mind and focus on enhancing our skills through regular and ongoing training we will pass up any temptations for distractions. We will eventually be rewarded by the many wonderful experiences that gliding offers to those who have acquired above-average skill and knowledge.

Possessing and implementing the highest level of commitment is what our top pilots do in preparation for tasks such as international competitions and record flights. It makes these pilots different to most others but being successful at this level is all about being better than others. Top achievers simply do things more thoroughly and professionally than everyone else and an undivided commitment is a big part of this. Our sport tends to reward deeply committed pilots by better flights.

6.10 Setting a goal and achieving it.

We will consider the subject further while discussing planning. (Refer 7.1) Now let us see how we can set a goal and how we can best achieve it. None of us is likely to invest a great deal of effort into a task with little or no chance of succeeding. So the first step is to set a realistic goal – one that we feel is within our reach.

The achievement orientated pilot tends to set difficult but doable tasks for himself while others tend to set themselves goals that are much easier to accomplish. Setting a goal such as winning the next championship is counterproductive as it is dependent on many external factors such as the strength of other competitors, equipment failures and perhaps the weather. Set a goal that is entirely within your own control. Ideally such goals should pull you out of your comfort zone and provide positive motivation. It follows that you need to develop a plan, because if you fail to plan you plan to fail.

Let me share my plan with you right now.

At first concentrate on one (1) particular aspect of your flying and pick a skill that you think could do with some enhancement. The next step is to <u>WRITE IT DOWN</u> and put it in a place where you see it at least once a day. Once you have done that, forget about all other possible areas of improvement in your flying, the decision has been made and you will stick with it. Do not get distracted, but focus on one skill refinement to the temporary exclusion of all others. Of course, this does not mean that you relax on safety or ignore the lessons learned during basic training, but it does mean that every opportunity must be used to increase your skill level in this particular area.

Let us look at an example together.

Say you have resolved to work on your angle of bank. Perhaps you have learned that you can improve your rate of climb just by optimising the angle of bank and you have also come to realise that you are usually thermalling at too shallow an angle. Now you have a realistic goal and you have just completed step one of your exercise. You can now move on to "stage two" where you collect information on the subject and polish up on your theory. Theoretical knowledge ensures that you don't have to go by trial and error but simply implement what very experienced and seasoned glider pilots have collated and written down in good books or gliding magazines.

As luck would have it, it just so happens that the subject of bank-angle optimisation was covered in detail earlier in this book. All you have to do is to spend an evening (or two) digesting it.

You have now completed "stage two" of your exercise without even stepping into a glider. It has cost nothing and you have already absorbed a lot of background information. In "stage three" you simply put theory into practice. You implement what you have identified as the correct course of action but also learn from your mistakes. Try as you might, sometimes you fall back into your old bad habits, but – with a bit of thought – you quickly remind yourself that there are better and more efficient ways of thermalling. Bad habits are often deeply ingrained and it is only too easy to give up. Obviously, you tell yourself, you are not made of the right stuff. Maybe other pilots can do it, but I just don't have the willpower to go through with it.

Nonsense!!! We are all humans and we all make mistakes, but the difference between success and failure is persistence. Don't be discouraged. When you return from a training flight, realise that you were too busy just trying to stay airborne and you did not find the time to experiment with a steeper angle of bank. There will be another opportunity next week or the week after – just don't give up, simply resolve to attempt it again next time. If this appears too pedantic and you think you can work on more than one skill simultaneously – think again. I have seen glider pilots with world records to their credit but with a note stuck to the instrument panel on a training flight. The note simply served as a reminder to focus on one particular aspect of their flying – very convincing indeed.

6.11 Our mood and its effects on performance.

Have you ever experienced a day when you thought that it would have been better not to get out of bed? Just too many things tend to go wrong! We feel "down" and conclude that we are having a "bad day", but in contrast there are days when we feel "just great". Obviously our assessment is highly dependant on our emotional state.

Most of us think that it is difficult, or even impossible, to change the mood we are in and some of us allow our mood to take control of our mental state. Clearly, there is a relationship between how we feel and how we perform. By learning to manipulate our mood we can bring about some positive performance changes. To perform great we must feel great!

Research has identified six dominant mood states. Separating them in terms of positive or negative contribution to performance we find that tension, depression, anger, fatigue and confusion are clearly detrimental, but vigour stands out as an extremely beneficial contributor. If we develop a better self-awareness of these moods we can assess ourselves more accurately and successfully implement some mental changes. The aim is to turn a negative frame of mind into a positive one.

Let's look at these contributors one by one.

Tension

A proven method to combat tension and anxiety in a competitive environment is not to focus on the outcome, but on the task at hand. As we have seen in Section 6.8 the outcome is always dependant on some external factors, such as the strength of our competitors. By focusing on performing to the best of our ability, we will not only stand a good chance to do well but also eliminate a lot of counter-productive mental ballast. Physical and mental relaxation (refer to Section 6.5) can also play a major role in tension and anxiety control.

Depression

Depression is an alteration in the brain's chemistry and is an increasingly serious health problem in western society. A pilot who is seriously depressed has no business flying until he or she has had treatment.

Temporary bouts of feeling down or bad is also commonly referred to as depression and that's what we are considering in this context. Glider pilots are not immune and need to combat such unhelpful mind-sets for optimum performance. By fortifying ourselves with our favourite piece of music, or a dose of recorded humour (or even from friends or members of our crew) we can manually over-ride those undesirable feelings. Positive imagery from past great performances is also a well-proven method and so are vivid memories of some enjoyable surroundings or favourite places. (For additional information on positive thinking refer to Sections 6.2 and 6.5.)

Anger

An anger-induced bad mood is also highly detrimental to performance for the vast majority of aviators. I say majority because some pilots are known to perform better while feeling a reasonable amount of anger. As this is an exception rather than the rule, we will not elaborate further other than to say that any anger or hostility must be well-focused and must not be allowed to become a safety issue. A technique called "parking" has proven to be the best solution for dealing with anger in a competition environment. It allows pilots to put the issue in the back of their minds, deal with it at a later stage and refocus on the task at hand. Humour or calming music are also well-proven methods for anger control.

Fatigue

Research has demonstrated that fatigue and poor decision making are closely related and feelings of fatigue and bad mood go also hand-in-hand. Genuine fatigue can have many reasons (refer to Section 3.3) but perceived fatigue is what we are considering here. To overcome the onset, we undertake some positive action and by doing so we can override our own mindset. We simply need to resume control over the way we think and remember that we feel fatigued when we focus on how tired we are. By concentrating on positive things and by focusing on the rewards from a successful outcome we can turn this negative mood into a feeling of excitement and confident anticipation.

Confusion

Uncertainty and insufficient preparation are major contributors to confusion in gliding. This confusion often leads to elevated levels of arousal through increased excitement and internal overload. If too much is going on in the pilot's head and if the high workload of competition flying is intensified by the need to rush through some final preparations, the stage is set for a mood-induced performance low. In particular, less experienced pilots competing at a new venue for the first time need to be aware of these traps. (Refer to Section 3.3, Equipment, 7P rule).

**Grob 109 over Mt. Fuji (Japan)
Photo: Hiroshi Seo**

Vigour

Vigour is a positive contributor to performance but extremely low levels of it are highly detrimental to achievement in gliding. A lack of incentive to perform well, or insufficient alertness can allow the mind to meander or even shut down altogether. The result is a less than ideal or even disappointing performance.

Personal energising techniques, such as strong and positive self-talk, can re-establish just the right amount of vigour and bring the pilot back into the mood for optimum performance. The same problem can occur when pilots are too stressed or burned out. In situations like these the mind just shuts down as it is incapable of absorbing any more stress. The only strategy to reactivate drive and vigour is to reduce stress levels by relaxation or a break from competition.

To sum it up, understanding the subject of mood control is vital for success and so is the ability to acquire the right mental attitude. Not every pilot is blessed with a stable mood including psychological fitness and emotional balance. However, knowing how to control these factors when necessary will give ambitious pilots the edge in any endeavour.

6.12 Formula for success

There are glider pilots who HOPE that things will happen, there are others who EXPECT things to happen and a select few who MAKE THINGS HAPPEN.

You have read through a large part of the book and already learned quite a few things about thermals, thermalling and cross-country flying. You have rolled up your sleeves and you have started – perhaps you have even identified areas of weakness and you have resolved that you will concentrate on improving one or two skills in particular.

You are on the right track; you are a person that makes things happen. Don't worry if the first weeks or months do not show immediate results. You have embarked on a long and difficult road with every chance of an occasional setback. But if you persist you will begin to see the benefits before long. You have every right to feel confident, you can step into a glider with a more positive attitude, and be assured that you have done all you can to succeed.

What we need to do first, though, is to give you some inside secrets for keeping on track. You might be lucky and have instant success when you try some of the suggestions, but it is more likely that you will not hit the jackpot on the first few attempts. There could be a number of reasons why your early attempts aren't met with success, but it is vital to persevere and try again. Winners never quit and quitters most certainly never win. Giving up after a few unsuccessful attempts is just like getting a prescription for 100 pills to cure a longstanding ailment but then throwing the pills away after taking only two or three just because they have not shown the desired effect immediately.

You can have every confidence that you are on the right path – you have read the book and you have acquired some vital background knowledge. You now have the pills in your pocket and as long as you don't forget to take them you will succeed – no question at all.

6.13 Analysing your flight

How often have you faced a tricky situation in the air and wished you had the right answer to a particular question or problem? "If only", you say to yourself, "I could think of the hints or suggestions I read some time ago, and quickly apply the solution right now, the chances of getting out of my current predicament would be much improved".

Well, if this story sounds familiar, you are not alone. The high workload of a cross-country flight, or perhaps even the added pressure of a threatening outlanding, makes it very hard to remain cool, focus on the problem and apply the correct measures. When you return from such a flight you have two options. Either you quickly forget the experience or you find a few moments to analyse the flight and find out what could have been done better. In some cases, this involves re-reading of the gliding literature but in others it is just a matter of standing back, reflecting on the flight and the decisions made prior to getting into trouble.

More often than not, the reasons become obvious and are very plain to see with the benefit of hindsight. However, in some cases this soul-searching exercise involves

Impressions of winter flying in Australia

(Photos courtesy of Simon Dallinger)

7 Flying competitively

7.1 Choosing a competition class

The first decision a competitively minded pilot has to make is the class in which to compete. As a result of different design rules, there is a wide range of gliders on offer, although personal preferences and financial constraints usually point the pilot quickly towards a particular class.

Anything from a low-cost glider with modest performance to Open Class aircraft with glide ratios better than 60:1 is available. But it doesn't have to be new; second-hand gliders have proven a very popular choice for pilots relatively new on the competition scene. Another popular way is part ownership in a syndicate. Provided good relations can be maintained amongst all members, such arrangements can be cost-effective as all expenses are shared between members. In most cases, such arrangements can provide substantial financial advantages and still allow sufficient access to the glider.

However, pilots keen on competition flying don't need to own an aircraft as long as they belong to a club that makes their gliders available to individual members for a week or two. Although most clubs do allow suitably qualified members to fly in competitions, it always pays to make inquiries first.

The following is an extract from the current FAI (Fédération Aéronautique Internationale) rules on competition classes:

Open Class

No special rules (other than a weight limit of 850 kg)

18 Metre Class

The only limitation is a maximum span of 18 000 mm

15 Metre Class

The only limitation is a maximum span of 15 000 mm

Standard Class

a) WINGS

The span must not exceed 15 000 mm. Any method of changing the wing profile other than by normal use of the ailerons is prohibited. Lift increasing devices are prohibited, even if unusable.

b) AIRBRAKES

The glider must be fitted with airbrakes which cannot be used to increase performance. Drag parachutes are prohibited.

c) UNDERCARRIAGE

The undercarriage may be fixed or retractable. The main landing wheel shall be at least 300 mm in diameter and 100 mm in width.

d) BALLAST

Water ballast which may be discharged in flight is permitted.

World Class

The World Class glider is the PW-5 design which was the winner of the 1994 World Class design competition. All gliders must be built to the IGC specifications for the World Class and must conform to all applicable IGC rules. No modifications are permitted except as approved and circulated in writing by FAI to all NACs (National Aerosport Control) on behalf of the International Gliding Commission.

a) ALTERATION TO AIRFLOW

Any alteration affecting airflow around the glider is prohibited. This includes, but is not limited to, the use of turbulation devices, fairings, and special surface treatment. The only exceptions are:

I.) a yawstring,
II.) a total-energy probe,
III.) adhesive tape to seal gaps between wings, fuselage and tail.
IV.) Sealing between moveable control surfaces and the airframe is not permitted.

b) ELECTRICAL DEVICES

Electrical and electronic devices are allowed, including instruments and navigational aids.

c) BALLAST

Ballast which can be jettisoned in flight is prohibited. In a World Class competition, a mass shall be specified by the Competition Director between the maximum gross mass and the lowest takeoff mass attainable by the heaviest entrant. To attain the specified mass each glider shall incorporate a fixed ballast system approved by the IGC, which may include tail ballast.

d) CENTRE OF GRAVITY CONTROL

Any device capable of altering the centre of gravity location of the glider during flight is prohibited.

Club Class

The purpose of the Club Class is to preserve the value of older high-performance gliders, to provide inexpensive but high-quality international championships, and to enable pilots who do not have access to gliders of the highest standard of performance to take part in contests at the highest levels.

a) ENTRY

The only limitation on entry of a glider into a Club Class competition is that it is within the range of handicap factors agreed for the competition. The handicap factor list for the country or region in which the competition is held shall normally be used. Any list of handicaps proposed for a World Club Class championship must be approved by IGC.

b) BALLAST

Water ballast is not permitted.

c) SCORING

A Club Class championship shall be scored using formulae which include handicap factors.

Flying competitively

The starting grid at a World Championship
Photo:
Hiroshi Seo

NEW

7.2 Preparing for your first competition

So you think that you have accumulated enough experience to enter a competition and find out how your soaring skills stack up against others? What a great idea! Competitions are an excellent way of creating a very steep learning curve. You get a chance to compare yourself to others on a daily basis and closely observe the effects of different flying styles and decisions. Just make sure you set yourself a goal – otherwise you have nothing to aspire to.

If bigger competitions are just a touch too intimidating for you it might be best to start by entering a club competition or a smaller regional championship. These competitions often attract less than 20 gliders and are usually scored on handicap. It means that the scoresheet will reflect your true standing very well - even if you don't have access to the latest hardware. In any case, the aim is to practice and build your skills in a competitive environment and at the same time learn a few tricks for higher ranked competitions in future.

What do we have to do in terms of preparation? Well, a good starting point is to have another close look at Chapter 3. Under the heading of "Preparing for cross-country flying" we have already discussed some vital points. Here they are again.

- Getting ready for road retrieves
- A partnership with your crew
- Preparing for longer flights
- Checklist for taking a glider away

But you would be well advised to take preparation one step further. Make yourself familiar with the competition rules and if you are hopeful of a top placing you had better pay particular attention to the section on scoring. Find out just how badly an outlanding will affect your overall scores and consider the virtues of flying less aggressively (i.e. being more conservative) in an attempt to make it home every day.

Also, make sure you know what penalties are applied to dangerous flying or airspace infringements and the like. Again, prior knowledge of the consequences might not only prevent disappointment but will also ensure that you study the maps more thoroughly and enter the current airspace files into your flight computer or PDA.

Ensure you are familiar with all your electronic gadgets – especially your logger. All too often pilots have returned from task only to find out that they failed to switch on their data logger or have forgotten to delete previous flights. Loggers are a wonderful invention but when the maximum memory capacity is exhausted the last part of the flight may no longer be recorded. The result is zero points for the day! Don't laugh; it has happened often enough that many pilots now carry two loggers on every flight.

The next step is to obtain a list of turn points, or better still, download the turn point data from the organiser's website and feed them straight into your flight computer. Finally, check whether a working Flarm unit is compulsory and, if so, fit it to your glider well before the competition begins. Also, make sure you know how to interpret the Flarm indications prior to the competition starting. (Refer to Section 10.6.)

But no job is finished until the paperwork is completed. Here is a list of documents organisers usually want to see:

- Entry form
- Radio licence
- Insurance confirmation
- Competition licence
- Certificate of registration
- Proof of glider airworthiness
- Current check flight
- CFI approval for participation
- Approval for use of club glider (if applicable)

These documents are best put together weeks, or even months, ahead of the event. A last-minute scramble might not only spoil the first competition day for you but will open the door to stress with all of its many negative consequences.

But whatever you do, you must not forget the most important part of the preparation process – PRACTICE and TRAINING. Practice as much as practical at your home site and implement the suggestions made in section 4.4. There is every chance that you need to share the sky with about 20 other gliders and find yourself in a thermal that is occupied by about half of them. Try to get comfortable with this – if necessary while conducting your final training at the competition site just prior to the event. It increases your chances of enjoying your first competition and doing very well indeed. If that happens you might even get bitten by the competition bug and enter higher ranked competitions in future. And wouldn't that be wonderful?

7.3 Getting to know the contest area

Just as important as thorough preparation of pilot and equipment is a good knowledge of the contest area. Preferably you should have a few flights prior to the official practice day to get familiar with the local area and learn about outlanding hazards etc. Also, talk to the locals and find out where the lift is best earlier in the day and which areas are best avoided. Have as many familiarisation flights as practicable for a better appreciation of the airfield layout and nearby navigational features.

All these flights will serve you well when the contest is underway and if you are forced to come home on a marginal final glide. Many airfields are embedded in areas unsuitable for outlandings, but having performed a few final glides from various directions not only provides a definite advantage but also improves safety.

Especially in areas of interesting geology, it pays to adopt flying tactics to stay in reach of reliable updraughts and safe outlanding areas. A good study of large-scale topographical maps is also beneficial.

Especially hilly or mountainous contest areas require pilots to be flexible and adjust speed and track to coincide with geological features on the ground. A good dose of local knowledge gained by a lengthy training period in the contest area is certain to provide a competitive advantage.

7.4 Starting a race

What happens prior to the beginning of a race has absolutely no effect on the competition scores. The clock only starts ticking after you have crossed the start line and therefore you want to be in the best possible position for starting. That position is as close to the start point as feasible with as much altitude as possible. Every foot of height gained prior to the start is valuable and translates directly into time savings on task.

Just as important is the optimum timing for the start, but forecasting that is easier said than done. A good start can have a big bearing on our chances of success and the majority of newcomers need help with this aspect of competition flying. Especially pilots new to competition flying tend to keep an eye on others and copy their decisions. In other words, they rely on their competitors for the optimum start time rather than reconciling the official weather forecast with their personal assessment and take matters such as approaching middle–level clouds, trough lines, cirrus development etc. into account. When thunderstorms are forecast it is almost always best to start early.

Let's look at an example and assume a 300km task with 6 kts thermals expected for the best part of the day. A good pilot may achieve an average climb rate of 4 kts and under such conditions a modern glider (with just the right amount of water on board) could achieve almost 60 kts or 110 km/h. (Refer to Section 5.4.2.) The time on task would therefore be in the order of 2h45min. In most parts of the world, the peak of the day is between 2:00pm and 5:00pm which means that the optimum start time would be around 2:00pm. If your best judgment of the climb rates on task is different you can adjust the duration of the flight accordingly.

But what happens when you get launched and find that the best average rate of climb is only 2 kts even though the maximum temperature of the day has long since been reached? In this situation your average speed would be down to about 45 kts or 85 km/h. Now the time on task will be in excess of 3½ hours and it would pay to leave well before 2:00pm. If deteriorating conditions are expected (or adverse weather is threatening later in the day) it might be better to leave earlier still – perhaps even as soon as the start gate opens.

You might ask what to do if you have started early and find that conditions are improving rapidly? Will you continue or return for a restart? The answer depends on the distance travelled and your assessment of the day ahead. Canny pilots often make an early start and return for a restart unless the conditions peak much earlier than expected.

Advanced competition pilots with ambitions for a top placing tend to entertain additional tactical considerations. They usually start after the majority of competitors have left; knowing that shaving off valuable seconds becomes easier with some thermal markers ahead on track. We will elaborate on that in the next section but other proven starting tactics include finding a thermal upwind of the start point and drifting towards the start line while extracting every bit of altitude possible. While close to and within close proximity of the start line, level out and cross the line at maximum altitude. This is easier said than done, as theory and practice are sometimes miles apart.

Working a thermal under a blue sky
Photo:
Noel Matthews

In practice, the starting altitude is often reached a fair distance away from the start line. In such cases it is prudent to approach the start at the speed of best L/D in order to conserve as much energy as possible. Every bit of altitude wasted needs to be regained on track at the expense of valuable time. Only after crossing the start line should you select the appropriate MacCready setting or cruise at speeds judged appropriate for the conditions ahead.

Just as important is to conserve mental energy. There is no point in working hard to extract the maximum climb rate out of a thermal prior to the start of the race. By far more important is to get a feel for the air, the effective ceiling and the conditions of the day. Fly around effortlessly prior to starting and venture a little towards the first turn point to get a few clues for the conditions on the first leg. Just make sure you don't burn yourself out before the start and don't forget to announce your start time after crossing the line.

Finally a quick word on sustenance in a pre-start competition context. The importance of maintaining appropriate blood sugar and fluid levels has already been highlighted in section 3.3. Therefore it should suffice to say that it is wise to eat something (even if you don't feel like it) before crossing the start line. Unpacking a sandwich and eating it during a race not only impacts negatively on your concentration but is a hassle that you can do well without while cruising fast or when in a gaggle with other gliders.

Whatever you do, stay away from sugary foods such as candy bars or cookies as they only provide a short term energy boost. Food with a high content of carbohydrates (found in most plant foods, like fruits and vegetables, legumes and whole grain bread) releases the energy more evenly and over a longer period of time and is therefore by far preferable when it comes to conditioning your body for a three to five hour racing performance.

7.5 Out on a competition task

In chapter 5 we have already discussed some vital issues under the heading 'Advanced cross-country flying'. All of these hints and suggestions are directly applicable to competition flying but there is a need to stress a few additional points here.

Earlier in this book I have already alluded to the need to thermal efficiently but selecting only the strongest of thermals is just as important. Fortunately this task becomes a fair bit easier if you can take advantage of the many thermal markers on

NEW

Climbing away on a promising competition day
Photo:
Hana Zejdova

track. If you see a better climbing glider while thermalling you better join it at once. If you are cruising and spot another pilot marking a thermal don't hesitate to inspect this thermal either - especially if the glider is thermalling steeply and the pilot has a proven track record. It can not only save centring time but might – at least on occasions – also allow a climb in an exceptional thermal that could have otherwise been missed. Even while cruising close to maximum altitude it is usually advantageous to detour slightly in order to extract valuable energy from a marked thermal. The lesson is to watch out for others and use them to your advantage. Help is always welcome – especially when it is provided by your competitors! High to very high average speeds in competitions can often be explained by the assistance competitors give each other on task – unwittingly, of course.

The next thing to remember is that the competition will last a whole week or even longer and it is therefore vital to pace yourself. After all, pilots are no robots and it is the total point tally that counts at the end. Going your hardest during the first few contest days is a common mistake. Experienced pilots know that only too well and often apply a self imposed rule to fly at only 95% of capacity on any given day. It ensures that they last the distance and it prevents burnout half way through the championship. This is not only vital if you don't want to ruin your chance of success but is just as crucial in terms of safety.

Like it or not, competitions and gaggles go hand in hand – especially on blue days with low convection. Some pilots thrive on it and fly more relaxed in the knowledge that nearby gliders might provide clues in difficult situations. Others hate it and prefer to go it alone. But successfully completing a task on a low and difficult day is more likely when a group of pilots work together and spread out to find the best available thermals. The price to be payed is a reduced rate of climb because sooner or later gliders are bound to get in each other's way. It goes without saying that under such circumstances pilots need to display great patience and vigilance. For this reason gaggle flying is seldom favoured by relative newcomers although the reward can be a higher speed around the task on tricky days. A word of warning though! Never neglect your own navigation. There are plenty of examples of pilots relying on each other and flying well past a turn point. Infringing airspace by a large part of the gaggle is also not uncommon for the same reason.

Because the race is normally run during the best part of the day it is usually beneficial to carry water ballast. Even if the climb rates are expected to be miserable and the thermals are likely to be narrow it pays to launch with water on board for two reasons:

a) conditions might improve later, and

b) water ballast speeds up your first glide after starting.

Dumping water is always an option when it becomes obvious that ballast is a hindrance rather than a benefit. But if you intend to dump only part of your water it pays to know the dump rate of your glider in litres per second. Only then can you calculate the remaining water ballast accurately. For further aspects of water ballast please refer to Section 4.8.

A few words on flying tactics with open class gliders might also be appropriate. These graceful machines might have impressive L/D figures but at medium to high speeds they are struggling to keep up with heavily ballasted modern 15 or 18 metre aircraft. Therefore open class gliders tend to cruise somewhat slower in an attempt to minimise the number of thermals and to utilise only the strongest ones. But there is another reason. Their agility and rate of roll is usually nowhere near as good as smaller wingspan gliders resulting in longer thermal centring times. Extracting energy in cruise and remaining in buoyant air for as long as possible (by seeking areas of high thermal density or other sources of lift) is a well proven tactic for any glider but for open class gliders in particular. Even longer detours are therefore often advantageous for high performance open class gliders provided it results in contacting more buoyant air.

Now let's talk about leeching. It is a term usually used by top pilots when referring to others following close behind. The better guys hate it with a passion and the reasons are as simple as they are obvious. Top pilots feel that they have to lead and do all the hard work while others just follow them to good effect. No wonder they often find such tactics irritating and invest considerable effort and energy into shaking off their 'shadowy nuisances'. Their followers in turn feel that they have entered the competition to learn something from pilots with a proven track record and are happy to be dragged along for as long as possible. Unfortunately leeching is part and parcel of competition flying and even happens at world comp level. It certainly doesn't make the sport any safer and will always remain a contentious issue. Decide for yourself whether you want to score a few extra points and get a dubious reputation for leeching or become a self reliant pilot and earn the respect of your peers.

Almost every competition has at least one day of extremely difficult and challenging conditions. If you are finding the thermals broken and hard to centre you can be sure that it is no different for all your fellow competitors out there. Just remain patient and get on with the task at hand. Do the best you can but confine yourselves to sharing your frustrations with others at the end of the day and consider the terrain. Remaining low but on a ridge can result in higher speeds compared to using broken convection higher up. Those tricky days tend to separate the boys from the men. At the end of the contest the daily scores make up the total points tally and the scores on these tricky days usually make the difference between winners and the also run. A true champion possesses the ability to adjust speed and flying style in line with changing weather conditions.

Finally let's put the final glide in a competition under the microscope again. We have already considered this part of a cross-country flight in chapter 5 and the points discussed apply here as well. But now you are racing and every second lost is a second your competitor gains on you. What can you do to save time on the final glide home?

Not to relax when your flight computer indicates sufficient height is the first and most crucial bit of advice. Meteorological navigation mustn't stop until you arrive at your destination. This is of major significance on longer final glides as even small amounts of additional atmospheric energy permit speeding up. In fact many competition pilots advocate leaving the final thermal prematurely as long as conditions allow obtaining the required final glide energy while cruising through pockets of lift on the way home.

This, of course, has lead to many outlandings just a few kilometres short of the airfield and should therefore only be attempted when uniform and reliable conditions prevail or when the topography favours such an approach. Keeping an eye on the true wind strength and direction is just as important. Don't forget that most flight computers calculate wind speed based on the drift in a thermal and because the wind outside of an updraught is usually stronger the resulting final glide calculations might be incorrect. Especially in costal areas it is common to encounter a sea breeze which can quickly turn a tailwind into a head wind. This has ruined quite a few final glides which were thought to be safe when the pilot left the last thermal.

The above comments already highlight that the final glide is the most demanding part of the flight. Just as you are beginning to get tired you have to monitor airspeed versus altitude while observing other incoming traffic. On top of that you need to keep the finishing rules in mind which might specify minimum or maximum heights for crossing the finish line. Additional radio announcements at certain distances from the airfield might also be compulsory and sometimes even airspace restrictions apply. And the race isn't finished until you are safely back on the ground. Countless wheel-up landings after a stressful final glide (and with several other finishers in the circuit) underline this comment.

**Low level finish
Photo:
Joost van Veelen**

7.6 Turning points

Regardless of whether we round FAI–style turning points with sectors or fly to an area turning point, the most important issue is not to waste time and altitude. The days when pilots performed spectacular aerial acrobatics to take their turn point photographs are thankfully gone forever but even when using dataloggers for flight verification valuable energy can be wasted. Turning cleanly and in the most efficient manner is what matters most. On days with assigned area tasks, for example, we can fly further into the sector and turn in an area of lift. This will improve our energy balance significantly.

The advent of dataloggers has allowed competition organisers to create a large number of different task options with a variety of turn point rules. The most popular ones are listed below:

a) Flying to a FAI sector

This turn point rule is basically a remnant of the old photo verification method but as it is still required for badge and record flights we will deal with it first. The FAI zone is best described as two 45° sectors located on either side of a line bisecting the inbound and outbound courses. Figure 94 shows a typical situation for a task flown in a clockwise direction. Provided the datalogger is programmed correctly it will give us an unmistakable audio signal as soon as it is recording

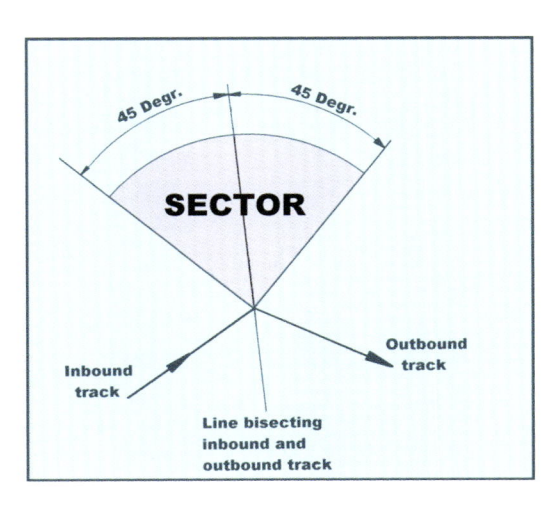

**Figure 94:
FAI Sector**

a position within the sector (shaded area). We can turn without looking at a feature on the ground. This is a big step ahead in terms of collision avoidance around turn points.

b) Flying to a 'beer can' sector

Rounding a turn point with a 360° sector is even easier. In glider pilot's jargon this zone is called 'beer can'. It is usually a cylindrical bit of airspace with a radius of 500m around nominated coordinates on the ground. These coordinates have to be programmed into the datalogger which allows it to provide an audio signal as soon as a point within the specified airspace is reached.

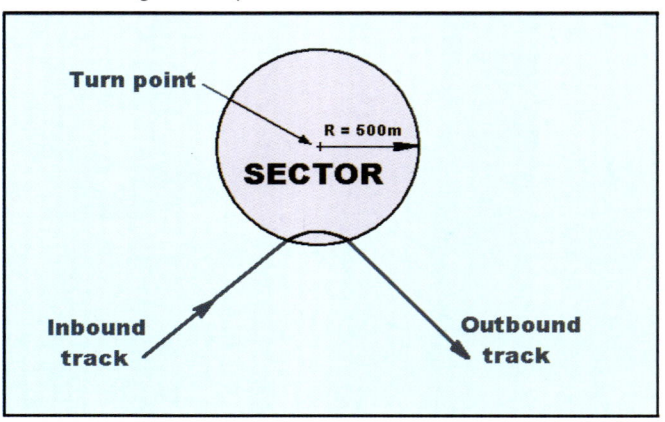

Figure 95: 'Beer can' sector

c) Flying to an area turn point

In an attempt to ease congestion near turn points, and in order to allow greater flexibility, the "Assigned Area Task" (AAT) was invented. Competition organisers nominate a task time and the aim of the pilot is to cover as much distance as possible within this timeframe. Turn points are still nominated but can be as big as 50 kilometres in radius around a certain point. This means that pilots are allowed to turn within a much larger area and get credited with the actual distance flown. The pilot can either extend or shorten the task distance according to his or her weather assessment at the time. Exceeding the nominated task time doesn't carry a penalty. However, it is seldom advisable, unless the additional distance can be covered in exceptional time and hence adds considerably to the average speed. Pilots returning before the task time has elapsed get scored on the minimum task time. As an example, if the nominated time period is 3 hours and a competitor returns after 3 ¼ hours the average speed is calculated by dividing the distance covered by 3 ¼ hours. A pilot returning before his 3 hour time has elapsed is scored on the full 3 hours and suffers a significant reduction of average speed. Tactical considerations can influence the scores greatly but, on the other hand, the AAT helps organisers of Club Class events to set achievable tasks for gliders with vastly different performances.

d) Pilot optional speed task (POST)

Contrary to the tasks mentioned above, the POST allows pilots to put together their own task from a list of approved turn points. This concept has provided pilots with greater flexibility, as the task distance can be adjusted based on the prevailing weather conditions and the performance of the glider. Again, a task time is nominated by the organisers and pilots are credited with the distances between all turn points rounded.

7.7 The problem of stress in competition

Although stress is an overused word, it is undoubtedly present in all facets of our lives. In particular, high–ranking competition pilots are usually far more stressed than in ordinary life. High expectations of outsiders plus the pilot's own ambition can lead to psychological stress, which is sometimes bordering on the extreme.

In anything we do we come under some degree of pressure – or "level of arousal" as scientists call it. If our level of arousal is too low we perform far below our best but, equally important, we will perform poorly when under too much stress or pressure. In other words, a certain level of arousal is required for optimum performance. When we feel 'comfortably challenged' we usually perform best. However, when we are challenged beyond the limits of our skill (or when we are pushed for time) we get stressed and the inevitable result is a very detrimental effect on our performance. (Refer to Section 7.9.)

A scientifically accepted definition of stress is "The arousal of mind and body in response to demands made on the individual". Put simply, stress occurs when we have to deal with more tasks than we can comfortably handle. In competitions this tends to happen frequently — especially when things don't go according to plan. Typical examples are last-minute equipment problems, extended searching for lift at low levels or deteriorating weather conditions while on task. To resolve such problems, it is vital to assimilate a lot of information in a very short period of time. This in itself is stressful enough, but the risk of making a wrong decision on top of this increases stress even further and we lose the ability to take in the broader picture.

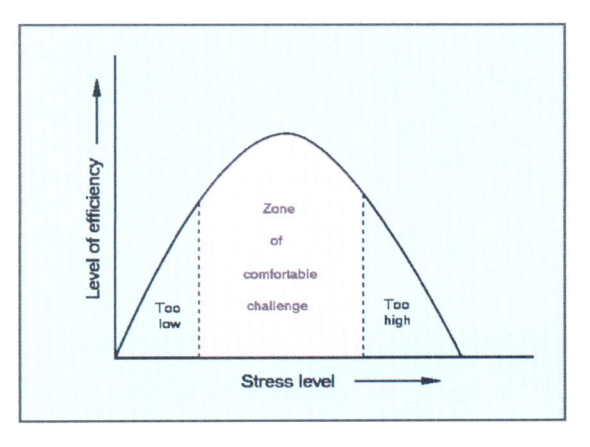

Figure 96: Zone of comfortable challenge

The body's natural reaction to stress is a release of adrenalin which, amongst other things, causes an increased heart rate. Blood is primarily directed towards the muscles in preparation for a fight–or–flight response. As a result our brain's blood supply is reduced and our capacity to think clearly is impaired. The short–term consequence is an increase in blood pressure as well as a higher breathing frequency. Prolonged exposure to such conditions can affect sleep patterns and may even have adverse behavioural consequences. Restlessness and anxiety can set in, but at the very least individuals tend to feel tense which is more often than not tantamount to poor decision making and bad judgement. Even the most refined flying skills count for very little if the pilot falls apart under pressure. In some cases pilots may even become depressed while others get angry or slightly aggressive.

**Thermalling over a salt lake in South Australia
Photo:
Noel Matthews**

Flying competitively

**Coming home in style
Photo:
Peter Weigelt**

Knowing what stress does to a pilot is one thing, but dealing with it successfully is quite another. Avoiding stressful situations wherever and whenever possible is by far the best approach. One way of doing just that is to reduce our physical as well as our mental workload. Delegating all routine work to our crew is part of this process and gives us time to attend to more relevant matters without haste.

Finding time to 'switch off' and relax is just as important as stress reduction and is unlikely to be successfully achieved if left to chance. Relaxing on cue is a difficult skill that can only be learned over time. The relaxation techniques discussed in section 7.9, such as deep breathing and progressive muscle relaxation, elicit the opposite to a stress response in the human brain. Both heart rate and blood pressure decrease almost immediately and as the need for oxygen is reduced, breathing also slows down. Stress hormones gradually disappear from the bloodstream and the brain produces alpha or theta waves which indicate deep physiological rest.

Therefore, most elite pilots attempt relaxation on a regular basis and in doing so they develop control over their arousal levels and thoughts. Finding a few hours without thinking about the competition, their opponent's tactics or other task-relevant aspects is vital. For example, enjoying social time or going for a forest stroll with a friend or partner after a demanding day in the cockpit goes a long way towards winding down and regaining valuable mental energy. Sharing thoughts or problems with friends can also be a great stress reliever.

Many of our top pilots manage to eliminate all thoughts about winning and instead focus on performing to the best of their ability. They realise that their final results are highly dependant on the performance of their competitors. This type of mental attitude allows them not to worry about their scores or ruminate over an average performance. They don't care what their competitors are doing but instead strive to achieve consistency and an optimum performance of their own. This often sees them very near, or even at the top of the score sheet at the end of the contest.

To further ease the load on our mind, we need to put a lot of effort into preparation.

Knowing that nothing was left to chance is a precondition for a relaxed state of mind and manageable stress levels. Having all our equipment in top condition is just as important. It will let us rest easy and will make unexpected failures less likely.

But even with the best preparation the first major competition can be very demanding on body and soul. Newcomers often struggle with a lot of time-consuming organisational procedures. In addition, they are likely to be flying at a site other than their home airfield, which also adds to the pressure. Therefore it becomes important to assess one's own state of mind from time to time and step back for a break when necessary.

7.8 Shaving off the seconds

Competition victory will usually go to the pilot who makes the least number of mistakes. It follows that winners have the skill and ability to avoid major blunders, although even a minor mistake can make the difference between winning and not making it onto the podium.

But winning a higher level competition takes more than just not making mistakes. The difference between being placed first or second is often expressed in less than one minute – one minute after a two-week competition period. The winner not only selected the best thermals and cruised in the most efficient manner but he or she probably saved a second or two in most thermals. These seconds add up quickly. For example, if only a single second is saved on 20 thermals in a race it represents a saving of 200 seconds over 10 competition days – almost a 3-minute advantage. The winning margins at major championships are often much less than that.

Where can we save the seconds? Seemingly minor matters such as entering and exiting thermals carelessly do attract time penalties. More specifically, slowing down too early (and crossing the sink surrounding the thermal at a low speed) is tantamount to wasting good time. The same applies if we do not accelerate the glider before contacting sink on leaving the thermal (Section 5.11).

Another time waster is the radio. Talking on the radio takes concentration and concentration is what makes you go faster. All top competition pilots have one thing in common, they are hardly ever heard on the radio and only press the transmit button when safety demands it or when they want their crew to know that they are on final glide.

Feeling minor updraughts in cruise and acting upon them before the instruments display the lift makes for much better energy extraction. Getting it right every time might even save a few turns in a thermal. Remember, a full circle takes approximately 20 seconds.

Making a mental note of the aircraft registration marks of the top pilots and being able to recognise their aircraft in the air can also save time. When two gliders are circling in relatively close proximity, it is usually best to join the pilot with the best track record and competition standing.

7.9 Risk management.

'Human factors' is presently the big topic amongst professional aviators and recreational pilots are well advised to tap into the lessons learned by our big brothers. Gliding accidents still occur despite ongoing efforts to avoid complacency in our sport. Every mishap should provide us with an impetus to review our attitude to the sport and the risk that comes with it. This healthy approach serves two purposes.

Flying competitively

ASK 21 Mi over Mt. Bogong on a fresh winter day
Photo: Simon Dallinger

First and foremost it reminds us to remain vigilant and, what is just as important, it helps us to avoid repeating the mistakes of others.

While flying gliders we are faced with two kinds of risks. The first and most obvious one is the risk of landing out. Here the pilot's ego and the placing on the score sheet might take a bit of a hammering but on the whole we can put it down under: "No big deal!" After all, a properly executed outlanding poses hardly any risk to aircraft or pilot – something we will examine much closer in chapter 8.

What we are really concerned about in this context is the risk to pilot and aircraft that some of us might be tempted to accept just to improve our chances of success. With almost every activity undertaken we accept a certain level of risk and in this respect gliding is no different to a lot of other sports. This is a very personal thing and means that every participant needs to decide what level of risk he or she is prepared to accept. No doubt experience, the quality of training, currency, know-how, theoretical knowledge and a host of other factors influence the level of risk and our attitude towards it, at lease subconsciously.

Risk tolerance can even change depending on the circumstances we are in at the time. For example, some pilots tend to fly even more conservatively with passengers or students on board. Obviously risk acceptance cannot only be rather fluid but it can also be influenced by our momentary motivation.

Let me give you an example. A few years ago I took part in a regional competition where the task involved crossing an unlandable area of scrubland. At my altitude and by my estimation it was only just safe to cross the scrubland at a low MacCready setting when I noticed another competitor at least 2000 ft below me and cruising much faster. He was clearly dependant on finding a thermal to make it across the scrubland. We both completed the task and met again for a drink at the end of the day. I enquired about his tactics and was shocked by the answer:" Well" he said, "I outlanded on the first day and figured that I need to take more risks if I still want to make it on the podium."

I'm sure you get my point now. Momentary motivation can lead to a severe reduction of safety margins to a point where they no longer exist. In the end our hero never made it onto the podium and even if he did he would have got a handshake by the competition director for his efforts. Food for thought isn't it?

Recognising that our individual motivation can affect our momentary risk profile empowers us to resist gambling with danger. Let's review our risk profile periodically – at least prior to every new soaring season.

It is also a known fact that humans are less inclined to abandon their goal the closer they get to it. Glider pilots have continued on a very marginal final glide to their intended destination although an outlanding would have been the only safe option. "Get homeitis" is the term often used to describe the phenomenon. Let's be aware of it and resist it when next it arises. Smart pilots are constantly assessing ways to avoid bad luck while flying. One poor judgment will increase the probability that another will follow and this holds true, especially in gliding. If the poor judgment chain is allowed to grow the chances of a safe outcome decrease rapidly.

The old saying holds true more than ever: "Superior pilots use their superior knowledge to avoid situations requiring the use of their superior skills."

7.10 Staying fit for the duration of the contest

Being removed from our daily routine and under competition pressure for a period of up to two weeks can put a lot of strain on body and soul. Therefore, a reasonable level of physical fitness is part of the necessary preparation for any high-level contest. For a competitive glider pilot, fitness is not only about body but largely about mind. Physical fitness favours a much quicker retrieve of information from memory and allows us to focus better on the task at hand – a very important issue in a highly competitive environment.

Competitions may require you to fine-tune your nutrition with special plans. This could include a substitution of heavy meals with easily digestible food or a special re-hydration pattern. Since you will be under pressure to be at your best, these tactics should be rehearsed beforehand. Practising in a training environment allows the body to become used to different nutritional intakes well before the contest begins.

Avoid any consumption of alcohol if possible. Studies have shown that it can take weeks if not months for the body to rid itself of toxic substances. Therefore it is not at all sufficient to refrain from drinking during the contest period. The temptation of celebrating a good performance with fellow competitors or crewmembers is ever present but it is up to the individual pilot how he or she deals with these matters. A wise pilot will have several glasses of water before fronting the bar – the benefits will come as early as the next contest day. Also avoid fluids which speed up dehydration by stimulating increased urination. A number of popular beverages containing caffeine, such as tea, coffee and cola drinks, fall into this category.

Of equal importance is to ensure regular rest periods and energy-restoring sleep. Being under competition pressure away from home and in unfamiliar surroundings can be enough to disrupt regular sleeping patterns. Therefore, even the hardiest of competitors can find it difficult to get sufficient rest. If, on top of that, an outlanding occurs far away from base, an additional sleep deficit might be forced upon you with all its consequences.

7.11 Is the mature glider pilot disadvantaged?

Unlike most sports, success in gliding is not primarily dependant on physical strength or stamina but on little more than skill and good decision making. This skill is accumulated over time by a mixture of experience, training, currency and application of theoretical knowledge as well as smart flying tactics. Experience plays a major role in gliding, more than in most other sports,– a statement underlined by the fact that most major competitions are won by mature pilots in the 40 to 50 year old age bracket.

Experience allows a more automatic response to a large number of tricky in-flight situations and can greatly contribute to safety – especially in stressful situations or in circumstances where quick action is essential. Most importantly, experience can avoid the pilot getting into difficult situations in the first place.

In contrast, less experienced pilots often need to put a much greater mental effort into their decision making processes. This results in a significantly greater workload with a risk of neglecting other important tasks. It follows that automatic responses are highly beneficial but a good analysis of every situation – regardless whether on the ground or in the air – cannot and must not be neglected.

Even mature pilots can still compete at the highest level, as long as they remain healthy and mentally fit. I'm quick to add that maturity doesn't equate to experience and experience doesn't necessarily equate to maturity. Often young pilots display maturity beyond their years and sometimes we meet older pilots who are repeating mistakes made years or even decades ago.

Mature pilots tend to be self-reliant and think for themselves but are keen and willing to tap into the know-how of others to enhance their knowledge and skills. Accepting responsibility for their own actions is just a sign of maturity as is recognising potential strength and weaknesses. To overcome these weaknesses, they are prepared to put in a persistent effort which is often rewarded by a remarkable consistency on the score sheet. Being consistent when others aren't usually results in a top competition placing. Mature pilots take control of their own lives and often make smarter decisions based on first class observations as well as past learning and experience.

Being aware of their perceptions and recognising them as such, while accepting that others, are different is another hallmark of mature pilots. They never try to be like others and have developed their own style while striving to progress to the very best of their ability. Also, they believe in their capacity to cope with difficult situations and recognise limitations by setting realistic and achievable goals. Failures and setbacks are seen as positive opportunities for performance enhancement and are used as stepping stones towards future improvement.

Mature pilots also stand out by managing their own affairs and their time very efficiently. Their energy is directed towards self-monitoring and overcoming any obstacles on the way to achieving their goals. In short, the sport of gliding allows competitively minded participants to gain pleasure and enjoyment from high-ranking competitions for decades. This sets our sport apart from most other activities and greatly adds to its attraction.

Chapter 7

Flying competitively

Winter flying in Australia
Photo:
Simon Dallinger

Impressions of New Zealand from the air

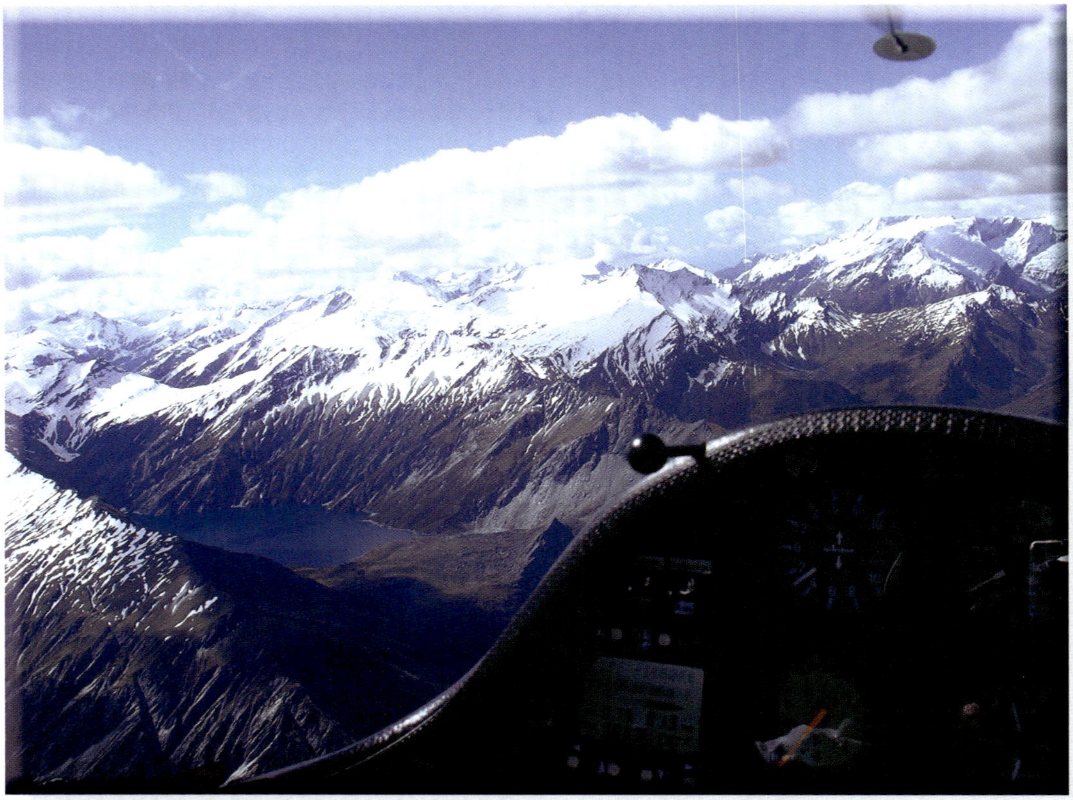

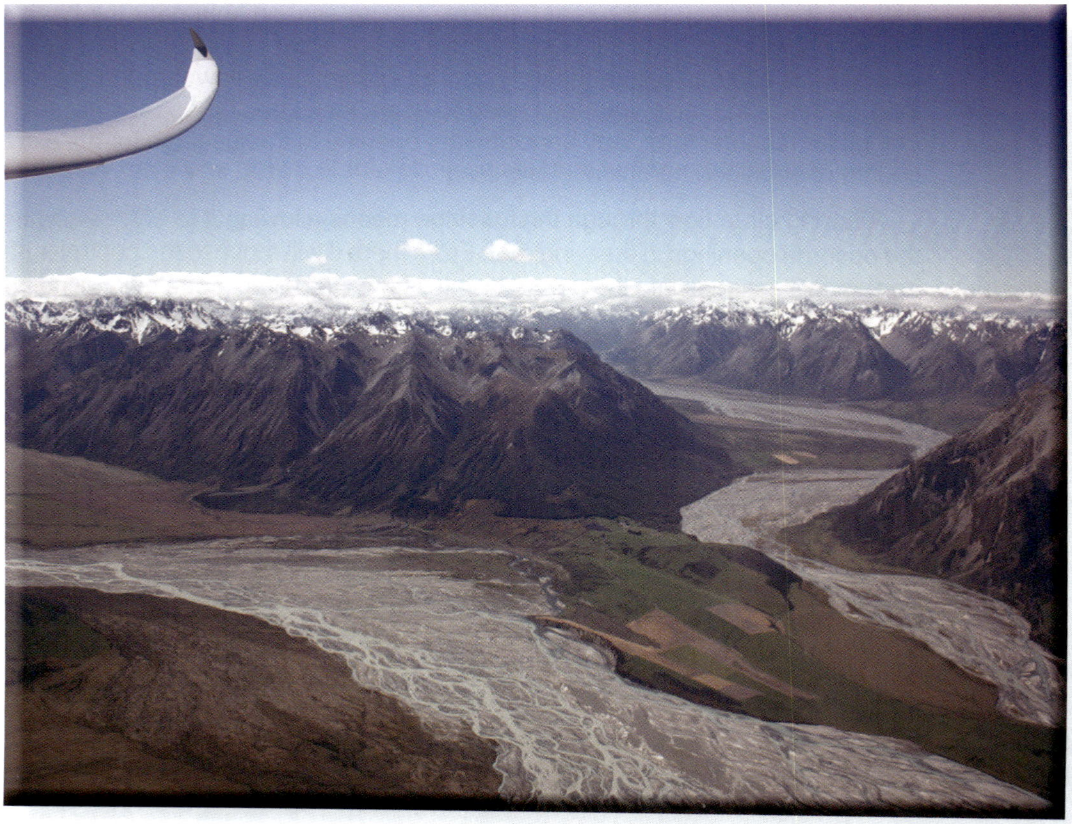

between unflapped and flapped gliders. Flying fast in a 'flapless' aircraft is always associated with a marked 'nose down' attitude. In contrast, the 'nose-horizon attitude' barely changes in a flapped glider. The nose always remains relatively high on the horizon and pilots new to flapped gliders can be forgiven for thinking that the glide slope is extremely shallow. However, reality is different – even flapped gliders come down rapidly at speeds of 100 kts or so.

In unflapped gliders we only have one mechanism for pitch control – the elevator. However, in a flapped glider we have elevator or flaps at our disposal. Selecting positive flap settings will make the aircraft climb and slow down and negative flap settings will, of course, have the opposite effect.

Leaving the elevator alone in a flapped glider avoids pitch changes which in turn eliminates unnecessary fuselage drag. The required amount of lift can be directly controlled by the flaps instead and, for this reason, the elevator deflection can be minimised for maximum efficiency.

Just to prove the point, let me tell you that a few pilots have saved their skin by applying this knowledge when they were on tow and realised that they had forgotten to connect the elevator. Flapped gliders are known to have landed without further incident thanks to the appropriate use of flaps. (Something I do not recommend copying)

In summary, the effect of flaps on performance is negligible in weaker conditions and tends to be overestimated by a large portion of the gliding movement. However, the picture changes somewhat in stronger conditions. Flying a flapped glider is not very difficult, but doing it efficiently is not as easy as it first appears. The secret is to fly the glider accurately and operate it efficiently throughout its entire speed range. No doubt, it adds considerably to the pilot's workload during all stages of flight but it sure is a lot of fun to squeeze a little bit of extra performance out of a glider.

Let's get technical

LS4 posing for
the camera
Photo:
Geraldine Clark

Chapter 8

ASH 25 over Lake Ohau in New Zealand
Image: McCaw Media.
(mccawmedia.co.nz)

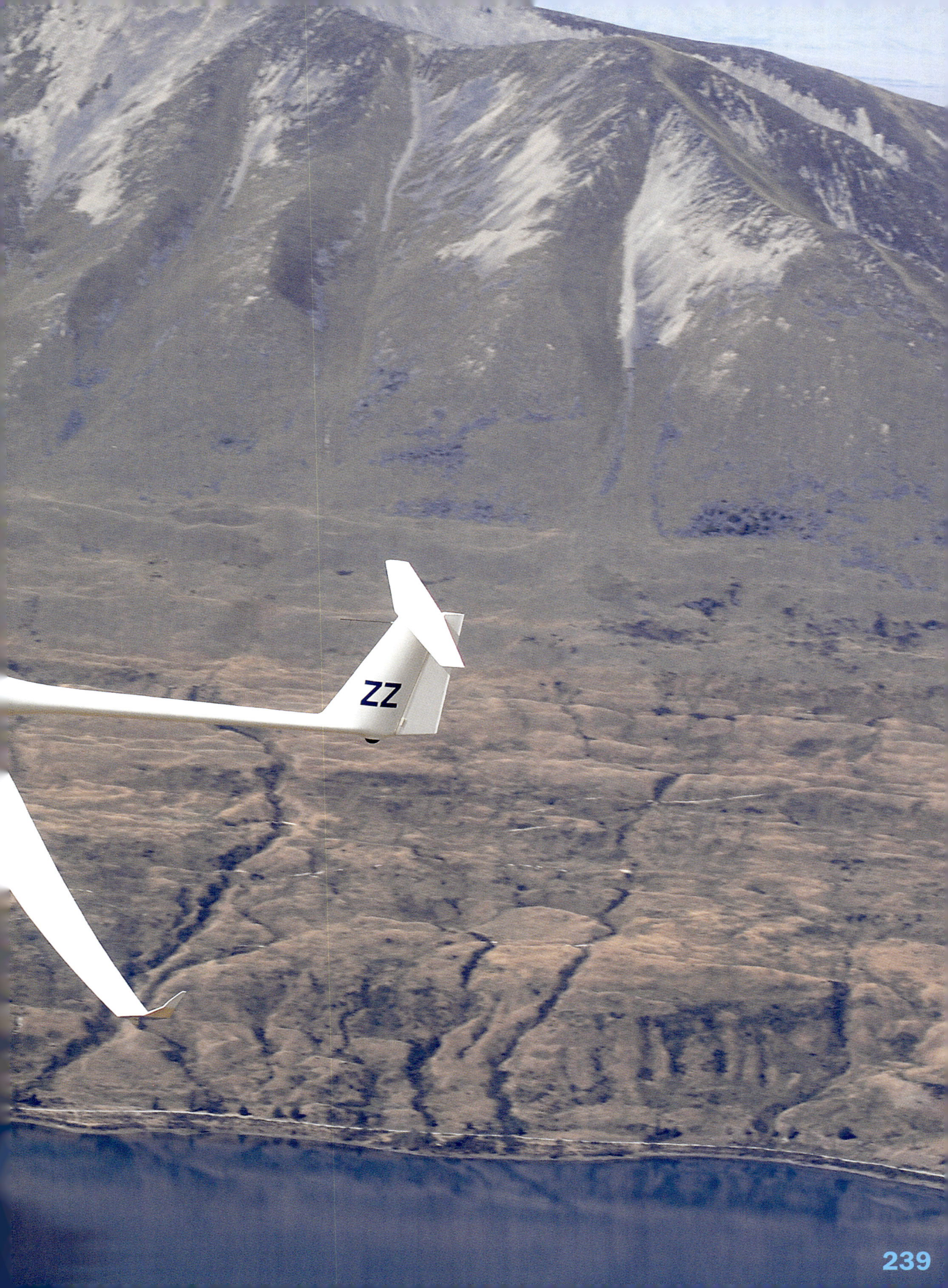
ZZ

9 Outlandings

9.1 Introduction

Wash yourself and you get wet; fly gliders far enough away from the airfield and you will outland one day. Landing out is nothing to be embarrassed about – it belongs to gliding just as the occasional flat tyre is part and parcel of cycling.

Whenever we outland we become ambassadors for the gliding movement. We are uninvited guests and, strictly speaking, we are trespassing although we are not doing it by choice but of necessity. The manner in which we conduct ourselves will be a reflection on all glider pilots. Every farmer I have met has been most helpful in every respect. Sure, a bit of psychology often goes a long way and therefore I suggest you tell onlookers about your flight and explain to them that you were unfortunate enough to run out of lift. Be diplomatic. You will soon have everyone's sympathy and if you then let one or two of the kids sit in the cockpit for a minute or two, you will also have an army of helpers going out of their way to make life bearable and to provide company and entertainment until your crew arrives. Think about it and make every attempt to notify the farmer if at all possible – it is a matter of courtesy.

Too many pilots look at outlandings with a great deal of reservation or even some degree of trepidation. Their approach to gliding is to stay in close proximity to the airfield and maintain a conservative glide angle back to the field at all times. There is no need to deprive yourself of the exhilaration and rewards that come with cross-country flying for fear of outlandings. Eliminating any possible concern or anxiety might allow you to go a bit further away in future and enjoy seeing countryside never seen before. If that happens you have managed to open new horizons and you are on the fast track to fully experience the beauty of our sport. Outlandings are not risky, nor do they require luck. It all comes down to mental preparation and application of know-how. It is a skill that can be acquired through practice and does not necessarily involve more than just a few "real" outlandings. Make every landing at the home airfield a precision landing, get to know the real performance of your aircraft and practise the following hints and suggestions at every opportunity. It will pay dividends later.

Gliders do not require bitumen runways. They were all designed to operate out of, or into, unsealed landing grounds or fields. It follows that outlandings do not represent a risk to aircraft or pilot as long as they are performed properly. They simply present another challenge in the quest to become more proficient and make for some very fast learning – something we will discover a bit later.

Back to outlandings now, or off-field landings as American pilots call them. If an off-field landing is performed properly it is not much different to a landing back at our home airfield. However, there are two important differences relating to the use of the altimeter and the detection of wind direction.

9.2 Misleading altimeter

Let us deal with the altimeter first. In fact, we can save ourselves talking about it because in an outlanding situation it is as superfluous as a crank handle on a modern motor car. Unless we know the elevation of the field we are landing in, our altimeter is not only totally useless but also very misleading.

The only thing we can be sure of is that the altimeter is incorrect and therefore we

**Coming home late
Photo:
Tim Lacey**

should force ourselves to ignore it. So what is the solution? Yes, you guessed it. We must rely on our own ability to estimate our height above ground and plan our circuit accordingly. You didn't have any problems when the instructor covered up the altimeter on your last check flight, did you? So what is the big deal? Just apply your best judgement and you will soon realise that missing an altimeter will not stop you from putting the glider down safely.

If you are still not sure about this, just check with your instructor and find out whether he (or she) will allow you to cover up the altimeter on the next few landings at your home airfield. It won't be long before you are perfectly happy performing landings without reference to the altimeter and only then you can consider yourself one step closer to cross-country flying.

9.3 Determining wind direction

Now let's discuss how to determine the wind direction away from the airfield. Back home, the duty instructor selected the runway after taking the prevailing wind into account, but when landing in a field 100 km away it's essential to check the wind direction ourselves. Not that that is a problem, because every self-respecting glider pilot should always know the wind direction on the ground. After all, this information is absolutely crucial if we want to position ourselves correctly in relation to thermal sources and thermal triggers.

Particularly when landing into an unknown field, we should point the aircraft nicely into wind. However, there are two exceptions to the rule. The first one is an uphill landing in hilly terrain and the second is a landing directly into the sun when it is low on the horizon. Landing directly into wind gives us the lowest speed above the ground, but if we are looking directly into the sun on our round-out we will have very poor forward visibility, which tends to become a safety issue in itself. If, on the other hand, we leave the sun 10 or even 20 degrees to one side we have traded improved visibility for a very small crosswind component. It is not hard to see why this is perhaps the better option in the far majority of into-sun landings.

Now back to landings into wind. Let's assume we are flying on a day with plenty of cumulus clouds around. Under these circumstances, we can be forgiven for keeping our eyes on the clouds and not on the wind at ground level. At this point, a word of warning on using the direction of travelling cloud shadows as a wind indicator is warranted. More often than not, the wind direction at cloud level is very different from that at ground level. In fact, a 100-degree difference in wind direction is quite normal, especially on days with a high cloud base.

Motor gliders – an ideal tool for outlanding training
Photo: Diamond Aircraft

As soon as we have to think about a possible outlanding, we need to establish where the wind is coming from. Unfortunately, only very few fields feature a windsock (although they are usually the best option) and it goes without saying that we cannot simply assume that the wind direction is roughly the same as it was back home. In fact, it is very seldom the case, making it necessary to check the wind right then and there.

By far the best option is to look out for cars driving on unsealed roads. A cloud of trailing dust enables us to determine the wind direction at ground level although the motion of the vehicle can give a misleading picture. Farmers working their fields also leave a trail of dust and sometimes the same applies to moving stock. Generally speaking, it is still common in the countryside to burn rubbish and the resulting smoke gives a glider pilot a useful indication of wind strength and direction. Last but not least, smoke from houses or factories serve as an excellent wind indicator.

If all else fails, we can look around for a dam or small lake. Wind produces small ripples on the surface of the water, but not close to the protecting windward shore. Again, we have found a wind indicator almost as reliable as a windsock.

9.4 Circuit planning

Landing a glider away from your home airfield and into a strange field is anything but boring. Unless you are the exception to the rule, you will find that the adrenalin is pumping because all familiar landmarks you used for reference at your home airfield are suddenly missing. All you can rely on is your best judgement of distance to the aiming point and your height above the ground. It is very easy for experienced outlanders to say that there is absolutely no need to get stressed about an outlanding, but doing it for the first time undoubtedly represents a real challenge.

The mind can play some funny games with us, especially in stressful situations. It can suddenly remember that there might not be enough fuel left in the car for the retrieve or it could remind us that the last time we looked at our trailer one tyre was a bit down in pressure. Don't laugh, because I'm not the only one to have experienced such distractions. Many other pilots have reported the same thing, and there is every chance that such minor details will flash through our minds when we need to concentrate most. The lesson is clear; we need to focus our mind on the job at hand and perform every single landing check calmly. More than anything else, a cool head is needed and it is important to remind ourselves of that. Why not calm yourself down and say aloud, "I have landed this aircraft many times before and I can do it again right here and now. My instructor would be very proud watching me now".

Once a decision is made to land in a chosen paddock, turn the radio off and the audio vario down to avoid possible distractions. Then calmly perform your FUBST check (Flaps, Undercarriage, Ballast, Speed, Trim) and consider this field your base of operation. In other words, make a decision and stick to it – even if you discover some unpleasant surprises very late in the circuit. This is no time for indecision, as experience shows that changing our mind at the very last minute is inviting disaster. Even if we find something troublesome on closer scrutiny, it is usually too late for an alternative course of action – we simply have to cope as best we can.

Over the years, I have done a fair few outlandings myself. To be frank with you, initially I was never very impressed with my circuits because, inexplicably, I was leaving out my base leg. Just a few days after such an outlanding, I was on my way to visit a nearby national gliding championship and happened to observe two pilots struggling to make it home into a sea breeze at the end of a long day. Slowly but steadily they were getting lower and eventually decided to outland next to the road I was travelling on. Both of them put the aircraft down quite safely, but without even the slightest hint of a base leg.

That made me think. I was not the only one struggling with proper circuits in outlanding situations and, when giving the matter a bit more thought a day or two later, it became crystal clear why pilots are performing unconventional circuits in such situations.

Let me share my findings with you right now. During outlanding training, we were all taught to have a final and thorough inspection of the field on the downwind leg. Plain common sense and self preservation

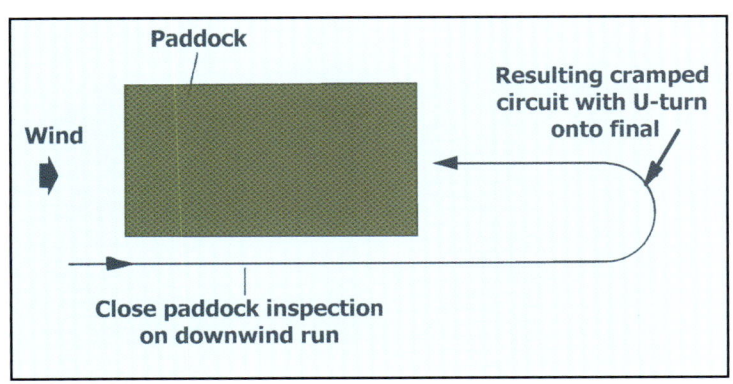

Figure 105: Circuit without base leg

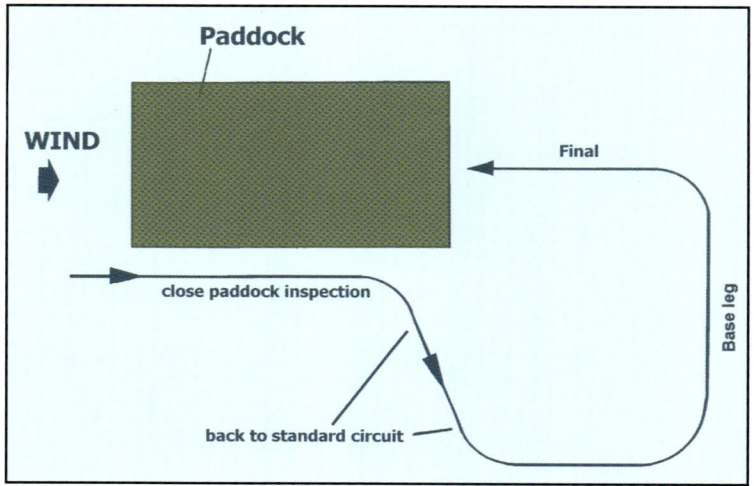

instincts would suggest that that is a very good idea indeed. However, performing such a visual inspection means that we must fly a very close downwind leg. The resulting circuit is illustrated in Figure 105.

Although the base leg was invented for very good reasons it is completely missing in the above circuit pattern despite the fact that it is especially important in an outlanding situation. No ifs and buts, we must get the base leg back into our circuit. My answer to the problem is a slightly modified circuit as shown in Figure 106 above, but I would like to stress that this should not be viewed as a recommendation for every outlanding.

Figure 106: Modified circuit after a close paddock inspection

In my view, such a slightly modified circuit solves the problem and offers the best compromise between being able to inspect the outlanding field at close proximity on one hand and performing an almost conventional circuit on the other.

9.5 Field selection

Let me say a few words on the old "wisdom" of landing near a farm or even a pub. Landing safely and without risk to our glider is what matters most and we would be well advised to put convenience very low on our list of priorities. A suitable field is more important than anything else at this point in time.

After all, we want to fly the glider the next day, not waste time making arrangements to get it fixed. Keeping the ground run as short as possible also minimises the risk of unpleasant surprises. My advice is to apply brakes to shorten the ground run as much as possible and refrain from taxiing towards the gate. The longer the ground run, the greater the chances of colliding with an obstacle or dropping into a depression hidden amongst the vegetation.

Perhaps now is the time to discuss a few specific outlanding checks. Over the years I have made it a habit of doing them every time I descend through about 2000 ft above ground level and strongly recommend that you do the same. Experienced "outlanders" have found an easy way to memorise this checklist because for some reason all items start with an "S" and I think that's why it's called "5 S checklist".

SIZE, SURFACE, SLOPE, STOCK, SINGLE-WIRE POWER LINES

Size

Without a doubt, size is the simplest part of this checklist. With a bit of experience and a good dose of common sense, every pilot should be able to judge whether the paddock is of a sufficient size to allow a landing without hitting the fence at either end. If it is at all doubtful whether the field is big enough consider landing diagonally across the field as it will add considerably to the available landing distance. In the unlikely event that you approach an obstacle (e.g. a fence) on your ground run it might be advisable to put one wing firmly on the ground. Although this will result in a deliberate ground loop, it is more often than not the lesser evil. Just make sure you push the stick firmly in the top right or left corner.

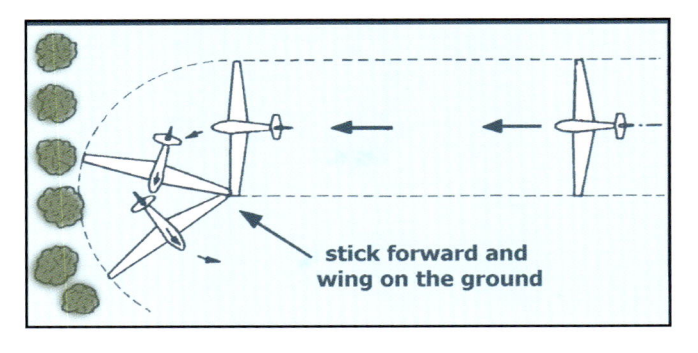

Figure 107: Deliberate groundloop to avoid obstacle

This will keep the wing down and the tail wheel or the skid off the ground. Your glider will definitely thank you for it but the above comment doesn't necessarily apply to a glider with a nose wheel.

Colliding with a fence is potentially very dangerous because, if the canopy fails, the pilot can potentially be decapitated by the wire. One European country has made it compulsory to fit a steel bar just below the perspex as a wire deflector for precisely this reason.

In this context, a word or two on visual illusions is appropriate. Relatively small fields will appear much bigger, especially after flying at a low altitude for some time. A narrow field can appear longer than it is and a wide one much shorter. These optical illusions should be taken into account especially if we have selected an outlanding field with obstructions in the approach path. The resulting touchdown further into the field could see you closer to the fence than you would like to be.

Surface

Pilots not born and bred on the land often find it difficult to judge the surface (or vegetation) of a field from the air, although this skill is much easier to acquire than first thought. Just remember to select a few suitable fields while driving to the airfield and later in the day look at them again from the cockpit of a glider. Repeating the

Mt. Cook, New Zealand's highest mountain hiding behind clouds.

exercise weekend after weekend will soon give you a pretty good idea on the suitability of certain fields for outlanding purposes. Ask yourself whether you would drive your car through the field at a speed of 100 km/h. If the answer is "yes", the field is suitable but if the answer is "no", you had better look for an alternative.

Generally speaking, fields with vegetation more than a foot high should be avoided. As a rough rule of thumb we can say that, if we can't see the ground between the plants in the crop it is too high. If we can see the wind waving the crop, it is clearly much too high and likely to result in a ground loop with some damage to the glider. However, if we have no choice but to land in a crop, we should act as if the top of the crop were at ground level and flare accordingly. Touch down with the slowest possible speed and keep the wings level.

Ploughed fields should be avoided as the ground is normally very soft or extremely rough. In case there is no other choice make sure you land parallel to the grooves. Some pilots advocate not extending the gear in such emergencies. As circumstances vary and the type of glider also plays an important role, I prefer not to discuss this subject in greater depth other than to say that good undercarriage designs absorb a lot of energy.

Not a good place for an outlanding

By far the best options are fallow or stubble fields. Fallow fields are left un-cropped for a season and when viewed from the air they appear to have a greyish colour. They are always my preferred option as the ground is generally quite firm with little risk of damaging a farmer's crop. The same applies, more or less, to stubble fields, but we will usually find that the ground is not quite so firm. Also there is a risk of starting a fire when driving a retrieve vehicle with a catalytic converter into them. On the other hand, stubble fields are easily recognisable from the air due to the tracks left behind by headers and tractors.

Slope

If we can detect any slope from the air, the field is simply not suitable. Only in an extreme emergency would we consider landing in such a field as slope detectable from the air will prove to be much worse in reality. Flying directly over a field makes it impossible to detect any slope and therefore I recommend viewing the field from about 30° to the horizontal. If committed to land in a steeply sloping field, consider landing uphill, but make sure to have extra speed for the uphill run and flare very close to the ground. The speed will wash off very quickly indeed.

Only when crossing a hilly part of the country with insufficient height can we possibly be faced with a difficult field selection. Less-experienced pilots in particular should keep this in mind at all times and only venture over difficult terrain if they have the altitude to cross it safely. How does that saying go? A superior pilot is one who uses superior judgement to avoid situations which require him to demonstrate his superior skill. In other words, never let a glider take you somewhere your brain didn't get to a few minutes earlier!

Stock

Avoid landing in a field with stock in it. Even if we are absolutely sure that we can avoid animals on our landing run, it is a good idea to select a different field, as some animals are known to have a tendency towards nibbling on the most expensive parts of our precious gliders. There are plenty of funny stories of pilots unable to get to a phone because they were kept busy chasing curious cattle away. Cattle seldom have third-party liability insurance, but still they seem to enjoy the company of gliders. They have managed to step on wings and seemingly enjoy the taste of ailerons or elevators and the like. Just imagine you are trying to contact base and notify your crew but are surrounded by cattle and you want to fly the aircraft another day. Also be very suspicious of a single cow in a field. It could be a bull unappreciative of the fact that you are invading his territory.

Horses are known to have bolted and jumped fences. I guarantee that the farmer will not be impressed if he finds you in his field and his horses in his neighbour's crop. Sheep are generally known to take little notice of gliders. When they see a glider dropping into their field they tend to run around a bit nervously at first but calm down quickly and reassemble in a remote corner of the field a few moments later. Still, it is a good idea to select another field provided this option is available.

Single– wire power lines

Overhead power lines are the almost invisible foe of glider pilots. They remain the principal method of delivering electrical power to remote locations but are extremely difficult to see from the air. In fact, many pilots (including myself) have given up looking for the wire but search for the poles instead. The poles stand out far better as farmers can't get their heavy machinery close to them. As a result a small area around the poles usually remains uncropped and often this shows up quite well from the air. Often these wires follow lines of trees with the result that even the poles are nearly invisible. Never land close to a farmhouse until you have located the power supply cable and never select a field without checking first whether it is crossed (or partly surrounded) by power lines.

9.6 Dos and Don'ts

Now that the theory and the "5 S checklist" are behind us, let's talk about common sense. But first a quick reminder that it is high noon to perform the cockpit check and dump any water ballast if we haven't already done so.

Sitting in a comfortable armchair and reading this book every sensible glider pilot would agree that it is prudent to prepare for an outlanding when approaching 2000 ft above ground level. I'm glad we all agree on that point, but experience shows that many pilots react very differently indeed when they find themselves in such a situation. Many of us get tense and start thinking about the expense, the inconvenience, the competition scores and a potentially long wait for the retrieve crew.

Impressions of Western USA from the air

(Photos courtesy of Gavin Wills - Glide Omarama)

Outlandings

Safety first

For very good reasons, lookout is very high on the list of priorities in training. However, glider pilots need to know the limitations of their vision and for this reason the recent publication "How to Avoid a Mid-air Collision" is reproduced in part with the kind permission of the Air Safety Foundation. Only minor alterations were made to include matters relating to gliding operations.

10.3.1 Putting the focus on vision.

Vision is vulnerable to just about everything: dust; fatigue, emotion, germs, fallen eyelashes, age, optical illusions and the number of drinks consumed at last night's party. In flight, our vision is altered by factors including atmospheric conditions, canopy distortion, too much oxygen or too little, acceleration, glare, heat, lighting and glider design.

Most of all, the eye is vulnerable to the vagaries of the mind. We can "see" and identify only what the mind lets us see. A daydreaming pilot staring out into space sees no approaching traffic and is probably the number one candidate for an in-flight collision.

One function of the eye that is a source of constant problems to the pilot (though he or she is probably never aware of it) is the time required for accommodation. Our eyes automatically accommodate for (or refocus on) near and far objects. But the change from something up close, like a dark instrument panel two feet away, to a well-lit landmark or an aircraft a few kilometres away takes at least one to two seconds for the eye to accommodate. That's a long time, given that you need about 10 seconds to avoid in fight collisions.

It can not get more exciting than this

Another focusing problem usually occurs at very high altitudes but it can happen at lower levels on vague, colourless days above a haze or cloud layer when no distinct horizon is visible. If there is little or nothing to focus on at infinity, we do not focus at all.

We experience "empty-field myopia" staring but seeing nothing, even approaching traffic. The National Transportation Safety Board (NTSB) has studied the effects of "binocular vision" during investigations of in-flight collisions, with the conclusion that this is also a causal factor. To accept what we see, we need to receive cues from both eyes. If an object is visible to one eye but hidden from the other by an obstruction, the total image is blurred and not always acceptable to the mind.

Another inherent eye problem is that of narrow field of vision. Although our eyes accept light rays from an arc of nearly 200 degrees, they are limited to a relatively limited area (approximately 10 to 15 degrees) in which they can actually focus on and classify an object. Though we can perceive movement in the periphery, we cannot identify what is happening out there. We tend not to believe what we see out of the corner of our eyes. This, aided by the brain, often leads to "tunnel vision".

This limitation is compounded by the fact that, at a distance, an aircraft on a collision course with you will appear motionless. It will remain in a seemingly stationary position, without appearing either to move or grow in size for a relatively long time, and then bloom into a huge mass filling your canopy. This is known as "blossom effect". Since we need motion or contrast to attract our eye's attention, this becomes a frightening factor when you realise that a large bug smear or dirty spot on the canopy can hide a converging aircraft until it is too close to be avoided. Also be aware that fashion sunglasses can be useless in reducing glare and in some cases, can obstruct clear vision.

The eye is also limited by environment. Optical properties of the atmosphere alter the appearance of traffic, particularly on hazy days. Terms like "Limited visibility" in aviation forecasts actually mean, "Limited vision". You may be operating legally when you have five kilometres of visibility, but at that distance on a hazy day, opposing traffic is difficult to detect. At a range closer than five kilometres – even though detectable – a very fast powered aeroplane on a collision course may be difficult to avoid.

Lighting also affects our vision. Glare, usually worse on a sunny day or during flight directly into sun, not only makes objects hard to see but it also makes scanning uncomfortable. And an object that is well lit will have a high degree of contrast and will be easy to detect. One with low contrast at the same distance may be impossible to see. For instance, when the sun is behind you, an opposing aircraft will stand out clearly, but when you're looking into the sun and your traffic is "backlit", it's a different story.

Another contrast problem is trying to find an aircraft against a cluttered background. If it is between you and terrain that is vari-coloured or heavily dotted with buildings, it will blend into the background until it is quite close. And of course, there is the mind, which can distract us to the point of not seeing anything at all, or lull us into cockpit myopia – staring at an instrument without "seeing" it.

Perception is affected by many factors. It all boils down to the fact that pilots, like anyone else, tend to over-estimate their visual abilities and to misunderstand their eyes' limitations. Since the number one cause of in-flight collisions is the failure to properly adhere to the see-and-avoid concept, we can conclude that the best way to avoid them is to learn how to use our eyes in an efficient external scan.

The above article already highlights quite a few limitations in terms of our ability to detect other traffic. Although the article was written with relatively fast powered aircraft in mind, the picture isn't fundamentally different in gliding. After being involved in a mid-air collision himself, the Australian glider pilot Harry Medlicott has devoted a lot of time to this particular subject and has published several articles to help his peers with effective lookout strategies. Harry needs to be congratulated, not only for his courage, but also for his determination to make the sport safer for all of us. The author feels very privileged to have permission to include one of his publications on lookout in a slightly modified form below.

10.3.2 Good lookout is no accident

For every mid-air collision there are probably a thousand incidents where a pilot's comfort zone has been compromised with an unintentional separation of less than 50 metres. In virtually every instance, at least one pilot should have had a clear view of the other glider, so why do we have such a poor midair collision record?

No pilot willingly exposes himself or herself to unnecessary risks and probably every pilot believes that his lookout is of an adequate standard, but obviously that's not the case. This article explores some of the optical factors involved as a help to developing an effective lookout program.

Our vision can be divided into three sections.

Foveal vision is that part of our eyesight which we use for examining detail and subtends less than 5°.

Binocular vision covers the 60° straight ahead of our face and is enhanced by having the benefit of having the input from both eyes. Let's call this 60° our "field of vision".

Peripheral vision extends about 90° to each side. In this part of our eye the nerves to the brain are bundled in a way which precludes fine vision, but picks up movement or a difference in light intensity, such as a flashing light.

When looking at one picture in a comic strip we do not take in the next or proceeding pictures even though the whole page is well within our field of vision. Even when reading the words in a picture, the adjoining figures are indistinct and not recognised. Exactly the same happens with our distance vision. We see the object which is the subject of our attention clearly, but anything else is not taken in unless it is moving or flashing. Unfortunately, gliders on a collision course do not move relative to the canopy and only expand rapidly in size when they are so close that a collision is a real possibility. The exception is when one of the gliders is turning.

How much time do we have to identify a possible hazard and take evasive action then? Gliders cruise at between 25 and 50 metres per second. In a head-on situation, 1 kilometre can be covered in 10 seconds and it is only in the last few seconds that it expands from being a small mark on the canopy to an unmistakeable and unavoidable object. US Naval Aviation estimates the time taken to see an object, identify it as an aircraft, recognise collision risk, decide to take avoidance measures and delay due to reaction and aircraft inertia at 12.5 seconds.

It is obvious that looking away from where you are going for more than five seconds is fraught with risk. Tasks with an out-and-return content, or POST where head-on situations can occur, are best avoided. They are a disaster waiting to happen. Joining or flying with other gliders in close proximity obviously requires great attention and the time span for a distraction is very short indeed.

What a delight! Photo: Manfred Muench

Now let's identify some common lookout faults, as follows:

a) Spending too much time looking at instruments is a common problem. It helps to have ASI, vario and GPS readouts at the top of the instrument panel. Can you change radio channels without looking? Keeping our heads in the cockpit for 10 seconds while changing channels is not an option.

b) Using an audio vario is a must when flying in or near thermals with other gliders.

c) Not looking into the airspace into which you are about to fly is just as common. First look for other traffic and only then initiate a turn – not the other way around. Look both ways prior to releasing from the tug and look up before you reduce speed. Most pilots continue to look straight ahead, or roll out of a turn without looking in the direction of the down going wing.

d) Fixation – probably the most common cause of mid-air incidents. We tend to spend too long studying a feature of interest to the detriment of looking where we are going. Pilots would not dream of driving a car at high speed without keeping their eyes on the road and only scan the rear vision mirror or side roads for a second or two before focusing back on the road again. However, some pilots seem quite happy to study clouds or the airfield on which they intend landing for 10 seconds or more while flying at speeds of up to 200 km/h. It is small wonder that a series of disasters have occurred near airfields.

e) Less common but not unusual is the pilot, generally inexperienced, who almost continuously moves his head in a random fashion without carefully studying anything. He is using his eyesight in an inefficient manner, probably not identifying an item of interest even though it was momentarily in his field of vision.

Scan definitions

a) Cruising scan

Forward conical scan of 60° to the right and left as well as up and down. This area

The old and the new!

ahead of the glider is a prime collision risk zone. While cruising we must regularly move our eyes around our 60° field of vision to identify objects of interest. This is not a continuous flowing action but a movement, stop and focus, move again, stop and focus, etc. We only identify objects whilst our eyes are stopped and see virtually nothing when they are moving. A scan around our 60° field of vision without moving our head will probably take about 3 seconds or so. When we are flying at a constant speed, an aircraft on a conflicting course will almost always be on or very close to the horizon.

b) Full scan

This is a scan of the complete visible sky. It should be conducted at regular intervals.

c) Targeted scan

The targeted scan is a scan concentrating on a specific area for specific reasons and must always be conducted prior to changing direction.

Speed and directional changes

Many pilots continue to look straight ahead when pulling up, although their vision is usually obstructed by a hat brim. Because there is every chance that another aircraft is above and behind you a targeted scan must be conducted prior to initiating speed changes. The same applies when initiating a turn or when we push the nose down for a quick acceleration on leaving a thermal for example. It is vital to perform the targeted scan prior to turning a glider and to ensure that the area is clear of any other traffic.

Circuit area

Don't stare at the airfield! One good look should take no more than a few seconds and then look out for traffic in the circuit area. By all means think about what you saw on the airfield and then look back again, but ensure that the high traffic density near the airfield does not create a conflict. If you see another aircraft, don't fixate on that either. It is the aircraft you haven't seen which could get you. Do a careful targeted scan both ways when joining down wind, base and particularly final. Your downwind radio call should be made as you enter that leg so that aircraft about to join the circuit, perhaps further on than you, are aware of your position.

Sources of lift.

Maintaining a careful scan is particularly important when studying clouds or turning gliders. Studying them for 10 seconds before scanning ahead and to each side is far too long. Have a good look and then think about other gliders which may also be attracted to the same lift source and are similarly distracted. Also think of aircraft other than gliders. A pilot following another glider has a special responsibility to fly in a manner which will not endanger the leading glider. Being to one side requires vigilance for when the leading glider turns a conflicting situation can arise very quickly. It is preferable to fly sufficiently to one side to allow the leading glider to turn without a conflict or to stay well back, about one kilometre.

Let's summarise our findings on collision avoidance.

- Train yourself to develop good scanning habits. Move your vision from point to point systematically.

- In level flight the area from which a threat is most likely to emanate will be 45° to each side and 10 to 15° above or below the horizon. Therefore a cruising scan can be performed with modest and untiring head movements. Give this area regular attention. You should not look away from the view in front of the glider for more than 5 seconds.

- Perform priority scans as you approach areas possibly occupied by other aircraft such as airfields, turning points, thermalling gliders or thermal markers such as cumulus clouds. A full scan involves looking as far to each side and behind as you can and upwards and downwards as well.

- When about to turn, carefully scan the airspace into which you will be flying. When reducing speed check the airspace above you. When accelerating you have a blind spot beneath you. Always perform targeted scans and accelerate smoothly.

- Except when one is turning, aircraft on a collision course start as a small stationary object and only increase in size rapidly when a collision is probably unavoidable.

- Minimise time looking inside the cockpit, arrange instruments thoughtfully, use an audio vario, remove obstructions to good vision such as a compass on top of the instrument panel and keep your canopy clean.

- Maintain situational awareness. Keep a mental picture of the aircraft around you. To do this you must be very familiar with your aircraft, in current practice and unaffected by fatigue, hypoxia or lifestyle excesses.

A good lookout is essential, but so too are safe flying manners. What you achieve on your next flight will only be a distant memory in a few years time. Just make sure you are around to enjoy it!

Harry Medlicott

A lovely new dusting of snow on the countryside

10.6 Using the radio to enhance safety

Listening to the radio on any cross-country flying day, one can't help but feel that there are two categories of glider pilots.

Group 1 seems to think that, as the radio is one of the most expensive instruments in the panel, it is important to get their money's worth, whereas Group 2 is only ever heard when circuit calls are to be made. Although lookout remains the main weapon against mid-air collisions, it does not mean that we can not also engage the radio in this process.

The risk of a mid-air collision is ever present as soon as several aircraft operate in the same airspace and it is especially in circumstances like these that a broadcast is most valuable. Typical examples are flying under conditions of streeting or gaggle flying of any sort. Knowing at what altitude another glider is operating, and knowing the intentions of its pilot involved can be of immense value. The exchange of this information, however, does not require a lengthy monologue and it is also totally unnecessary to repeat such broadcasts at short intervals.

When two or more gliders fly along a cloud street, for example, and the leading aircraft pulls into a thermal the broadcast could be as follows.

"Alpha Bravo Charlie abeam X–town 5000 ft climbing." The follower(s) could either reply: "Delta Echo Foxtrot 3 km behind – got you sighted" or he could simply press the transmit button twice in short succession as a sign of acknowledgement, although this gives the faster pilot no indication of the relative position of the follower.

Another prime example of the sensitive use of radio is when one glider joins another in a thermal at roughly the same level. As an example the message could be as simple as: "Alpha Bravo joining glider abeam X–town from the north."

Radio messages of that kind can go a long way towards making the sport safer for all participants. Competitively minded pilots need to decide for themselves whether a perceived impact on their competition scores outweighs the bonuses in terms of added safety.

10.7 Radio procedures

When using the radio it is important to realise that there are many users on the same frequency. Messages must be kept brief and to the point. However, in general, most glider pilots do not pay enough attention to proper radio procedures for a variety of reasons. Especially to assist newcomers to gliding the most important procedures are reproduced below.

a) For callsigns and individual letters, the Radio Phonetic Alphabet should be used.

Letter	Word	Spoken as
A	Alpha	ALF AH
B	Bravo	BRAH VOH
C	Charlie	CHAR LEE
D	Delta	DELL TAH
E	Echo	ECK OH
F	Foxtrot	FOKS TROT
G	Golf	GOLF
H	Hotel	HOH TELL
I	India	IN DEE AH
J	Juliet	JEW LEE ETT
K	Kilo	KEY LOH
L	Lima	LEE MAH
M	Mike	MIKE
N	November	NO VEM BER
O	Oscar	OSS CAH
P	Papa	PAH PAH
Q	Quebec	KEH BECK
R	Romeo	ROW ME OH
S	Sierra	SEE AIR RAH
T	Tango	TANG GO
U	Uniform	YOU NEE FORM
V	Victor	VIK TAH
W	Whiskey	WISS KEY
X	X-ray	ECKS RAY
Y	Yankee	YANG KEE
Z	Zulu	ZOO LOO

Note: Emphasis should be given to the syllables underlined.

b) Numbers should be pronounced as follows:

Number	Spoken as
0	ZE-ROH
1	WUN
2	TOO
3	THREE
4	FOW-er
5	FIFE
6	SIX
7	SEV-en
8	AIT
9	NIN-er

All numbers except thousands should be sent by pronouncing each digit separately. For example an altitude of 6200 ft should be transmitted as SIX, TWO, ZERO, ZERO feet.

c) Certain standard phrases and words should be used where applicable:

Affirm	Yes or permission granted
Negative	No or that is not correct or permission not granted
Correction	An error has been made – here is the correct version
Acknowledge	Tell me you have received and understood my message
Roger	I have received your message
Wilco	Your message received, understood and will be complied with. (Will comply)
Verify	Check that the message is correct
Go ahead	Send your message (Continue your message)
I say again	Self explanatory
Say again	" "
Speak slower	" "
Stand by	" "
That is correct	" "
How do you read?	This is a request to gauge effectiveness or serviceability of radio and should not be used in normal radio messages. It should be answered by:

Readability

Wun: your transmissions are unreadable

Two: your transmissions are readable now and then

Three: your transmissions are readable with difficulty

Fower: your transmissions are readable

Fife: your transmissions are perfectly readable

The station being called should be named first, followed by the call sign of the caller and then the message given, e.g. "Waikerie Base this is Alpha Bravo Charlie – Morgan, six thousand".

Certain messages must not be sent – e.g. those that:

1) are of a personal or private nature,

2) use obscene or improper language,

3) use the call sign of another station improperly,

4) are false or intended to deceive, or

5) are not related to operational requirements.

d) are emergency related

Should you have an emergency situation arise, the call to use is:

Mayday – repeated three times if possible, followed by call sign, position and nature of the emergency. Should an urgent situation arise, but not immediately involving the safety of the aircraft, the call to use is "Pan" three times, followed by the call sign and nature of the situation.

On cross-country flights, gliders should give a position and height at regular intervals (approx. 1 hr) to indicate their progress and thus allow the base to be of assistance if necessary. These calls should come from the glider so that the pilot can choose a convenient time to transmit. Calls from base, or others, could be at times when the pilot needs to concentrate and thus be a nuisance. Should this happen, the pilot should acknowledge and indicate they will call back when less busy.

Range to be expected for air to ground station is relative to height and under good conditions, can be:

1000 ft - 70 km

2000 ft - 90 km

3000 ft - 120 km

5000 ft - 160 km

8000 ft - 200 km

VHF radio gives "line of sight" range and ground–to–ground ranges are usually only a few kilometres.

10.8 Open class manoeuvrability

Compared to a 15 m wingspan glider, all Open Class aircraft have a significantly slower control response. With a wingspan of over 25 m and a weight of approx. 800 kg, these gliders are more difficult to fly and lack the agility that pilots of smaller gliders have come to expect. Particularly, their slow rate of roll needs to be taken into account by other pilots. Even if the pilot of an Open Class glider is taking evasive action it will not result in an instant change of direction.

For this reason, it is vital for all pilots to keep all changes of direction predictable and give Open Class gliders a little more space. Their thermalling speed is not significantly different to other ballasted gliders, but thermalling flap settings further reduce their already slow rate of roll. A change of speed also happens more slowly due to much higher inertia. On the other hand, their slow and graceful motion allows a good anticipation of their movement and is unlikely to give you any surprises.

Safety first

**Open class:
Graceful
but often
lacking agility
Photo:
Peter Selinger**

10.9 Gliders with retractable engines

The growing popularity of gliders with retractable engines is evident when looking around gliding sites today. The self–launching variety offer greater independence and convenience but even gliders with smaller sustainer or 'turbo' engines can be used to explore areas otherwise out of reach.

We will leave the pros and cons of the different types aside but instead concentrate on the safety aspects. Statistics clearly indicate that having a retractable engine does not equate to enhanced safety. In fact, we see outlanding accidents despite built-in engines for a number of reasons.

First, the increased sink rate of gliders with extended engines seems to catch many pilots by surprise. A decision to start the engine must be made in good time, as the sink rate with an extended engine can be even higher than that caused by extending the airbrakes. The resulting loss of height might lead to a close encounter with the ground if the engine fails to start promptly.

Second, we need to consider the notorious unreliability of two–stroke engines. Well-known starting problems after lengthy periods of inactivity (sometimes combined with less-than-perfect engine management) have resulted in numerous starting failures. The very high levels of vibration have been proven to play havoc with ignition systems as well as the extension mechanism. Automated extension and retraction systems rely on a large number of sensors and switches, all of which are well-known to create serviceability and reliability problems.

Older power plant designs do not feature fixed engines but instead lift the whole drive unit out of the fuselage. This engine tilting contributes to the reliability problems mentioned above. Pilots should think twice before they put all their trust in two–stroke engines. In contrast, modern installations only extend the propeller and leave the engine in place in the fuselage where it is permanently connected to an effective muffler system.

Retractable engines offer independence and also allow contacting areas normally out of reach. They are also a convenient means of getting home after the day has died but they don't extend the daylight!

Safety first

10.9.1 Take-offs in self-launching gliders

Self-launching gliders are usually equipped with engines just powerful enough to satisfy the design rules and to perform quite satisfactorily at "standard atmosphere" conditions. (Sea level pressure of 1013.25 hPa at a temperature of 15°C, and an initial lapse rate of −6.5°C/km.) The aircraft's flight manual nominates take off distances based on these conditions but we need to keep in mind that we often operate under circumstances which are very different indeed. High ambient temperatures, soft runways, long grass, uphill slopes, low ambient pressures, tailwinds, and a high airfield elevation can increase take off distances considerably.

The following table provides some guidance.

Table 12: Approximate increase in take off distance over an obstacle of 50 ft.

Circumstance	Factor	Multiple
per 10% increase in aeroplane weight	20%	1.2
an increase of 1000 ft in airfield altitude	10%	1.1
an increase of 10C in ambient temperature	10%	1.1
dry grass on firm soil	20%	1.2
wet grass on firm soil	30%	1.3
2% uphill slope	10%	1.1
a tailwind of 10% of lift-off speed	20%	1.2
soft ground or snow	25%+	1.25 +

Air density is the single most important factor affecting any aeroplane's performance. It is dependant on the ambient temperature, airfield elevation as well as the atmospheric pressure and has a direct bearing on:

- The lift generated by the wings
- The efficiency of the propeller
- The power output of the engine

As a result of a density altitude which is higher than the actual physical altitude, the following effects are observed:

1) The aircraft will accelerate more slowly as a result of reduced engine power production.
2) The aircraft will need to achieve a higher airspeed to attain the same lift. This implies both a longer acceleration period on the runway before lift-off and requires a higher airspeed while climbing.
3) The aircraft will climb more slowly as a result of reduced power production and lift.

Because all adverse effects are additive it is perhaps best if we look at an example together to demonstrate this:

A pilot of a self launching glider carrying water ballast amounting to 20% of the aircraft's normal weight wants to take off from a wet grass runway at an airfield with an elevation of 1000 ft, a 2% uphill slope and with an ambient temperature of 25°C. What percentage increase in distance can the pilot expect for his climb over a 50ft obstacle?

Safety first

a) 20% higher weight - increase of 40% = Multiple of 1.40
b) Wet grass runway - increase of 30% = Multiple of 1.30
c) Elevation of 1000 ft - increase of 10% = Multiple of 1.10
d) 2% uphill slope - increase of 10% = Multiple of 1.10
e) 25°C temperature - increase of 10% = Multiple of 1.10

Total = 1.4 × 1.3 × 1.1 × 1.1 × 1.1 = 2.42 - almost 2.5 times the take off distance compared to standard atmosphere conditions and flight manual figures. If in doubt, pilots with self launching gliders should err on the side of caution and opt for an aero-tow or winch launch. Safety first!!!

Warming the engine......

..... and climbing away. Photo: Manfred Muench

Safety first

ASW 28-18
heading towards
the vast westerm
plains in Australia
Photo:
Paul Wiggins

Chapter 10

11 Ridge lift and slope soaring

11.1 Introduction

Thermals are by far the most commonly used sources of lift, but glider pilots are frequently blessed with meteorological conditions that provide alternative forms of updraughts. Ridge lift is very common in areas of suitable topography and therefore an entire chapter is devoted to this subject.

Many spectacular flights have been performed by pilots making full use of the mountain ridges that in some parts of the world can be hundreds, if not thousands, of kilometres in length. The Appalachian Ridge in the north-east of the United States is a prime example. But even a much shorter and seemingly unspectacular mountain range can provide useful lift as long as pilots combine some experience and skill with a basic theoretical understanding of the subject. For this reason we will first touch on the theory and examine the best conditions for ridge lift. The most appropriate flying tactics will be considered the in the second part of this chapter.

11.2 Theoretical fundamentals

Ridge soaring (sometimes referred to as slope soaring) is the art of keeping a glider in a patch of air that rises at least as fast as the sink rate of the glider. If the updraught on the upwind side of a ridge or mountain is stronger, the aircraft climbs, but the glider will inevitably come down if the surrounding air ascends at a slower rate.

**Slope soaring the cliffs at Torrens Pines, California
Photo:
Marshall Martin**

Ridge lift and slope soaring

Rather than performing tight circles we simply fly parallel to the hill or mountain and gain altitude in the process. Of course we must eventually turn back, but there is nothing that stops us from completing this 180° turn in an area of a strong updraught. If indeed a certain part of the hill works exceptionally well, we can even fly some figure-of-eight patterns to take advantage of strong pockets of lift.

Only about two wingspans from the mountain face

Although ridge lift seldom provides spectacularly strong updrafts, the lift generally covers a relatively large area and hence presents us with less of a challenge compared to conventional thermal soaring. Provided the wind is strong enough, we can slope soar from first to last light and gain height effortlessly by flying straight and level without worrying about bank angles, thermal sources, thermal triggers and the like. After all, this is how gliders stayed airborne in the 1920s, before the development of the variometer and the discovery of thermal lift. When meteorologists talk about ridge lift they often refer to it as orographic movement of air. Although this sounds a bit more scientific, it simply means that when a wind strikes an obstacle it has no choice but to divert around or over it. If the obstacle is a conical mountain, the air can divert to the right or the left of it without being deflected in a vertical direction. No vertical airflow – no workable lift – no joy for glider pilots.

However, if the mountain is long enough and the wind strikes it at the right angle, the air has no

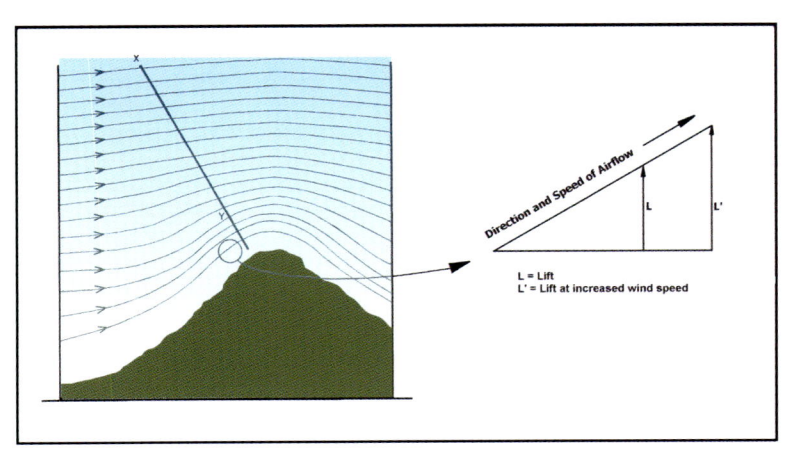

Figure 108: Airflow over a mountain ridge

Chapter 11

275

choice but to rise and flow over the top. When that happens, we only need to fly the glider into this area to soar with comparatively little effort.

The strongest updrafts are always found where the steepest deflection of air occurs – not right above the top of the ridge but along the X-Y line extending approximately 45° out from the crest of the ridge as shown in Figure 86. When we look at the airflow over the ridge more closely and divide it into horizontal and vertical components, the following three fundamentals spring to mind almost immediately.

- We can only expect to gain altitude if the vertical component (Lift L) is stronger than the sink rate of our glider.
- The rate of lift increases in direct proportion to the wind speed.
- At lower levels, the air is deflected approximately in line with the gradient of the underlying ridge.

It is important to note that the wind speed not only dictates the strength of the lift but also has a major bearing on the maximum possible altitude. Provided we are not troubled by a low inversion, we can usually climb a little higher when the wind is stronger.

11.3 Conditions affecting ridge soaring

There are numerous other complicating factors, which do not make ridge soaring a straightforward gliding activity. So far we have only looked at a perfectly shaped ridge with the wind blowing onto it perpendicularly. However, in the real world there exist uneven mountains with changing gradients and varying peak heights. On top of that, we are usually confronted with a wind blowing from a less than ideal direction. As might be expected, changes in the topography also have a bearing on the local airflow, which not only influences the characteristics of the ridge lift, but also its precise location as well as its strength or its vertical extent.

Although there are only very few sure things in gliding, we can be absolutely certain that:

a) moving air always travels along the path of the least resistance, and

b) air moves fastest where it can flow relatively unimpeded.

Implementing this knowledge takes us a huge step closer to predicting the presence of updrafts and, indeed, the likely position of them. Reputable meteorologists such as the late C. E. Wallington closely examined ridge lift more than 40 years ago and theoretically determined the location for the strongest updrafts in relation to the mountain ridge.

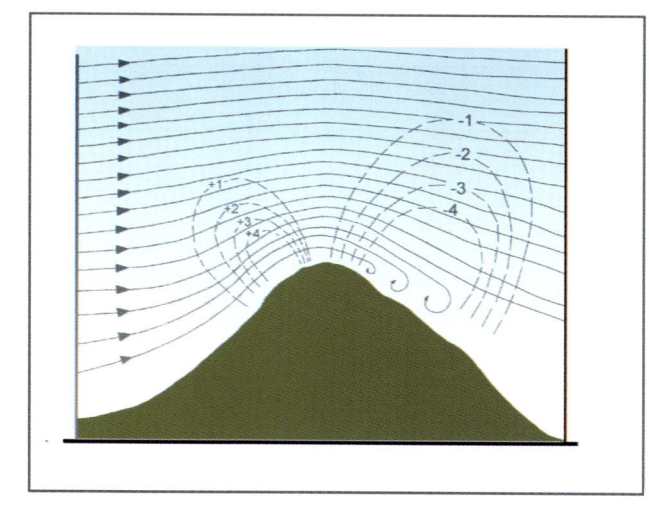

These findings were based on a semi-circular shaped ridge but, as such mountains are almost never found (perhaps with the exception of Australia's Uluru, formerly Ayers Rock); a careful attempt was made to transfer the results into a more realistic cross section of a ridge as per Figure 109.

Please note that Figure 109

Figure 109: Lift / sink distribution

Ridge lift and slope soaring

Getting ready for a day of slope soaring in the far North of South Australia

shows a lift/sink distribution partly adopted from the Wallington findings and based partly on two decades of practical experience. For this reason, it has limited scientific relevance and should only be regarded as an attempt to show a typical lift/sink distribution around an average mountain ridge by taking the typical sink rate of a glider into account. Note that the position of the lift upwind of the ridge mirrors the sink downwind of it and that the latter is most severe just behind the crest.

Figure 109 also highlights the fact that lift and sink are strongest very close to the ridge and diminish steadily with increasing altitude or horizontal distance. This explains why we always experience a steady reduction in the climb rate with increasing altitude and why we eventually reach a point where the rate of lift approaches zero. This does not mean that the air around us has stopped rising but that we have reached a level where the air is ascending at a speed equal to the sink rate of our glider. Climbing any higher requires either a miracle or an engine.

The shape of a ridge also has a major bearing on updraughts. Although even a strong wind is unlikely to produce useful lift on a very shallow mountain, a steep escarpment doesn't necessarily guarantee strong lift either. Severe turbulence can spoil the all-important smooth airflow sufficiently to prevent the generation of reliable and usable lift. To put it differently, a nice streamlined flow around a moderately high hill can often produce stronger and more reliable updraughts than a rather turbulent airflow around a big and rather steep escarpment (Figure 110).

Mountain ranges are far from uniform and generally feature changing gradients and different peak heights. The usual bends, gaps, protrusions and saddles tend to divert the wind or even funnel it into a particular spot. Therefore, it shouldn't come as a surprise that areas of particularly strong updraughts are right next to stretches of weak or nonexistent lift. Even areas of sink need to be crossed from time to time but, as long as such ups and downs results in a net gain of altitude, these changing vertical airspeeds are of little consequence.

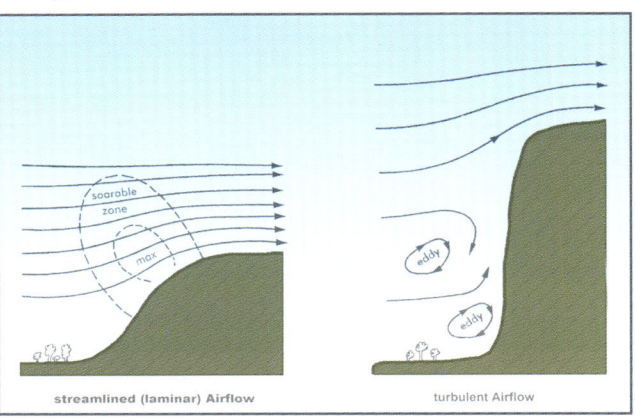

Figure 110: Turbulent and streamlined (laminar) airflow

Ridge lift and slope soaring

Figure 111: The funnel effect produced when wind strikes a ridge at an oblique angle

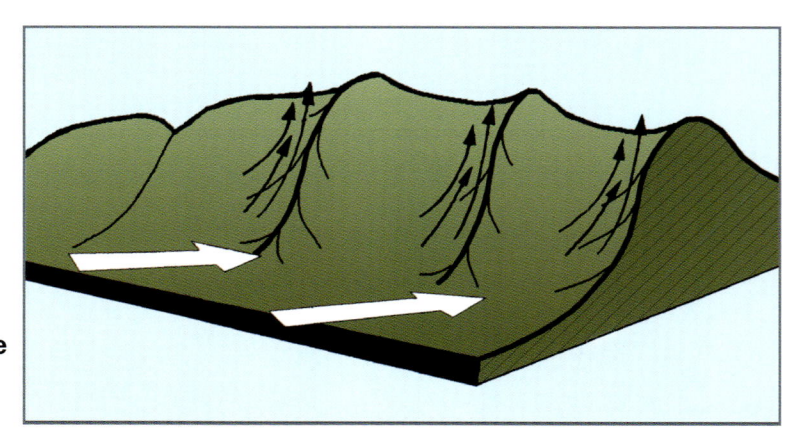

When the wind is blowing against the ridge at an oblique angle, protrusions in the face of the ridge are of particular interest as they favour a mini-venturi effect, which is basically a significantly faster local air-flow. The phenomenon is often referred to by ridge soaring glider pilots as a "funnel" simply because the air is funnelled into pockets of particularly strong updrafts (Figure 111). It is also worth noting that there can be downdraughts and turbulence on the lee side of these funnels.

11.4 Obstacles upwind of the ridge

Extra care is needed when mountains are in clusters and glider pilots are attempting to fly in the midst of them. Upwind obstacles almost always influence the airflow in mountainous areas, especially on days with a low inversion level.

Rather than following the contours of the landscape, the air is often channelled through valleys instead. Air will only rise if rising represents the path of the least resistance. This means that the flow tends to detour through valleys even if these valleys are not properly aligned with the general wind direction. For this reason, it is worth remembering that the air can bypass a particular ridge even if it appears to be located almost perpendicularly to the general airflow.

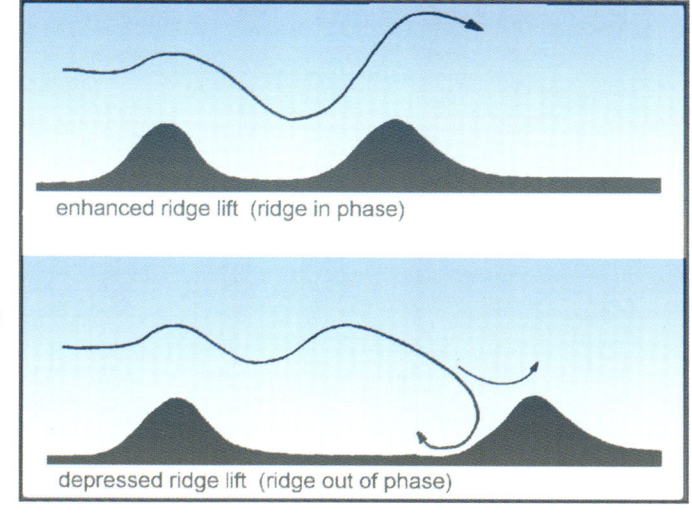

Figure 112: Vertical excitement of air by an upwind obstacle

Another complicating factor is the excitement of air in a vertical direction by another upwind mountain. In this case, the air can assume a wave-like flow pattern. The upstream vertical excitement of the air can have the welcome effect of enhancing the lift as shown in Figure 112.

But when the position of a particular ridge is not in phase with the upper airflow, extremely turbulent and unpleasant conditions can be encountered. It is not uncommon for pilots to be faced with either severely depressed ridge lift or possibly no usable lift at all. Even worse, with even a small change in wind strength, there is a real danger of one condition being replaced very quickly by the other without prior warning. One minute there can be good lift but only moments later we find nothing but turbulent sink. If that happens, glider pilots can find themselves in danger.

Therefore, enough height must be maintained for a return to a landing field within safe gliding distance of the ridge. For this reason, it is necessary to re-evaluate the ridge on each pass, looking for signs of change in the way the ridge is working. Most ridges will change their character throughout the day and it should never be assumed that the ridge will work the same way with every pass or "beat" along it.

Before we leave the subject, let us investigate the reduction in lift strength with variations in wind direction. Of course, we always prefer the wind to be blowing at a right angle to the mountain ridge, but more often than not the wind is striking the ridge at a considerably shallower angle.

Sunset at a ridge soaring camp

An example:

On Day 1 perfect ridge soaring conditions prevail. The wind is right on the ridge, which has an average gradient of 25° and the wind speed at the top of the ridge is averaging 15 kts. Overnight the wind has changed direction and is now striking the ridge at 45° although we still measure the same wind speed.

What would be the likely reduction in lift strength?

Basic calculations reveal that on Day 1 the wind is deflected upwards at a rate of 3.2 m/s or approx. 6.5 kts – a good day. Allowing for a glider's sink rate of, say, 1.5 kts, we still find lift of approx. 5 kts in close proximity to the ridge and that means that we are likely to climb to a comfortable height above the summit.

On Day 2 the wind is striking the ridge at 45° and we will experience a lift reduction of about 30%. In other words, the lift drops to around 4.5 kts and, if we make allowance for a 1.5 kts glider sink rate, only approx. 3 kts of real lift remains. Sure, there is nothing wrong with a 3 kts climb rate, but the maximum altitude is unlikely to be very much above ridge-top level. Also the speed above the ground on the into-wind run will be significantly reduced. The net result is that we can still use the ridge but we can never afford to relax and we will get a much closer look at the trees.

Ridge lift and slope soaring

Table 13: Lift reduction in relation to wind direction

Angle of wind direction towards the ridge	90	80	70	60	50	40	30
Lift reduction (%)	0	2	6	14	24	36	50

Just to get a feel for the reduction in lift, the above table was produced indicating that relatively small deviations from the optimum wind direction have only a very minor effect on the strength of the lift.

However, winds striking the ridge at a 45° angle or less result in a significant lift reduction and for this reason they should be treated with a fair degree of suspicion. Even the slightest worsening in wind direction can lead to a situation where the air starts flowing parallel to the ridge and, if that happens, we see an instantaneous collapse of updrafts.

11.5 Ridge lift and thermals

It is not hard to see how thermal activity can be embedded in ridge lift, especially if the ridge is facing the sun and hence experiences some heating during the course of the day. In the northern hemisphere, ridges facing east-southeast through to west-southwest would fall into this category. South of the Equator ranges facing east–northeast through to west-northwest are well suited.

For the ridge-soaring pilot this is a mixed blessing because thermals will inevitably increase the amount of turbulence significantly. On the other hand, ridge thermals will usually allow us to climb much higher and that should be enough reason for finding out how we can best contact these ridge-lift-embedded thermals.

Although the strongest ridge lift is found well upwind of the crest (Figure 108), the same can't be said for ridge thermals. We already know that the ground below generates thermals and it is not hard to imagine that a warm air pocket originating from the base of the ridge is pushed against the mountain face by the prevailing wind. While rising in close proximity to the mountain, it usually receives further warming and, when it finally arrives at the top, the parcel of hot air has little choice but to separate from the ridge and continue upwards as a strong thermal.

This theory is supported by everyday experiences of pilots operating in a mountain ridge environment. A weak thermal found near the foot of the ridge will almost always pick up strength as it moves closer to the crest and the strong interaction between ridge lift and thermal activity is another reason for this phenomenon. Further proof can be drawn from the fact that the lift usually weakens again as soon as the thermal drifts downwind of the crest.

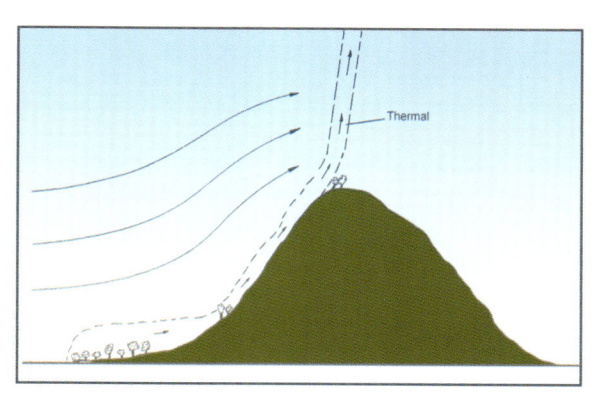

Figure 113: Ridge thermal

If we want to intercept such ridge thermals, our best chance of contacting them is to fly above or even slightly downwind of the ridge top. (Refer to Figure 113.) However, as Figure 109 shows, welcome lift upwind of the ridge is always accompanied by severe downdrafts on the downwind site. As this can constitute a serious hazard we will deal with it again under the heading "Flying tactics".

Ridge lift and slope soaring

What ridge-soaring glider pilots are faced with is often very different from what is shown in Figure 92. The vast majority of mountain ridges are not as evenly shaped as pilots would like them to be and exhibit steps, ledges and undulations of various shapes and sizes. On top of that, ridges are often overgrown with patches of tall trees. Although that does not affect ridge lift to any great extent, it has a major bearing on the location of thermals. Knowing that a heated pocket of air clings to the surface and requires a trigger to make it leave the ground, any major undulation in the face of the ridge is ideally suited to assume the role of such a thermal trigger.

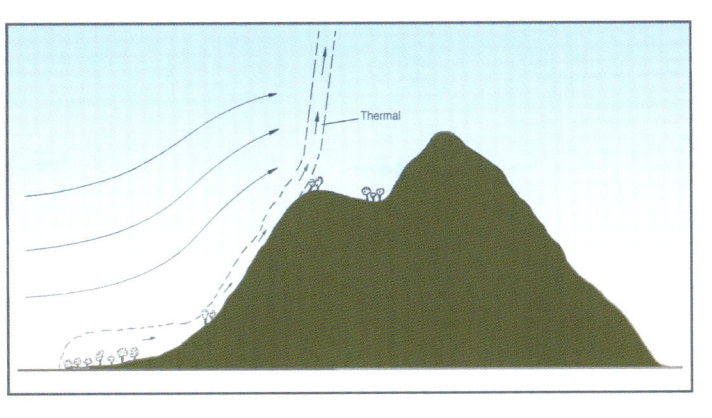

Figure 114: Thermal triggered by step in mountain face

However, once the buoyant air has separated it will continue to rise and never re-attach itself to the surface (Figure 114). Under such circumstances, the thermals are not found just above the top of the ridge but further upwind where they are more than likely mixed up with ridge lift.

11.6 Katabatic and anabatic Winds

If "katabatic wind" doesn't mean anything to you perhaps the term "mountain wind" or "drainage wind" rings a bell. In some parts of the world, the term "gully wind" is used, but people living at the bottom of hills know that rather cool and sometimes very strong down-slope winds occur. They have a tendency to spring up suddenly during the evening as a result of nocturnal radiation. The impact on ridge soaring is simple – as soon as the air starts flowing downhill, slope soaring comes to an abrupt stop.

On the other hand, down-slope winds can have a positive impact on gliding in mountainous terrain. Katabatic wind tends to displace the slightly warmer air in the centre of a valley. This usually results in smooth lift on quite a large scale. The updraught is often found near the valley centre, although seldom stronger than 2-3 kts. "Anabatic wind" describes an airflow moving upslope. The theory behind it is straightforward. As soon as the sun has warmed the ground sufficiently, the air closest to the slope becomes less dense and starts flowing uphill. The effect is strongest in areas of bare soil or better still over rocky outcrops.

According to Wallington, an anabatic airflow is usually confined to a shallow layer of about 500 ft depth, but this is more than enough to reinforce any wind generated ridge lift. It also explains why it is often possible to soar a mountain slope even if the prevailing wind at ground level appears too weak for ridge soaring. The wind speed usually picks up significantly with increasing

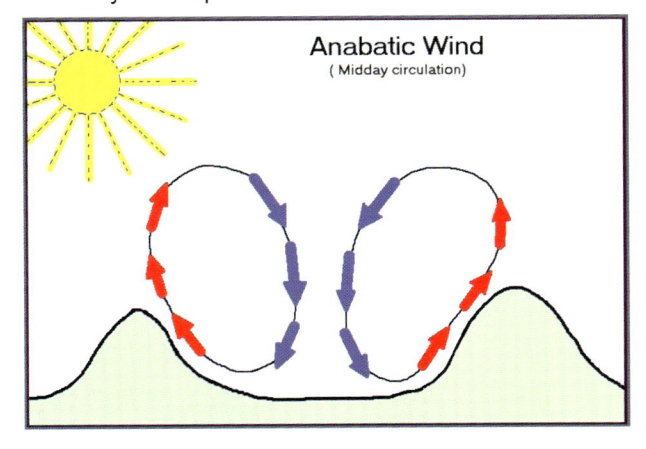

Figure 115: Anabatic wind

281

Ridge lift and slope soaring

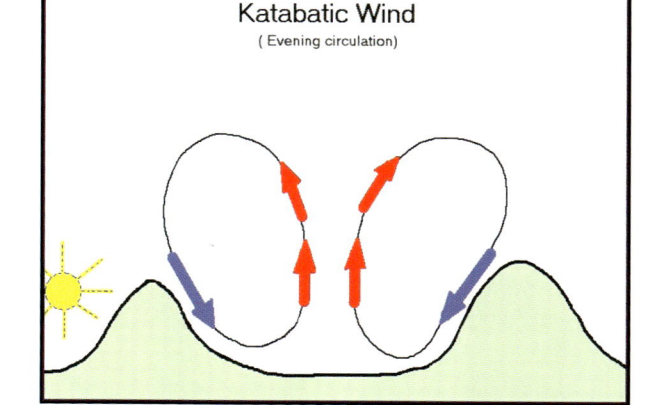

Figure 116: Katabatic wind

Katabatic Wind
(Evening circulation)

altitudes. Although a windsock located at the bottom of a hill might appear lacklustre, the ridge can still work remarkably well due to the combination of anabatic winds and the stronger wind at ridge-top level.

Due to the Coriolis Effect, wind changes direction with increasing altitude. Pilots in the southern hemisphere can rely on the fact that the wind backs with altitude. (The wind "backs" when it changes in an anticlockwise direction and "veers" when it changes direction clockwise) In other words, as we stand at the bottom of a ridge and with our back to the wind we can assume that the wind at ridge-top level is blowing further from our right. Of course, the opposite holds true in the northern hemisphere.

A rule of thumb says that the wind at 3000 ft above ground is approx. twice as strong and changes roughly 30 degrees anti clockwise. Of course, in the northern hemisphere the wind would veer approx. 30 degree in a clockwise direction.

A colourful mountain backdrop

In other words, as we stand at the bottom of a ridge and with our back to the wind we can assume that the wind at ridge-top level is blowing further from our right. Of course, the opposite holds true in the northern hemisphere.

11.7 Flying tactics

Having dealt with the fundamentals of ridge lift, we can now turn our attention to flying tactics and safety matters. In the normal course of events, we approach a slope below ridge-top level and therefore I suggest we cover flying tactics while in fairly close proximity to the ground first. According to triple world champion Helmut Reichmann, the best lift over smooth hills is found close to the hill whereas rougher slopes tend to form a turbulent layer close to the surface, resulting in better climb rates a little further from the ridge.

In any case, if we enter ridge lift fairly low, our utmost and undivided concentration is required. As long as we are within a few wingspans of rugged terrain we must expect eddies severe enough to unnerve even highly experienced glider pilots. Operating close to the rocks is best left to the experts and experienced pilots able to fly with only an occasional glance at the instruments. Glider pilots who find this difficult are well advised to contact ridge lift well above ridge-top level. Above the summit, we can expect to get into somewhat smoother air which often goes hand in hand with improving climb rates.

First, we want to find the area of the strongest lift, which can be done by comparing the climb rates at different distances from the crest of the ridge. In the process we usually gain further altitude and soon we have a few thousand feet of buffer between us and the top of the ridge. Now we can relax, enjoy the scenery and thank God for giving us gliders and the right conditions for ridge soaring.

Let us now turn our attention to safety matters and speed. I know of hardly any aviation accident caused by excessive speed but, sadly, I know of a number which have resulted from insufficient airspeed close to the ground. Every self-respecting glider pilot instinctively adds a few knots in an environment of severe turbulence.

The reasons for that are well known. First and foremost, we maintain the safety buffer above stall speed which allows us to convert speed into altitude if required. In addition, speed significantly improves the glider's control effectiveness – a welcome by-product when it comes to ridge soaring. While in close proximity to the ground, we are exposed to rotor-like eddies with occasional severe downdrafts. To prevent a close encounter with the ground, we take advantage of the topography and execute an instant escape by rolling the glider away from the hill into clear air. Even shallower ridges provide a fairly rapid increase in ground clearance. Although it cannot be denied that operating close to the ground contains a greater element of risk, we can almost completely eliminate such risks by strictly adhering to the above.

Turning away from the ridge

Needless to say that we never approach a ridge (or any obstacle for that matter) head on. Instead we fly towards it at an acute angle which much better allows us to quickly turn away from it and maintain a safe distance.

11.8 Ridge soaring rules

Ridge soaring is often conducted as a club activity. This makes it likely that several gliders will operate on the same ridge simultaneously and the need to thoroughly brief all pilots new to ridge soaring on these rules becomes paramount. Knowing exactly what the rules are is a precondition for implementing them and is an important step in making ridge soaring as safe as possible for all of us.

Rule No. 1: **All turns must be made into wind, i.e. away from the hill.**
Never turn towards the ridge, even though it might seem to be a long distance away.

Rule No. 2 : **A glider overtaking another glider when hill soaring shall do so by passing between the overtaken glider and the hill.**
If the slower glider decides to turn away from the hill and the overtaking glider is between the overtaken glider and the hill, there is no danger of a collision. Still, we must make it a habit to look over our shoulders before performing any turn. It must become second nature whether we know the position of other gliders or not. In aviation we never assume, we always check.

Rule No. 3: **If two gliders approach each other head-on while hill soaring, the glider which has the hill to its left shall give way by turning away from the hill.**
(Right wing to the ridge has right of way)

Rule No. 4: **When hill soaring, a glider shall not be flown lower than 100 feet above ground when within 100 metres horizontally of a person, dwelling or public road.**
Please remember that the rules might be different in some countries and keep in mind that the lift can suddenly die without any prior warning. Do not assume that the ridge will be working just because it was working a few minutes earlier and always have enough height to get to an airstrip or at least to a safe landing area.

11.9 Flying well above ridge top level

Provided we are flying several thousand feet above the summit, we can adopt tactics akin to flying in conditions of streeting. In other words, we can employ the classic MacCready Theory of speeding up in bad air and slowing down again as soon as our backside senses an updraft. Flying in this fashion is called "dolphin soaring" because, viewed from a distance, it very much looks like the up and down swimming motion of a cruising dolphin. (Refer to Figure 84.) When we do it right, it cuts down on time in sink but at the same time maximises time spent in lift and that tends to improve our cruising speed substantially. Just make sure the control inputs are not too severe, as aerodynamic losses can otherwise cancel out any such gains.

Needless to say, dolphin flying does go hand in hand with altitude variations and therefore it is essential to keep one's eyes out for other traffic and not on the instruments. After all, our backside and our audio-vario provide us with more than enough information on the vertical movement of air. This makes it totally unnecessary to keep a close eye on the variometer. In fact, a reliance on the vario is counterproductive, as it gives us misleading information on the location of the strongest pockets of lift due to the lag time in our instruments. Readers can find additional information on the subject in Sections 1.2 and 8.2.

Just below ridge-top level

11.10 Dangers

It is important to stress that ridge soaring pilots face danger if they under-estimate the strength of the upper wind and fail to realise that they are slowly drifting across the ridge and into sink on the downwind side. The sink downwind of the ridge is even stronger than the lift upwind of it because of the additional sink rate of our glider. Don't be surprised if the rate of sink downwind of the ridge is more than twice the rate of lift on the upwind side and don't forget that there is always a strong headwind on the way back towards rising air.

There are plenty of stories of pilots rapidly losing altitude in the downwash of mountains and getting a very close look at the ridge from the wrong side. It usually happens much quicker than expected. In situations like this, pilots have reported high levels of stress, knowing that there is almost no chance of finding lift downwind of the ridge.

Sadly, some of these stories had very expensive and even tragic consequences when landings in unsuitable terrain had to be attempted. Let's not forget that ridge soaring is often conducted in the most inhospitable areas. The countryside might be beautiful, but the unforgiving nature of such terrain calls for extreme caution and dictates conservative safety margins at all times.

> The soaring season was at its peak when a promising weather forecast and a near-optimum synoptic situation provided suitable conditions for a long-distance flight over South Australia. I managed to convince a friend of mine to join me for a 1000 km attempt in our medium-performance 15m gliders. Being mid-week, we had to talk a fellow Club member into coming out to drive the winch for us, but he made it clear that he could not hang around to come and get us in the event of an outlanding.
>
> We quickly agreed that we could live with this and headed due north, where even better conditions were expected. The day improved in line with the forecast, allowing us to progress reasonably well despite the fact the forecast cumulus clouds were missing. Approximately 250 km north of our home airfield, I took a climb to 8000 ft for a glide into more mountainous terrain, when extremely strong sink set in. It did not matter what I tried – the total-energy variometer seemed to be stuck hard against the bottom stop and the altimeter kept winding down at an alarming rate. My Pik 20D

never liked to be driven much above 85 kts, but the McCready ring called for well over 100 kts to get out of sink quickly.

Soon I was down to 2000 ft and looking for a field. The scenery in the far north of South Australia might be truly beautiful but the outlanding possibilities are few and far between. No wonder I was feeling uneasy and was beginning to wonder whether I would make it onto a rather low ridge where a farmer was reaping his meagre crop. The dust coming off his header indicated that the wind was right on the little ridge but the question was whether the lift was good enough to prevent me from getting to know the farmer personally.

Yes, I just made it onto the ridge, but it soon became apparent that it would only allow me to maintain altitude around ridge-top level. The fact that I had no retrieve crew back at the airfield and the knowledge that someone had to do a 600 km trip to retrieve me made me dump even the last drop of water and forced me to concentrate as I had seldom done before. Although I was constantly getting a very good look at the trees, I was able to regain my composure and began to evaluate the options available. Only then it occurred to me that I had none. If I were to prevent a meeting with the farmer in his paddock, I had to test my patience and play the waiting game until the ridge produced a thermal for me to climb away in.

Although my mate was high and advertising that he was having a great time, I was getting ever more determined to cling to this ridge for as long as necessary. After what seemed to be a very long time, the ridge did eventually give birth to a rough but welcome thermal which got me back to more comfortable altitudes.

The flight never got me anywhere near my 1000 km diploma on that occasion but it is still fresh in my mind after more than a decade. A good knowledge about ridge lift is bound to come in useful one day for recreational and performance-orientated glider pilots alike.

Tense moments amongst the rocks

Ridge lift and slope soaring

Impressions of Patagonia from the air

(Photos courtesy of Dr. Rick Agnew)

Wave lift

12.1 Introduction

Not long ago, the gliding world was astonished with the news of a spectacular world record of just over 3000 km at a speed of 200 km/h. Such enormous distances were considered impossible only a few years ago, but a few European glider pilots, assisted by meteorological scientists, changed gliding history. Their work has set new standards and extended the boundaries of gliding.

Extensive research into mountain waves dates back to the 1940s although Walter Geogii had already suggested wave-type airflow in the early 1920s. The Sierra Wave Project (USA) resulted in a series of still unbroken altitude records and outstanding distant flights. Further work on lee waves was done in New Zealand and resulted in the first 2000 km flight in the history of gliding. In the late nineties, the OSTIV Mountain Wave Project research project was initiated. It was aimed at improving knowledge of orographic turbulence and hence allowing better forecasting of mountain wave conditions. Although mainly of interest to sports aviation, it has also contributed to enhancing safety in the commercial and general aviation arena. Using a modern two-seat touring motor glider, the initial field research took place in the Argentine Andes back in 1999 when lift of 20–30 kts to 33 000 ft was recorded. The Andes seemed to provide ideal conditions for long-distance flights at previously unheard of average speeds.

A stunning wave cloud in Argentina
Photo:
Dr. Rick Agnew

Wave Lift

After the first 3000 km flight in gliding history, record hunters began to study meteorological data and maps of South America. If past experience is anything to go by, we will hear of even greater distances in years to come. Even without going into the details of these record flights, we can see the tremendous potential that wave lift has to offer for the performance-oriented glider pilot. But even the recreational pilot can see that by directing the flight path through large areas of strong wave lift, altitude is gained as a by-product of cruising. This in turn allows high-speed runs at maximum speed between various bands of wave lift. In addition, strong lift is available from first light till last light and at a rate that makes the average flatland pilot shake his head in disbelief.

**Another stunning picture
Photo:
Dr. Rick Agnew**

It is certainly not hard to see that flying in such conditions for 15 hours or more and at altitudes between 20 000 and 30 000 ft can lead to new, fabulous world records. Having said that, I hasten to add that only very fit and experienced first class pilots with tremendous mental stamina and almost limitless funds stand a chance of successfully conducting such extreme flights in such unforgiving environments.

The first time I heard about "wave" was during my training days, when one of my fellow students asked our instructor: "What's the difference between ridge lift and wave lift? " The instructor thought about it for a while and then said: "Ridge lift is only found upwind of a mountain and lee wave always occurs downwind of it."

A very good answer if you were to ask me. After all these years I still think it is impossible to explain the fundamental difference any better in just a single sentence. But there is a lot more to wave lift than this. There are many different forms of wave lift such as thermal wave, shear wave and lee wave and, although some forms of wave have limited practical use for cross-country flying, most of them allow glider pilots to climb in silky-smooth air to great heights. When it comes to development of soarable waves, the three main ingredients are the shape of the terrain, the stability of the air and the velocity of the wind.

But before we talk about such details as wavelength, amplitude, stability etc, we had better make an attempt to visualise the lee wave effect. By far the best way of doing just that is to think of a boulder in a stream of water. As the water flows over the boulder, it descends on the downstream site, only to rise sharply again soon afterwards. Usually this oscillation occurs several times downstream of the boulder, although the effect diminishes with increasing distance from it. What hardly changes at all is the position of these crests and valleys, which explains why they are sometimes referred to as "standing waves". However, because these forms of wave are most commonly known as lee waves, we will retain this name throughout this chapter.

12.2 Topography

Sufficiently strong winds and favourable meteorological conditions will result in lee wave if the shape of the mountain is suitable. In Figure 117 the various types of mountains are ranked in terms of their suitability for generating lee waves. At the top of the list is topography where two mountain ridges are one or two full wavelengths apart. This allows resonance to create a reinforcement of the wave amplitude and under such conditions we can get a very steep and strong vertical airflow. Although ideal for gliding operations it occurs rarely.

Just as the upwind side of the ridge is of prime importance for the generation of ridge lift, the downwind side of the mountain significantly affects lee wave development. All other things being equal, a steep lee escarpment is clearly best, but near-vertical escarpments or very shallow downwind slopes tend to inhibit lee wave.

Large mountains are not necessarily superior when it comes to initiating lee waves. Small hills can be just as effective when mountain shape and wavelength match well. Smaller ridges can generate useful wave lift at lower wind speeds although, compared to large mountains, the height gains are limited. Good wave lift can even be experienced downwind of a tableland with a suitable downwind slope. Least desirable are mountains with a shallow downwind slope or, even worse, a pair of ridges out of phase. In such a case, the second ridge cancels out the lee wave triggered by the upwind hill.

Figure 117: Suitable and unsuitable mountain shapes

12.3 Lee wave airflow and terminology

Figure 119 shows a typical lee wave generating flow pattern and includes most of the terminology used below. Near the ground, there is a turbulent layer which transitions to a smooth flow pattern with parallel streamlines higher up. Clearly, Figure

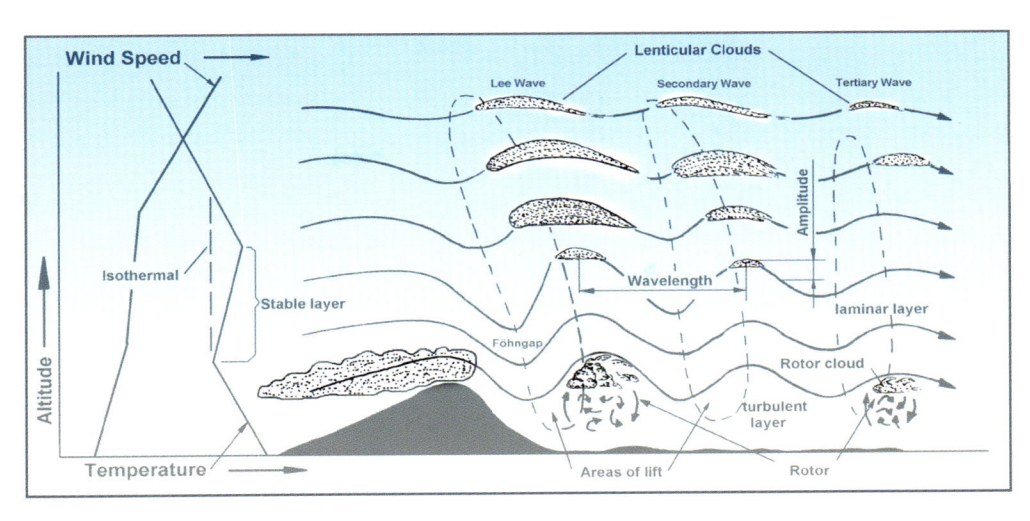

Figure 119: Typical airflow during lee wave conditions

119 describes an ideal scenario. If we wait until such textbook situations occur, we might only ever contact lee wave if we base ourselves in one of the wave capitals of the world for a long time.

The amount of cloud varies on a day-to-day basis and can range from complete cloud cover to a totally blue sky. Although we will deal with "Foehn Gap" later, we should explain the phenomena right here and now. The word "Föhn" originates from the German language and describes unusually warm down-slope winds. Down-slope winds are always relatively dry, descending winds.

When the air upwind of the mountain is laden with moisture, it is usually lost as precipitation. On its way down the air compresses again, and as there is little moisture left it warms considerably. This causes condensed water particles to evaporate leading to very few clouds or no clouds at all. For this reason, a gap in the clouds just downwind of a mountain often appears. This is usually a telltale sign of wave activity, especially on days when the wave is not otherwise indicated.

A relatively frequent occurrence is an airflow pattern as depicted in Figure 120. The airflow doesn't necessarily follow the contour of a rugged landscape. Sometimes the airflow creates an eddy which serves to fill the gap on the lee side. This is frequently the case with very steep (or near vertical) escarpments, .

Figure 120: Effective shape of a mountain changed by an eddy

Such a peculiar airflow has the effect of extending the mountain and hence allows the streamlines to assume a smooth shape which in turn helps to establish the pattern for lee wave. Such an airflow is not confined to lee wave conditions but can be experienced quite frequently downwind of a suitable mountain range.

12.4 Meteorological conditions

The best time for well-developed lee waves is in the morning and late in the afternoon. Thermals penetrating high into the atmosphere tend to inhibit strong development of lee waves. Another important requirement is a sufficiently strong wind increasing in strength with altitude. Fortunately this is the case more often than not.

Aerotow in progress Photo: Manfred Muench

It can easily be explained by the frictional resistance of the wind in the lower layers of the atmosphere. A favourable wind profile is illustrated on the far left of Figure 119, although it is by no means necessary that the wind speed continues to increase to high altitudes. As long as the wind strengthens up to the level of approximately twice the height of the mountain, useful lee waves can be expected.

In any case, the mountain should be more or less perpendicular to the general wind direction, although wind deviations of up to ±30 degrees will still allow the formation of lee waves. It is important though that we search for wave bands parallel to the mountain and not at right angle to the wind. The minimum wind strength at mountain-top level should be in the order of 15 to 20 kts but just as crucial is a constant wind direction – at least in the lower levels. Even if all these conditions are met, lee waves will not develop without a layer of stable air embedded between layers of lower stability. If that sounds complicated, just refer back to Figure 119, which illustrates the most favourable temperature profile on the left.

Remember that:

a) the lowest layers of the atmosphere should feature a relatively stable air mass,

b) a more stable air-mass (an inversion or at least an isothermal layer) must be present above the lower layer, and

c) the upper layer must feature stability again.

For obvious reasons, glider pilots like inversions as much as they like a toothache, but when it comes to wave flying these same inversions are most welcome indeed. Sandwiched between layers of stability, inversions are a very important ingredient for lee waves to form.

11.5 Wavelength

Where can we expect to find rising air in a lee wave and where is the dreaded sink? We can get a small clue by having another good look at Figure 119, although in practice a more precise prediction can only be made when the wavelength is known.

Wavelength is defined as the distance between one wave crest and the next. According to Wallington, it varies between 4 and 35 km.

More than anything else, the wind speed tends to determine the wavelength, although, according to Tom Bradbury (UK), the period of oscillation depends also on the stability of the air. For standard atmosphere conditions and unsaturated air, the oscillation period amounts to 590 seconds and for a wind speed of 25 kts this translates into a wavelength of 7.6 km.

However, more stable air has a shorter oscillation period and the same applies to moister air. Therefore scientists such as Scorer and Casswell have developed methods to calculate lee wave behaviour. As accurate forecasting requires precise meteorological data such calculations are seldom conducted. A rule of thumb formula states that the wavelength is approximately 1/6 (or 15%) of the wind speed at altitude. For example, if the wind speed at 10 000 ft is 40 kts (75 km/h), the wavelength would be of the order of 12 km.

Short wavelength over Waikerie airfield

By knowing the position of the lee-wave-triggering mountain and by using this formula, we can get a rough idea of the position of the wave lift, although a lot of guesswork is still involved. On the other hand, very good indicators of the position of the wave crest are lenticular clouds; they are a telltale sign of wave and help us to pinpoint its approximate position.

According to Wallington, the shape of the mountain has a major bearing on the location of lee wave. Depending on the gradient of the downwind slope, the best lift can be located even closer than a 1/2 wavelength downwind of the summit (for an asymmetrical ridge with a steep lee escarpment). However, in the case of a gentler slope, the lift is often found significantly further downwind.

12.6 Amplitude

Amplitude is defined as half the vertical distance from wave trough to wave crest. It not only depends on the height of the ridge but it also tends to vary with altitude (Figure 119). It is normally at its maximum in the most stable layer of the atmosphere where the strongest lift is also found.

Amplitude also diminishes with increasing vertical distance from the stable layer, due to the compressibility of air. As lift strength is closely associated with amplitude, it is not difficult to imagine that the rate of lift reduces steadily above and below its stable layer maximum.

While flying in the turbulent lower layer, glider pilots often notice not only a reduced rate of sink but also significantly smoother thermals over an unusually large area. This is often a sign of operating under the influence of upper wave airflow. (Refer to Section 4.11). However, down low, the amplitude of the wave (and hence the lift) is not usually strong enough to compensate for the sink rate of even the very best of gliders. For this reason, it remains a challenge for glider pilots to gain enough height through other forms of lift prior to contacting the wave.

12.7 Moisture

If the atmosphere contains just the right amount of it, the sky features lens-shaped or "lenticular" clouds similar to the beautiful specimens photographed at Queenstown, New Zealand. But that raises an interesting point. Why do we often witness several layers of lenticular clouds, as in the photo?

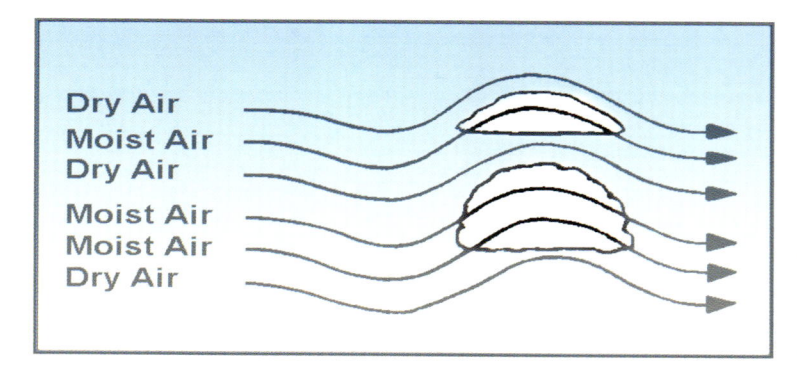

Figure 121: Moisture distribution in lee wave airflow (example only)

The phenomenon can be explained by the different moisture levels at various altitudes. Only when the air contains the appropriate amount of moisture can we expect lenticular clouds. If the moisture content is significantly higher, we will have overcast conditions which tends to hide any visual clues of lee wave. Conversely, if the atmosphere doesn't contain enough moisture, the sky will remain blue – also depriving us of visual indicators. In both cases, we still get lee wave, although it is much harder to identify and hence more difficult to exploit.

Lee wave near Queensstown in New Zealand

12.8 Dangers

Although all pilots know that the air gets thinner (i.e. less dense) as they climb higher, there is often only a vague appreciation of the dangers associated with flying at high altitudes. The higher we climb, the closer we get to the limits of pilot and aircraft alike.

12.8.1 Limitations of the human body

Most humans have evolved to live close to sea level. Our physiology is not adapted to prolonged exposure to an environment to which it is not accustomed. For example, it will respond with a marked loss of performance if exposed to high altitudes.

Regardless of altitude, the composition of air (21% oxygen, 78% nitrogen plus 1% of other gases) remains unchanged, but the ambient pressure does not. At 18 000 ft, for example, the pressure is half that of sea level – and that means that there is only half the amount of oxygen in a given breath. Reduced pressure at altitude not only decreases the actual number of oxygen molecules per unit volume of air but an insufficient ambient pressure also restricts the blood's carrying capacity of oxygen. If the blood oxygen saturation level drops to approximately 93% all of us suffer from a noticeable deterioration in our mental and physical performance. Even well below a supposedly safe altitude of 10 000 ft the effects are evident to an observer, though not the person suffering from the lack of oxygen. The general medical term for an oxygen deficiency is hypoxia, but the specific type we will consider as part of this article is "altitude hypoxia". Also called "hypoxic hypoxia", it is a condition that results when there is a lack of available oxygen or lowered partial pressure of oxygen.

Individual responses to hypoxia vary considerably, not only between individuals, but also in the same person at different times. These can be dependant on such factors as diet, physical condition, body chemistry, age, general wellbeing, stress factors, dehydration, current blood sugar levels etc. The severity and onset of hypoxia can vary. However, not even the fittest or youngest of us remain unaffected.

Now let's look at the main factors one by one.

Altitude

As gliders are non-pressurised aircraft, the severity of hypoxia will first and foremost depend on the operating height above sea level. Hypoxia can degrade mental and physical performance. We know that athletes are affected when sports take place at higher altitudes. Even as low as 5000 ft, a pilot's night vision is already impaired. Although we only operate gliders during daylight hours, the fact remains that the body reacts to a marginal supply of oxygen at surprisingly low altitudes. The brain consumes as much as 30% of the available oxygen, but an even higher percentage of oxygen is consumed by the retina of the eye. In other words, the organs that are most critically dependant on oxygen concentration are those which are by far the most important ones in terms of safety.

At **10 000 ft** the blood saturation of oxygen has dropped to approx. 90% of normal levels. Even after a short stay at this altitude, our performance and our judgement is starting to be significantly compromised. The body's initial response to a lack of oxygen is a sense of mild intoxication. We can be lulled into a false sense of wellbeing. Our pulse rate increases and a true self-assessment of our abilities are clouded by euphoria although physical symptoms are not yet apparent. Above 10 000 ft our performance degrades increasingly steeply.

At **15 000 ft** our blood oxygen level is down to a dangerous 85%. Memory, normal vision, decision making and proper judgement have degenerated and, if no

The aftermath of an avalanche from a safe distance

corrective action is taken immediately, we are in serious danger. General clumsiness sets in, vision is seriously degraded and we are likely to experience problems with the general handling of the aircraft, especially speed control, although we are unable to notice this loss of performance.

At **17 500 ft** our blood oxygen saturation will have dropped below 80% of normal levels but we continue to feel just fine. In fact, we might even be euphoric but at the same time disorientated, irrational, fatigued or even nauseated and therefore in extremely serious danger. We will definitely pass out within 20 minutes or so, possibly even quicker if we have to perform any physical activities.

At **20 000 ft** blood oxygen saturation drops to an almost lethal level of about 70% and we will lose consciousness within the next few minutes. Death is waiting around the corner. Considering that it will take at least a few minutes to descend to a safe altitude, the chance of survival is very slim indeed.

Rate of ascent / acclimatisation

It is common knowledge that even the world's tallest mountains have been conquered by climbers without carrying oxygen. Such extreme physical activities are possible even at around 28 000 ft without supplementary oxygen. However, climbers on their way to Mount Everest, for example, take their time and stop for several weeks at intermediate altitudes to acclimatise. This gives their bodies time to increase their blood haemoglobin concentrations by increasing their red blood cell count, and hence improve their oxygen carrying ability. Needless to say, such a long adaptation period is out of the question for glider pilots.

Level of physical activity

Any form of muscular activity uses up oxygen and further deprives the brain of an already limited supply. As a consequence, the onset of hypoxia will be much faster. Fortunately, flying gliders does not demand much physical effort, but prolonged exposure to rotor, for example, requires quick reactions and repeated inputs with full control deflections. If this continues for some time, the body's oxygen reserves would have to be drawn on which in turn decreases the supply to the brain and hence brings the onset of hypoxia forward.

Temperature

Flying high is always associated with low temperatures, but flying very high indeed means that the ambient temperatures are usually well below zero. For example, 21°C (70°F) at sea level turns into an ambient temperature of minus 19°C (−2°F) at 20 000 ft. The extreme cold of a glider cockpit will cause the body to use up energy just to keep its temperature within acceptable limits. The energy usage is comparable to an increased level of physical activity and it is therefore not surprising that the body's tolerance to hypoxic conditions is decreased.

Duration of exposure

All the effects become worse the longer we deprive our body of an adequate supply of oxygen. Scientists have established a benchmark and determined the Time of Useful Consciousness (TUC) for the average person at various altitudes. As the name implies TUC is the time span during which we can remain conscious but it does not necessarily mean that we are well enough to make the right decisions or take proper corrective action such as donning an oxygen mask.

Here are some typical figures:

Table 14 : Time of useful consciousness

ALTITUDE		TUC (min)
15 000 ft	(4600 metres)	30 or more
18 000 ft	(5500 metres)	20 to 30
22 000 ft	(6700 metres)	5 to 10
25 000 ft	(7600 metres)	3 to 5
28 000 ft	(8500 metres)	2 to 3

Carbon monoxide

If you smoke, you will be affected by hypoxia at a much lower altitude than a non-smoker. According to some research findings smokers are affected approximately 5000 ft earlier than non-smokers. Carbon monoxide combines with the haemoglobin in our red blood cells much more readily than oxygen does and this in turn limits the blood's capacity to carry oxygen. To refrain from smoking for a day or two does not make the slightest difference, as it takes a long time for the body to rid of the toxic substances.

Fatigue

A mentally or physically fatigued pilot will always display a greater susceptibility to the effects of hypoxia. Getting into a glider in an already fatigued state sets up a cycle that puts us on a downward spiral of increasing fatigue and a rapid degradation of performance.

Alcohol

Alcohol, or even the after-effects of alcohol, will diminish a pilot's tolerance to hypoxia even after our blood alcohol reading has returned to zero. Only one ounce of alcohol in the blood of an average adult will raise the body's perceived altitude by 2000 ft. Many independent tests on air force pilots have shown that pilot judgement and performance are affected for up to 5 days after a heavy consumption of alcohol.

A few valuable lessons were learned during a seminar with a hyperbaric chamber run at the Edinburgh Air Force Base in South Australia. A simulated flight to 22 000 ft was arranged for eight glider pilots. After a fairly quick ascent to 22 000 ft, we were instructed to take the oxygen mask off and keep subtracting 7 from a figure of 1000 while recording all intermediate results on a piece of paper. The instructor suggested stopping the exercise when this mental arithmetic was getting too hard and asked all of us to sign the paper afterwards.

The results came as a rude shock. For most of us the mental arithmetic became too hard somewhere near 850 and all of us had to admit to making mistakes before we even got down to about 900. Some of us forgot to sign the paper altogether and hardly any of us were able to recognise our own signatures afterwards. Symptoms ranging from tiredness to blurred vision and a total mental blackout were reported.

The insidious nature of hypoxia

Of even greater concern to recreational pilots is the insidious nature of hypoxia. The most dangerous aspect of altitude hypoxia is that pilots do not, and cannot, detect the deterioration in function. Even worse, they lose their ability for critical judgement. Our very limited ability to recognise the onset of hypoxia must be kept in mind if we don't want it to become a silent killer. While operating above 10 000 ft, we need to check the proper function of our oxygen equipment on a regular basis.

Any feelings of euphoria should give rise to suspicion and trigger corrective action immediately. Altitude-induced exuberance must be replaced by rational thinking. Imagine you are in strong wave lift and are beginning to think that you can detect the curvature of the earth. No wonder you are ecstatic, especially if you are only a few thousand feet away from diamond height, but in a situation like this you must remain cool, calm and rational and remember that the difference between perceived and actual performance is unbelievably large.

Lately, small "Pulse Oximeters" have come onto the market for non-invasive measurement of oxygen levels in the bloodstream. These small gadgets simply clip onto a finger (or earlobe) and provide a digital readout of oxygen saturation levels as well as pulse rate. Their accuracy is affected by body movement or cold. Also they tend to overstate the blood oxygen saturation in smokers by a few percent. In spite of their limitations, they enhance safety considerably and are therefore highly recommended – especially for flights above 15 000 ft.

Oximeter for non-invasive measurement of oxygen levels in the bloodstream.

Hyperventilation

Why can't we just breathe a little faster or deeper to make up for the lower oxygen intake? After all, that is what athletes are doing subconsciously every time peak performance is demanded from their body. The answer is closely linked to the way our body measures the oxygen levels. Our body doesn't actually measure the oxygen concentration in the blood but the carbon dioxide concentration. It then adjusts the breathing frequency automatically. That works just fine at or near ground level, but unfortunately not at altitude while sitting almost motionless in the cockpit of our glider.

Wave Lift

Even if we are breathing twice as fast (or twice as deep) the oxygen saturation doesn't increase and our blood remains seriously depleted of oxygen. Hyperventilation does, however, lower carbon dioxide concentration and thus can lead to other undesirable effects such as dizziness.

**Extreme altitude flying
Photo:
Dr. Rick Agnew**

Carrying oxygen in gliders

In order to remain safe, we need to adhere to the rules which require us not to climb above 10 000 ft AMSL without breathing supplementary oxygen. The history of aviation is full of oxygen starvation related losses of human lives. This chapter only deals with hypoxia and does not touch on technical matters such as airworthiness requirements etc. Portable oxygen dispensing systems are not recommended as restraining relatively heavy oxygen containers has proved to be very problematic in gliders.

Carrying of oxygen in gliders does not come without risks due to the oxygen's explosive potential. Therefore, prior to the installation of any oxygen system expert advice should be sought. The final selection of equipment and dispensing unit comes down to intended mode of operation. An oxygen system used for cross-country flying up to a maximum of 15 000 ft can be very different from a system that is intended for wave flying to twice this altitude.

12.8.2 Aircraft limitations

Air density decreases as altitude increases. Pilots are aware of this, but it is probably not so well known that the maximum speed of gliders is limited by flutter. Flutter might best be described as a high frequency oscillation of aircraft control surfaces (or other components) which usually leads to structural damage or a total loss of control. The reduction in air density is responsible for the earlier onset of flutter at altitude. Flutter is a very serious problem as it destroys aircraft, and it kills, but provided the glider is properly maintained it only occurs when pilots ignore the placarded airspeeds. Therefore we must accept a reduction of permissible speeds at higher altitudes and refer to the flight manual which usually contains a table like the one reproduced below.

Table 15: Speed limitations with increasing altitude

ASH 25 SPEED LIMITATIONS	
Altitude (ft)	Vne (kts)
0 – 10 000	150
10 000 – 16 000	130
16 000 – 23 000	120
23 000 – 30 000	106

As we can see, Vne (Velocity never exceed – or "maximum permissible speed") decreases with altitude. Please note that other gliders might have an even greater restriction on airspeed. At an altitude of 30 000 ft, the speed of a Hornet, a Libelle or an Astir, for example, is limited to 81 kts – only about 2/3 of the speed permissible at sea level. But it doesn't really matter what glider we fly, we need to keep a close eye on the speed as altitude increases. By law, all aircraft equipped with oxygen must have a Vne placard fitted in view of the pilot. (Refer to sample above.)

While we are on the subject of speed and altitude, we must keep in mind that the stalling speed goes up as air density goes down. In other words, the higher we go the faster we need to fly in order to avoid a stall, although it still occurs at the same indicated airspeed.

Seemingly we face a dilemma, but it is only a problem at first glance. Our airspeed indicator is also affected by the lower density and indicates a lower speed because there are fewer air molecules available to operate it. In other words, the real speed (or true airspeed) is higher than the indicated airspeed and for this reason we are flying

Curl-over of wave cloud near Mt. Cook in New Zealand. Photo: Adam Dalziel

faster at altitude without really being aware of it.

To convert indicated airspeed into true airspeed we need to add a correction factor of approximately 2% per 1000 ft. For example, a glider cruising at an indicated airspeed of 100 kts at 12 000 ft is in reality cruising at 124 kts. It is important to note that the glide ratio of our glider is totally unaffected by altitude. Lift and drag are both equally affected by the lower air density but the glide performance of the glider improves at medium to high speeds. The effect is similar to the displacement of the polar curve by higher wing loadings.

Figure 122 shows the reduction of ambient pressure with altitude. Although there is an almost linear reduction in pressure up to an altitude of 18 000 ft (5500 m) the rate of pressure drop is by more pronounced at higher altitudes. This needs to be taken into account not only for the wellbeing of the pilot but also for flutter considerations.

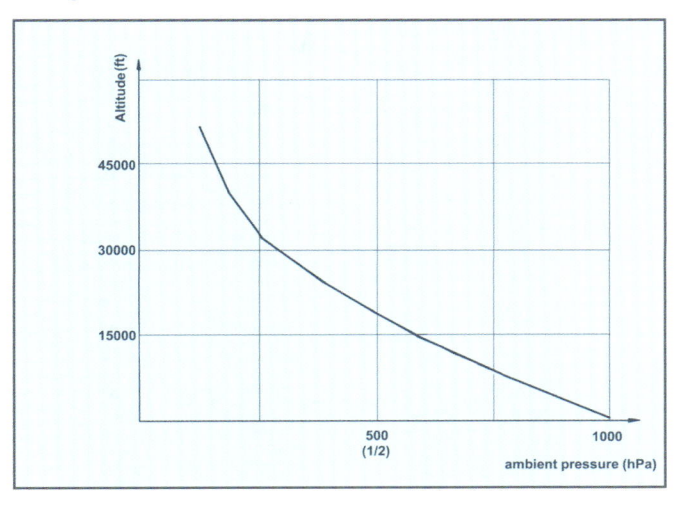

Figure 122: Reduction of pressure with altitude

12.9 Cloud formation

A) THE ROTOR CLOUD

Rotor clouds (sometimes also referred to as roll clouds) can form upwind and below lenticular clouds. The picture below shows a rotor cloud formation just in front of the wave crest. Often these rotors appear in bands and can often be observed to rotate along their longitudinal axis in a somewhat chaotic fashion. Adiabatic cooling and heating of the air in the rotor cloud is responsible for the instability within the rotor zone, where lift of 10 m/s (20 kts) on the ascending side can be quickly replaced by the same amount of sink on the opposite one. As a result, strong lift and sink with extreme turbulence can be encountered and this puts tremendous strain on aircraft and pilot alike. In the lower part of the rotor, the airflow is directly opposite to the prevailing wind. This can make flying hazardous and requires quick reactions with full control deflections to remain in station behind a tug or prevent our glider from performing some unwanted manoeuvres.

Over relatively low mountains, we might encounter only mild turbulence, but the other extreme is the violent rotor turbulence often found on windy days downwind of very steep escarpments. Also, let's keep in mind that we can encounter rotor activity in the blue and for this reason we are well advised to tighten our harness and to carefully stow all loose items prior to take off if lee wave conditions are expected.

B) THE LENTICULAR CLOUD

Air rising in a wave updraught cools adiabatically and clouds will form if this cooling is sufficient to cause condensation. However, the nature of wave-type airflow dictates that air which has gone up must come down again. As the air is descending, it is compressed and the resulting warming causes all condensed water droplets to

Lenticular clouds over New Zealand's South Island

evaporate again. Due to this ongoing process, a lenticular cloud forming at the leading edge dissipates just as quickly at the trailing edge. Lenticular clouds are actually a constantly moving air stream revealed only by condensation in the airflow. This explains why these clouds remain stationary, even though they are actually subjected to very strong upper winds. The bottom of lenticular clouds can be concave, convex or even flat.

Lenticular clouds are often mixed up with other forms of clouds and are therefore quite frequently very difficult to identify. Contrary to popular belief, lenticular clouds are neither indicative of lift strength, nor do they indicate the level at which the wave lift is strongest. They form along the crest line of the wave and indicate that a particular parcel of air was lifted to its condensation level.

12.10 The practical aspects of wave flying

Dr. Rick Agnew is one of Australia's best known and most experienced mountain wave pilots. He flies with the Canberra Gliding Club and has already set 18 Australian gliding records. Rick currently holds the Australian altitude record and is the fastest, highest and longest flying Australian standard class pilot. He has published numerous articles on wave flying and has kindly given permission to include the following extracts of his work in this publication.

There are basically two different flying techniques that can be utilised to exploit the lift generated in a wave system depending whether you are flying in:

- the underlaminar air mass (turbulent layer), or
- within the laminar layer air stream.

Lift exploitation in the turbulent layer air mass

There are several forms of underlaminar layer lift, but they all stay almost immobile above the ground. To utilise this type of lift, it is advisable to fly upwind of the lightest clouds, even if they are tiny and short lived. I call these the rotor or roll cloud. These sometimes nearly invisible small bits of 'fluff' delineate the leading edge of the laminar flowing air mass. It is important for the wave pilot to recognise these rotor clouds and react appropriately. The success of the wave flight may depend upon both the quick recognition of it and the decision to move to that area of the air mass.

By maintaining your airspeed so as not to be forced backwards (i.e. greater than wind speed) you can remain above the same location with reference to the ground. Choosing some distinguishing landmarks on the ground will assist you to maintain your position. Frequent checking of your location in reference to your chosen landmarks will assist you maintaining any lift. By manoeuvring either forward, back or laterally you may encounter stronger lift. Again, by checking your position relative to some chosen features on the ground may assist in maintaining this new advantageous position of lift. GPS may also make this process easier for those who have such gadgets. Your position by reference to the rotor is also dependent on the development of the cloud. You must get a mental picture of the lift structure quickly, by using the variometer (quantitative but delayed information) and your sensations (qualitative but immediate information).

Figure 123: Thermalling into wave

Tight lift, often rough, used with steep turns (at times very steep thermalling technique), reduce bank angles in the upwind direction in areas of lift and conversely quickly steepening the turn and increasing your speed in the downwind sinking areas. By this method (seemingly two steps up, one step down!) you will gain height!

Usually you will have to use several techniques within a short time span, as flying the rotor lift changes quickly with time. Flying a glider in such conditions requires good handling as well as a short time response to the indications given by both the instruments and your sensations. Avoid arriving low in this kind of lift. Climbing is nearly always difficult, and there is sometimes an altitude below which it is impossible to climb altogether.

Lift exploitation in the laminar layer

The atmosphere becomes calm when you reach the laminar layer. The strategy is then to stay in the area where the maximum rate of climb is. Like in the underlaminar layer, using landmarks to stay in the same location above ground is essential. If the wind speed is less than the speed of minimum sink of the glider, you will need to fly parallel to the obstacle triggering the wave, compensating for the crosswind. The best location is usually below the leading edge of the lenticular, or slightly ahead of it. When the lift is localised, use wide figure 8-shaped turns, like in front of a slope.

If the wind is equal to or greater than the speed of minimum sink of your glider, you will have to stay in front of the wind, stationary above the ground. To adjust your speed to wind speed, choose two landmarks as close as possible to the glider, and check your relative position often. Do not forget that wind speed usually increases with altitude. You may have to increase your speed to

Figure 124: Surfing the cloud

Having fun

stay stationary above ground. Only frequent checks of your position will prevent you from being pushed backwards into sink. As the lift is not the same everywhere in the rising zone, you may have to move sightly upwind, downwind or laterally until you find the best rate of climb. If you lose the lift, you are either downwind or upwind of the zone of best lift. For safety reasons, you will need to search for the lift upwind. Indeed, if you searched downwind and found nothing but sink, you may lose too much height when you cross the zone of sink again with the penalty of a strong headwind.

An example...

Let us consider that you fly at 40 kts and your variometer reading is 0 kts. You increase your speed to 60 kts, your variometer will go up slowly to reach a maximum value and will then go down if you fly on. You have just crossed the zone of best lift. Aha! So you must go back to 40 kts as soon as your variometer readings begins to drop. Do not get impatient, as your speed is low while flying into a headwind. You may have to fly for several minutes in this manner. This example is typical whenever wind speed increases with height.

Let us now consider another example with the same speed of 40 kts and the same variometer reading of 0 kt. You increase your speed to 60 kts. The variometer shows the sink getting stronger and stronger: you therefore deduce that you are upwind of the rising area. So you turn back and look carefully at the variometer. Downwind, your speed, in respect with the wave system, is high and the changes in variometer readings are much faster than in the previous example. As soon as your readings become positive, turn through 90°. The drift will take you to the zone of best lift. When the variometer tends to drop, turn upwind, set a 40 kts speed and choose new landmarks for position references.

When you have reached a comfortable height, move a little laterally to find the best climb area. As a general rule, the best rates of climb are upwind of clouds with high vertical extension and downwind of the highest obstacles.

Flying cross-country in wave

For an experienced wave pilot, long cross-country flights are possible. These flights can exceed the average speeds of flights in convective conditions by a great margin. Such flights normally require the use of several wave systems, triggered by different obstacles. I will try and explain how to fly in a single system, but also jumping from one system to another.

Once you are above your safety height (i.e. you are confident that you won't drop out of the bottom of the laminar air flow), you can move laterally along the wave, crabbing to compensate for the crosswind. This is usually rather easy when you have clouds to mark the wave. In blue sky, you must imagine an alignment parallel to the obstacle triggering the wave on the ground. If you lose the lift, you must search upwind.

These movements imply a change of wave. Between the zones of lift, you will cross strong sink. Adjust your MacCready settings accordingly and follow your instrument's indication. You will have to fly pretty fast in sink. Be careful not to fly above the gliders Vne, remembering that Vne indicated decreases as you gain altitude! The height loss between waves varies, depending on the wavelength, the rate of sink, and your trajectory.

Figure 125: Flying cross-country in wave

As an example, with a 40 kts wind and a wave length of 8 km, a change of wave upwind can cost up to 3000 to 4000 ft for a 35:1 glider. Flying downwind, the loss of height is lower, as the areas of sink can be crossed very quickly and the loss is limited to approx. 1000 feet. To keep the height loss to a minimum, you can sometimes change wave at one edge of the system you are aiming to move to. When flying from one wave system to the other, always stay parallel to the wind direction, in order to follow the shortest trajectory in sink. You can jump to another wave system following a trajectory where the clouds are thinner or less organised. These clouds are indicators that the wave system is weaker, so the sink should be reduced, and therefore you should lose less height.

When flying upwind to another wave system, allow for a large safety height above the clouds. The glide ratio in sink can be deceptive and you will have the feeling of going down without going ahead. If you realise that you will arrive below the cloud summit of your target wave system, turn back to the previous wave. Top up your height before trying again. Avoid reaching the next wave system below the roll cloud, as you will probably find heavy sink and turbulence. Then you will have to attempt to 'thermal' the rotor to re-contact the laminar air flow again. Reaching the smooth lift may be difficult, if at all achievable!

In wave, outlandings are easily possible. At many gliding sites every wave flight is treated as a fully fledged x-country flight. Your safety heights (altitude below which you will try not to go) will be chosen depending on the landscape and the make up of the wave system. Such a safety margin should be higher than in normal thermal conditions. Selection of an outlanding paddock downwind should only be used as a last resort.

12.11 The effect of crosswind on our speed above ground.

Does a crosswind affect the true speed above the ground, and if so, by how much? As usual, the answer depends on a number of factors.

With low to moderate wind speeds (and under normal convective conditions) crosswinds can be neglected, but the situation can be fundamentally different when flying cross-country in wave. Here we often cruise at a considerable altitude where winds of 60 kts (110 km/h) are common. They blow at a right angle to our track for most of the flight which necessitates pointing the glider's nose into wind to compensate for drift. For example, we want to counteract a 20 kts crosswind while cruising at 80 kts. To compensate, we need to turn the glider about 15 degrees into wind and this depresses our true speed above the ground as per table 16a and 16b below. However, the significant altitude advantage (already discussed in section 12.8) usually more than compensates for it.

Table 16a: True groundspeed along track (kts)

Crosswind (kts)	True airspeed TAS (kts) along heading							
	50	60	70	80	90	100	110	120	130
10	49	59	69	79	89	99	109	119	129
20	46	56	67	77	88	98	108	118	128
30	40	50	63	74	85	95	106	116	126
40	30	45	57	69	81	92	102	113	124
50	-	30	49	62	75	87	98	109	120
60	-	-	37	53	67	80	92	113	115
70	-	-	-	39	56	71	85	97	110

The above tables show that crosswinds of up to 20kts have little effect on our ground speed but also indicate that the situation worsens considerably at stronger crosswinds and slower cruising speeds. Flying more slowly than the crosswind effectively means that we will get blown off track and never regain it!

We can conclude that under strong crosswind conditions the glider's heading will be considerably different from its track. Maintaining track is much easier with a moving map GPS unit displaying the actual track. Once the ideal track line is established it can usually be maintained as long as wind velocity and cruising speed remain largely unchanged. The real skill is in varying speed or track to ensure that the glider remains in the strongest updraught.

For readers preferring metric measurements another table is printed on the opposite page.

Table 16b: True groundspeed along track (km/h)

Crosswind (km/h)	True airspeed TAS (km/h) along heading								
	80	100	120	140	160	180	200	220	240
20	77	98	118	138	158	179	199	219	239
40	69	92	113	134	155	175	196	216	237
60	53	80	104	126	148	169	191	212	232
80	-	60	89	115	139	161	183	205	226
100	-	-	66	98	125	150	173	196	218
120	-	-	-	72	106	134	160	184	208
140	-	-	-	-	77	113	142	170	195

In this context: a word of warning on using the classical MacCready theory for wave flying. The theory was developed for maximising speed in convective conditions but for a number of reasons it is of limited value for wave flying. One of them is that it doesn't take the effects of crosswind into account.

12.12 Safety in Wave

An ecstatic, and even hypnotic feeling associated with wave flying should be regarded with suspicion and not make you forget the safety rules associated with this type of flying.

On tow

Takeoff and towing most often occur in the under laminar turbulent air mass. As such, they can be quite rough. Therefore before take off, check your harness and secure any loose objects in the cockpit (including that camera to capture the epic flight!). An experienced tug pilot can sometimes soften some of the roughness by avoiding the worst of the rotor. Be familiar with emergencies and potential landing areas in case either you have to release from the tug, or if the rope breaks – it may happen.

In flight

Throughout your flight you should have a contingency plan, i.e. where to land if you lose the wave or if the cloud (or the Foehn gap) starts to close in. By maintaining a safe height, and being mindful of outlanding strips, is probably the best insurance.

A headwind of 30 to 40 kts affects the average glider's glide ratio quite markedly. The glide ratio can be as low as 10:1 and quite often more like 5:1. Flying low downwind to a landing zone is dangerous. If you have to fly back to a landing area after missing the lift, do not fly across the wave system. Obviously, spending more time in sink reduce your chances of making it back. It is better to try and fly upwind of any roll clouds as long as possible.

Outlanding

Outlandings in normal conditions should present no problems. However, to the uninitiated, outlandings in wave conditions may involve strong turbulence near the ground, wind shear giving you a tailwind on final when you expected a strong headwind, as well as poor visibility. Beware of these possibilities and fly accordingly.

Wave Lift

Rotor clouds under high level lenticular Photo: Dr. Rick Agnew

Last light

You may still be basking in the sun at some incredible height, but remember that it may take some time to decent – even with full dive brakes and in areas of strong sink. The light on the ground fades especially fast in winter time! Respect last light by making provision for the return flight.

Clouds

You are often near the clouds when you fly in wave. If you are next to the leading edge, be careful not to be pushed downwind, as you may disappear into the cloud. If you see clouds forming in front of you this is where the lift is! If this happens, quickly try to fly upwind of these clouds to re-contact the area of lift.

Always watch out for changes in airmass humidity which is known to increase within minutes. The Foehn gap (refer to Figure 119) can shrink and even disappear altogether at an alarming rate. If this starts to occur, make sure you have an access area clear enough to safely descend in clear air. If you are stuck above the clouds after the Foehn gap has closed, radio your situation to your base, notifying your intentions.

Normally there will be still some gaps downwind that will allow you a safe decent. However, this too might not be an opinion. By quick reaction and recalling where the gap was, it may get you down in the thinnest area of cloud. Alternatively, if the situation gets worse, descend straight away, crossing the cloud where the Foehn gap was. Before being engulfed by the clouds, set the trim to 60 kts, deploy full airbrakes, and let the controls go loose. The glider will stabilise itself in its decent. As you are a trained pilot, well versed in unusual attitudes, you may need that skill to recover once below cloud base. Obviously this emergency procedure can only be attempted if you are certain that the clouds do not reach the ground. Otherwise I would probably recommend your last resort is to use your parachute. This scenario should never be encountered, and therefore, this is the reason why you must be very careful when flying above cloud.

Radio

A (working) radio increases safety substantially. Tell other pilots your altitude, your position and your intentions. Giving a position at altitude to your ground crew assists in letting other know where you are, the best areas of lift, and allows them to monitor your progress as well as your levels of situational awareness. This last point I can not stress too highly. High altitude flying is advanced flying and not totally without potential risks. These risks can be minimised and controlled, leading to some of the most memorable flights you will experience.

Isn't it nice to tap into the expertise of a record holder and benefit from decades of wave flying experience? My sincere thanks is extended to Rick for his contribution and for his practical hints. I might add that wave flying is almost always conducted at altitudes above freezing level. For this reason, we would be well advised to dump all water ballast, as structural damage to the wing might occur if the water freezes.

Another very important safety issue is adequate clothing – keeping in mind that even in the middle of summer, temperatures are usually well below 0° Celsius. Serious lee wave pilots sometimes wear heated boots and even fit double – glazed clear vision panels to their gliders. Because most greases will freeze at such low temperatures, it becomes necessary to lubricate all control linkages with specially formulated grease.

Our discussions on wave would not be complete if we did not at least touch on two other forms of wave lift – shear wave and thermal wave.

12.13 Shear wave

Shear wave usually forms when an inversion separates winds at different altitudes although it sometimes occurs when two different air masses converge. A significantly different wind direction (or wind velocity) above and below the inversion layer is also required. If we have a wind of, say, 270/10 (Wind blowing from 270° at 10 kts) below the inversion and a stronger wind of 200/25 above, this could be illustrated as per Figure 69 in Chapter 4. The resulting friction causes the air to oscillate and generate small-amplitude waves which can be compared to ripples on water in conditions of moderate wind. Independent of any obstacles on the ground, these shear waves travel with the wind and are therefore often called 'moving waves'. Not surprisingly, they are generally regarded as unsuitable for gliding purposes.

However, when thermals extend high enough to leave a substantial hump in the inversion layer the situation is fundamentally different. A major distortion of the inversion layer can trigger a significant downstream airflow oscillation which, in turn, makes shear wave useful for gliding purposes.

Provided that pilots correctly identify such conditions and employ the same flying tactics as for thermal wave, they can climb far above convection level and enjoy effortless flying in silky-smooth air. The phenomenon can even exist on days with blue skies. Without any visual clues, however, it is extremely difficult to make use of it.

12.14 Thermal wave

One of the most beautiful experiences in gliding is to fly well above the clouds or along a wall of towering cumulus clouds. Some pilots call it slope soaring of clouds; some call it thermal wave or shear wave while others make no distinction between thermal wave and usable shear wave.

Let us touch on the meteorological requirements first and as a second step investigate suitable flying tactics for taking advantage of this truly awesome experience. Ideally, solid cumulus clouds with substantial vertical development and an inversion layer well above condensation level are called for. Just as important is a wind profile with a maximum velocity between the tops of the clouds and the inversion layer above. The trained eye can detect the presence of thermal wave by the lopsided shape of the clouds and, at least sometimes, by the curl-over at its trailing edge (Figure 126).

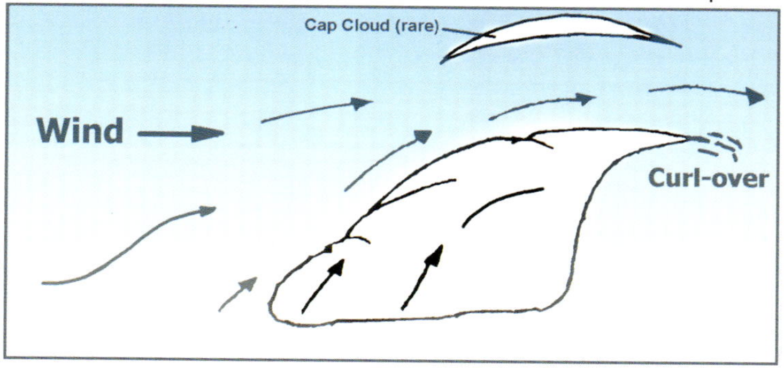

Figure 126: Shape of cumulus clouds under thermal wave conditions

If a cap of silky smooth cloud is forming above the cumulus cloud, (called "Pileus", Latin for cap) we can be almost certain that thermal wave conditions exist. Thermal wave has precious little to do with better-known mountain waves. Thermal wave is triggered by a large cumulus cloud which assumes the role of an obstacle to the airflow at the same level. The cloud acts as a kind of ridge, forcing the air to rise and flow around it. The path below the cloud is blocked by the updraught and therefore the air has little choice but to be deflected over the top.

As long as the vertical component of the deflection is strong enough to exceed the sink rate of our glider, we can take advantage of it if we are in the right place at the right time. The standard entry procedure is to climb as high as is legally possible under a cloud suspected to be producing thermal wave. The closer we can get to the underside of the cloud the better, as contacting thermal wave is often impossible much below cloud base.

When, for whatever reason, we can't climb any higher, we point the glider exactly into wind and fly at the speed of best L/D. In this context, it is important to note that the wind direction just below the cloud can be very different from the wind direction on the ground. For this reason, we need to keep an eye on the direction of travel of the cloud shadows, or consult a GPS-based navigation system for the wind direction at this level. Flying into wind will eventually make us cross an area of relatively smooth but rising air.

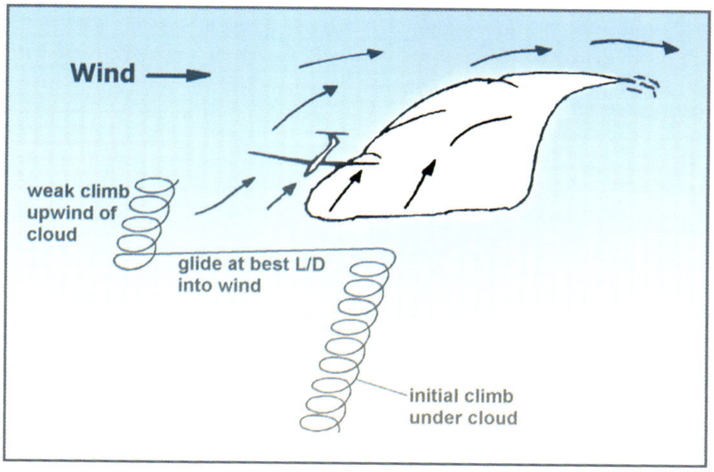

Sometimes the lift is located only a few wingspans in front of the cloud, but on other occasions it can be up to a kilometre upwind. Initially, the lift is very weak and might only be strong enough to climb at a rate of half a knot or so. However, we must accept this weak lift and remain

Figure 127: Entering thermal wave

**Half way up the cloud
Photo:
Yuji Higuchi**

patient. This patience will pay off when we slowly gain altitude in clear air just upwind of the cloud.

Once level with cloud base, we usually experience a significant increase in the rate of climb, but even then our rate of climb is seldom as good as it was while climbing up under the cumulus cloud. However, this welcome strengthening of the lift allows flying tactics akin to ridge soaring. Fly a figure-of-eight pattern in the strongest part of the updraught, just as you would do while ridge soaring, and before long the magic carpet of fluffy and brilliantly white cumulus clouds is gradually left below. Soon a stunning world of breathtaking beauty and overwhelming grandeur opens up in front of our eyes. In unusually smooth air, we can relax and, provided our glider is trimmed correctly, it hardly requires any control inputs.

Such excursions do not come without dangers. More often than not, thermal wave conditions extend to altitudes which require the use of oxygen. Another serious trap can be an unexpectedly strong downwind drift at higher altitudes which, in combination with impeded navigation (due to clouds below), can become serious. In mountainous terrain, we must be conscious of "Cumulus Granitus" and never descend near clouds. Remember, other glider pilots are keen to contact the thermal wave as well and that should be enough reason for descending in an area known to be clear of other aircraft.

**Pileus cloud marking thermal wave
Photo:
Martin Feeg**

perfect for lee wave. A rather strong inversion was apparent between 4500 ft and 5000 ft with less stable air above and below this level. Again, almost perfect conditions for the development of lee wave were present.

That only leaves the terrain. The Adelaide Hills feature a rather shallow downwind gradient in a westerly airstream, but history shows that lee wave formation is not uncommon under favourable meteorological conditions. We knew of past flights up to 25 000 ft in the area, but none of us realised the situation earlier in the day.

The depressed and very broken thermals near the airfield could be attributed to the downflow of air as a result of overlying wave conditions. (Refer to Section 4.11 and Figure 70) This was confirmed by other gliders pilots, who reported climbs in the tertiary wave to 12 000 ft and also found much stronger and smoother lift in areas that had come under the influence of the upper wave airflow.

Looking at the datalogger later that night, it was confirmed that we had cracked Diamond height, but the truly remarkable aspect was the use of thermals, thermal wave and lee wave in just a single flight. This doesn't happen every day, but getting the opportunity to share such a beautiful experience with a relative newcomer to the sport only comes once in a lifetime.

**The shape of the clouds clearly points to the presence of thermal wave
Photo:
Yuji Higuchi**

12.15 Bands of cumulus wave

Provided that the air around cloud level adopts an oscillating behaviour, and a wind shear of 5 kts (10 km/h) per 3300 ft (1000 m) exists, we already have the two most important conditions for bands of cumulus wave. Also, a near-constant wind direction above convection level is required. (E. Lorenzen, 2002)

When the first Cumulus cloud is big enough to form a major obstacle to the upper airflow (and the air is mainly deflected over the top) conditions are right for an oscillating airflow downwind of the cloud. Under the ascending part of this airflow, convection is greatly enhanced. The result is a series of downstream cumulus clouds as per Figures 129 and 130. Such conditions can provide breathtakingly beautiful soaring above walls of towering clouds. It can also make for some very fast cross-country flying, especially when the track is nicely aligned parallel to the cloud bands.

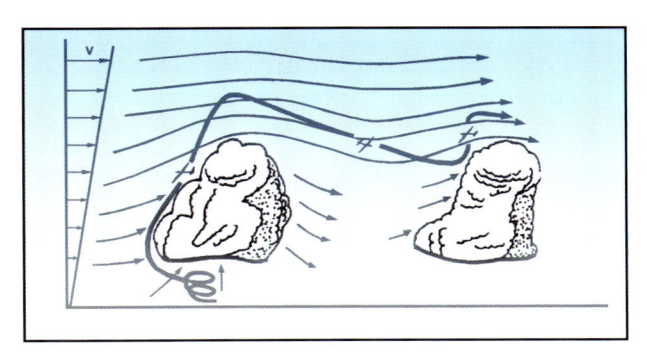

Contrary to mountain lee waves, such bands of cumulus clouds are not stationary, but travel roughly with the wind speed at convection level.

A different reason for bands of cumulus wave exists when an inversion separates a lower layer of well-developed cloud streets from the wind above. Provided the upper wind is blowing at almost right angle to the cloud streets, a wave pattern as per Figures 130 and 131 can develop. However, the wind induced oscillation above the inversion must be in phase with the distance of the cloud streets below.

Figure 129 & 130: Graphic illustration of airflow under cumulus wave band conditions.

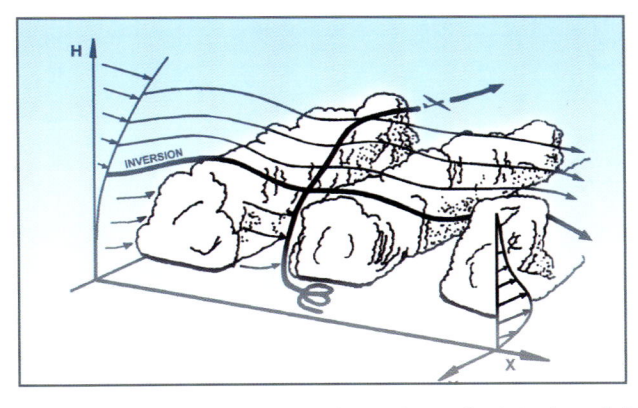

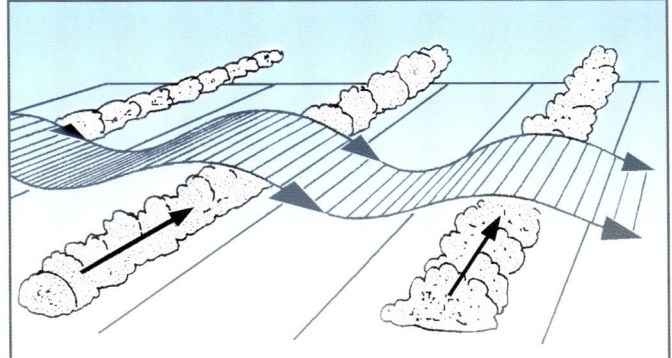

The required wind speed can be calculated as follows:

V = 5 x (H + 1)

Where

V = Wind speed above inversion level (m/s) and

H = Height of inversion level (km)

Figure 131 & 132: Wave flow above an inversion and streets of cumulus

12.16 The Morning Glory

This chapter would not be complete without a mention of pressure waves producing roll clouds in several places around the world. One of the better known occurs each spring in Northern Australia and is known as "The Morning Glory". It is associated with the impending onset of the monsoon season.

The Morning Glory may be considered as the gliding equivalent to the "endless wave" which surfers occasionally find in various locations around the globe. They are often referred to as "Dynamic waves" (or shockwaves) although scientists like to call them "Highly nonlinear giant waves". The Morning Glory in Northern Australia occurs unheralded around dawn and attracts a growing number of glider pilots each year. It often appears in the form of one or more, rapidly advancing, rather formidable

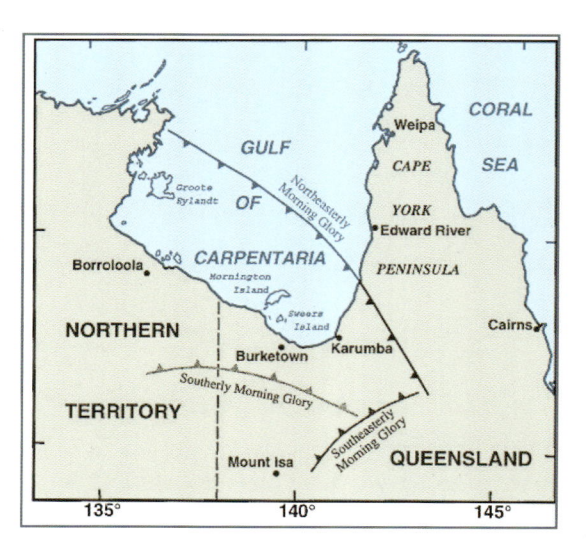

Wave Lift

Figure 133: Map of Northeast Australia with different roll cloud formations (Courtesy of Dr. Doug Christie of the Australian National University)

roll cloud formations which extend from horizon to horizon in a long line as far as the eye can see. In fact, it has occasionally been observed to exceed 1000 km in length and 10 000 feet in height with a base at about 1000 feet above the surface and typically about 3000 feet in depth. However, on occasion, the base of the cloud may lie below 300 ft AGL and the depth may exceed 6000 ft. The Morning Glory wave is believed to contain the energy equivalent of several nuclear devices and similar waves higher up in the atmosphere are one of the causes of clear air turbulence which can sometimes make commercial air travel uncomfortable. It is a natural wonder and ranks amongst the world's most exotic and interesting meteorological phenomena.

**Let the fun begin
Photo: Al Sim**

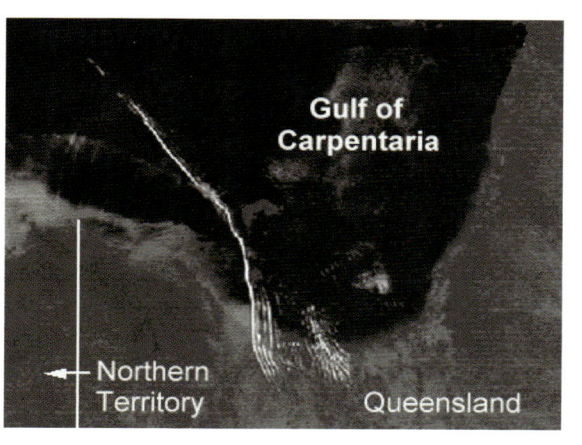

Satellite picture of Morning Glory roll cloud over the Gulf of Carpentaria.

While quite common in the Arabian Gulf region it also occurs infrequently in other parts of the world, including the Kimberly region in Western Australia and in South Australia. However, it most frequently occurs in the sparsely populated southern margin of the Gulf of Carpentaria when the weather starts to alternate back and forth between wet and dry season patterns. These patterns, combined with high humidity levels and the development of the seabreeze fronts around the Gulf signal the onset of the brief Morning Glory season. The roll cloud formation is even big enough to show up clearly on satellite images.

On average Morning Glories propagate at speeds of about 40 kilometres per hour, but are occasionally observed to travel at speeds of over 60 kilometres per hour. Sometimes Morning Glories occur on a daily basis at Burketown (Northern Queensland) over periods ranging from three to seven days in succession.

Soaring the leading edge of a Morning Glory Photo: Al Sim

12.16.1 Soaring the Morning Glory

The Morning Glory was not known to be soarable until 1989 when Robert Thompson and Russell White pioneered soaring it in a touring motor glider. Other experienced glider pilots have since made regular trips to Burketown and completed successful flights on Morning Glory waves lasting for more than three hours at average air speeds exceeding 80 kts (150 km/h) and covering several hundred kilometres. These flights have generated considerable interest in the gliding community and have made Burketown a Mecca for gliding enthusiasts from around the world.

Roll cloud formations are visible manifestations of large amplitude solitary waves. They propagate as exceptionally long-lived disturbances and are aided by the presence of a surface based stable layer in the lower atmosphere. While 'solitary wave' is the term used, the primary wave is normally accompanied by secondary and several tertiary waves – each of which are soarable. There is considerable variability from occurrence to occurrence in the rate of movement across the ground and the distance between waves.

Wave Lift

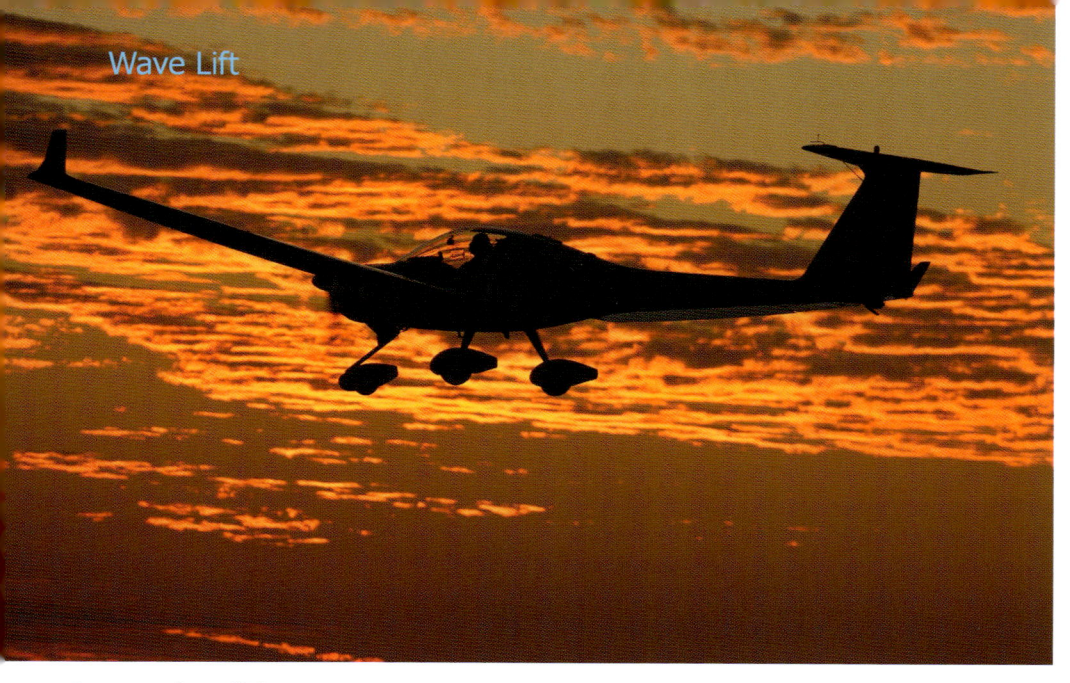

**Dawn take off for an encounter with The Morning Glory
Photo:
Al Sim**

A typical flight starts with a take-off at first light from the sealed strip at the Burketown aerodrome. Most flights to date have been carried out with medium performance touring motor gliders on north-easterly Morning Glories. In most cases, the Morning Glory is first encountered over the Gulf as a moving mountain of cloud while the aircraft is cruising towards it. On arrival the aircraft is directed along the axis of the wave. Remaining in front of the roll cloud the glider then ascends very rapidly in the strong updraft along the face of it – providing exciting and very scenic flying at the same time.

The strong updraft along the leading edge of the wave extends over a broad area ahead of the wave above the top of the cloud. Useful lift to an altitude of up to 10 000 feet AGL can often be provided although the top of the roll cloud extends to only five or six thousand feet. This means that the flight direction along the axis of the roll cloud can be safely reversed with ease at any time but the wave eventually disappears as it moves inland over very inhospitable terrain with very few possibilities for a safe landing. It is important to note that the trailing edge of Morning Glory waves harbours potentially dangerous down-draughts which could leave any aircraft which has been unfortunate enough to end up on the wrong side of the wave in a precarious position with the safest action being to fly away towards the leading edge of the next wave. Attempts to fly under Morning Glory roll clouds could also lead to disaster and should be avoided.

**A nice specimen rolling over Waikerie airfield
Photo:
Gavin Wrigley**

12.16.2 Solitary Waves

(Article partly adopted from the Burke Shire Council Website)

Solitary waves commonly occur throughout much of the arid interior of the Australian continent and elsewhere. When sufficient moisture is present near the surface, as is often the case over the southern Gulf of Carpentaria region, large amplitude waves of this type may be accompanied by what appears to be a propagating roll cloud formation. In this case, cloud is created continuously in the up-draught along the leading edge of the wave as moist ambient air from near the surface is lifted to condensation level. Cloud elements are then eroded away as air parcels descend in the down-draught along the trailing edge of the wave. The clearly visible upward motion of cloud elements along the leading edge and the downward motion of cloud elements along the trailing edge of the wave combine to give the impression that the cloud formation is rolling backwards as it advances.

**A roll cloud as far as the eye can see
Photo:
Al Sim**

Conditions over the tropical southern margin of the Gulf of Carpentaria between the months from August to November prior to the onset of the 'wet season' are particularly favourable for visible solitary waves. Roll cloud formations probably accompany more than eighty percent of all Morning Glory disturbances during the spring months as they propagate off-shore over the southern Gulf.

Three distinct types of Morning Glory waves have now been identified: north-easterly Morning Glories which appear most frequently just before sunrise over the Burketown area, southerly waves which can appear over the Burketown region at any time of day, (except during the afternoon and early evening) and south-easterly waves which tend to be active primarily during the early morning hours.

More than half of all disturbances observed at Burketown belong to the category of north-easterly waves. These disturbances originate during the previous evening in the collision between two opposing intense tropical sea-breeze fronts over the highlands of the Cape York Peninsula. Waves of this type propagate at night towards the southwest over the Gulf of Carpentaria, arriving near dawn over Burketown. The cloud formation associated with north-easterly Morning Glory waves dissipates fairly rapidly as the disturbance moves inland into drier air over northern Queensland. Even

**Flying in pairs below Mt. Cook
Photo:
Marty Taylor
(GlideOmarama.com)**

after the cloud dissolves, however, the disturbance continues to propagate inland, often for distances in excess of two hundred kilometres, as a clear-air wind squall.

There is clear evidence to show that some southerly disturbances originate over the interior of the Australian continent in the interaction of a mid-latitude cold front with a developing nocturnal radiation inversion. Some of these waves have very large amplitudes and may be accompanied by spectacular roll cloud formations; other southerly waves take the form of relatively minor disturbances with amplitudes of only a few hundred feet.

The origin of Morning Glories arriving at Burketown from the southeast is thought to be thunderstorm down-draughts impinging on a stable layer at the surface. These thunderstorms often develop in the late evening over the region to the northeast and to the east of the inland town of Mount Isa.

The origin and propagation of Morning Glories is controlled by synoptic conditions which turn out to be nearly identical for all types of wave. Thus, north-easterly, southerly and south-easterly waves may occur simultaneously over the southern Gulf region. Favourable conditions for the occurrence of Morning Glory waves at Burketown include a significant pressure ridge over the east coast of the Cape York Peninsula, absence of storm activity over the Burketown region and a well-developed sea-breeze regime over the south-eastern Gulf area on the preceding day.

These conditions are enhanced by the presence of an inland heat trough and an advancing frontal trough system south of the Gulf of Carpentaria. The presence of an inland heat trough and ridging over the eastern Cape York Peninsula will almost always guarantee that a north-easterly Morning Glory will arrive at Burketown on the following morning. It has proven to be fairly difficult, however, to predict the precise arrival time of north-easterly Morning Glories over the Burketown area, the size of these disturbances and whether or not these disturbances will be accompanied by a spectacular roll cloud formation.

12.17 Dynamic soaring

Dynamic soaring is another method of extracting energy from the atmosphere, although very few glider pilots have investigated this closely, and even fewer aviators have made practical attempts to utilise it.

The theoretical fundamentals have been analysed, based on the flying style of the albatross, a truly magnificent sea bird capable of crossing entire oceans without flapping its wings. It has obviously mastered the art and demonstrates how energy can be extracted very efficiently from a wind shear near the surface of the ocean. Admittedly, albatrosses fly at a very high wing loading and their wings have a very high aspect ratio, but much the same applies to modern sailplanes. This is enough reason to look into the matter and find out how a wind shear can possibly be utilised by sailplanes.

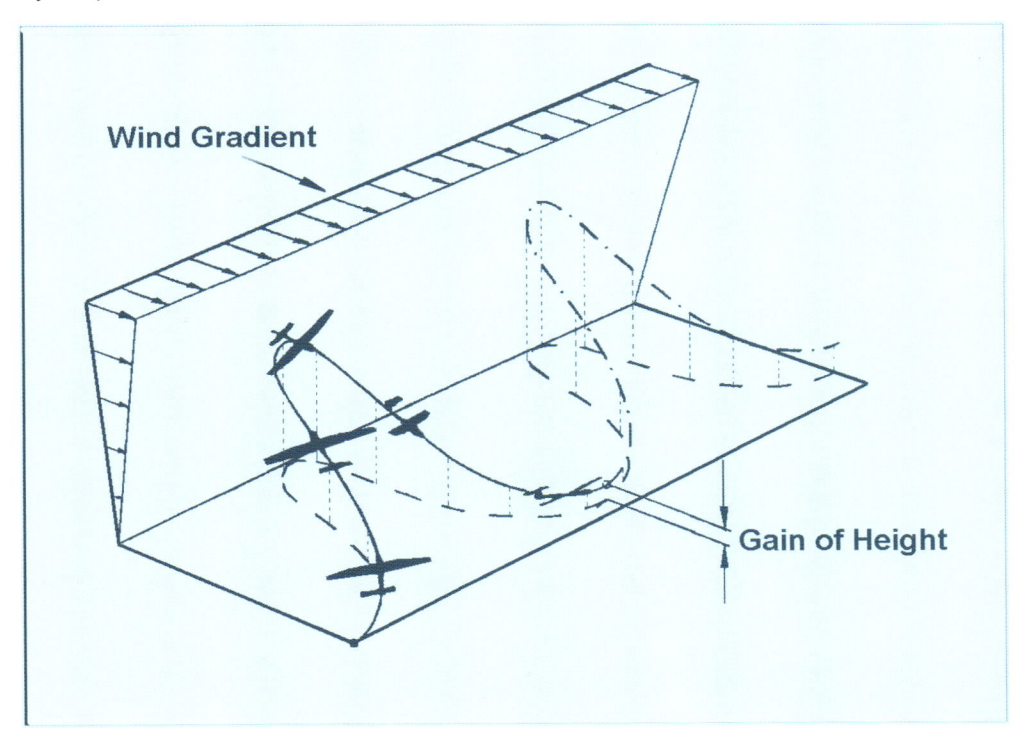

Figure 134: Optimum trajectory for dynamic soaring

In Section 4, it was said that a wind shear exists when either wind speed or wind direction changes significantly within a relatively thin layer of air. Typical examples are regions of temperature inversions or even jet streams. In the case of the highly efficient albatross, a normal wind gradient just above the water (as a result of surface friction) is sufficient to sustain flight. For safety reasons, such low-level operations are out of the question for aircraft of any kind, but the good news is that strong wind shears also exist at higher levels. Let's for example, take a temperature inversion where the wind speed above the inversion is frequently much higher than just below it. A pilot speeding up while descending through the inversion layer can point the glider into wind before initiating a steep pull-up. The subsequent transition into the strong headwind above the inversion increases the airspeed of the glider by a significant margin. As a result, the aircraft gains energy despite all associated aerodynamic losses.

Example:

If we assume that a pilot starts his pull-up in still air at a speed of 100 kts and reduces his speed to just 50 kts at the top of the climb, he would have gained several hundred feet of altitude. Ignoring aerodynamic losses, the pilot has simply converted kinetic energy into potential energy and his total energy balance remains unchanged. However, if the glider enters a level of increasing headwinds, the picture is fundamentally different.

For example, a strong wind of 50 kts (blowing opposite to the glider's direction of flight) at the top of the climb means that an airspeed of 100 kts is retained. The glider has gained several hundred feet and still operates at an airspeed of 100 kts. If the process is repeated, the accumulating energy gain can not only be utilised for soaring but quite conceivably even for cross-country flying (Figure 134).

Ingo Renner has demonstrated that sustained dynamic soaring is possible, although his tests were conducted in an unusually high wind shear of 40 kts. Renner's practical research dates back to 1974 and was first conducted in a Libelle and later in a PIK sailplane. Subsequent calculations have revealed that, with more modern and more efficient sailplanes, a wind gradient of 0.03 m/s per metre of altitude would be sufficient to sustain dynamic flight. However, the big question is whether pilots can endure sustained g-loading variations ranging between approx. 0.5 and 3g for any length of time and whether this style of flying is deemed enjoyable enough for pilots to want to practise it.

**Over the Roehn mountains in Germany
Photo:
Manfred Muench**

Wave Lift

Homecoming just before sunset at Lake Keepit
Photo:
Geraldine Clark

"Winners in society".

"Advanced Soaring Made Easy" was primarily written to improve the retention rate in our sport. Even though the second edition has put a much higher emphasis on performance-orientated soaring (and the all-important psychological aspects) it should be seen as a bonus and a result of readers' suggestions. The original intent, however, has certainly not changed.

After all, only a minority of glider pilots is involved in the competitive side of gliding and by far more of us are working as instructors and coaches or as volunteers in various capacities. We are all blessed with a potential to be productive and all of us have a capacity to win in life - not necessarily as competition winners, but as genuine persons committed to helping others. In other words, we can all be valuable members of our sport and act as trustworthy, credible and authentic people, or 'winners in society'.

Why are comments like these made at the end of this book? Well, our volunteers are the real backbone of our sport and they deserve recognition for their untiring efforts to improve the skills and hence the enjoyment of their fellow pilots. For these people, real achievement is in helping others. Without them our beautiful sport would long be dead and buried.

'Winners in society' never play the blame game and always accept the uniqueness of others. Enjoying their own accomplishments is as much a part of their characteristics as gaining enjoyment from the accomplishments of others. 'Winners in society' are real champions when it comes to improving the quality of life for their fellow glider pilots. They deserve our admiration just as much as celebrated pilots on the podium. For this reason, I would like to dedicate this book to all volunteers acting in the name of gliding.

Where to go from here?

When selling a glider pilot a book on gliding, you don't sell him 1 kg of paper, ink and glue – hopefully you sell him a whole new outlook on the sport. In this book we have discussed a wide range of topics, and I trust that pilots of all levels of experience will have found a few hints or clues. We have also touched on various training methods including mental training, covered the preparations for badge flying and looked into such issues as outlandings, safety and meteorological matters. Hopefully, all glider pilots will have gained a bit of motivation. Without fail it makes the difference between what a glider pilot can do and what he or she will do. Success is almost assured with the right amount of motivation and some basic theoretical knowledge.

My instructor hit the nail on the head after sending me solo over 25 years ago. "Soaring can only be learned by soaring" he commented and then went on to say: "Nothing will improve your gliding more than time in a glider, but if you fail to learn something out of every flight you fail to make progress. If on top you want to make progress real fast you had better go and buy some books on gliding". No doubt, my instructor was a wise man, and his unmistakable message was to keep learning and digest every flight, especially if it was shorter than intended or if it only turned out to be a circuit.

Soaring skills can't be developed overnight – we all know that. We also know that there are a few talented and very determined pilots who make it to the top without ongoing long–term support, training and coaching. These pilots seem to possess the willpower and the determination to acquire the necessary skills on a trial and error basis. However, such pilots are the exception — not the rule. Therefore, it is up to all of us to provide new pilots with further practical and theoretical training, as well as the occasional gliding treat, which makes them see what the sport really has to offer.

Unfortunately, statistics on gliding club membership retention make for some depressing reading in most countries. Sport scientists offer plausible explanations and tell us why a large number of pilots drop out of our sport every year. Their research indicates that dropouts occur as soon as the expectations of participants are not met and other activities appear more rewarding or more satisfying. The lesson is clear - people want to have fun in their precious spare time and we need to ask ourselves whether we are providing enough of it.

Over recent years I have earned myself a reputation for not only advocating a more modern and more efficient method of training, but also for taking the requirements of the 'Satisfaction NOW' generation into account. I'm the first to admit that this reputation is not entirely undeserved. If only a small percentage of dropouts could be retained, gliding would experience real growth again. No doubt, all dropouts were quite enthusiastic at some stage and have put their hard–earned money on the table to join our ranks. They had every intention of becoming glider pilots but have thrown in the towel part way through their training, or soon after going solo.

Gliding: the sport females can compete in without disadvantage over their male competitors

I know that we are always quick to rattle off a convenient list of reasons, but are we really hitting the nail on the head or are we falling into the same old trap of blaming others for our own failures and shortcomings?

Questions immediately coming to mind are:

- Are we teaching our new pilots the skill of soaring or is our training primarily consisting of takeoffs and landings?
- Are we doing enough to provide fun and enjoyment for newcomers to the sport?
- Are we neglecting advanced training to the detriment of long term member retention?
- Are we supportive enough and are we putting enough effort into theoretical training?
- Are we training newcomers in a way that makes them not only see but also experience the full spectrum of our marvellous sport?

I'm sure there are cases where the answer is "yes", but if we find that the answer to any of these questions is "maybe" it might be a good idea to look more closely at ourselves and our approach to training. Sure, our trainees can see that more experienced pilots are having loads of fun on their seemingly effortless flights, but, as far as trainees are concerned, they find it hard to see the light at the end of the tunnel. In too many cases, they have only done circuits, something that gets very boring after only a few weeks. Circuits hardly meet the definition of fun and hence fails to excite the majority of new aviators.

The world is changing rapidly – and with it the expectations of newcomers to the sport. In today's society, the focus is on efficiency and successful outcomes and when it comes to training, the gliding movement is well advised to embrace exactly the same strategy. Unless we manage to train newcomers efficiently and get them on the road to success quickly, we will continue to see large numbers of glider pilots turn their back on gliding. Make no mistake, nothing seems to motivate glider pilots more than success. Early success promptly translates into improved confidence and into a desire to attempt those long and memorable flights that the more seasoned pilots undertake on a regular basis and almost take for granted.

So what is the solution? Well, the bad news is that I don't have the magic answer either but I'm sure that all of us – especially instructors and coaches — need to work smarter to enable newcomers to fulfil their dreams and ambitions.

As a well-known American president once said:" My fellow glider pilots; don't ask what newcomers can do for you, ask what you can do for newcomers".

Yes, you are right, that's not exactly what he said, but I'm not too far off the track. Or am I?

Don't follow where the path may lead.

Go where there is no path

And leave a trail.

Acknowledgements

There are quite a few distinguished authors, specialists and fellow pilots who have in some form or another provided valuable assistance and should be recognised for their contribution to this book.

Let me begin by acknowledging the late C. E. Wallington for his book on meteorology, the late Helmut Reichmann for his truly excellent publication on cross-country flying, Ronald B. Stull for his book "An introduction to boundary layer meteorology" and Tom Bradbury for his publication "Meteorology and flight". All of these books served as a valuable source of inspiration. Special thanks must go to Fred Thomas (Professor at the German Research Centre for Aerospace) for giving his consent to include a number of graphics from his book "Fundamentals of Sailplane design" and Assoc. Professor J. Hacker of Flinders University for his permission to include extracts from his research paper "Inside Thermals". Although reproduced in a slightly modified form ,Figure 108 was taken from G. Sachs, A. Knoll and K. Lesch's 1989 OSTIV paper "Optimal utilisation of wind energy for dynamic soaring".

My sincere gratitude also goes to Dr. Rick Agnew for allowing me to include extracts of his various publications on the practical aspects of wave flying and his photos on mountain waves and roll clouds. Also I would to acknowledge the advice of glider designers Gerhard Waibel and Martin Heide for their help for on matters relating to dynamic soaring and C of G optimisation. Figure 6 is courtesy of John Hall, HRA, UK and Anthony Smith of the Adelaide University Gliding Club contributed Figure 11 and 68. Mike Hancy deserves enormous credit for helping me to refine my knowledge on meteorological matters over the years and for giving me valuable advice in relation to Chapter 2. The same applies to Carsten Lindemann, lecturer at the Free University of Berlin. I'm also grateful to the Bureau of Meteorology for granting permission to reproduce some of their excellent photos and graphics for chapter 2 of this book. Parts of chapter 8 were kindly provided by Norman Kennedy. Harry Medlicott and the Air Safety Foundation deserve a special mention for granting permission to include publications on lookout.

Special thanks must go to Ingo Renner for his advice on matters relating to thermal behaviour. He kindly reviewed the manuscript and let me tap into his enormous wealth of practical experience. Rob Thompson provided valuable advise on section 12.16 of the book and Al Sim contributed some of his excellent photos. Dr. Doug Christie of the Australian National University not only contributed figure 133 but also offered valuable advise on the different types of Morning Glory roll clouds. Thank you all.

Also I would like to express my appreciation to a number of fellow writers who published material on a long list of topics – both in German and English – on the Internet. Please forgive me for not listing all of them all individually. The excellent publications of all these people helped me to delve deeper into various subjects and develop the intellectual framework for this book.

My sincere appreciation is extended to my friends Catherine Conway, Graham Parker, Martin Feeg, David Wilson and Craig Vinall for their input and assistance and David Lawley for his help with computer and software issues.

Martin Simons, Franko Fonovic, Anne Philcox, Lesley Snell and Jon Millard have provided valuable advice on the structure of the book as well as editing and proofreading it. Knowing that English is not my mother tongue, they did an excellent job of polishing the text for the benefit of the international readership. Any remaining mistakes are the author's own.

Finally I would like to express my appreciation to Hiroshi Seo, Yuji Higuchi, Rick Agnew, Geraldine Clark, Jill and John Mc Caw and the team around Gavin Wills in New Zealand as well as the many other photographers from around the world who have given permission for publication of their truly excellent photos.

In this context I would like to thank my wife, Chris, not only for being my assistant but also for enduring the countless hours I've spend in bringing this task to completion.

Last but not least, I would like to thank the many fellow glider pilots who have nourished my thinking about gliding and the various topics of publication over the years. Your input, your ideas and your comments are very much appreciated and your moral support as well as your many suggestions have contributed to this book in a way that can not be emphasised highly enough.

Disclaimer

The information contained in this book is believed to be reliable, but its completeness and accuracy is not guaranteed. The author does not accept any liability, whether direct or indirect, arising from the use of this information.

No part of this publication is to be construed as a solicitation and should be viewed as the author's personal opinion only. Views expressed may change without notice, and where the information is in conflict with other documents the reader is referred to current operational guidelines.

Copyright

All rights to this book are reserved by the author in accordance with the Copyright, Design and Patents Right Act of 1988. No part of this book may be reproduced or transmitted in any form or by any means, neither electronically nor mechanically, including photocopying, recording, scanning, or any other data storage or retrieval system without prior written approval by the author.

The author would warmly welcome any suggestions for additions to a future edition of "Advanced Soaring Made Easy"

All photos taken by the author, unless otherwise noted

Close to sunset at Uluru (Ayers Rock, Australia)

Table of Contents

Preface to second edition		2
About the Author		3
Foreword by Ingo Renner		4
Foreword by Michael Sommer		5
Content at a glance		6-7
To my family / The use of icons		8

1. Training in the vicinity of the home airfield

1.1	Introduction	10
1.2	Thermal recognition & thermal detection	11
1.3	Centring a thermal	12
1.4	Using other gliders as lift indicators	16
1.5	Thermalling at a steady rate of climb	18
1.6	Audio variometers	19
1.7	Thermalling speeds	20
1.8	The effect of different wing loadings	22
1.9	Angle of bank	22
1.10	Drag	26
1.11	Practical hints	29
1.12	Problems arising while thermalling steeply	30
1.13	Avoiding sink after releasing	31
1.14	Structure of thermals	32
1.15	Thermal formation and thermal behaviour on a calm day	35
1.16	Finding thermals on blue days	36
1.17	Efficient centring of thermals in blue conditions	38
1.18	Thermal behaviour on windy days	38
1.19	Lift towards the end of the day	40
1.20	Lift under cumulus clouds	42
1.21	Finding the core under larger cumulus clouds	43
1.22	Spacing of thermals	45
1.23	Tactics just before and after launching	46
1.24	Over-development and cycling	47
1.25	Dissipating cumulus clouds	47
1.26	The self-stoking effect of cumulus clouds	48
1.27	Dust devils	48
1.28	The effect of a strong wind on thermals	51
1.29	Thermal re-centring in windy conditions	51
1.30	The importance of flying accurately	52
1.31	Other sources of energy	53

2 Weather and Gliding

2.1	Introduction	56
2.2	The sun hard at work	57
2.3	The upper air temperature profile	58
2.4	The importance of inversions	59
2.5	The Dry Adiabatic Lapse Rate (DALR)	59
2.6	The Environmental Lapse Rate (ELR)	59
2.7	The role of the dew point	63
2.8	Prediction of thunderstorms	65
2.9	Over-development of cumulus clouds	66
2.10	Strength of thermal activity	67
2.11	Highs, Lows, troughs and ridges	69
2.12	Weather patterns in Australia	74
2.13	Soaring conditions in Central Europe	76
2.14	Sea breeze fronts	85
2.15	A clue from the clouds above	92
2.16	The "skew T – Log P" diagram.	95
2.17	The Tephigram	96

3 Preparing for cross-country flying

3.1	Getting ready for road retrieves	100
3.2	A partnership with your crew	100
3.3	Preparing for longer flights	101
3.4	What is a reasonable task for the day ahead?	108
3.5	The point of no return	110
3.6	What did I learn today?	110
3.7	Checklist for taking a glider away	113

4 Extended local soaring

4.1	Introduction	114
4.2	Stepping out of your comfort zone	114
4.3	Dealing with fear	115
4.4	Training	116
4.5	Getting help from a coach	118
4.6	Lead & follow coaching	120
4.7	Team flying	123
4.8	Flying with water ballast	125
4.9	Looking for lift when low	128
4.10	Wind shear	129
4.11	Influence of airflow above the convection level	131
4.12	Operation in Cumulonimbus/Thunderstorm conditions	133
4.13	Drift	135
4.14	Navigation with modern instruments	136
4.15	Certificates and Badges	138

5 Advanced cross-country flying

5.1	Introduction	144
5.2	Getting the speed up	144
5.2.1	Are we using too many thermals?	145
5.2.2	Are we hanging on to a thermal for too long?	145
5.2.3	Are we centring a thermal quickly enough?	145
5.2.4	Are we thermalling efficiently enough?	146
5.2.5	Yawstring corrections	147
5.2.6	Is our meteorological navigation up to scratch?	148
5.2.7	Is our thermal selection good enough?	148
5.3	The effect of detours	149
5.4	Speed to fly	152
5.4.1	Maximising glide distance	152
5.4.2	Maximising average cross-country speed	153
5.5	How important is cruising at optimum speed?	156

5.6	Flying tactics on track and height bands	157
5.7	Thermal streets	160
5.8	Dolphin flying	164
5.9	Haze domes	165
5.10	Mountain thermals	165
5.10.1	Ground inversions in mountainous terrain	167
5.11	Exiting a thermal	168
5.12	Final glide	169
5.13	Low level finishes	170
5.14	Flight analysis	172

6 Winning the mental game

6.1	Planning	180
6.2	Positive thinking	182
6.3	Making decisions	183
6.4	Thinking ahead	186
6.5	Concentration & Relaxation	187
6.6	Learn how to learn	190
6.7	Confidence and over-confidence	190
6.8	Mental rehearsals	191
6.9	Commitment	192
6.10	Setting a goal and achieving it	193
6.11	Our mood and its effect on performance	194
6.12	Formula for success	197
6.13	Analysing your flight	197
6.14	Learning from the experts	198
6.15	Believe in your ability to succeed	198

7 Flying competitively

7.1	Choosing a competition class	202
7.2	Preparing for your first competition	204
7.3	Getting to know the contest area	206
7.4	Starting a race	206
7.5	Out on a competition task	208
7.6	Turning points	211
7.7	The problem of stress in competition	212
7.8	Shaving off the seconds	215
7.9	Risk management	215
7.10	Staying fit for the duration of the contest	217
7.11	Is the mature glider pilot disadvantaged?	218

8 Let's get technical

8.1	Getting the most out of a glider	222
8.2	Variometers and their limitations	223
8.3	Getting the variometer set-up right	227
8.4	Optimising your sailplane's Centre of Gravity	229
8.5	Why do winglets work?	230
8.6	Flaps	232

9 Outlandings

9.1	Introduction	240
9.2	Misleading altimeter	240
9.3	Determining wind direction	241
9.4	Circuit planning	243
9.5	Field selection	244
9.6	Dos and Don'ts	247
9.7	Aero–tow retrieves	249
9.8	Long-term benefits	250
9.9	Outlanding training and motor gliders	250

10 Safety first

10.1	Introduction	254
10.2	Thermalling etiquette and thermal approach procedures	254
10.3	Effective scanning	255
10.3.1	Putting the focus on vision	256
10.3.2	Good lookout is no accident	258
10.4	Flarm	263
10.5	Are we fit for flying?	264
10.6	Using the radio to enhance safety	266
10.7	Radio procedures	267
10.8	Open class manoeuvrability	269
10.9	Gliders with retractable engines	270
10.9.1	Take-offs in self launching gliders	271

11 Ridge lift and slope soaring

11.1	Introduction	274
11.2	Theoretical fundamentals	274
11.3	Conditions affecting ridge soaring	276
11.4	Obstacles upwind of the ridge	278
11.5	Ridge lift and thermals	280
11.6	Katabatic and anabatic winds	281
11.7	Flying tactics	283
11.8	Ridge soaring rules	284
11.9	Flying well above ridge top level	284
11.10	Dangers	285

12 Wave Lift

12.1	Introduction	290
12.2	Topography	292
12.3	Lee wave airflow and terminology	292
12.4	Meteorological conditions	293
12.5	Wavelength	294
12.6	Amplitude	295
12.7	Moisture	296
12.8	Dangers	297
12.8.1	Limitations of the human body	297
12.8.2	Aircraft limitations	301
12.9	Cloud formation	303
12.10	The practical aspects of wave flying	304
12.11	The effects of crosswind on the speed above ground	308
12.12	Safety in wave	309
12.13	Shear wave	311
12.14	Thermal wave	311
12.15	Bands of cumulus wave	316
12.16	Morning Glory	317
12.17	Dynamic soaring	323

Winners in society	326
Where to go from here	326
Acknowledgements	329
Table of contents	333
Order form	335

www.alexander-schleicher.de

Alexander Schleicher Segelflugzeugbau

Alexander-Schleicher-Straße 1
D-36163 Poppenhausen (Wasserkuppe)
Germany

Ph. ++49 (0) 66 58 / 89-0
Fax ++49 (0) 66 58 / 89 40
e-Mail: info@alexander-schleicher.de

Dear fellow aviator!

In an attempt to reduce costs and hence make the book affordable to as many pilots as possible, this second edition of "Advanced Soaring Made Easy" was self published. As costly advertising is out of the question, I kindly ask you to recommend it to others if you think it was useful and informative.

In case you would like to purchase another copy for a friend (or buy the book for your club library) please contact a distributor in your country. In case you are unable to source the book locally please contact the author. We would gladly arrange for a dispatch by one of our distributors or we will submit your copy directly in case there is no sales outlet in your area.

Our electronic contact details are: **eckey@internode.on.net**
and our phone number is: **08 84492871**
(For calls outside of Australia + 61 884492871)

Postal address:

Bernard Eckey
10 Antigua Grove
West Lakes SA 5021
Australia.

All orders will normally be dispatched within 48 hours of receipt of your remittance.

Please do not forget to pass on your mailing address:

Name:..
Street address:..
Town (with postcode):..
Country:..
e-mail:...

Many thanks for your order.

Bernard Eckey

PS: Trade enquiries for orders of 10 or more books are always very welcome!

KOMET

Sailplane Trailers by Anschau

The Standard of Quality Worldwide

- Originators of clamshell trailer design
- Outstanding protection for your sailplane
- Ease of loading and unloading
- Excellent road handling

Anschau Fahrzeugbau

WWW.ANSCHAU.DE